*A Theological
and Historical Introduction
to the Apostolic Fathers*

A Theological and Historical Introduction to the Apostolic Fathers

JOHN LAWSON

Wipf & Stock
PUBLISHERS
Eugene, Oregon

Wipf and Stock Publishers
199 W 8th Ave, Suite 3
Eugene, OR 97401

A Theological and Historical Introduction to the Apostolic Fathers
By Lawson, John
Copyright©1961 by Lawson, John
ISBN: 1-59752-315-1

Publication date 7/26/2005
Previously published by The Macmillan Company, 1961

*Dedicated to my proved friend
and valued encourager in learning*
WILLIAM RAGSDALE CANNON
*Dean of the Candler School of Theology
in Emory University, Atlanta, Georgia*

Preface

The purpose of this book is to introduce the study of the Apostolic Fathers to theological students, to the clergy, and to the reading Christian public generally. The aim of the writer is to cover the whole of the subject in a single compendious volume. This involves a certain delimitation of the subject matter. There is a very large technical literature connected with the Apostolic Fathers. Were an attempt made at every point to give full references to all that has been written upon a given passage, we should soon have the proverbial narrow stream of text meandering through a wide and marshy flood plain of learned footnotes! This would be to defeat one of the chief purposes of this book, which is to arouse the student to the great interest of this subject by opening to him a conspectus of the leading points of the whole. It is presumed that the research student who wishes to press beyond the scope of this work to make an exhaustive examination of some passage of the text will wish to refer to the standard monographs, rather than to content himself with the partial information which can be given in brief references. The author hopes, however, that this class of reader will find something of substantial value in this work, in that the conclusions stated upon not a few of the major issues presented by the Apostolic Fathers are the results of his own reflection.

From the point of view of the more general student, it should be said that the arrangement of the subject matter is as follows: Technical questions of the establishment of the text of the Apostolic Fathers are only treated in so far as this is essential to the understanding of the intention of these writers. Historical matters are dealt with in greater detail, particularly when they relate to issues which are still of living importance to the Church, such as the witness of the Apostolic Fathers to the development of the Christian Sacraments and Ministry. The central point of the study, however, is a discussion of the theology and spirituality of these venerable figures. It is the conviction of the author that herein is the greatest need for a general introduction to this subject. The technical monographs in general naturally concentrate their chief attention upon linguistic and historical points. This is a necessary preliminary study, but it needs to be brought to fruition in a reconstruction of what this very important body of writings has to offer by way of theological and spiritual understanding of the Christian Church and the Christian religion. This surely is the aspect which should arouse the mind to interest in the Apostolic Fathers. It is likewise the attitude which leads to an intelligible understanding of them, for these writings are not primarily data for historical reconstructions. They are the witness of Christians to the faith that was in them, and must be read as such in a spirit of reverence and sympathy.

It is a healthy tradition of the British Parliament that a Member must "declare his interest" before he takes part in a debate the outcome of which might affect his personal fortunes. The same discipline should be required of Church historians! Particularly is this so when they write upon matters in which the firm historical evidence may at times be fragmentary, and the issues which arise controversial as between different schools of thought and Christian denominations. Such is certainly the case with the Apostolic Fathers. Let the present writer, then, not be accused of immodesty if he "declares his interest", theological and ecclesiastical. The student will then at least know where he is with the book! The writer finds himself partially detached from the main stream of traditionalist Catholic Christianity, because he belongs to a nonepiscopal branch of the Church. Yet he writes as one who feels the liveliest sympathy with the historic Catholic tradition of doctrine and Churchmanship. One would submit to the discriminating reader that this "central" position is in some respects an advantageous one for writing of the ancient Fathers of the Church. A great bulk of fine, scholarly work upon the Fathers has naturally been carried out by writers of the stricter Catholic tradition, in its various persuasions. These scholars are, however, under the difficulty that in relation to certain quite limited yet very important issues the requirements of ecclesiastical loyalty may commit them in advance to the defence of traditional positions which preferably require a more dispassionate investigation. At the other end of the ecclesiastical spectrum, moreover, there are many scholarly experts who have worked over the ancient Fathers in pursuit of various academic and critical theories which go far to assail the integrity of historic Christianity as it has been understood down the ages. Yet others have hammered the Apostolic Fathers upon the anvil of purest Reformation theology. Both the too strictly traditionalist and the too critical points of view are, one believes, a disadvantage in approaching the present subject. The ancient Fathers of the Church were Catholic traditionalists indeed, but not strict traditionalists as so many have later been. They are best understood by making the attempt to sit where they sat, hard to do though this is across the gulf of the centuries.

The present writer would therefore profess that he is an exponent of a flexible traditionalism. It is his conviction that the ancient visible institution of the Catholic Church was intended and founded by our Lord, has been preserved by divine providence, and today constitutes an essential part of the Christian religion. He declares his allegiance to the ancient Catholic Faith. He would write as one whose calling it is to uphold these venerable sanctities, yet to do so by reasoned historical and theological argument rather than by dogmatic assertion. The most he can hope for from his indulgent readers is that in the end they will find themselves of the same mind as was John Wesley, when upon a day great with fateful consequence he read Lord King's *Account of the Primitive Church*, and concluded, "I was ready to believe that this was a fair and impartial draught."

The author wishes gratefully to acknowledge permission to quote the Greek text from Lightfoot's *Apostolic Fathers*, published by Macmillan, and also to reproduce a number of passages from Dr. T. F. Torrance's *Grace in the Apostolic Fathers*, published by Oliver and Boyd, Edinburgh, and Wm. B. Eerdmans Publishing Co., Grand Rapids, Michigan.

CANDLER SCHOOL OF THEOLOGY
EMORY UNIVERSITY, GEORGIA
Epiphany, 1961

Texts and Bibliography

1. The student will find a chapter-by-chapter commentary on all the writings generally regarded as comprised in the Apostolic Fathers. These commentaries are arranged so that they may refer to the Greek original at all suitable points, and yet be fully intelligible to those who have no knowledge of Greek. Each comment opens with a quotation from the English translation that is long enough to identify the passage in question. Important Greek words or phrases are also inserted into the quotation, with reference to the text.

2. The most convenient Greek texts for the study of the Apostolic Fathers are as follows:

The Apostolic Fathers, revised text with short introductions and English translation, by J. B. Lightfoot (completed by J. R. Harmer), one volume, 1891, and subsequent editions. (The English translation in this edition is used in the present work for identification, and the references to the Greek are made to this edition.) English text alone re-published by Baker Book Co.

The Apostolic Fathers, by J. B. Lightfoot, five volumes, Cambridge, 1869–1890, with full introductions and commentary, is still the standard edition of 1 and 2 Clement, Ignatius, Polycarp, and the Martyrdom of Polycarp.

The Apostolic Fathers, with an English translation in parallel, by Kirsopp Lake, two volumes, in the Loeb Classical Library, 1912-1949, Harvard University, and Heinemann, London.

3. Further English translations, without the Greek, are as follows:

In volume one of *The Ante-Nicene Christian Library*, ed. Roberts and Donaldson, twenty-four volumes, Edinburgh, 1867–1872; also the American edition of the same, ten volumes, 1899–1905, and reprint, 1953.

In *The Fathers of the Church*, Cima Publishing Co., 1947; the volume *The Apostolic Fathers* being translated by F. X. Glimm, J. Marique, G. C. Walsh.

The Apostolic Fathers, an American translation, E. J. Goodspeed, New York, 1950.

4. A Select Bibliography:
Blakeney, E. H., *Epistle to Diognetus*, S.P.C.K., 1944.
Clarke, C. P. S., *St. Ignatius and St. Polycarp*, 1930.
Clarke, W. K. L., *The First Epistle of Clement to the Corinthians*, Macmillan, 1937.
Harrison, P. M., *Polycarp's Two Epistles to the Philippians*, 1936.

Hort, F. J. A., *Six Lectures on the Ante-Nicene Fathers*, Macmillan, 1895.

Mackinnon, J., *The Gospel in the Early Church*, Longmans Green, 1933 (Chapter iv).

Meecham, H. G., *The Epistle to Diognetus*, Manchester, 1949 (Greek text with detailed commentary).

Oxford Society of Historical Theology, Clarendon Press, 1905, *The New Testament in the Apostolic Fathers*.

Robinson, J. A., *Barnabas, Hermas, and the Didache*, 1920.

Schilling, F. A., *The Mysticism of Ignatius of Antioch*, 1932.

Srawley, J. H., *The Epistles of St. Ignatius*, 1919.

Stark, A. R., *The Christology of the Apostolic Fathers*, 1912.

Taylor, C., *The Witness of Hermas to the Four Gospels*, Cambridge, 1892.

Torrance, T. F., *The Doctrine of Grace in the Apostolic Fathers*, Oliver and Boyd, 1948, and Wm. B. Eerdmans Publishing Co., Grand Rapids, Michigan (contains a valuable further biography).

Vokes, F. E., *The Riddle of the Didache*, Society for Promoting Christian Knowledge, and Macmillan, New York, 1938.

Contents

	Preface	vii
	Texts and Bibliography	xi
I	Introduction	1
II	The First Epistle of S. Clement of Rome to the Corinthians	21
III	The Teaching of the Twelve Apostles	63
IV	The Epistles of S. Ignatius of Antioch	101
V	Literature Concerning S. Polycarp of Smyrna	153
VI	Homilies and Hortatory Literature	
	i. The Second Epistle of S. Clement and The Epistle of Barnabas	179
VII	Homilies and Hortatory Literature	
	ii. The Shepherd of Hermas	219
VIII	An Apology: The Epistle to Diognetus	269
	Index of Subjects	313
	Index of Scripture References	323
	Index of References to Ancient Writers of the Church	334

I Introduction

It is necessary first to define what is meant by "the Apostolic Fathers". The Fathers are the leading figures in the story of the devotion, the life, the thought, and the discipline of the Christian Church in its early formative centuries. They are those to whom we look back with veneration as the more eminent instruments used by God in the shaping of the Church of the first heroic and creative ages, which Church is the Mother of all our present orthodox Christian denominations. In token of this, many of them are accorded by long usage and general consent the title of "Saint". Though incipient divisive influences were certainly at work in the age of the Fathers, the Church of that time is one in which we may see still held together in a comprehension and unity those various spiritual and intellectual interests which in modern Christianity are naturally regarded as the characteristics of particular Christian communions, now unhappily divided from one another. No study, therefore, is more rewarding in balanced understanding of the Christian Faith, and in consequent promotion of Christian unity, than is the study of the Fathers. The walls which divide us, and all too often cause us to dwell in partial light, do not reach up to Heaven. In the study of the Fathers, if anywhere, we may look over the top of those walls, and refresh ourselves in fellowship one with another.

Among the Fathers, the Apostolic Fathers are the earliest. They are the Fathers who were the personal disciples of the Apostles, or at least those who were sufficiently early that the common tradition of the ancient Church could regard them as the disciples of Apostles. Needless to say, modern critical scholarship has questioned the date and authorship of many of the writings we are presently to discuss. Some of them were written by authors who could not have met the first leaders of the Church. Nevertheless, there is a sufficiently distinctive body of orthodox Christian writings, not included in the authoritative Canon of the New Testament, yet answering to the life of the Church in the period immediately succeeding New Testament times, that it may conveniently and intelligibly be designated "the Apostolic Fathers".

This statement has already raised a number of issues which must be discussed if the nature of these writings is to be understood. First, the Apostolic Fathers are the earliest writings which are not in the Canon of the New Testament as authoritative Scripture. This important distinction between "Scripture" and "the Fathers" is not simply a matter of the time at which different works were probably composed. If the reliable and conservative judgments of critical New Testament scholarship be compared with similar scholarly judgments upon the Apostolic Fathers, it will be found that some of the latter were composed at a date earlier than the writing of some of the later books of the New Testament. Nor is the distinction that the New Testament writers were "more inspired" than the Apostolic Fathers, in the sense that the canonical authors were necessarily of deeper spiritual insight, or more accurate in their literary methods, than those who came after them. As we proceed with our study we shall find that, as a class, the New Testament writers were possessed of more constructive spiritual genius than the Apostolic Fathers. Yet this is not invariably the case. There are not a few passages in the Apostolic Fathers which, considered as specimens of spiritual devotion or theological thought, compare very favourably with some parts of the New Testament. Furthermore, though it is to be admitted that the interest of the Apostolic Fathers is characteristically in the sphere of Church discipline and organization, rather than in stirring thoughts of new Christian truth, it does not follow that for this reason the work of the Fathers is of less spiritual value to the Christian religion. The judgment of history upon Mary's gift of spiritual devotion, and Martha's admittedly less charming gift of ecclesiastical discipline, surely is: "This ye ought to have done, and not to have left the other undone." Nearly as many Churches have gone astray through failure of sound discipline as through dearth of sound doctrine, and the guidance of the Holy Spirit may perhaps be seen just as truly in the zeal of S. Clement and S. Ignatius for an ordered Ministry as in the zeal of S. Paul for the principle of "justification by faith". It is not easy to say. Nevertheless, the distinction between the New Testament and the Apostolic Fathers is not the simple one that the writers of the former are demonstrably "nearer to God" than the latter. The distinctive authority and inspiration of canonical New Testament Scripture lies in what these writers characteristically have to say, rather than in the way they were enabled to say it.

The Apostles did not all possess the same spiritual gifts, nor did they all serve in the same way. However, the essential qualification and basic function of an Apostle is plain. He was one who could give authoritative testimony to the facts concerning the life, death, and resurrection of Christ, upon which facts the Gospel stands (Acts i, 21–2). By the nature of things, this was a passing office in the Church. Despite the circumstance that to a large extent the Apostles took up the work of travelling missionaries, even to the extent that we almost trace a tendency to treat the work of a travelling missionary as that which constituted the office of apostleship, the growing number of local Churches made it harder for each congregation to enjoy the personal guidance of an Apostle. Thus the Apostles sought to make up for their absence by their letters. Later on death took away from the Church the original witnesses to the facts about Christ. The Church then had perforce to fall back upon the precious written testimony of the Apostles. That the "memoirs of the Apostles," as S. Justin so fittingly calls them (1 *Apology*, lxvi), were at first looked upon only as a substitute for the personal presence and word of an Apostle does not involve that they in any way lacked spiritual authority. The Christian authority was the Apostolic principle, and the "memoirs" were the Apostolic principle in written form. Nevertheless, they were not at first looked upon as "Scripture," in the same sense as the ancient Jewish Scriptures inherited by the Church. Their authority lay not in the fact that they were enshrined in a sacred Canon, but that they went back reliably to a certain circle of authoritative witnesses.

This is the basis for the later theory of the ancient Church concerning the writings which became enshrined with the passage of time as a New Testament Canon of Scripture alongside the Old. The claim was that New Testament Scripture was the work either directly of Apostles, or at least of the intimate amanuenses and representatives of Apostles. This idea first comes clearly to expression during the last quarter of the second century, in the words of that very representative figure S. Irenaeus, who names the four Gospels, attributing the first and fourth to members of the Twelve, and the second and third to the amanuenses of S. Peter and S. Paul respectively (*Adversus Haereses*, III, i, 1). There was indeed a natural tendency in the Church to make the facts square more completely with this attractive theory. Some books from the original circle of witness which were of such merit that the Church could not bring herself to cast them out from the incipient Canon, yet which lacked "apostolic" names, were gradually supplied with them, doubtless through the operation of "wishful thinking." The leading example of this is doubtless the attribution of the Epistle to the Hebrews to S. Paul. Nevertheless, the instinct of the primitive Church is found to be true, and her effective position to be upheld, and this in light of the findings of modern scholarship regarding the authorship of various of the books. We may uphold with confidence the basic proposition that the New Testament is the sole and the sufficient witness to the all-important facts about the birth, life, character, words, works, death, and resurrection of Christ. As it was the essential function of an Apostle to give this witness, so in a unique and proper sense the New Testament is "the Apostolic writing."

It is not the purpose of this book to go deeply into the question of the authenticity of the portrait of Christ in the New Testament. For many decades past this has been a subject of the strongest and most intricate controversy, and continues so at the present time. This is not surprising, considering that the whole validity of the Christian religion depends intimately upon the substantial reliability, though not of course the detailed inerrancy, of the New Testament witness to the facts about Christ. Hence those who would reject the yoke of Christ are desperately concerned to erode away the scriptural figure of our Lord, and those who would uphold the Faith are as deeply committed to vindicate the authenticity of the witness. Suffice it to say that it seems to the present writer incredible that the majestic portrait of Christ in the Gospels, which admittedly haunts the imagination of the world, should have been conjured up out of the slender resources of the "group mentality" of a circle of sincere, well intentioned, excitable, and rather dim Galilean peasants! Only those who are "sinking under the dread that possibly the Gospel may be true" would clutch at this desperate conclusion. The primitive Church was not lacking in men of spiritual insight, intellectual agility, or literary talent. We can test the merit of S. Paul, S. John, S. Luke, and the writer to the Hebrews under these headings. Their work at its best is excellent. Yet it has not that uniform and peerless excellence which we find in the portrait of Christ. S. Paul was one of the world's spiritual geniuses, but we can judge from what he did write that he could not have constructed the Sermon on the Mount out of his own imagination. How then could S. Mark, that good and faithful servant with but two talents, have constructed the awful and disconcerting scene of Calvary? Yet we are in effect asked by some critics to suppose that the "group mentality" was adorned by geniuses superior in gift to S. John and S. Luke, the memory of whom has now entirely perished, who were responsible for piously transfiguring the martyred Man of Galilee into the living and commanding Christ of the Gospels! It appears more credible to suppose that the humble and limited scribes who composed the documents which lie behind our Gospels were able to write as they did, though patently they did not always fully appreciate what they wrote, because they were copying from the authentically remembered Life.

This New Testament witness to the all-important facts about Christ is a sufficient witness. It was not composed by biographers, and most provokingly does not supply material for a complete and consistent biography of Jesus of Nazareth. Nor was the material which is supplied miraculously preserved from the minor infirmities and obscurities of recording and transcription which are inevitable in the work of men who were certainly not expert professional biographers, as the art of biography is scientifically understood today. Nevertheless, the written witness is magnificently sufficient for the purpose for which it was recorded. It suffices for the preaching as Lord and Saviour of the Christ who went about doing good, who spake as never man spake, and who died and rose and ascended to glory.

The sufficient witness is likewise the sole witness. The curious student may read that which has survived of the so-called "Apocryphal Gospels." These are writings purporting to be accounts of the life of Christ, which come to us from the early days of the Church, but not immediately from the original circle of authentic Christian Apostolic witness.[1] Of the information therein given about Christ, that which bears upon it the marks of good sense, credibility, and authenticity is manifestly copied from the canonical Gospels, while that which is not contained in the canonical Gospels usually betrays itself as the pious imaginings of not very well instructed or farseeing disciples by its manifestly lower level of spiritual insight and good sense. Everything, then, that is known with any degree of certainty about Christ is made known by the Scripture. There are many and various precious and beautiful things to be found both in the Old and the New Testament,

[1] *The Apocryphal New Testament*, M. R. James, Oxford, 1926.

but the treasure hid in the field of Scripture is Christ. The record of the facts about Christ is the element of irreplaceable worth in the Bible. This is the element in the Bible which is the basis for the Christian doctrine that the Scripture is "inspired of God" in a manner different from other worthy Christian writings composed by saintly men acting under the influence of the Holy Spirit, and that the Church is for ever bound to the authority of canonical Scripture, so that no doctrine can be rightly promulgated which is contrary to Scripture.

There is, then, an important discontinuity between the temporary office of the Christian Apostle and the permanent office of the Christian teacher. Answering to this is the discontinuity between canonical "Apostolic writings" and the noncanonical "Apostolic Fathers." There is indeed no "sharp edge" between writings which manifestly qualify for the rank of New Testament Scripture and writings which do not, so that in no case is there ever any marginal difficulty in classification. It is perhaps not easy to establish a clear, logical case why, for example, 2 Peter should be included in the Canon and the Epistle of the venerable Polycarp left out. In accord with this is the historical circumstance that the ancient Church did not find herself possessed of an unquestioned guidance as to which books were canonical New Testament Scripture. Some books which finally were acknowledged as part of the Canon were subject to questioning and to delay in universal recognition. As we shall find, some of the writings which we are to study as the Apostolic Fathers were regarded as Scripture, or almost Scripture, by some responsible teachers in the ancient Church. It is possible that certain choices were finally made largely on the ground of tradition and sentiment rather than from reasons of logical consistency. Yet ambiguity of detail by no means abolishes the general principle. The writers of the Apostolic Fathers, and their early readers, felt that in these books one all-important formative age had come to an end in the Church, and that another had begun.

As we read today we have to admit that they were right in their judgment. There is indeed no vital difference in literary origin between the two classes of books. Each was largely composed by "the disciples of Apostles." Nevertheless, the Apostolic Fathers do not add anything to the original Apostolic witness to the facts about Christ, but have a different value for the Church. There are many things of great value in the Apostolic Fathers, but there is no passage which, as we read, we say, "The New Testament as we have it is decidedly the poorer for the purpose proper to the New Testament, because this was not included." And there are some things in the Apostolic Fathers which we may be profoundly grateful did not get into the Canon! In like manner, as we read the New Testament we find some minor writings which, to us at any rate, seem to be of less value than the average. Yet it would be hard to find a writing which would bring any wide consensus of responsible Christian opinion to the judgment: "We wish this had not been included." The Holy Spirit did not work through inerrant human instruments in the ancient Church's choice of the New Testament Canon any more than in other ecclesiastical decisions. Nevertheless, the spiritually valid and sufficient guidance is seen to be there.

There is, however, in the New Testament another element of great importance, as well as the irreplaceable historical witness. The first Christians reflected upon the deeper meaning of the facts regarding Christ, and sought to think out ways of explaining them to others. They argued, and did not always see eye to eye. They also held more formal discussions, resulting at times in formal definitions or decisions, sometimes arrived at by dint of compromise (as in Acts xv). This intellectual process went on through the normal medium of the human mind, and was by no means immune to the influence of human presuppositions, and even of human infirmity and prejudice. Yet it also took place under the prevailing guidance of the Holy Spirit. This was the process of doctrinal development and formulation. There is in the New Testament not alone a record of the facts about Christ, but also of the first great formative ventures in the doctrinal interpretation of those facts. In particular, we recognize in the distinctive work of S. Paul, S. John, and of the writer to the Hebrews three creative, distinctive, and complementary schools of Christian thought. This element in the New Testament is continuous with the work of doctrinal interpretation as it is found in the Apostolic Fathers, and in the later Fathers, and in principle down to the present day. The mental and spiritual processes which led S. Paul to render Christ's teaching about the free forgiveness of the penitent sinner into the legal formula of "justification by faith," and which, following from this, moved the primitive Church to decide that Gentile Christians need not be circumcised, are not to be regarded as in any way differing in principle from the processes which have led the Church to other weighty and responsible decisions, recorded elsewhere than in Scripture. In this sense we allow that the New Testament confession that Christ is the divine Son, or the apostolic resolution of the "circumcision question," are Christian theological decisions which lie in one continuous process with non-Scriptural decisions such as the adoption of the episcopal Ministry in the age of the Apostolic Fathers, the insertion of the *homoousios* clause in the Creed at Nicaea, the formulation of the Book of Common Prayer, or even the enunciation of the Lambeth Quadrilateral. However, this gradation down the centuries illustrates that the earlier decisions in the continuous process were the weightier in effect, even though the means of arriving at them were the same in principle. This is because the Church is a continuous living spiritual organism, the Body of Christ.

By way of illustration, we observe that organic life is continuous. The one thing which cannot be done with life is to cut it off, so as to start *de novo*. It cannot be expected of an organism that its future evolution should take place in any way other than in terms of its past evolution. In response to change of environment, life has produced an endless succession of evolutionary modifications. Each differentiation has as its point of departure the result of all previous differentiations. It is never possible to go back. The first leading differentiation was presumably that between primitive animal and primitive vegetable life, from a common ancestor. A further momentous differentiation, as that between the first vertebrate life and invertebrates, had to take its rise in a differentiation of distinctively animal life. It could not go back to the common ancestor of all life. And so on, for the differentiations of vertebrate animals. All the responses to environment are like in kind. They are part of a continuous process. Yet the nearer one gets to the beginning of the continuous process, the more far-reaching in consequence for all later times is each response.

The same is true of the development of Christian doctrine. Thus, the primitive Church came to confess that Jesus the Christ is the divine Lord and Son. The Church of the Councils defined the doctrine of two natures in Christ, one truly human, the other truly divine, perfectly joined yet distinct. Yet the later decision had to be made within the context of the primitive decision, which could neither be ignored nor reversed. In light of ampler scientific views of what is meant by "human nature," the modern Church might conceivably someday amplify the Conciliar doctrine of the two natures, but she would have to do so within the context of the Conciliar decision, which likewise can neither be ignored nor reversed. The nearer to the source are the dogmatic decisions, the weightier they are in effect. Thus the doctrinal interpretation recorded in canonical New Testament Scripture is not "more inspired" than that recorded later, in the sense that the Apostles were necessarily wiser, or more completely under divine constraint, than all later Christians. Yet the New Testament doctrinal interpretation of the facts about Christ is of plenary authority, in the sense that the primitive decisions, being irreversible, are determinative for all later time, and provide the context for all later doctrinal decisions.

The doctrinal interest of the Apostolic Fathers lies in the circumstance that in them we see this process being continued immediately from the New Testament. It has been well said that the second generation of a movement is the time of peril. A movement usually starts with a great creative genius, or at least a man of forceful personality. As such are rare, the followers are likely to be men of sincerity but of limited ability. Thus the Franciscan movement took its rise in a romantic and unconventional spiritual genius, a Saint who has captured the imagination of mankind. His followers, though they did invaluable humanitarian and teaching work, swiftly turned into a monastic movement much on the accustomed pattern. This has been repeated endlessly. One of the great issues of Church history is the extent to which this judgment is to be passed upon the Church as a whole. Did the whole Church succumb to the peril of the second generation, so that we are to find a great gulf fixed between the religion of our Lord and the religion of the Catholic Church known to history? There is an inherent likelihood that there will be found some degree of painful discrepancy between the Lord and His Church. The greatest saints have been the first to agree that they followed far behind the Master, and with faltering steps. Yet there is also Christ's promise to the Church, that the gates of Hell shall not prevail against it. Here are two opposite principles working within historic Christianity. On the one hand, the Church is a human society, subject to the failings of human movements. On the other hand, it is a divine society, expressly founded by Christ as the means by which the sovereign Rule of God is to work in this world of men, and assured by Him that it will endure until His coming in glory. That the historic Church should follow her Lord with faltering and at times wayward steps is inevitable, and does not of itself impugn her claim to be the divine society. The crucial question is: Did the Church not only stumble, but fall? It is surely from the Apostolic Fathers, the writers of the perilous second generation, that this momentous issue is if anywhere to be determined.

The charge that the Church of history is a fallen Church has been levelled in various ways. For example, at the Reformation the Anabaptists traced the fall of the Church to her association with secular society. The Deists advanced the view that the original religion of Jesus was an allegedly simple moral teaching, but that this was later decked out by an interested and covetous priesthood in the gay feathers of borrowed pagan ceremonial in order to gratify the vulgar multitude. A similar charge made by sceptical scholars nearer to our own time is the familiar plea that original Christianity was a simple and untheological message concerning the Fatherhood of God and the brotherhood of man, but that this was perverted into a sacrificial, sacramental, and theological Mystery by Saul of Tarsus, through the introduction into the Christian religion of elements derived from the pagan Mysteries. It is not too hard to show the fallacy of these arguments, based as they are upon complete misunderstanding of the message of Jesus as recorded in the Gospels. However, there are current today more cautious and better informed variants of the theme of the fallen Church, advanced by reputable historical and theological scholarship, and these charges are of the more force because it has to be agreed that there is at least some measure of truth in them. The liberal evolutionary school of historical theology, in such vogue a few decades ago, and ably represented by the great figure of von Harnack, made the basic assumption that "the spiritual" is the inward, the individual, the spontaneous, and the ethical; in contradistinction to the outward, organized, ceremonial, and dogmatic aspects of religion, which are inferior in spirituality. The interpretation of Church History given upon this assumption was that the authentic religion of the first disciples of Jesus was a somewhat informal and enthusiastic "movement" of devotion to Christ, and of brotherly love, which was not very interested in regular ecclesiastical discipline or dogmatic theology. The rise of a regular and disciplined official Ministry as an essential element of the Christian religion was a shift of interest away from the spiritual. It was a symptom of the fossilization of Christianity into a mere institution. The development of an official theology likewise represented the rendering of the primitive Christian preaching into the fundamentally alien categories of Greek thought. This "Hellenization" of Christianity was in fact the partial paganization of Christianity.

The force of these arguments lies in the fact that there is some truth in them, though the present writer would state his conviction that we have here the overstatement of a case in a manner quite unfair to the Christianity of the ancient Fathers. There is and always has been a place in authentic and healthy Christianity for a legitimate care for a regular Ministry and ecclesiastical discipline. Christianity always has been, and ought to be, an "organized Church," and not just a "movement." Nevertheless, zeal for due ecclesiastical order can easily crowd out an appreciation for "the religion of the heart," and in the long story of the Church has often done so. Whenever this happens there is a deteriorating movement away from "the spiritual." Likewise, the rendering of the primitive Christian preaching into the categories of Greek thought was beset by certain dangers, into which some schools of Christian theology at times fell. Pagan and non-Biblical presuppositions about the nature of God, man, sin, and salvation did at times creep into theology, and cloud the vision of the Church. Nevertheless, the exposition of Christianity by the use of the subtle thought-forms of the ancient world was in itself a constructive activity which has enriched the Christian faith, and which was necessary for the communication of the Gospel in that world. A fall into the dangers of paganization was not inevitable, and was not characteristic of the best ancient Christian thought. Here then is one of the leading issues to be examined in the Apostolic Fathers. It will also be found in these writings, as compared to the New Testament, that there is a greater proportional degree of interest in the organized Christian Ministry, and in ecclesiastical discipline. This may be due to the providential strengthening and legitimate development of New Testament Christianity, or, as others would argue, a dangerous symptom of incipient fossilization, or perhaps something of both. At any rate, here is a leading issue for the reader to have in mind as he approaches the Apostolic Fathers.

The charge that the Church known to Catholic history is doctrinally a fallen Church has in the distinctively modern period been levelled in an even more fundamental manner, and with a good deal of persuasive force, by some of the theologians who in recent years have turned with refreshed interest to the study of the great Protestant Reformers. The fundamental assumption of the neo-Reformation school, which has been most fertile and constructive in its renewed appreciation of the real issues of the Reformation, and the real interests of the Reformers, is that the eminent criterion of authentic Christianity is an uncompromised doctrine of salvation by grace. This proposition has only to be stated to be recognized as an important truth. One of the fundamentals in the spirit and teaching of our Lord is that God, who is the righteous Judge, is eminently the loving Father. He deals with sinful man not first and foremost as a judge in a court of law, or as an accountant in a bank, but as a father dealing with a prodigal son. The religion of divine grace is indeed of the essence of the Christian Gospel, and it is to be admitted that any representation of Christianity which is unsound in its doctrine of divine grace is to that extent vitiated. Nevertheless, it is often possible to criticize the way in which this criterion has been applied to the study of the ancient Fathers of the Church. Some theologians of grace have at times verged upon theological anachronism by requiring that ancient writers such as the Apostolic Fathers should express themselves on the doctrine of salvation by grace with that emphasis and clarity which would be natural in an evangelical writer of the Reformation period, when phraseology had been reduced to precision by the exigencies of controversy. If they fail to do this, it is tacitly assumed that they are "unsound" on grace! This is to make the mistake of asking a writer who lived before a particular doctrinal controversy, which gave rise to some formula of orthodoxy, to use the language which he possibly would have done had he lived afterwards. Of course, neo-Reformation writers do not state the matter in this way. They first make and defend the assumption that a strict Reformation understanding of grace is the essence of New Testament religion, and then judge such writers as the Apostolic Fathers by what is taken to be the religion of the New Testament. This involves a number of assumptions which plainly require to be examined.

The first of these is the tacit assumption that S. Paul is so far the Prince of New Testament theologians that his distinctive attitude is determinative for the rest of the New Testament. The second of these is that the doctrine of "justification by faith and not by the works of the Law" is so large a part of the living religion of S. Paul that it is in fact "the quintessence of Paulinism." It is the doctrine which is determinative for the understanding of Paul. Both these assumptions have sufficient of the truth in them to make of them weighty and arguable theological propositions. Nevertheless, they both incline to error through overstatement. This is the mentality which prompted Martin Luther to open his celebrated "Preface to the Epistle to the Romans" with the self-revealing observation, "This Epistle is really the chief part of the New Testament and the very purest Gospel. . . . It is, in itself, a bright light, almost enough to illumine all the Scripture."[1] He then goes on to concentrate most of his attention, albeit with great insight and power, and not a little moving eloquence, on a part only of this Epistle, namely, chapters i–vii. The circumstance behind this choice is that God had used meditation upon Romans i, 17, "For therein is the righteousness of God revealed from faith to faith: as it is written, The just shall live by faith," to bring to Luther a great experience of divine confrontation and spiritual release. He responded by heightening the effect of S. Paul's doctrine to a small but significant degree by rendering the Apostolic formula "justification by faith and not by the works of the Law" into the Reformation formula "justification by faith *alone*." The first formula is S. Paul addressing himself to a particular, important, but passing controversial episode in the history of the Church, namely, the "circumcision question." The second formula has been treated as more than this: as a universal guiding theological principle. It is to be questioned whether "justification by faith" was so large a part of the vital religion of S. Paul as this. Luther then took his formula "justification by faith alone" and treated it as the leading criterion for the understanding of the whole Bible, because it had brought to him this experience of spiritual release. This is a somewhat hazardous subjective judgment, and places upon Romans i, 17, leading text though it admittedly be, more theological weight than it will bear.[2] Romans i, 17, is vital to the understanding of Paul, but it is not in effect the whole of the Apostle.[3] Furthermore, S. Paul is certainly one of the most important New Testament writers,

---

[1] Luther's *Works*, Philadelphia ed., vi, p. 447.
[2] Cf. R. E. Davies, *The Problem of Authority in the Continental Reformers* (London, 1946), pp. 55 ff.
[3] Thus it can hardly be doubted that a leading incentive for questioning the Pauline authorship of Ephesians has been the feeling that the Apostle of individualist "justification" "*could not*" have been responsible for such Catholic theology of incorporation into the Church as is characteristic of this Epistle.

but he does not to this degree dominate the whole of the New Testament scene. Thus it is at least arguable that the Sermon on the Mount, with its statement of the eternal integrity of the Law, has as good a claim as the Epistle to the Romans to be treated as the Gospel "bright light." Neo-Reformation scholars have followed Luther in this out-of-proportion reading of the New Testament, and erred by applying it as the standard by which the ancient Fathers of the Church are to be judged regarding their faithfulness to the authentic Christian religion.

It is not our present intention to argue fully the question of the New Testament doctrine of grace. The study starts, as all Christian study must, with the Person, the character, the actions, and the words of our Lord. The whole drift of sound critical scholarship would appear to vindicate S. Paul as substantially a faithful theological interpreter of his Lord. If the theological implications of our Lord's spirit and teaching are drawn out, and cast into formulae comparable to those used in later theology, it would seem that Christ taught a "strong," and in the sense "Pauline," doctrine of grace. Nevertheless, He did not teach that severe and rigid doctrine of grace which so much later exposition has assumed to be "Pauline." Christ certainly taught that man was sinful, and could not save himself. Yet His teaching does not answer to the notion of "entire depravity," or to the total inability of "the natural man" to do *any* good thing. Christ likewise taught that man is totally dependent upon God for all good things, but certainly not anything from which a doctrine of Election could be inferred. He demolished the idea that man can accomplish his own salvation by the accumulation of religious merit, but He was not scrupulous to abolish the very idea of merit. In fact, the attitude of Christ answers to the theological formula "salvation by grace," but not to a supposed Pauline "salvation by grace *alone*." This should make us cautious in accepting the latter formula as in fact "Pauline," and still more reserved in treating it as a chief canon for the interpretation of Scripture.

As we come to judge the Apostolic Fathers in light of the New Testament, there arises the further consideration of how far S. Paul speaks for the whole of the New Testament. That he was one of the most commanding minds in the primitive Church none will dispute, or that his writings form one of the most important and valuable constituents of the New Testament. Nevertheless, it is at least arguable that he was in point of fact somewhat in the position of a "left-wing" leader in the Church, with the most fully representative opinion being in consequence a little to the "right" of his distinctive personal point of view. If this were so, he would be in the same position as that of many honoured and influential theological leaders, who have held a legitimate but not exclusive place in the counsels of their day. This very issue of the "circumcision question," with which is associated the formula "justification by faith," is the case in point. This controversy seems to have been settled, as so often in the later history of the Church, by a measure of compromise in the attempt to secure comprehension. The solution was an essential victory for Paulinism, in the sense that circumcision was not required of Gentile converts. Nevertheless, it was the victory of a prudently modified Paulinism, for in the interest of unity and discipline obedience was required of Gentile believers to *some* commandments, ceremonial as well as moral, though not to circumcision and the whole Jewish Law (Acts xv, 1-29). What happened here doubtless happened in relation to other issues of the time, of which we know less. The authority for the Church is the whole New Testament, and for a balanced comprehension of that authority we can no more assume that S. Paul is in effect the whole of the New Testament than we can that "the article of justification" is in effect the whole of S. Paul.

The student of the Apostolic Fathers should not fail to read such an able and scholarly work as *The Doctrine of Grace in the Apostolic Fathers* (London, 1948), by T. F. Torrance. This book, which is one of the leading works upon the Apostolic Fathers to appear in the modern period, is a good example of the neo-Reformation attack upon the ancient Church. The writer first makes a most careful reconstruction of the meaning of the word "grace" in the Classics, in the Old Testament, and in the New (pp. 1-35). He then goes through the Apostolic Fathers in turn, examining passages where they speak about divine grace, and salvation by grace, to discover whether they understand the Gospel. The general conclusion is that, while some of these writers are further sunk in error than others, as a class the venerable Fathers have no secure grasp of the essential and characteristic principle of the Christian message. This was lost, apparently with the passing of the immediate Apostolic circle, and "never recovered till the Reformation" (p. 136, footnote). "That was not understood by the Apostolic Fathers, and it is the primary reason for the degeneration of their Christian faith into something so different from the New Testament. Failure to apprehend the meaning of the Cross and to make it a saving article of faith is surely the clearest indication that a genuine doctrine of grace is absent" (p. 138). It is hard to imagine a more radical criticism of historic Christianity than this, and if this be the sober truth it is difficult to see why the Church should have survived at all as a spiritual force.

Dr. Torrance clearly displays the reason for this criticism: "Their theology represents a corrosion of the faith both from the side of Judaism and from the side of Hellenism, because the basic significance of grace was not grasped." "As opposed to both, the Gospel of Christianity was so astounding just because it taught a doctrine of justification by grace alone. This was unpalatable to both sides" (p. 137). The tacit assumption is plain. To pass muster as an understanding Christian a Father of the ancient Church must not only follow his Lord, and acknowledge with Christ that man cannot be saved apart from divine grace. He must also go a little further with Martin Luther, and teach that the action of salvation is solely that of the sovereign grace of God, in which human effort after good has in principle no part at all. The Apostolic formula "justification by faith and not by the works of the Law" is not strict enough as a canon of criticism. We must apply to the Fathers the Reformation formula "justification by faith *alone*." This is the anachronism which can easily vitiate modern thought upon the ancient writers. We are sometimes not sufficiently willing to let them express themselves in their own way, and ourselves to judge them by the canons of their own time. We would not be thought to argue that the Apostolic Fathers are invariably clear on the doctrine of grace or the principles of the Gospel. A dispassionate reading indicates that they were not immune to the peril of the second generation. There are some passages where they express themselves most unhappily. Nevertheless, it is important to read the Fathers without strong initial dogmatic prepossessions, or it may be hard to give due weight to other passages where the intention may be sound, but the language inexact. An examination of Torrance's arguments from particular passages will indicate that his case often has much force, but the present writer feels that the general conclusion is unfair to the Apostolic Fathers because it is an overstatement of this case. The error is to try to put both S. Paul and the Apostolic Fathers through the sieve of Reformation doctrine.

This discussion has brought us back to another part of our definition of the Apostolic Fathers as "*orthodox* Christian writings, not included in the authoritative Canon of the New Testament, yet answering to the life of the Church in the period immediately succeeding New Testament times." We must consider the force of the word "orthodox" as applied to these early Fathers. We shall, for example, find in the writings of these venerable figures statements about the Person of Christ, and of the Holy Spirit, which, taken literally, would be condemned as heretical in light of the definitions of the General Councils. However, this by no means involves that the Fathers are "heretical." It may only mean that they lack the clear terminology developed in later times, and are sometimes careless in their expressions. It has never been easy in any period to say, in relation to questions under current discussion, that one view is "orthodox" and another "heretical." The temptation is to be resisted to look upon the leading Councils and Synods of the ancient Church as though a gathering of bishops and theologians was held, a decision speedily made, and that this there and then became "orthodoxy." The actual Councils and Synods were only the decisive moments of a continuous process, and the clear foci of a much more widespread and general process of discussion. The circumstance that a Council or Synod was held was itself a mark that there had already been much discussion, and also usually that there was now some influence at work pressing for a decision. The discussion itself was held in terms of previous decisions, both those which had stood the test of experience, and those which had not. Nor was it possible at the time to appreciate just how significant the decision of a particular Synod was. Some gatherings of the Church, not conspicuous at the time for their representative or weighty character, have produced decisions which have come to be more and more significant and authoritative for the Church because of the way in which they have appealed to the judgment of the Church in later ages and in wider circles. Other gatherings, not at the time of meeting apparently less authoritative, and perhaps making high claims for themselves, have had their decisions undermined by the experience and thought of later times. That which is authoritative for the Church is not barely the decision of certain clearly defined official gatherings. It is the growing consensus of all the Church down the long centuries, as she responds to the lessons of experience and discussion. The official historic gatherings have their dignity as the decisive exemplars of the consensus.

We have already likened the development of doctrine to the evolution of an organism. The organism may pass through a number of outward forms, perhaps very different in aspect, but because it is one organism each form is the logical outcome of the preceding ones. This is true of orthodox doctrine, and also of the essential and Catholic institutions of the Church. The means of expression and mode of practical outworking may vary, perhaps at times markedly. Yet each stage follows logically from what has gone before, and there is a certain persistence of type running through all superficial changes. The real intention and inward spirit remains the same, though the thought forms or ecclesiastical machinery may alter. For example, in a matter of doctrine, there has been a succession of theologies of the Atonement. All have been alike in this, that they have conveyed to the believer a reasonable ground for supposing that in Christ God has done all that needs to be done for man to be forgiven, reconciled to God, and delivered from the power of his spiritual adversaries. This is the persistence of type. Yet this essential intention has been expressed in very various thought forms, derived from the mental background of various ages and cultures. The ancient world represented the Atonement as a victory over personal satanic adversaries, the Middle Ages in terms of the honour of a feudal potentate, the Reformation in terms of legal jurisprudence, while the modern world, with its interest in the psychology of human personality, has essayed to treat the same theme in terms of the persuasive effect of the Cross upon the human mind, feeling, and will. All the theologies have been used for the preaching of the Cross, and honoured by God to the salvation of souls. The orthodoxy, then, of a theology of the Atonement does not depend upon the intellectual apparatus employed to convey to the believer his "reasonable ground," but upon the circumstance whether the "reasonable ground" is in fact effectually conveyed. An example may likewise be taken in a matter of ecclesiastical institution. There has been a succession of rituals for the celebration of the Eucharist, developing one from another. The outward form has reflected the very various temperaments, aesthetic tastes, and intellectual apprehensions of many centuries and peoples. Yet wherever there has been a persistence of type, in an abiding intention to do what the Lord commanded to be done, the Lord has honoured the ordinance to its proper spiritual effect. The orthodoxy depends on the sincere and intelligent intention, not the details of the rite. The consequence is that one cannot determine the "orthodoxy" of a Father by asking: "Does his doctrine accord with the findings of this or that later Council?" The question always is: "Does his doctrine intelligibly lie upon the central track of development which is now seen to have led to the later orthodox Council?" The Apostolic Fathers are the Christian writers of their period who in light of the long centuries since are found to have passed this test.

The Church of that time did not march forward with even tread in the apprehension of Christian truth, or in its practical expression in Christian life, any more than it does today. Therefore we do not look back uncritically to "the early pure days of the Church," with the proverbial rose-coloured spectacles. These men are not all spiritual heroes, nor are their writings all works of clear spiritual insight. Some of them stumble, on occasion badly. Yet this is not to the discredit of the age of the Apostolic Fathers. It has not always been considered what an immense spiritual and intellectual task faced the primitive Church. The infant Faith took root within the sheltered seedbed of Judaism. It grew within the confines of a closely knit community, prepared for the coming of Christ by a firm foundation upon the principles of ethical monotheism. Yet if the world was to be evangelized with a universal Gospel, the Faith had to be planted out in the wide and exposed fields of the pagan world. This presented problems. The Church was new, yet continuous with the old. In some things she was free to break the bands of Jewish particularism, and to give herself to men of every race and culture as a free spiritual religion. Yet in other things she was bound to preserve the intellectual and moral discipline which was her priceless heritage from Judaism. It was not always easy to see which was which.

At the same time there was something to be brought into the Church from the Gentile world in the course of this evangelistic process. S. Justin Martyr, the first major theological apologist for the Christian Faith, had the insight to see that though the Law and Prophets were the chief preparation for the Gospel, there was also a true preparation in the intellectual treasures of Greek philosophy. This too had been inspired by the divine Word, so that "whatever has been uttered aright by any men in any place belongs to us Christians" (*Apology* ii, 13). Here is the great original charter of all Christian and Classical culture, which is the foundation of our civilization. Without the incorporation of these treasures the Faith would have been immeasurably the poorer, and without the use of the intellectual apparatus of the secular thought of the time the problem of the communication of the primitive Christian message to the pagan would have been all but insoluble. Yet here again it was not always easy to see how far to go. Where was the line to be drawn between the legitimate presentation to the Greeks of Christ in a Greek dress, and the illegitimate transformation of the original Biblical Christ into a false and subtly paganized Christ? The first type of movement is the true development of doctrine, the second the lapse into heresy, and to distinguish the one from the other required insight of the first order. The "Young Churches" of the mission field are today beset with similar perplexing problems, and the risk of the compromise of Christian with non-Christian religion is an inevitable one when the Church ventures into new cultures. Today missionaries whose training has centuries of theological experience behind it can go out to give friendly guidance, and key students from the mission field can come for higher education in countries of an established Christian culture. The Church of the Apostolic Fathers was like a "Young Church" without a "home base." As the cynic has observed, "It had nothing but the Holy Ghost to guide it!" That the Church of the first ages did not move forward with even tread is not to be wondered at. The marvel is that she did not fall altogether. The Apostolic Fathers are the leaders among those whose steps are now seen to be set in the main track forward. To grasp this is to appreciate the importance of this study, and the reverence which is due to these venerable men.

II The First Epistle of S. Clement of Rome to the Corinthians

1. Character of the Writing

This magisterial Epistle fittingly introduces the student to the Apostolic Fathers, for it takes one straight to the problem of the second generation. S. Clement deals with the issues of ecclesiastical discipline. It is for this reason that a reading of the Epistle comes as a slight disappointment to some people. Yet this is to do a great injustice to the writer. We instinctively compare his Epistle with the Epistles of S. Paul to the same Church, and we soon observe the absence of some things in Clement. There is nothing comparable to those moving and agonized passages in 1 and 2 Corinthians where the apostolic founder and father in God pours out his soul in exhortation to his erring children in the Gospel, in passion, in irony, in rebuke, in testimony, and in invitation. Clement is a deeply concerned father in God, but he writes as a dignified pastor. As we look into the future we see the figure of an archbishop! In the Epistle of S. Clement there is no lyrical hymn to love; there is no daring and poetic speculation upon the mystery of the Resurrection. The writer is no visionary prophet, but an earnest and competent preacher who has his feet firmly planted upon the solid earth. The Church to him is not so much a family as an army. There is then a great difference in ethos between the Apostle writing to the Corinthians, and the presiding presbyter. We are out of the great spiritually and intellectually creative period of the first apostolic witness, and have passed the great divide into the no less formative period when the Christians began to consolidate themselves into a Church.

The prepossessions of many readers lead them to see in this transition an element of anticlimax. The lyrical and visionary gift provides its own commendation to the awakened and sensitive spirit. The ecclesiastic with his gift of government is less immediately attractive. Nevertheless, he has his place. S. Paul puts "governments" seventh in the list of "the works of the Spirit" in the Body of Christ (1 Cor. xii, 28). In these days of ecclesiastical filing cabinets there are doubtless some who would put it first, even as there have been others who would put it nowhere! They are both wrong. The spiritual gift of government is not to be given the highest place, but it has a due place, and in that due place it is virtually indispensable. It is a mark of the age of the Apostolic Fathers that the time had come for the exercise of this gift.

This development answers to the peril inherent in that great and venturesome transplantation of the Faith into the exposed fields of the Gentile world. There was a need for some principle which would keep the Gentile converts true to the original and authentic tradition of Christianity, and thus shepherd the rapidly growing Gentile flock into one fold. There was need in the Church for that spirit of prudent management which can strike the happy mean between, on the one hand, unreasoning and rigid attachment to old ways when changing times demand flexibility, and, on the other, that error of irresponsible innovation which casts away the treasure of the past. The spirit of corporate discipline, of government, was original to the Christian Faith. No error is more perverse than the oft-repeated statement that Jesus did not intend to found a Church, and that original Christianity was a vague "movement," not interested in organization. In the teaching of our Lord the Church is "the New Israel," symbolically twelvefold like the Old, her distinctive rite a Christian Passover, the memorial of the founding of a nation. As the Old Israel was the disciplined community of the People of God, so is the New. The Church was from the beginning a body corporate, organically continuous with the Old Israel, yet made gloriously new with spiritual life. Nevertheless, this spirit of organic unity and corporate discipline, like other original and authentic elements in the Christian Faith, was not fully explicit in detail from the beginning. It had to undergo "doctrinal development" under the guidance of the Holy Spirit, and at the promptings of experience and practical need. The due time had now come for this development. That the attention of S. Clement is more taken up with problems of Church government and pastoral discipline than is that of S. Paul is not rightly to be regarded as a mark of the fall of the Church. It is a token that the season had now come for God to fulfil Himself in another way. There is a certain propriety in the circumstance that this Epistle was written from Rome. Many nations have brought gifts into the Church. The Hebrews brought the Christ. The Greeks brought the gift of contemplation. And more than anyone else, perhaps, the Romans have brought the gift of government. It is a moving spectacle to see them exercising it so early, and with such accomplishment!

The occasion of the writing of this Epistle was a dispute which had broken out in the Church at Corinth, in which duly appointed presbyters had been put out of office by insubordinate action. S. Paul would have recognized the Corinthian Christians as running true to form! On hearing of this, the Church at Rome wrote a brotherly letter (or one might perhaps say a "fatherly" letter, for it is couched in a certain tone of leadership), exhorting the Corinthian Church to discipline, unity, and respect for constituted authority in the Church. The first matter of significance is that one local congregation should write to another in this way. This plainly shows that though there was as yet in the Church no accepted and permanent visible administrative machinery of central government, yet the sentiment of corporate cohesion was strong. Many commentators, and of more parties than one, have been guilty of theological anachronism in discussing this salient issue. Some, having observed that to outward view the primitive Church looked like a chain of "independent-type" congregations, have instinctively assumed that the early Christians felt and behaved much like modern "Independents." On the other hand, some to whom it is a matter of deep conviction that the first Christians must have cherished "Catholic-type" values in their thought regarding the Church have at times too readily assumed that these spiritual values can only exist as and when they are outwardly embodied in the Church by those ecclesiastical institutions marked out by later Church usage as the due means for this embodiment. This has presented a temptation to wrest the history of the ancient Church, in the endeavour to show that the Church invariably possessed "Catholic-type" institutions, such as an unbroken succession of ruling bishops. On both sides there has been confusion between the outward form and the inward spirit of corporate cohesion, and an illegitimate attempt to compress the life of the ancient Church into the familiar categories and distinctions of the modern period. We submit that a study of the Apostolic Fathers will illuminate this matter, and show wherein the antagonists on both sides have erred.

The Epistle of S. Clement presents us with the fascinating spectacle of a Church thinking and behaving in an essentially "episcopal" and "Catholic" manner, yet without any officer which a modern Churchman could well recognize as a "bishop." The Epistle argues in a most compelling way that the Church is to be ruled by an authoritative ministry of divine appointment, which is in continuous succession to the Apostles. It shows the Roman Church acting in an authoritative manner. Yet the Roman Church appears to be governed not by a single bishop but by a presbytery, that is, by a body of substantially equal officers who comprise in their persons the office of both presbyter and bishop, the two names still having the same significance. Thus these early Christians certainly felt, thought, and behaved in a thoroughly Catholic manner about the Church, and not at all in what we would today call a "sect-type" way. Yet they practised this strong Churchmanship without it being visibly embodied in some of the institutions which to the modern mind are inseparably associated with "Catholic churchmanship." Some modern exponents of "Catholic churchmanship" find it genuinely hard to open their minds to the thought that these values which they cherish can be preserved in the absence of the traditional ministerial order of the Church. They thus feel a deep reserve toward nonepiscopal modern Christians. Such a writing as this Epistle stands as a warning to them not to be overconfident in this judgment. This very venerable and authoritative Roman Church appears to have been at this time in just this position of a Catholic Church with no single ruling bishop. And if there could be such then, it is not altogether impossible that there may be such now!

Yet the salutary warning goes with equal force the other way. There are some modern Christians who, in the supposed interests of primitive New Testament and spiritually "free" Christianity, are at times too much inclined to resist the claim that the historic episcopal institutions of the Catholic Church are the due and proper embodiment for the spiritual cohesion of all believers in one body. They may see in this Epistle a salient example of the principle of doctrinal development. This first venerable Church did in fact think, feel, and behave in a thoroughly "churchly" manner. As and when the primitive Church had time to reflect upon her own nature, and to respond to the lessons of experience, the institutions of authoritative corporate Churchmanship spontaneously arose, and by unerring instinct made their universal appeal. They did this because, though not originally explicit in the Church, they were from the authentic beginning wholly implicit. In the Epistle of Clement we see primitive Christianity displaying this nature, and undergoing an early stage of this logical development. This is surely a standing warning not to be overconfident in the rejection of the venerable institutions of traditional Christianity. History has made them the due and accepted embodiment of many of the values of authentic original Christianity. And both ways we are warned against trying to portray that ancient Church which is the Mother of us all after the inevitably partial patterns of our modern separated denominations. The issue posed by the age of the Apostolic Fathers has only to be stated for one to observe what practical import it has within the modern situation.

We cannot say for certain why the Roman Church wrote to Corinth upon this particular occasion. We may surmise that most probably the aggrieved party at Corinth had appealed in some way to the Church at Rome for the assistance of her good offices in securing respect for due order. It is interesting to observe the manner in which the Church in Rome exercises the gift of government. She does not write as though she could command. There is no Roman sovereignty here. Still less is there anything of the spirit of those ecclesiastical anathemas which lesser man in later times have too often used to assert their authority. The Apostles themselves after the Council of Jerusalem had written to advise, not to command (Acts xv, 29), but they wrote as those who knew that their grave and considered advice would come with immense compulsive force upon the conscience of their readers. The Church of Rome likewise writes to her sister at Corinth in this truly apostolic spirit, not claiming sovereignty, but with awareness of prestige and moral authority. It is notable also what is the foundation of this prestige. The Church of Rome does not assert her position as the Church of the imperial capital, or as a large or influential Church. The claim made is that she was the witness of the teaching and the martyrdom of two of the greatest of the Apostles, S. Peter and S. Paul. The authority of the whole Church lies in the fact that she treasures the heritage of the first authentic apostolic witness to the facts of the Gospel. The Church of Rome is the eminent though by no means exclusive example of this general principle.

2. Authorship and Date

It will be observed that, though the name of S. Clement of Rome has always been attached to this Epistle, and this traditional authorship is almost universally accepted by modern scholarship, the Epistle is in no sense a personal one, like those of S. Paul. The author does not name himself, and he writes expressly in the name of the Church at Rome. The earliest testimony that the Epistle was the work of one "Clement" appears about A.D. 170 in the writings of Dionysius, Bishop of Corinth, as they are reported and cited in the *Church History* of Eusebius (*H.E.*, IV, xxiii, 11). The passage cited says of the Epistle "that it had been the custom from the beginning to read it in the Church." This would be to read it as in effect an "apostolic writing," and in the same class as those writings which were at this time being formed into the Canon of the New Testament. That some circles in the early Church regarded it as canonical New Testament Scripture, or as almost canonical, is also perhaps indicated by the circumstance that a MS of it occurs at the end of the New Testament in the Codex Alexandrinus. In his own account of Clement, Eusebius first states that he succeeded Anencletus (or Anacletus) in the twelfth year of the Emperor Domitian, that is, A.D. 93 (*H.E.*, III, xv). This date agrees with the internal evidence of the Epistle, which appears to indicate that it was written toward the end of the persecution which took place under that emperor, that is, about A.D. 95. It is thus one of the very oldest Christian writings outside the New Testament, and perhaps the oldest. In the same passage Eusebius further claims that this Clement is the Clement mentioned by S. Paul as his "fellowlabourer," in Philippians iv, 3. This is, of course, not impossible, but it is the sort of thing which pious supposition of later times would be likely to imagine, and we do not know upon what authority Eusebius makes his statement. In this account of S. Clement, Eusebius then goes on: "There is extant an Epistle of this Clement, which is acknowledged to be genuine, and is of considerable length and of remarkable merit. He wrote it in the name of the church of Rome to the church of Corinth. . . . We know that this Epistle also has been publicly used in a great many churches both in former times and in our own" (*H.E.*, III, xvi).

S. Irenaeus, furthermore, writing only a little later than Dionysius, in the celebrated passage in which he affirms the apostolic foundation and spiritual prestige of the Roman Church, goes on to give a list of the Bishops of Rome. First he records Linus, and claims that he is the Linus mentioned in 2 Timothy iv, 21. Next there is Anacletus, "and after him, in the third place from the apostles, Clement was allotted the bishopric. This man, as he had seen the blessed apostles, and had been conversant with them, might be said to have the preaching of the apostles still echoing in his ears, and their traditions before his eyes" (*Adv. Haer.*, III, iii, 3). Irenaeus then goes on to give an account of the Epistle. It is well possible that the author might in his youth have heard SS. Peter and Paul teaching in Rome, as Irenaeus says. There is, however, an element of anachronism in the designation of these early Roman figures as "bishops," for the Epistle itself appears to indicate that there was at Rome at this time no "bishop" in the sense in which S. Irenaeus uses the word, that is, a single ruling bishop, presiding over the presbytery. Nevertheless, we can hardly doubt that S. Clement was a leading figure among the company of the "presbyter-bishops" which governed the Roman Church at this time. Thus he was *almost* a "bishop," but Irenaeus naturally reads back the conditions of his own time into this earlier period.

3. Manuscript Sources

(i) The most ancient and the best authority for the text is the MS which is found at the end of the famous Codex Alexandrinus, the fifth century uncial MS of the New Testament in the British Museum. However, this copy of Clement has lost its end, and is illegible in parts. (ii) The Constantinopolitan MS dated A.D. 1056, and published by Bryennios in 1875, contains the whole of the text, together with other important texts of the Apostolic Fathers. (iii) There is a Syriac translation of A.D. 1170, now at Cambridge.

4. Commentary on the Epistle of S. Clement to the Corinthians

Note.—The newcomer to Patristic studies is advised that the Fathers of the Church commonly quote the Old Testament from the Septuagint, the traditional ancient Greek version of the Scripture. There are many variations of wording, sometimes considerable, from the Hebrew text, which is the foundation of our accustomed English versions of the Old Testament. This is the normal explanation why so many of the Old Testament quotations in the Apostolic Fathers appear in a form unfamiliar to the reader of the English Bible, even at times to the point of being hard to recognize.

Salutation. "The Church of God which sojourneth": This reflects the New Testament doctrine that the local Christian congregations at Rome and at Corinth are not properly local independent "Churches." They are local parts of the one Church.

"Grace to you and peace . . . be multiplied": This greeting is manifestly a union of the typically Pauline greeting, as in Romans i, 7, with the Petrine, in 1 Peter i, 2.

"Grace . . . be multiplied": To Dr. T. F. Torrance this is an initial example of the way in which Clement uses Pauline evangelical language without grasping its essential meaning. He writes: "The addition of πληθυνθείν is also worth noting. It is not Pauline, but is found in First and Second Peter and Jude. To Clement's Greek mind this word might imply the idea that one can have more or less of grace which, of course, on a Pauline doctrine, is impossible."[1] The student is referred to Dr. Torrance's more detailed argument as to the meaning of the word "grace" in S. Paul (pp. 26 ff.). It will suffice here to indicate that the statement that one cannot have *degrees* of grace carries the implication that the common theological notion of "grace" as a divine power working in man to renew his character is to be rejected as false to the Pauline understanding of the Gospel. Dr. Torrance would restrict the Pauline (and therefore, for the purpose of his argument, the Christian) definition of grace to the notion of a decisive divine act whereby God, for the sake of His unmerited mercy and love, chooses to place sinful man on a reconciled relationship to Himself. Manifestly, if "grace" is almost exclusively a divine declaration in Christ of love, forgiveness, and release from the burden of guilt, there cannot be degrees of it, though there may be degrees of human realization of God's attitude toward man. Equally, if as has been usual in Christian theology, the notion of "grace" is allowed to comprehend, in addition

[1] *The Doctrine of Grace in the Apostolic Fathers*, p. 51 (hereafter cited as *Grace in the Apostolic Fathers*).

to God's gracious favour, the idea also of a *power* flowing into man's life to change his character, then there can be degrees of "growth in grace." It would seem that the first usage is typical of S. Paul, though Dr. Torrance himself would appear to admit that the idea of "grace" as a power communicating itself is not wholly alien even to the Apostle (p. 32).

Whatever be one's judgment in this technical matter of the use of language, two things ought to be said. First, it seems to be placing more upon the New Testament language than it will bear to make a precise distinction between a presumed true idea of "grace" as the unmerited favour of God, and a presumed false idea of "grace" as an infused power. If the load which prevents the spirits of men rising to brave new moral endeavour is chiefly the weight of a guilty conscience, and of self-despisings before God, then to be liberated from it releases into the human personality a power which changes the character and moral will, and this power works by progressive stages. Grace as manifested divine favour, and grace as infused divine power, can hardly be separated, save in thought. Second, we place more weight upon S. Clement's language than it will bear if we draw from this passage the conclusion that he has departed from a true understanding of the Christian Gospel of salvation by grace. His terminology is not so exact as the critic would assume. Whether or no he teaches "salvation by grace" is to be determined from whether he holds that man is to be renewed with the assistance of divine power, or simply by human effort in self-improvement. It is not to be settled by seeking to find fine distinctions of language in a nontechnical vocabulary.

1. "Sudden and repeated calamities and reverses which have befallen us": This may be taken as referring to the persecution of the Church at Rome, under the Emperor Domitian, in A.D. 95.

"The elect of God": The Church is the New Israel; compare 1 Peter ii, 9.

"To the older men"; πρεσβυτέροις (Lightfoot, p. 5): In this Epistle the rulers of the Church are called "elders" and "bishops" without apparent distinction (see chapters 42, 44).

2. "More glad to give than to receive": An apparent allusion to Acts xx, 35. The very numerous Biblical quotations in this Epistle are chiefly from the Old Testament, together with a number of the sayings of Jesus, apparently cited from the canonical Gospels. Other New Testament quotations are very few. This is the usage we would expect at this very early period, when "the Scriptures" were still in effect what they were in the New Testament Church, namely, the Jewish Scriptures. The words of Christ Himself were from the beginning naturally remembered and quoted as an authority, but the Apostolic writings are still not more than the written substitute for the personal testimony of an Apostle. As there are still numbers of persons in the Church who distinctly remember the Apostles, the need for citing Apostolic writings is only just arising. The New Testament quotations in S. Clement are interesting, as they may be presumed to be the first appearances in Christian literature of the New Testament books. This allusion to Acts is to a celebrated and most authentic-sounding "word of the Lord" not recorded in the Gospels. This raises the question as to whether Clement is in fact citing Acts, or independently remembering the same orally transmitted saying of Christ as is recorded in Acts.

"And giving heed unto His words . . . His sufferings were before your eyes" (cf. 2 Cor. iv, 6, 10; Gal. iii, 1; and so on): Despite the observations of some critics, it may be confidently affirmed that there is a strong evangelical principle in this Epistle. Salvation by divine grace is clearly centered in the spectacle of the divine sufferings in Christ, as here.

"A profound and rich peace was given to all, and an insatiable desire of doing good. . . . Ye had conflict day and night for all the brotherhood": In a truly evangelical and Pauline manner (cf. Phil. ii, 5 ff.), Clement's mind moves in this paragraph from the thought of the Cross to that of Christian mutual responsibility and long-suffering. This flows from the principle of the Cross, and is the cement of that Church unity which he is writing to enjoin upon Corinth.

"Ready unto every good work": A quotation of Titus iii, 1.

"Written on the tables of your hearts": Compare Proverbs vii, 3.

3.4. "That was fulfilled which is written"; τὸ γεγραμμένον (Lightfoot, p. 6): By contrast with the allusive use of the Apostolic writings, this solemn formula indicates an express quotation of authoritative Scripture, that is, the Old Testament. It will be noted that S. Clement uses the Greek (LXX) canon of the Old Testament, as does the ancient Church in general, and quotes the Wisdom of Solomon as Scripture, without distinction. The theology of chapters 3 and 4, with their citations of Deut. xxxii, 15; Isa. iii, 5; lix, 14; Wisd. ii, 24; Gen. iv, 3–8;

and Ex. ii, 14, is a demonstration that the spiritual experiences of Old Israel were a rehearsal for the guidance of the Church. In the Old Testament there is a "type" of everything in the New. It will be observed that S. Paul himself had notably made this point to the Corinthian Church (1 Cor. x, 11). Thus the experiences of the Church bring the Old Testament to its fitting climax, and "fulfil" the Scripture. The moral of the quotations is that in Old Israel, and even right back to Cain and Abel, pride worked insubordination and strife, which is the undoing of God's people. And this is what has happened at Corinth!

5. "Those champions who lived nearest to our time... which belong to our generation": This moving passage presupposes a vivid memory of the martyrdom of SS. Peter and Paul at Rome. It is moving to feel that these historic events are here written of as experience, not as history. The suffering of the Christian martyrs at the hands of an evil world, which is moved by an irrational jealousy of the righteous, is the supreme historic example of, and so is the "fulfilment" of, the principle seen in the sufferings of Abel, Jacob, Joseph, Moses, and David. It is noteworthy that a Christian with a Latin name, writing from an essentially Gentile Church, should have preserved this strong sense of the spiritual and organic continuity of the Church with Old Israel.

"The greatest and most righteous pillars of the Church": A clear tradition fixes upon Peter and Paul as eminent among the founding Apostles of the Church. It is interesting that we get the same impression from this Epistle as from Acts. S. Peter is given pride of place as the first of the Apostles, but S. Paul has more deeply impressed the memory of the Church as foremost in missionary enterprise, labour, and suffering. We see that the primitive Church judged these things on traditional grounds. An Apostle owes his place of honour to the choice of Christ, not, as in the modern manner, to the quantity of useful activity for which he is responsible. In the same way, the Roman Church owes her prestige not so much to her activity as to her traditional foundation. The implicit plea of apostolic foundation in this chapter is indeed Rome's mandate for writing as she does to Corinth. There were Christians in Rome before the arrival of either Peter or Paul, as is evidenced by the Epistle to the Romans. However, this in no way precludes the idea that the two Apostles were influential in founding the Church at Rome.

"After he had been seven times in bonds": This account may

possibly be largely derived from Acts, though it could well have been remembered independently.

It is notable that as we pass from the martyrs of the Old Covenant to those of the New, Christ Himself is not cited as the supreme example of martyrdom, though the writer is mindful that He did suffer. In the thinking of the primitive Church Christ was not, as so often to the modern mind, the supreme Martyr. First and foremost He was the sacrifice for sin, and the conqueror of the devil. In this He was in a class by Himself. The early martyr Church had a strong sense of the relationship of their own sufferings to those of their Lord, but the connection was from man to Christ, not Christ to man. It was not that Christ suffered as the supreme example of the sufferings of the Christians. The Christians were called to suffer in order that they might fully be one with Christ as He offered His unique sacrifice, and waged His decisive warfare.

6. "A vast multitude of the elect": The reference here is doubtless to the earlier and more severe persecution at Rome under Nero, A.D. 64, associated with the deaths of SS. Peter and Paul.

"Danaids and Dircae": This corrupt text is of obscure meaning. We know that sometimes the Christian victims were in mockery dressed up as figures in heathen mythology (for example, in "Passion of SS. Perpetua and Felicitas," xviii).[1] Possibly there were cases in which they were done to death in the enactment of a sort of grim stage "play," and there is some such reference here. This would accord with the famous account given by Tacitus of the Neronian persecution, where it is stated that "besides being put to death they were made to serve as objects of amusement," though the details do not elucidate this passage.[2]

"This now is bone of my bones": Genesis ii, 23.

7. "For we are in the same lists": This is doubtless an appropriate application of S. Paul's metaphor in writing to the Corinthians, where he likens the Christian life to the famous Corinthian Games (1 Cor. ix, 24–7).

"Let us fix our eyes on the blood of Christ and understand how precious it is unto His Father, because being shed for our salvation it won for the whole world the grace of repentance": Some have felt that

---

[1] *Acts of the Early Martyrs*, ed. E. C. E. Owen, p. 89.
[2] *Annales*, xv, 44.

the somewhat restrained references to Christ's atoning death, of which this is the first, are inadequate to their theme, and betray a lack of evangelical understanding in S. Clement. There is some force in this case. If the standard of comparison be S. Paul, we have to admit that there are passages where the Apostle speaks of the Cross with more passion that does S. Clement (for example, Gal. ii, 20). However, it is not easy after all these years to make allowance for the subtle difference of ethos between an urgent personal appeal of S. Paul to his friends and a dignified official communication from one Church to another in a matter of ecclesiastical discipline. Nor are we lightly to assume that Clement did not feel about the Cross as we think he ought to have done, because he does not express himself as we would. Western Christianity has long associated the appeal of the Cross with religious sentiment, in the Middle Ages with a million agonized crucifixes, since then, and in evangelical circles, with a million "awakening revival sermons" about "the blood." In this primitive period the Gospel indeed spread marvellously, but there is no evidence whatever that the appeal was made through sentiment (though we are not arguing that sentiment has no due place). The primitive "Gospel appeal" was a statement of objective fact, of a sacrifice offered, a victory won. It was declared objectively, in the Sacraments. This is indeed the spirit of S. Mark's Gospel, which paints its grim scene of Calvary, but sheds no tear, holds up no hands in horror. We are in that ancient world here, and it is dangerous to judge the evangelical insight of the Apostolic Fathers by the standards of our time. What is significant is that the objective fact is here, though stated with classic restraint. The blood of Christ is of infinite merit in the sight of the Father, and has brought to all mankind the power and opportunity of repentance. A doctrine of atonement is indeed not stated in the careful language of later times, but the essential is there, because Clement teaches that God freely forgives the penitent sinner, and that in the Cross there is a prevailing incentive to penitence, and also that which emboldens sinful man to come to God in his penitence. It is a little severe in judgment on Clement to write: "What Christ's death is said to procure is not atonement, but an opportunity for repentance."[1] It is notable also that in light of the work of the Cross the whole human race is a unity. The

[1]Torrance, *Grace in the Apostolic Fathers*, p. 46.

offer of the grace of repentance is for all. There is no notion of the particular Election of individuals to salvation, and this is the invariable attitude of the primitive Church.

"From generation to generation the Master hath given a place for repentance unto them that desire to turn to Him": We observe that the preaching of Noah and Jonah (both preachers, be it noted, to those who were outside the Covenant, and so "aliens from God") is a preaching of Christ. This is another illustration of the solidarity of the Church with the righteous of old time. This solidarity can indeed be misconstrued to give a doctrine that the work of Christ was only to bring a clarification of the old Law. This, however, was not the true mind of the ancient Church, and there is no necessity to see this in Clement. His real intention here is to affirm that righteous men of old time, who faithfully followed such light as they had, will in the end be found to belong to Christ, and to have been in their day and generation "Christians before Christ." It is not denied that there is something radically new in the Incarnation and the Cross, but it is affirmed that the saving effect of the Incarnation and the Cross extends backward in time, as well as forward (Heb. xi; 1 Pet. iii, 19–20).

8. This theme naturally leads Clement into an Old Testament sermon on repentance and faith, leading up to the thought that the fruit of penitence is humility, and the fruit of humility unity within the Church. If we ask why the sermon on faith should be from the *Old* Testament, the answer is, as with Hebrews xi, that at this early time the only authoritative Scripture which could be quoted in the Church was the Old Testament. However, as is the case with Hebrews xi itself, the argument suffers from an inevitable limitation. Faith in the Old Testament is "the faith of Abraham." It is fidelity: the committing of one's life to a course of action based on obedience to God, in trust that God will fulfil His promise to guide, to strengthen, and to bless. This is indeed a large part of "Christian, saving faith," but it is not quite the whole. Being "faith before Christ," it inevitably lacks the central element of personal loving trust in, and loving unity with, Christ the Saviour. The danger of faith considered as fidelity is that it is in constant danger of slipping into faith considered as obedience, and nothing more. Clement's Old Testament exhortation to repentance and faith does not entirely escape this danger.

"The ministers of the grace of God through the Holy Spirit": The inspired writers of the Old Testament were preachers of *grace*. How far S. Clement can show that this is so remains to be seen.

"For as I live, saith the Lord": This is aptly quoted from Ezekiel xxxiii, 11, one of the great prophetic passages on free and loving divine forgiveness.

"Repent ye, O house of Israel": This is apparently a citation from some apocryphal Jewish book.

"Wash, be ye clean": Isaiah i, 16–20. This beautiful and eloquent passage of prophetic morality is not perhaps quite so clear on the theme of grace, as it assumes that man can make himself well pleasing to God by doing social right.

"Seeing then that He desireth all His beloved to be partakers of repentance, He confirmed it by an act of His almighty will": It is not quite explicit what this "act" is, but the most natural construction is that it is God's saving act in Christ. If so, S. Clement may well realize that there is more to be said about salvation by grace than Isaiah i, elevated morality and beautiful poetry though this passage be.

9. "Wherefore let us be obedient": Here we see the weakness of the Old Testament argument of faith in terms of fidelity. It easily becomes represented as no more than obedience, which is what happens here.

"Them that ministered perfectly unto His excellent glory": Compare 2 Peter i, 17.

10. "Abraham . . . was found faithful in that he rendered obedience": Following S. Paul, S. James, and the writer to the Hebrews, Abraham is set forth as the Old Testament type of faith, with citations of Genesis xii, 1–3; xiii, 14–16; and xv, 5, 6. We note that Clement does not say that faith is simply obedience to God, which would be an unevangelical error. He rightly affirms that Abraham's obedience was the fruit and mark of his faith.

11. We are less convinced about Lot as a type of faith!

12. The same applies to the story of Rahab, despite the weighty precedent of Hebrews xi, 31. We have quotations of Joshua ii, 3 ff.

"A scarlet thread, thereby showing beforehand that through the blood of the Lord there shall be redemption unto all them that believe": We have here a "type of Christ." A detail of the story is regarded as holding a hidden meaning, as well as the literal and historical, which in some way answers to the principle of Christ. In this way the Old Testament is read as a Christian book. Such exegesis, though poles asunder from modern critical methods, is characteristic of the ancient Fathers. It answers on the one hand to their conviction that the Scriptures spoke of Christ, and on the other to the obscurity, and sometimes the offensiveness, of the literal and historical meaning of certain passages.

"Not only faith, but prophecy, is found in the woman": Prophecy here is not a supernatural power to foresee the future, but a faculty granted by God whereby "types" answering to Christ were inserted into the narrative. This is a somewhat unscientific way of stating the fundamental Christian proposition that the Old Covenant and Old Testament Scriptures came from the same God as did the New.

13. The argument is now coming round to its destined aim. The fruit of penitent submission to God is humility. Those who are aware that they have been forgiven will forgive. Humility works submission to the brotherhood, and in particular to duly constituted authority in the Church. It is therefore the active principle of Church unity and discipline, for which Clement pleads.

"For the Holy Ghost saith": We have apt quotations on the theme of humility before God from Scripture, which is the voice of the Holy Spirit: Jeremiah ix, 23, 24.

"Most of all remembering the words of the Lord Jesus": We come now to what are perhaps the earliest quotations of the words of our Lord in Christian literature, from S. Matthew v, 7; vi, 14; vii, 1, 2; S. Luke vi, 31, 36–8. It would be hard for S. Clement to attribute to them a higher degree of spiritual authority, for they follow as its due climax the very voice of the Holy Spirit in authoritative Scripture. It is noteworthy that the Church came to this point long before the writings of the Apostles could be quoted as "Scripture." This indicates that the primitive Christian message (the so-called "kerygma") was by no means confined, as some have tended to argue, to an announcement that Christ's incarnation, death, and resurrection had brought the Kingdom of God to man. Doubtless this was the central point of it, but an essential part of the Christian message was a rule of life for the redeemed, based upon our Lord's moral teaching. The Christians were in the first place the redeemed followers of a victorious Risen Lord, but in this strength they were also the disciples of a teaching Master. This provided the motive for remembering the moral teaching of Jesus, as here.

"Upon whom shall I look": Isaiah lxvi, 2.

14. Rebellion against duly constituted authority in the Church is disobedience to God. Citations of Proverbs ii, 21, 22, and of Psalm xxxvii, 35–7.

15. Further citations on the theme of obedience to God: Isaiah xxix, 13; Psalm lxvii, 4; lxxviii, 36, 37; xii, 3–5.

16. It is interesting to speculate why the author should have considered it worth while to fill up a whole chapter with a long quotation of Isaiah liii, 1–12, and Psalm xxii, 6–8, though the Corinthian Church must have had copies. We may perhaps see in the Epistle echoes of the sermon-method of the ancient Church, with impressive recitals of Scripture *in extenso*. It is at least plain that S. Clement lays great store by the authority of a Scriptural argument in vindicating ecclesiastical authority and the tradition of the Church. Scripture and ecclesiastical authority are in no sense opposite quantities in his view. S. Clement is quite characteristic of the ancient Fathers in that, following our Lord Himself (S. Luke xxii, 37), and the first Church (Acts viii, 30–35), he clearly connects Isaiah liii with the sufferings and death of Christ, yet does not draw from it any substitutionary theology of the Atonement, which was not known in the Church at that early period. (See Irenaeus, *Adv. Haer.*, IV, xxxiii, 11; *Demonstration*, 67, 69.) The sufferings of Christ are here treated primarily as a pattern of humility, and of obedient submission to God. This by no means involves, however, that Clement sees in the Cross only "a good example," which Christians have to try to follow. He is on the same ground as S. Paul himself, in his great theological passage Philippians ii, 5–11. The Cross is an objective victory over evil, wrought not by force, but by the divine power of suffering love. The Christian is to be one with Christ in this.

17. The theme of obedient faith in the Old Testament is continued, with quotations from Genesis xviii, 27; Job i, 1; xiv, 4, 5; Numbers xii, 7; and Exodus iii, 11; iv, 10.

"And again he saith, But I am smoke from the pot": This appears to be cited as "Scripture," but it must be from some apocryphal Jewish book.

18. The scriptural argument is continued by consideration of the case of David, introduced by a brief citation of Psalm lxxxix, 20, with an allusion to 1 Samuel xiii, 14, leading into a long citation of Psalm li, 3-19.

19. The scriptural argument for the virtue of humility closes with an appeal, enforcing the blessedness of those who walk in this way, and the favour of God toward them.

20. Clement has covered one branch of the preparation for the Gospel. In considerable detail he has surveyed Israel as the precursor of the Church, and her prophets as speaking of Christ. He now significantly turns from revealed religion to a brief survey of the other branch of the preparation for Christ. We have divine truth argued and demonstrated from the rational order of nature. This is "natural religion." What we have here is not a distinctively Christian argument. It is one which could be shared by a Jew, or indeed by many other exponents of the higher religions. Nevertheless, we are reminded by this chapter that rational argument to demonstrate the truths of religion from the constitution of the world, and of man who lives in it, has always had its due place in the best-considered and most-balanced tradition of Christian theology and preaching. Natural theology is indeed not more than the substratum of Christian theology. It cannot speak of the profoundest and most distinctively Christian truths of the faith. However, it is an important part of the introduction to the Christian faith. Thus we may see from the sermons recorded in Acts that when the primitive Christian preachers addressed themselves to pagans, who had no preparation through knowledge of the Law and the Prophets, they opened the case by arguing as Jews to Gentiles. They were reticent about the specific Christian doctrine of Christ the crucified Son of God. Rather by argument from the order of nature and divine providence did they enforce the folly and impurity of idolatry (Acts xiv, 15-17; xvii, 22-31). Clement's interlude of natural theology is brief, but it is one of the noblest and most impressive passages in the Epistle. The argument is that the world which God has made, and which He rules by His providence, is a world of law and order. It displays the principle that subjection to law produces order. If this indeed be the nature of God, the moral is plain: Subjection to law must be found working order in the Church of God!

"Into its reservoirs": Genesis i, 9.
"So far shalt thou come": Job xxxviii, 11.

"Doing good to all things, but far beyond the rest unto us who have taken refuge in His compassionate mercies through our Lord Jesus Christ": It is pleasing to find that at the close of the little essay in natural religion the higher truth of Catholic and evangelical dogma is remembered. The Christian lives not only by divine law and divine providence, but chiefly by divine grace, made known in Christ.

21. This truth is applied in an explicit appeal for the observance of ecclesiastical order in Corinth.

"The Spirit of the Lord is a lamp": Proverbs xx, 27.

"Let us reverence our rulers; let us honour our elders"; τοὺς πρεσβυτέρους ἡμῶν (Lightfoot, p. 17): If there had been in Corinth a single ruling bishop of the later pattern, the writer could hardly have failed to mention him in a context such as this, where he is so explicitly enforcing the claims of Church order. If there had been a ruling bishop at Rome, a mention here might have been fitting. This is part of the evidence that in the Churches known to Clement there was at this time no clear distinction, and perhaps no distinction at all, between the elders (presbyters) and the bishops. The local Church was governed by a corporate body of substantially equal "presbyter-bishops." See also chapters 42, 44, with notes.

"What power chaste love hath with God, how the fear of Him is good and great and saveth all them that walk therein": It is to be admitted that by the standard of the carefully considered language of later theology regarding "salvation by grace," this is a faulty statement. God is not moved toward us by our own initial goodness and love, nor are we saved by the "fear" of God, that is, by our own obedience. It is, however, altogether too critical to condemn Clement on this account. All he means to say here is that a life of submission to God, and of strict virtue, is well pleasing to God. Christ plainly said this much, and S. Paul himself would have agreed.

22. The chapters thus far have been introductory, being concerned with the prophetic preparation for the Gospel. The life of Israel, the Law and the Prophets, have for Clement this use: they enforce the lesson of submission to God, and of unity in the Church. The writer now opens the central section of his Epistle (chapters 22–36), which we may call doctrinal, because it deals with some salient points of more distinctive Christian belief. It is, however, by no means a comprehensive treatment of Christian doctrine, but takes up certain points which can be used for the enforcement of the lesson of submission and unity. We have a survey of divine grace, the resurrection of the dead, justification by faith, and of the atonement, treated from this point of view.

"Now all these things the faith which is in Christ confirmeth": We have a certain degree of departure from the more usual Pauline usage here, for in this passage we have mention not of "faith," in the sense of personal saving trust in Christ, but of "the Faith," that is, the Christian way of life and body of doctrine, as in Acts vi, 7; Galatians i, 23; Ephesians iv, 5; Jude 3. Some critics strongly maintain that for a writer to use "faith" in this second sense betrays a decline in understanding of the essential nature of the Christian life, because it indicates a dangerous confusion between saving faith in Christ and mere orthodoxy and good Churchmanship. Our judgment is that this may be so in some cases, but is not necessarily so, nor invariably so. The case of each Apostolic writer must be considered on its own merits, for the matter is largely one of what is meant by different words. It is not to be presumed that a writer like S. Clement, who can speak of "the Faith," is lacking in understanding of "faith."

The citations are from Psalm xxxiv, 11-17, 19, and xxxii, 10.

23. The chapter opens with a declaration of God's grace. It is somewhat hypercritical to object that this is not truly "grace," because it is given to those who "draw nigh to God with a single mind." This degree of strictness in definition would condemn our Lord Himself for being "unsound on grace" in S. Matthew vii, 7.

"Wretched are the double-minded": Though this is called "Scripture," ἡ γραφή (Lightfoot, p. 18), it is not known whence the quotation comes. Lightfoot considers that possibly it comes from the lost Jewish apocryphal "Book of Eldad and Modat" mentioned in Hermas, Vision ii, 3 (see p. 229).

"He shall come quickly": Isaiah xiii, 22.

"The Lord shall suddenly come into His temple": Malachi iii, 1.

24. In the survey of the Christian faith we now come to a more extended treatment of the doctrine of the General Resurrection, as a sanction for good conduct. Two tokens are found for the truth of the General Resurrection, the fact of Christ's own resurrection, and the order of nature with its renewal of life. This is substantially the argument of 1 Corinthians xv.

"The sower goeth forth": We presumably, though not certainly, have allusion here to the word of the Lord in Matthew xiii, 3; Mark iv, 3; Luke viii, 5.

25. The legend of the Phoenix is treated as a type of the Resurrection. We may perhaps be thankful that this story did not find its way into the canon of Scripture! This may be suggested by a word-play between φοῖνιξ=phoenix, and φοῖνιξ=palm-tree, as it occurs in the Septuagint of Psalm xcii, 12.

26. "Holiness in the assurance of a good faith": The Resurrection is granted to those who, in the power of Christian faith, have lived a righteous life; cf. Matthew xxv, 31-46.

"And thou shalt raise me up": We observe that the early Church interpreted these texts, Psalm xxviii, 6; iii, 5; xxiii, 4; Job xix, 26, as prophecies of the General Resurrection.

27. "With this hope therefore let our souls be bound unto Him that is faithful in His promises and that is righteous in His judgments": The mention of the General Resurrection naturally leads to the doctrine of God's righteous Judgment, and this in turn to a renewed exhortation to the moral life (chapters 27-31).

"Let our faith in Him be kindled within us": Clement believes that faith is kindled in the heart by a conviction of the sovereign majesty of God, the all-seeing ruler of all things, and by a trust in His faithfulness to His promise. Taken in isolation this is less than a full saving faith in Christ. It is "the faith of Abraham." It is trustful obedience to God, rather than to "God in Christ." Nevertheless, the next section shows that Clement has not forgotten that God has made His salvation known in Christ.

"By a word [ἐν λόγῳ, Lightfoot, p. 20] of His majesty He compacted the Universe": The allusion is doubtless to Genesis i, 1 ff., and perhaps also to John i, 1-3. There is here at least an incipient doctrine of creation by the Logos (Word) of God.

"Who shall say unto Him": Wisdom xii, 12; xi, 22.

"The heavens declare the glory of God": Psalm xix, 1-4.

28. "For where can any of us escape from His strong hand? ... Whither then shall one depart, or where shall one flee, from Him that embraceth the universe?": Here is the salutary force of Jewish Biblical ethical monotheism to Gentile ex-polytheists. A doctrine of many gods presupposes a "sphere of influence" for each. Not one has an absolute claim. However, if there be but one sovereign Judge of the universe His claim is absolute, and morality is based absolutely. Dr. Torrance is probably right in observing that this impressive doctrine of ethical monotheism, now happily emancipated from its former association with unwelcome Jewish particularism, was one of the chief sources of appeal in early Christianity, and perhaps equally with the distinctively Christian message of salvation in Christ. It is to be admitted that there was herein a certain danger that Gentiles would be converted to faith in God, not faith in *Christ*.[1] As to S. Clement himself, he certainly devotes a good deal of space and loving care to the indispensable foundation of ethical "faith in God," but it is unfair to him to imply that he fails to recognize the distinctively Christian "faith in Christ."

"Where shall I go": A citation of Psalm cxxxix, 7–10, most appropriate to the context.

29. The grace of this sovereign Judge is shown in His loving choice of Old Israel, and after them the Church, to be His "elect People." This is the thought of Deuteronomy vii, 6–9. Scripture references are appropriately quoted to support this theme, from Deut. xxxii, 8–9; iv, 34; Num. xviii, 27; Ezek. xlviii, 12.

30. "God resisteth the proud": Prov. iii, 34, as cited in Jas. iv, 6, and 1 Pet. v, 5.

"Being justified by works and not by words"; δικαιούμενοι (Lightfoot, p. 21): This interesting and important phrase introduces us to a matter in which many have been found at cross-purposes, alike in the primitive Church, and at the Reformation, and today. S. Paul's characteristic formula was "justification by faith and not by the works of the Law." The intention of this is plain. Man is saved by faith in Christ, not merely by being a good Jew. The Christian religion is more than a reformed Judaism. It is to be affirmed that the Apostle is right in this fundamental point. However, his formula depends for its truth upon a right understanding of what he means by justification. In S. Paul's normal and characteristic usage it is man's *initial* acceptance with God. Justification is God's free forgiveness of the penitent sinner, for Christ's sake, but expounded in legal terminology. This position is also to be accepted as an important aspect of the Gospel of grace. Sinful man

---

[1] *Grace in the Apostolic Fathers*, p. 44.

cannot of his own unaided human resources do anything that will earn God's forgiveness, and establish his status before God. Acceptance with God can only be by free and unmerited forgiveness. It may be argued with some cogency that "justification" being S. Paul's characteristic word, it is only rightly used in his characteristic sense. The fact remains, however, that the New Testament itself is not invariable in this usage. Our Lord Himself (at least as reported in Matt. xii, 36–7) could use the term "justified" of man's *final* acceptance with God, at the Judgment. Later Church writers have often used the word in this way, as does official Roman Catholic theology today.[1] However, if justification be taken to include man's final acceptance with God, and made almost the equivalent of salvation, then to say "justification by faith and not by works" is open to dangerous misunderstanding. It may be understood as implying that man is accepted at the Judgment by his sincere profession of a "religious experience," or even by a mere acceptance of orthodoxy, rather than by a changed moral character and a righteous life. This is to sever the link between Christian faith and morality, and is contrary to the teaching of our Lord (as in Matt. vii, 21–3; xxv, 31–46). If it once be allowed that the word "justification" may be used of man's final acceptance with God, then it must be admitted that of the alternative formulae, "justification by faith and works" is nearer to the truth than is "justification by faith alone" (though S. Paul's original phrase, kept strictly to its historical context, is preferable to either). It is significant that even within the New Testament we find the Epistle of S. James objecting on these grounds to the formula "justification by faith," or, as some would prefer to say, objecting to what is wrongly taken to be the meaning of the Pauline formula (Jas. ii, 14–26). James' objection is the stronger because to him

---

[1] This is the chief ground of the familiar divergence between Roman Catholic and Lutheran theology in the matter of "justification by faith". Lutherans limit "justification" strictly to the initial act of acceptance of sinful man by God on account of grace. They naturally speak of "justification by faith alone". Roman Catholics extend "justification" to cover man's final acceptance with God, and therefore just as naturally speak of "justification by faith and works" (Council of Trent, v. 797, 24). As so often in these matters, there is between the two sides some real degree of difference in proportion and emphasis regarding spiritual intention, but this difference in proportion is heightened into an apparent one of principle by confusion of terminology. There is therefore between Roman Catholics and Protestants some genuine difference of spiritual apprehension, but it is not nearly so great or important as it superficially appears, or as is commonly supposed!

the definition of faith is "acceptance of the truth about God," but not necessarily including "loving obedience to God on the basis of that truth" (v. 19). If this be "faith," then "salvation by faith" is plainly antinomian. It need hardly be said that S. Paul includes much more within the notion of faith than does S. James.

The issue is that the Catholic Church in framing her accepted doctrine, as in so many other things, sought for a compromise and a comprehension. In token of this, both S. James and S. Paul are in the Canon as authoritative Scripture, despite their superficial contradictions. The Church in general accepted S. Paul's position, but tried to guard it against misunderstanding, by emphasizing the necessity of the discipline of good work as requisite to salvation. (We would not be supposed to imply that S. Paul, *rightly understood*, is in fact careless of good works, but the Church from the beginning has recognized some things in him which some have misinterpreted in this way.) Thus the main tradition of Catholic Christianity has established itself upon a substantial Paulinism, but a guarded and cautiously modified Paulinism. This is where S. Clement is. As compared to the Epistle of James we have a moderating position. The Pauline formula "salvation by faith" is not directly assailed, as in the Epistle of James, but "justification" is correctly affirmed to be not upon the basis of a profession of faith only. As in S. Matthew vii, 21, etc., deeds are required by God, as well as words. Yet S. Clement certainly does not intend to affirm the "unevangelical" position that salvation is by human good works, and not by divine grace (see chaps. 32, 38, and 49, with notes). We are warned against viewing Clement anachronistically with Reformation eyes, and forming from the phrase "justification by works" a too hasty judgment that he is a Christian Pharisee!

"He that saith much": Job xi, 2, 3.

31. "Abraham wrought righteousness and truth through faith": Here again we have faith as "fidelity." It is faith, but not full Christian faith. The passage is Scriptural but not absolutely Pauline.

32. Here, however, we have a thoroughly Pauline passage on "justification by faith," though the objections of Dr. Torrance merit consideration.[1]

"Thy seed shall be as the stars of heaven": Genesis xv, 5; xxii, 17.

[1] *Doctrine of Grace*, p. 50.

"They all therefore were glorified, not through . . . their own works . . . but through His will": The sons of Jacob were a priestly people by divine grace, and the same is true of the Church.

"Are not justified [δικαιούμεθα; Lightfoot, p. 22] . . . through our own wisdom or understanding or piety or works which we wrought in holiness of heart, but through faith": This is admittedly Pauline language. It may with some show of reason be claimed to bear a Pauline sense.

33. "Must we idly abstain from doing good, and forsake love?": Clement clearly sees that the principle which connects faith with its necessary good works is that faith works love in the heart, and love prompts to obedience (see particularly Chap. 49, and note).

"By His exceeding great might He established the heavens": This is a passage based on Genesis i, and containing quotations of verses 26, 27, and 28.

"The Lord Himself having adorned Himself with works rejoiced. Seeing then that we have this pattern, let us conform ourselves with all diligence to His will": We have an interesting application of the doctrine of divine creation. The existence of the Creation is the self-expression of God's good will, and man is to do good for the same reason. Human morality is a participation in God's work of creation.

34. Clement passes to an enforcement of the theme of zealous and joyous service, which service is also the rule of the angels. The quotations are from Isa. xl, 10; lxii, 11; Rev. xxii, 12; Dan. vii, 10; Isa. vi, 3; lxiv, 4; and 1 Cor. ii, 9.

35. "If our mind be fixed through faith towards God": In this context "faith" appears to be "fidelity."

"But unto the sinner said God": Psalm l, 16-23.

36. The doctrinal section of the Epistle closes with a brief and reticent, but effective, treatment of the saving work of Christ, based upon the doctrine of the Epistle to the Hebrews.

"Jesus Christ the High-priest of our offerings [τῶν προσφορῶν ἡμῶν; Lightfoot, p. 24], the Guardian and Helper of our weakness": It would appear that the Christian "offerings" are in the first place the acts of Christian obedience made by the believer in virtue of his union with Christ, as the Son offers to the Father His sacrifice of obedience (cf. Heb. ii, 9-18; v, 7-9). We cannot exclude, however, the distinct possibility that the "offering" is also that particular act of Christian obedience, the Eucharist, which is the appointed means whereby the Church makes herself one with Christ as He makes His sacrifice. Thus the "offering" here may be the same as the manifestly sacramental "offering" of Chapter 41, and the "gifts" of 44. The thought would then be that Christ is the High-priest who established the Christian sacrifice of the Eucharist, and whose self-offering is celebrated by the Church in the Eucharist. It is clearly stated that the Christian Highpriest is a Saviour, who helps frail man to come to God (cf. Heb. iv, 15–16).

"Through Him we behold as in a mirror His faultless and most excellent visage": This is certainly a much more profound notion than that Christ's office as Saviour is to reveal to man the true doctrine about God. The great High-priest is the One who gives man access to the heavenly sphere, even to the mysterious and invisible God Himself (cf. Heb. i, 3; ix, 24).

"Who being the brightness of His majesty": The usage of these quotations is interesting, and seems to shed light upon the distinction still felt to exist between full Old Testament Scripture, and an authoritative "apostolic" writing such as Hebrews, which was not yet regarded as Scripture. Hebrews i, 3, 4, 7, 5, and 13 are quoted without special introduction. These quotations in turn contain quotations of Psalm civ, 4; ii, 7, 8; cx, 1, and these are introduced with the solemn formula "for so it is written," indicating that they are properly "Scripture."

37. At this point the doctrinal section of the Epistle gives way to what may be designated the ecclesiastical section. Introduction having been made by the laying down of general principles, we now come in chapters 37–48 to the real purpose and particular application of the Epistle, in a pointed appeal for obedience to duly constituted authority in the Church at Corinth, and for the consequent unity of the Church.

"Let us mark the soldiers . . . Let us take our body as an example": This is a very "Roman" passage, and the contrast between it and S. Paul, upon whose writing it is manifestly based, is most revealing. The Apostle had written of the interdependence of believers with gifts great and small, within the unity of the Church, under the figure of the members in the Body of Christ. This is alluded to by S. Clement, but to him the Church is first and foremost an army rather than an organism. He expatiates upon the virtue of exact military obedience.

In principle he is on the same ground as S. Paul, but his conception of the Church is plainly less mystical, more external and ecclesiastical.

38. "According as also he was appointed with his special grace": It will be observed that "grace" has here not its primary meaning of the undeserved favour of God, but its derived meaning of a power at work in man, granted by that favour. Thus we here have not "grace" so much as "a grace," which is almost the equivalent of "a spiritual gift" in the writings of S. Paul. Those who have different and complementary "gifts" or "graces" are to help one another, and build one another up in the unity of the Church.

"Let him . . . not boast, knowing that it is Another who bestoweth his continence upon him": This is a clear reflection of the doctrine of salvation by divine grace. A correct consequence is drawn from the doctrine of grace, namely, the lesson of humility.

39. The virtue of Christian humility before the holy God is enlarged upon in a long citation of Job iv, 16–v, 5; xv, 15.

40. "Now the offerings and ministrations He commanded to be performed with care . . . at fixed times and seasons": The constitution of the Church corresponds to that of the Old Israel, but at a higher spiritual level. As there was an ordered ecclesiastical discipline in Israel, so there is to be in the Church, and the divinely appointed ministerial institutions of the Law are a "type" or prophecy of those in the Gospel. This is the fundamental theme of the Epistle to the Hebrews, which is the principle source of that theology which has spoken of the Christian ministry as a priesthood, and of the Eucharist as the Christian sacrifice. We cannot exclude the possibility that at times the nomenclature of pagan worship influenced the Church, but it is a fundamental error to look to the pagan sacrifices and Mysteries as the effective source of the Christian doctrine of the Ministry and Sacraments. Christ's own doctrine of the Church as the "New Israel" is the sufficient and intelligible source. However, like other Christian doctrines, the original needed to be developed, and this is what S. Clement here does.

"They therefore that make their offerings at the appointed seasons are acceptable and blessed": On the surface Clement seems to be reconstructing the religion of Israel; actually, he is applying his results to the Church as he goes along. Clement knows nothing of a supposed "free and easy" period in the first days of the Church, when "organization did not matter." To him duly appointed officers and duly celebrated ritual were an original part of Christianity, and one is strongly disposed to agree with him. Indeed, the notion of an original "unorganized" and "unincorporate" Christianity is the figment of the imagination of modern liberal historians! However, it is important herein to remember the principle of development. There is a difference between an accepted and authoritative ministry and a precisely organized ministry, and between a due and significant ritual and a complicated and rigidly fixed ritual. The two do not necessarily go together. The primitive Church had the first from the beginning, while the second was later developed.

"For unto the high-priest his proper services have been assigned...": It is pressing Clement's parallel too closely to say that he implies that to the Jewish high priest corresponds the bishop, to the priests the Christian presbyters, and to the Levites the deacons. Indeed, the passage is the strongest possible evidence that in the Church known to Clement there was no distinction in rank between a bishop and the presbyters, for a parallel between a threefold ministry in the ancient Scriptures and a threefold Ministry in the Church would have been so tempting that the writer could hardly have avoided drawing it, had he been able.

"The layman is bound by the layman's ordinances": The implication surely is that the whole body of the laity has a proper share in the sacramental ministry carried on by the whole Church. Yet this "universal priesthood" (1 Pet. ii, 9) by no means precludes some particular and representative limbs of the body from having a special office and ministry.

41. "Let each of you, brethren, in his own order give thanks"; εὐχαριστείτω, Lightfoot, p. 27: The "giving of thanks" (1 Cor. xiv, 16) in which every member of the Church is to take his due and united part is the Eucharist.

"But in Jerusalem alone": The allusion is doubtless to Deuteronomy xvi, 5–6.

"In proportion as greater knowledge hath been vouchsafed unto us, so much the more are we exposed to danger": There is spiritual danger, that is to say, if the Christian sacrifice be profaned (cf. 1 Cor. xi, 27–31). Clement plainly sees that the Christian ritual is at a higher spiritual level than the Old Testament sacrifices, but he shows little sympathy with the notion that the "Gospel freedom" of the Church allows carelessness in the manner of celebrating the Christian sacrifice to be a matter of relative indifference. The Church is to be more careful in discipline than the religion of the Law!

42. In this important chapter S. Clement elaborates his doctrine of the Apostolic Ministry. It is necessary carefully to observe both how much he says and what he significantly does not say. We must remember, moreover, that as he writes he has no idea of bringing his venerable authority to bear on this side or on that in later ecclesiastical "strife over the name of the bishop's office." He addresses himself to a practical and a much simpler problem, and it is an anachronism to expect his inexact language to correspond to later distinctions.

"So then Christ is from God, and the Apostles are from Christ": The ultimate reason in principle why the Christian Ministry is hierarchical, and has an authority from above, is that this corresponds to the heavenly plan. Christ was the personal representative upon earth of the invisible God. The Apostles were in turn the personal representatives of Christ. They therefore speak with an authority derived from the divine authority, and are to be reverenced as such.

"Having therefore received a charge": The constitution of this primitive Apostolic Ministry is now described. It is to be observed how S. Clement follows the New Testament. (*a*) The Apostles were chosen and commissioned by Christ (Matt. xxviii, 19; John xx, 21–3). (*b*) The qualification for this commission was that they were witnesses to the fact of the resurrection of Christ (Acts i, 21–2). (*c*) The equipment for the work was the gift of the Holy Spirit (Acts i, 8; ii, etc.). (*d*) The work they characteristically did was "preaching everywhere in country and town." They were travelling missionaries.

"They appointed their first-fruits . . . to be bishops and deacons" (cf. Acts xiv, 23; 2 Tim. i, 6): The last stage in this Ministry of derived divine authority is that of local officials in every place, appointed by the travelling Apostles as their permanent personal representatives. Again, there is no mention of presbyters as distinct from bishops. As in the New Testament, the two names appear to be alternative titles for the same office (Acts xx, 17; cf. 28). Thus Clement knows two ranks only in the ministry, bishops and deacons, as in Philippians i, 1. We may see a reason for the coupling of the title of "bishop" with that of "deacon" in this context in the quotation of Isaiah lx, 17, to which Clement proceeds. The Greek Septuagint translation, as used by the ancient Church, reads "bishops" and "deacons."

There is hardly space here to go into the interesting but obscure question of the origin of the ministry of deacons. It would appear to go back to the Seven mentioned in Acts vi, 1–6, chosen by the Church at Jerusalem, and ordained by the Apostles, to have charge over the administration of the Church's charity. However, later mention in Acts of members of the Seven represents them as preachers, much after the manner of the Apostles themselves (Acts vi, 8–10; viii, 26 ff.). It would even seem that at first they were the effective leaders of the Greek-speaking section of the primitive Church under the Apostles, while the Twelve had immediate leadership of the Hebrew-Christian section of the Church. However, with the movement of the Church into a body separate from Judaism this distinction, if indeed it existed, lapsed, while the office of administration of charity, and hence of the Church's finance, continued. Thus as the Diaconate emerges into the light of history it is found to be a ministry derived from the Apostles, but inferior in rank to the "presbyter bishops," engaged in financial and charitable administration, and assisting in the administration of the Eucharist (Justin Martyr, *Apology*, 1, lxvii). The primitive ministry of deacons gradually ceased, and it became in fact an introductory ministry to the priesthood. The work of the deacons known to Clement is unfortunately not described.

43. "A faithful servant in all His house": Numbers xii, 7, and Hebrews iii, 5.

"For he, when jealousy arose concerning the priesthood . . .": Having defined the character of the Christian Ministry, Clement continues his doctrine of the Ministry by a consideration of the reason why the Apostles should have appointed a Ministry to succeed them, and a Ministry embodying the principle of succession. This is because the holding of office in the Church can easily become the occasion of jealousy and strife. Clement shows that the Church cannot be at peace without an accepted and continuous Ministry. A Scripture "type" of this is seen in the "gainsaying of Korah" (Num. xvi) and the story of Aaron's rod which budded (Num. xvii, 1–10).

44. "Our Apostles knew through our Lord Jesus Christ": We may perhaps regard this statement as an indirect and implied claim that it was by express command of the Lord that the Apostles appointed a regular Ministry in succession to themselves. Clement would clearly like to feel that the Ministry is of express dominical foundation, but he has no "word of the Lord" which he can expressly quote here. It is fruitless to speculate what Christ may have said on this subject, which has not been recorded. The likely supposition is that we have here another example of development. Christ established the principle. He founded the Church as the New Israel, a corporate body. He gave to it its first simple but sufficient authoritative government, the Apostles. He warned His disciples very plainly of the danger of "seeking to be greatest," and enforced the virtue of humility in service. Then He left His Apostles to develop these principles in the light of experience.

"There would be strife over the name of the bishop's office": There are few words in the Fathers more truly spoken than this! This strife is still very much with us. It is no accident that when in the modern situation the more farseeing leaders of the separated parts of the Church take counsel as to how "our unhappy divisions" may be healed, the main stumbling block is found to be the question of ministerial and sacramental order. In the first place, while the divisions in the Church are without doubt in part due to genuine differences of spiritual apprehension in Christian belief and worship, they are chiefly due to the invasion of the Church by sinful human pride and selfishness. And this pride and selfishness naturally manifests itself more readily in the desire to be in office, and to enjoy prestige, power, and wealth in that office, than in any other way. In the second place, and at a profounder level, the unity of the Church is more intimately associated with unity of ministerial and sacramental order than with any other factor because order reflects the outward and expressive form of the Church. A difference of apprehension as to what it means to be a Christian will be reflected in a difference of theological emphasis within the Church, but this discussion will not harm the Church until sharpness of temper develops to the point where brother parts company with brother in the public worship and the organizational discipline of the Church. A breach of outward order, a dispute as to who ought to be in office, is the eminent mark that a theological difference has passed "the point of no return."

Certainly the unity of the Church is not merely organizational. It is unhappily all too possible to have folk nominally within the same ministerial and sacramental order, and yet possessed toward one another of "envy, hatred, and malice, and all uncharitableness." This is a poor sort of "Church unity"! Nevertheless, as long as the common order holds, there is always hope that wiser counsels may prevail, and the dialogue of belief be renewed in charity and mutual edification. Thus in the case of the modern separated communions of the Church, such as the Anglican, the Presbyterian, the Methodist, we find that there are within each great divergences of theological apprehension, including the doctrine of the Ministry and Sacraments. Experience shows that so long as men who sincerely think differently on certain points can charitably agree to remain loyally within the same ecclesiastical discipline, irreparable harm is never done to the truth. As soon as visible separation is added to difference of understanding, then the prestige of competing organizations partially inhibits joint worship and theological dialogue, and folk grow further and further apart in sympathy. The long experience of history shows that the leading (though not the sole) duty to theological truth is the maintenance of the organic unity and brotherly cohesion of the Church. Apprehension of the truth in all its variety and balance increases in brotherhood, while separation, even supposedly for the sake of theological truth, generates the error of an unbalanced apprehension of partial truth (John vii, 17). Visible "organic" unity, expressed in ministerial and sacramental unity, is by no means the whole matter of Church unity, but it is the eminent "case in point." What we find today was true in the primitive Church. As the Church ventured out into the pagan world, there were differences of interpretation and sentiment. As and when these became spiritually dangerous, they focussed themselves in disputes as to who should be the bishop. Therefore as the Church faced the danger of the second generation she had to turn her mind with more self-conscious attention than before to issues of ministerial and sacramental order. It is a perverse misreading of history to treat this undoubted transfer of interest in the Church of the Apostolic Fathers as a symptom of the spiritual decline of Christianity. It is the development of authentic Christianity to meet the new needs of a new generation.

"They appointed the aforesaid persons, and afterwards they provided a continuance, that if these should fall asleep, other approved men should succeed to their ministration": This celebrated passage in

S. Clement demonstrates the sheer impossibility of stretching the primitive Church upon the procrustean bed of modern denominational differences. Some today uphold the continuous episcopal Ministry, and the traditional doctrine of Apostolical Succession as the reason for it. Others uphold "the historic episcopate," but reject the traditional doctrine of Apostolical Succession. Yet others reject both the necessity for the continuous episcopal Ministry, and the doctrine of Apostolical Succession. S. Clement for his part has a clear and intelligible doctrine of Apostolical Succession, but knows nothing about a "bishop," in the traditional sense of the word at least! The Church as he knows it is governed by a continuous authoritative Ministry going back to the Apostles. This Ministry expresses the theological principle of hierarchy. It is the earthly visible representative of divine authority. Yet the authority operates through a body of equal "presbyter-bishops," of whom S. Clement is at most the very leading spokesman, but certainly not a ruling bishop. He does not match exactly to any modern denominational policy. It is clear that the principles of succession and of authority are inseparably linked. The idea of succession involves that only those can be admitted to authoritative office who commend themselves to those who are already in authoritative office. This is the principle which denies the right of an individualist section to rebel, and make for itself, *de novo*, a doctrine, an organization, or an officer. Ministerial succession is in fact one of the chief operative principles of sacramental and disciplinary unity, and one of the chief expressions of "organic unity." Thus Clement stresses the principle of continuous succession in office from the Apostles.

The question will be raised: "Is he right, in point of historical fact?" It is clear that this cannot strictly speaking be *proved*. Properly speaking, no piece of historical evidence can be more than *probably* genuine. Therefore, however much evidence be mustered, an historical position can never be demonstrated to more than a high degree of probability— apart from the experiential test, that it may be impossible to give an intelligible account of certain later events if certain earlier ones did not take place. This is the position of the primitive Ministry. There are no records for all the appointments of all the presbyter-bishops in all the Churches. Therefore no one can ever prove that the succession was maintained everywhere intact in the primitive Church. Indeed, the whole historical probability is that there were at certain places and at certain times mistakes, and even deliberate irregularities. Human programmes are not commonly executed perfectly in a fallen world! It is for this reason highly dangerous to seek to elevate a doctrine of a mechanically perfect ministerial succession in the Church into an article of Christian belief, and it is contrary to our experience of God's working in the Church to suppose that the saving operation of the Holy Spirit is in some way limited to a mechanically perfect organization. Nevertheless, in theological principle S. Clement is right in the claim which he makes for the primitive Ministry. The substantial history of the Church is as he says, though not in every detail. He was near to the events he describes. It is not to him a matter of gradually accumulating pious legend. There is no other historical evidence to impugn his testimony. And the Church at large certainly behaved as though he were right in this judgment. As the Church emerged into a clearer light of history, and as she became more conscious of her nature, she is seen to have moved by general consent and unerring instinct to the conception of a continuous authoritative Apostolic Ministry.

"Those therefore who were appointed by them, or afterward by other men of repute with the consent of the whole Church": This loose phrase is a warning against trying to go beyond judgments of probability in the course of actual historical event in the primitive Church. The natural construction to place upon the phrase "men of repute" is that ordinations to the office of "presbyter-bishop" performed after the passing of the first Apostles were by those who were already "presbyter-bishops." Ordination was by "the laying on of the hands of the presbytery" (1 Tim. iv, 14). However, S. Clement is not so careful as a later writer might have been to make this explicit. We notice also that the choice and ordination of new bishops is by consent of the Church. There is an authoritative government in the Church, but it does not act "as being lords over God's heritage" (1 Pet. v, 3). This is before the days of constitutional democracy, but the whole congregation has a right to be consulted, and by general acclamation to consent to what appears to be the leading of the Spirit in the government of the Church.

"It will be no light sin": Loyal obedience to the duly appointed ministry is a matter of vital importance in Christian discipleship.

"Those who have offered the gifts of the bishop's office"; προσενεγκόντας τὰ δῶρα τῆς ἐπισκοπῆς (Lightfoot, p. 29): That is, those who have been admitted to the office of celebrating the Eucharist, which is the Christian sacrifice.

45. Those who with a high hand thrust out duly appointed presbyters are in the position of the wicked persecutors of righteous Daniel and his companions.

46. "For it is written; Cleave unto the saints": Here Clement quotes, apparently as Scripture, from an unknown passage.

"With the guiltless man thou shalt be guiltless": Psalm xviii, 25, 26.

"Have we not one God and one Christ and one Spirit?": This is not the later language of careful trinitarian orthodoxy, but it amounts to the same intention. The undivided Trinity is a type of Christian unity.

"Remember the words of Jesus our Lord": Again we have the words of Christ solemnly quoted as a Scripture-like authority. The passages are Matthew xxvi, 24; xviii, 6; Mark xiv, 21; ix, 42; Luke xxii, 22; xvii, 1, 2.

47. "Take up the epistle of the blessed Paul the Apostle." This is a telling appeal. S. Paul himself had written to this same Church on this same issue. His letters were doubtless their most prized possession. That the Apostle had founded their Church and had written so weightily to them were their chief grounds of repute in the Church. Clement reminds them that he is treading in the steps of the great Apostle. In expelling presbyters they are following the course of those rebuked by S. Paul, and with much less excuse than they. So he comes to his affectionate and stirring appeal: "It is shameful, dearly beloved, yes, utterly shameful and unworthy of your conduct in Christ, that it should be reported that the very stedfast and ancient Church of the Corinthians, for the sake of one or two persons, maketh sedition against its presbyters."

48. "That He may show Himself propitious and be reconciled unto us"; ὅπως ἰλέως γενόμενος ἐπικαταλλαγῇ ἡμῖν (Lightfoot, p. 31): Clement carelessly slips into an un-Pauline phrase here, for S. Paul speaks of man being reconciled to God, not God to man (2 Cor. v, 20).

"Open me the gates of righteousness": Psalm cxviii, 19, 20.

49. "Who can declare the bond of the love of God": The appeal for unity within the Church is now pressed in perhaps the most evangelical passage of the Epistle. S. Clement shows, once he comes to unbend a little from his customary judicial and ecclesiastical appeal, and when he addresses a more personal and pointed appeal, that he is well aware that the faith which produces good works is "the faith that works by love." It is those who have love, and they alone, who can fulfil the commandments of Christ. Love of the brethren, and no mere responsible sense of ecclesiastical duty, is the true and effective bond of unity in the Church. It is, after all, the family of God, and not just the army of God!

"Love joineth us unto God": Compare 1 John iv, 7, 8, etc.

"Love covereth a multitude of sins": A quotation of 1 Peter iv, 8, which is notable as one of the few verbal quotations of New Testament Scripture in Clement, apart from words of Christ. This is very early evidence for the existence of 1 Peter. We notice also that it is not cited formally as "Scripture."

"Love endureth all things": Appropriately joined to the above is a more extended passage, manifestly allusive to S. Paul's hymn to love in 1 Corinthians xiii. Clement has already naturally linked SS. Peter and Paul as chief "pillars of the Church" (Chap. 5). That he here so pointedly joins together allusions to these two Epistles may indicate that he is a witness to the opinion that 1 Peter was indeed written by the Apostle, and is in this way, comparable to 1 Corinthians.

"For the love which He had toward us, Jesus Christ our Lord hath given His blood for us by the will of God, and His flesh for our flesh and His life for our lives." The first clause is not explicit, but the context is quite plain. The atoning death of Christ is the fruit of the love of God. This is the thought of John iii, 16, to which there may be here an allusion. Thus the end of this chapter aptly complements the beginning. How may the member come to that love of God which enables him to obey the commandments, and which binds him in the brotherhood? Plainly it is the believer's response to that love of God which provided the Atonement in Christ. Thus at the climax of his appeal S. Clement is found securely based upon the Gospel of divine grace. The last clauses are not framed in precise theological language, and we cannot be perfectly certain what further meaning Clement saw in the death of Christ. He gave His "blood" for us. That is, our salvation was accomplished eminently by His death. He gave His flesh for our flesh. The thought here is probably that an Atonement wrought out by an *incarnate* divine Son, and in human conditions, suffices for salvation in the conditions of this life, and accomplishes the salvation of the body and the resurrection of believers. This at least is the general patristic thought on the subject. Christ also gave His life for our lives. This is an echo of the prevailing New Testament conception that the death of Christ is God's victory over the power of death, which releases believers into life eternal.

50. "How marvellous a thing is love.... Who is sufficient... save those to whom God shall vouchsafe it?... But they that by God's grace were perfected in love": Clement clearly sees that Christianity does not consist merely in telling men that it is a blessed thing to love one another! This love which produces willing obedience and the unity of the Church is the gift of God, and nothing less. Here is the religion of grace, of which S. Paul himself would surely have approved.

"Enter into the closet...": Isaiah xxvi, 20; Ezekiel xxxvii, 12.

"Doing the commandments of God in concord of love, to the end that our sins may through love be forgiven us": The purist may claim that this statement is contrary to the doctrine of salvation by grace. We do not earn our forgiveness by our love, and our obedience to the commandments. Yet to press the matter thus far is to condemn also the Lord's Prayer, with its petition "forgive us... as we forgive." Here is the language of devotion, not of precise theology, and it indicates in a common-sense and unspeculative manner that God looks for a response to His initial grace by the doing of good, that man may grow in grace.

"Blessed are they whose iniquities are forgiven": Psalm xxxii, 1, 2.

51. A call is made to penitence, and confession of sin.

"Death shall be their shepherd": Psalm xlix, 15.

"Their chariots and their horsemen": Exodus xiv, 23, 26, 28; xv, 19.

52. The sacrifice which is pleasing to God is penitence: Psalm lxix, 30–2; l, 14, 15; li, 17.

53. "The oracles of God": The Old Testament Scripture.

"O mighty love! O unsurpassable perfection! $\tau\epsilon\lambda\epsilon\iota\acute{o}\tau\eta s$ (Lightfoot, p. 33): The "perfection" of the Christian is love (cf. Chap. 50). This is the Pauline doctrine (1 Cor. xiii, 10) and the Johannine (1 John iv, 12, 17, 18).

"Moses... than this": Deuteronomy ix, 12–14.

"Nay, not so, Lord": Exodus xxxii, 32.

54. True greatness in the Church is shown in vacating office if necessary, so that unity and obedience to authority be preserved (Luke ix, 48, and so on).

"The earth is the Lord's": Psalm xxiv, 1.

55. The pagan world is not without shining examples of public spirit and self-sacrifice for the good of the community. There are also examples in the history of Israel of the self-sacrifice of heroines such as Judith and Esther (Esther iv–v; Judith viii–xiii).

"Many among ourselves": The context seems to refer this to the heroines of Israel rather than to Christians who have sacrificed themselves to emancipate their fellows, though doubtless there were cases of the latter. The Church is so much one with Old Israel that Judith and Esther are heroines of the Church.

56. "The admonition which we give one to another . . . joineth us unto the will of God": The corporate discipline of the Church is the expression of the will of God.

"The Lord hath indeed chastened me": Psalm cxviii, 18.

"For whom the Lord loveth": Proverbs iii, 12.

"For the righteous shall chasten me in mercy": Psalm cxli, 5.

"Blessed is the man whom the Lord hath reproved": Job v, 17–26.

57. A call for the factious party to submit in humility to the presbyters.

"Behold I will pour out": Proverbs i, 23–33.

58. "For as God liveth, and the Lord Jesus liveth, and the Holy Spirit, who are the faith and hope of the elect": We have here a simple statement of the Christian doctrine of the Trinity, as the Faith of the Church.

59. "The number that hath been numbered of His elect throughout the whole world": This is the New Testament doctrine of Election, not the later Augustinian. It does not involve that a certain fixed number of individual souls have been chosen by God to be saved. It means that God, in His foreseeing sovereign wisdom and goodness, has appointed a certain community, a Chosen People, to be the instrument for the accomplishment of His purpose in the world. Only the Chosen People can fulfil the appointed task of the Elect, but it does not follow that any individual soul will enjoy an eternal reward simply because he happens to be part of the chosen community, or that any soul will suffer inevitable loss simply because the lot of his life is cast outside the community.

"Called us from darkness to light": Compare Acts xxvi, 18.

The Epistle then leads into a long prayer, extending to chapters 60 and 61. It is interesting to have this very ancient example of a Christian prayer written out at length, and to be able, as it were, to overhear the primitive Church at its devotions. The prayer illustrates in yet another way the extent to which the ancient Church was nurtured upon the Old Testament. Just as those ancient Christian hymns preserved in their beauty in the first chapter of S. Luke are plainly built upon Old Testament models, so these prayers are catenae of Old Testament invocations. The prayer starts with invocation of the God of creation, the bringer of restitution upon earth, and the God of providence.

"Abidest Highest in the lofty. . . . Layest low the insolence of the proud": Isaiah lvii, 15; xiii, 11.

"Scatterest the imaginings of nations": Psalm xxxiii, 10.

"Who settest the lowly on high": Job v, 11.

"Bringest the lofty low": Isaiah x, 33.

"Makest rich and makest poor": 1 Samuel ii, 6–7.

"Killest and makest alive": Deuteronomy xxxii, 39.

"Lookest into the abysses": Ecclesiasticus xvi, 18, 19.

"Saviour of them that are in despair": Judith ix, 11.

"Chosen out from all men those that love Thee through Jesus Christ": The prayer then turns its address to God as He is now known in the New Covenant. God now has a new Chosen People composed of those who love Him, out of every nation without distinction, and they are called together in Christ. The prayer then turns to intercession for the unfortunate, and for the progress of the Gospel.

"Our help and succour": Psalm cxix, 114.

"Let all the Gentiles know": 2 Kings xix, 19.

"We are Thy people": Psalm lxxix, 13 and c, 3.

60. The prayer continues in praise to the God of providence and forgiveness:

"Pitiful and compassionate": Ecclesiasticus ii, 11.

"Guide our steps to walk in holiness": 1 Kings ix, 4.

"To do such things as are good": Deuteronomy xiii, 18.

"Make thy face to shine upon us": Psalm lxvii, 1.

"By Thy mighty hand": Exodus vi, 1.

"When they called on Thee in truth": Psalm cxlv, 18.

61. The prayer continues for "our rulers and governors upon the earth." It is not explicit whether these are the governors of the state or of the Church, but we would judge that it is the latter.

"King of the ages": Cf. 1 Tim. i, 17.

62. The prayer ended, S. Clement composes his epilogue (chaps. 62–5). He reminds the readers of his arguments in behalf of righteousness and concord, on the basis of the example of the men of old time.

63. Clement renews his pointed plea for submission to authority in the Church.

"We have sent faithful and prudent men": The message of the Epistle is to be seconded by a dignified and official deputation, doubtless of mediators in the dispute.

64. "Who chose the Lord Jesus Christ, and us through Him": On the face of it the first clause appears "adoptionist," and certainly does not accord with later orthodoxy. It is probably a reference to the divine voice at Christ's baptism, "In whom I am well pleased." Christ, who considered from the point of view of His human life is eminently the "Chosen Man," is the Head of the new Chosen People.

"Our High-priest": Compare Hebrews vii, 26; viii, 1; x, 21.

65. The deputation is named, and the expression of hope that peace will be restored almost takes on the tone of a command, as S. Clement takes his leave of the subject with a benediction.

5. A Summary of the Doctrine of the Epistle of S. Clement

This outstanding writing from the Church of the period immediately succeeding the New Testament is most valuable for its own sake, and also as evidence for developing Christian life and thought at a most important and formative time. It is a noble piece of writing, dignified in tone and broad in outlook. We sense, however, that it lacks some of the artistic beauty, the deep spiritual insight and constructive genius, and the passion of the greater books of the New Testament. It is the work of an able, enlightened, and devoted Churchman rather than of a fiery prophet like S. Paul or a mystic like the Beloved Disciple. Though the Epistle is neither so ruggedly uncompromising, nor so clear in expression, upon the doctrines of salvation by grace and justification by faith as is S. Paul, the teaching is essential Pauline. The doctrine is, however, a "central" Paulinism, prudently modified to take account of other strands in the Christian tradition. This is characteristic of the position of the later Church, and thus S. Clement is in the line of development of Catholic doctrine. When he speaks about "faith" it is usually from the ground of the Old Testament, and therefore "faith" is often fidelity before God rather than the more personal and mystical "faith-union" with Christ. However, this latter is not neglected, and Clement shows that he understands the idea that Christian salvation is based upon "the faith that works by love," in response to the offered love of God in Christ. There is in this Epistle a clear doctrine of the saving work of Christ through His death and resurrection, but it is not elaborated in detail, nor is it expounded at length or with passion. This, however, is doubtless largely due to the purpose and interest of the Epistle, which is not a devotional address, but an appeal for order and unity in the Church.

If S. Clement is undoubtedly evangelical, it is equally true that he is genuinely catholic. The two sides of authentic Christianity are united in his teaching. The interest of the Epistle leads him to say much about the Church. This change in balance of interest, as compared with much of the New Testament, is by no means to be regarded as a symptom of the incipient spiritual decline of early Christianity. It is the rightful development of the life and thought of authentic primitive Christianity, in response to the taxing problems of the second generation. Following our Lord, and the New Testament writers in general, the Church is for S. Clement essentially the New and True Israel, the spiritually reconstituted ancient People of God. The Gentile Church for which he speaks is one company with the true Hebrews of old, and is the rightful heir to all the promises made to Israel. The Church and her doctrine, Ministry, and Sacraments are prefigured and typified in the Old Testament. The Old Testament writings are alone in the proper sense authoritative Scripture, the written "oracles of God." However, the sayings of the Lord Himself are also regularly quoted as in the fullest sense authoritative, and a number of New Testament books are alluded to with respect, but not cited expressly as "Scripture." S. Clement views the Church as a unified and disciplined corporate body, having a dominically established and apostolically ordained continuous authoritative ministry of Word, Sacraments, and ecclesiastical discipline. This Ministry is still, however, constituted in two orders, the "presbyter-bishops" and the deacons. The traditional threefold Ministry of ruling bishop, presbyters, and deacons has not yet appeared in the Churches known to S. Clement. However, although Clement does not claim to rule the Church at Rome, or even to preside over it, but writes as the mouthpiece of the presbytery and general body of the Church, we can see in him the figure of the bishop that is to be. He is an eminent exponent of the Roman genius for government, and of authoritative Churchmanship. Experience shows that the principle of spiritual authority most fittingly presupposes a "father-in-God," who shall be the effective embodiment in the Church of the divine authority upon which the Church rests. Clement of Rome clearly was such an one, even though he was not called a "bishop." In his person we may see the development of the Ministry actually taking place. To S. Clement reverence for the Ministry is the key principle of Church order and unity. He saw the need of the time, and he fulfilled the need, for manifestly he was a minister of Christ who could be so reverenced.

III   The Teaching of the Twelve Apostles

1. Manuscript Source

Possibly the greatest value in the celebrated early fourth century *Ecclesiastical History* of Eusebius is that he makes mention of, and sometimes gives precious citations of, ancient Christian books which he had read, and which are now lost. In this *History* he gives a list of νόθοι, "rejected writings" (*H.E.* III, xxv, 4). These were not to be regarded as dangerous heretical works, but were orthodox Christian writings which had been quoted to a greater or less degree as "Scripture" by various of the Church Fathers before his time, but which were not in Eusebius' own time accepted as authoritative canonical New Testament Scripture. Among the number of these writings rejected as Scripture, but not thereby condemned, are "the so-called *Shepherd*," "the extant Epistle of Barnabas," and "the so-called *Teachings of the Apostles*."[1] Until the modern period it was considered that this latter writing had perished in the wreck of history. However, in the year 1873 Philotheos Bryennios, Metropolitan of Nicomedia, discovered in the Jerusalem Convent in Constantinople a MS dated A.D. 1056, and now called the Constantinopolitan, or Hierosolymitan, MS. This contains the complete text of the genuine and pseudonymous Epistles of S. Clement, the Epistle of Barnabas, the Epistles of S. Ignatius and the pseudonymous Epistles of Ignatius, S. Chrysostom's Synopsis of the Old and New Testaments, and in particular the long-lost *Teaching of the Twelve Apostles*. Thus our sole authority for the text of this work is this single document, apart from a short fragment of a Latin translation. This may possibly be acclaimed the most important single discovery ever made of a document bearing upon the history of the Church, at the very least rivalling in interest the now famous Dead Sea Scrolls.

It may seem strange to some readers that so important a MS could linger unknown for many centuries in an ancient monastic library.

---

[1]This work is also commonly called the *Didache*, *didache* being the Greek word for "teaching", as used in the original title.

It must be remembered, however, that these old libraries often contained great accumulations of uncatalogued material. Until the rise of modern critical scholarship there was often no incentive to examine this with any degree of care, if it was of no apparent practical value to the life of the monastery. In any case, a careful scholarly examination, such as would alone indicate the precise nature and value of particular documents in a miscellaneous accumulation, is a highly expert and extremely laborious and lengthy proceeding. Hence it has been easy for the owners of old libraries to continue sometimes for centuries unaware of the character, interest, and value of some of their possessions. *The Teaching of the Twelve Apostles* was published in 1883.

The MS does not ascribe the work to any author, and gives no direct indication of the place or date of composition. These have been matters of much controversy, the issues turning upon one's judgment of the contents. The question of date will therefore be deferred.

2. Contents of "The Teaching of the Twelve Apostles"

Didache is a manual of Church discipline and ritual, and, according to most judgments upon its date, the earliest such book known to us. Its evidence, therefore, for the organization of the Church in the post-Apostolic age is extremely important, for there is provided a systematic and reasonably complete, though brief, description, as opposed to the scattered hints and allusions given in other writings of comparable age, and in the New Testament itself.

The manual consists of two parts. (i) The work opens with a moral treatise, giving a summary of Christian conduct, apparently adapted for the instruction of catechumens. This has a strongly Biblical, and indeed Jewish, flavour. It is widely held that it is based upon an older and possibly Jewish moral work, but amplified for Christian use by extensive quotations of the words of our Lord. This moral treatise, called "The Two Ways," sets forth the path of righteousness and life, and of unrighteousness and death, a natural and common mode of moral exhortation. (ii) The *Didache* then leads into a Church Order, giving instructions for Baptism, prayer, and fasting, the celebration of the Eucharist and Agape, the treatment of apostles and prophets, and of bishops and deacons, closing with a short epilogue exhorting to watchfulness, in view of the Second Advent of Christ.

3. "The Teaching of the Twelve Apostles" and the "Charismatic Ministry"

Possibly the most controversial issue connected with the *Didache* lies in the witness which it makes to the so-called "Charismatic Ministry" of the primitive Church. This term is derived from the Greek word χαρίσμα, "charisma," rendered "spiritual gift" in 1 Corinthians xii, 4 ff. It is plain from the New Testament that prominent among the spiritual gifts bestowed upon the Church by the Holy Spirit was the "gift" of an ecstatic "speaking with tongues" (1 Cor. xiv, 1–40). This was not, as some have supposed, a supernatural power of speaking in foreign languages without the normal process of learning. Rather was it, as we may plainly judge from S. Paul's account, that in times of special religious fervour some of the believers would pass into a state of ecstasy, and utter strange speech unintelligible to the ordinary hearer. We may observe in passing that this phenomenon has been by no means confined to the Apostolic Age or to the Christian religion, but can take place whenever religious emotion rises to the point of ecstasy. To those in the ancient Church who looked upon this phenomenon with the eye of faith it was by no means a mark of mental instability. It was a most manifest token of the presence, power, and blessing of the Holy Spirit. This "charisma" of "speaking with tongues" was manifestly in some way connected with the ministry of the Christian "prophets," and yet was to some degree in contrast with it, for the proper "charisma" of the "prophet" was to preach in plain speech, and also to interpret to the congregation the significance of the "tongues" (1 Cor. xiv, 2–4, 22–4). It is to be admitted that S. Paul and the other New Testament writers do not make the situation completely plain to us. Nevertheless, the undoubted fact emerges that there was a double Ministry in the primitive Church. There was the permanently appointed, and in this sense "official," Ministry of "presbyter-bishops" of Apostolic appointment, with an essentially sacramental and disciplinary ministration. Alongside this there was in the Church a more spontaneous and occasional ministry of "prophecy," "tongues," and "signs." This was regarded by the early Christians as immediately authorized by the divine action of the Holy Spirit, who bestowed the "gift." Although he did not place the highest value upon the "gift of tongues" (verse 5), S. Paul professed the highest regard for the ministration of the Christian prophets, placing them next to the Apostles themselves (1 Cor. xii, 28–9, Eph. iv, 11). This estimate is reasonable if the "gift" be regarded as the immediate operation of the Holy Spirit. It by no means follows, however, that a high estimate placed upon the ministry of prophets involves a low estimate upon the ministry of presbyter-bishops.

This more occasional, enthusiastic, and spontaneous type of prophetic Ministry in the primitive Church has been described by many modern writers as the "Charismatic Ministry." Such writers have frequently been found advancing the supposition that in the first days of the Church the "Charismatic Ministry" was the predominant and most valued Ministry, but that as the Church settled down from its early spiritual "freedom" into an organization this Ministry was displaced in influence and repute by the formerly subordinate Ministry of bishops, presbyters, and deacons. It will readily be appreciated that here is an issue charged with controversy. Church historians of Catholic sympathies, who have wished to vindicate the Church as authentically and from the beginning a disciplined corporate body, and the later development of ecclesiastical institutions within the Church as a legitimate and providential development, have inclined toward reserve regarding the notion of a primitive "Charismatic Ministry." They will allow that such existed, for the evidence is plain. They will not allow that in the primitive Church the "Charismatic Ministry" was so predominant that the continuous and corporate "official" Apostolic Ministry was purely subordinate, and of little repute. On the other hand, historians writing from the standpoint that original Christianity was in no sense an "organization," with a fixed Ministry, sacramental system, and creed, but rather a free-and-easy "group movement," and with the assumption close to hand that the development of ecclesiastical and "Catholic" Christianity represents in some sense the spiritual decline of the Church, have shown much more sympathy with the doctrine of the "Charismatic Ministry." It represents to them the idea of an original so-called "free" and "spiritual" Christianity, before the bishop took charge.

There is no space here fully to debate this interesting issue. We may say that, as usual in these matters, there is some truth on both sides. In the spiritual pilgrimage of the healthy and balanced believer, and in the life of the Church at large, there is a place both for emotion and spontaneity, and for discipline and fixed principle. In times of spiritual revival there has normally been an increase of emotion and spontaneity, but it by no means follows from this that to advance the claims of discipline is a mark of second-rate spirituality. Spontaneity is good, but it is not the only good. The primitive Church was in such a condition of spiritual revival, and showed much of emotion and spontaneity. As time went on, the claims of ecclesiastical discipline waxed greater in proportion, and less was heard of "tongues" and Christian "prophecy." Thus by the times of S. Irenaeus, at the end of the second century, the "Charismatic Ministry" is acknowledged indeed, but largely as a matter of pious memory. The regular and continuous episcopally ordained Ministry is the effective Ministry of the Church.[1] Though in a fallen world the possibility of spiritual decline in the Church is never to be excluded, this undoubted change of ecclesiastical emphasis is not necessarily to be accounted a symptom of the departure of the Church from the authentic mind of the Lord. It is just as likely to be found a mark that

" . . . God fulfils Himself in many ways,
Lest one good custom should corrupt the world."

Possibly the chief historical importance of the *Didache* is that alone among surviving Christian literature outside the New Testament it appears to reflect an order in which this so-called "Charismatic Ministry" was a vital element in current Church life, and the spontaneous and itinerant "prophetic" Ministry an influential and honoured body, alongside the permanent local "Apostolic" Ministry. Those historians who have wished to find a large place for "free" and nonecclesiastical Christianity in the first days of the Church have found in *The Teaching of the Twelve Apostles* a most important piece of their evidence, and have treated it as a writing of which the most serious account is to be taken. It is by them regarded as a representative, authentic, and priceless testimony to a primitive Christian polity, soon to be buried beneath the growth of later ecclesiastical Christianity.

[1] See Lawson, *Biblical Theology of S. Irenaeus*, pp. 97–9, with references.

The tendency of such writers has been to give the book an early date, immediately after the New Testament period. On the other hand, writers who seek to vindicate the integrity of the "Apostolic" Ministry of "presbyter-bishops" as the essential polity of the Church from the beginning tend to give somewhat less weight to the evidence of *Didache*, though all admit its great interest to the Church historian.

Three possible positions naturally belong to the latter point of view. (i) *Didache* is early in date, archaic, and represents an essentially impermanent order of things. (ii) *Didache* represents not the main stream of developing Christianity, but rather a somewhat rustic and backward local Church, and possibly a naïve and even eccentric congregation. It does not wholly speak for the real life of the Church. (iii) A stronger variant of this second view is that *Didache* is later in date than has usually been held, and is definitely nonrepresentative of orthodox Catholic Christianity. It is, in fact, a semiheretical book. In this connection it is worthy of note that the author of the most weighty modern monograph on *The Teaching of the Twelve Apostles*[1] adopts this view. The Church from which *Didache* sprang "was one which supported a moderate Montanism which it expressed in as respectable and apostolic form as possible" (*The Riddle of the Didache*, page 8). The so-called "Phrygian heresy" of Montanism was a recrudescence of violently charismatic religion within the Church, taking its rise from about A.D. 172 onward among the population of Phrygia, the old pagan religion of which had a strong ecstatic element. It rapidly spread, inevitably broke the bounds of customary ecclesiastical discipline, and developed into a vigorous, well-organized, and enduring schismatic body.[2] Montanism was not properly a doctrinal heresy but a disciplinary schism, though the apparent claim that the supposed utterances of the Holy Spirit through the Montanist prophets and prophetesses were an authority equivalent to the Apostolic Writings manifestly contains the seed of heresy. Clearly it might not be too easy to distinguish between a "moderate" and "respectable" Montanism and an orthodox and Catholic congregation which retained some measure of sympathy with the New Testament charismatic ministry. If the development of Montanism in the ancient Church is in any way

[1] *The Riddle of the Didache*, by F. E. Vokes, published for the Church Historical Society, 1938.
[2] An account, naturally most hostile in tone, of Montanism is given by Eusebius in his *Church History*, Book V, Chap. xvi.

to be compared with the natural history of revivalistic sects in the modern, we may assume that after the initial enthusiastic separation from the Church many Montanist congregations would thus grow increasingly "moderate" and "respectable," and lose the characteristics which caused them to secede. Mr. Vokes finds the origin of *Didache* in such a background, and his case merits the student's careful attention. (iv) Another interesting suggestion is that *Didache* is the work of an early representative of the long tradition of religious antiquaries. Years afterward he is trying to reconstruct in pious imagination that which he thinks "ought" to have been the Church polity of the Apostolic Age, possibly with a view to commending this polity to a Church he felt had deserted it. This would make *Didache* a misleading view of a Church which never actually existed!

In criticism upon these points one would say: (*a*) If *The Teaching of the Twelve Apostles* is in any sense within the main stream of Christianity, it must be very early, and immediately after the Apostolic Age, because, like 1 Clement, it apparently knows nothing of the single ruling bishop. "Bishop" is still used as synonymous with "presbyter," so that "bishops" are coupled with "deacons," as in 1 Timothy iii, 1–13, Philippians i, 1. (*b*) If *Didache* is "central," representative, and early, its evidence is most important. (*c*) The evidence of *Didache*, if taken seriously as representative, indicates the insuperable difficulties attendant upon the functioning of a spontaneous "Charismatic Ministry," and the inevitability of its speedy passing from a position of eminence in the Church, just as certainly as it does the honour in which this ministry was originally held. On balance, *Didache* is not really as favourable toward the ministry of "gifts" as some have supposed. The same is true, of course, of S. Paul's chapter in 1 Corinthians, xiv. (*d*) It can hardly be disputed that *Didache* breathes an atmosphere of naïveté, although a not unattractive naïveté, which contrasts most forcibly with the magisterial dignity of the Roman Church of this period, as reflected in 1 Clement. We can hardly imagine S. Clement having to resort to the very practical and hardheaded, but somewhat simple-minded, expedients advocated by *Didache* in order to discover whether a travelling "prophet" was a true man or an impostor. Rome would surely have wanted an official testimonial! However, *Didache* was widely received in the Church, venerated almost as Scripture by some, and incorporated into later works, so it must have struck a chord in general Christian sentiment. It may well represent the life of a relatively unsophisticated congregation, but these must have been much more numerous in this early period than more developed congregations like the Roman, which displays so much of the shape of things to come. (*e*) It is a little hard to suppose that the *Didache* could have been for a time received by some almost as Scripture, and cited with deep respect by theologians of care and wide experience like Clement of Alexandria and Origen, if it was indeed under serious suspicion of being either semiheretical or "phony." In conclusion, there are many questions raised here for which there is no certain answer. That this should be so in the case of so important a work as *Didache* is a standing warning against oversimplification and too confident dogmatism, in relation to this period of Church history.

4. Date of "The Teaching of the Twelve Apostles"

As there is no certain evidence on this point, it is only possible to cite the opinions of various reputable authorities. The reliable Roman Catholic scholar F. Caryé writes: "In all probability the *Didache* was composed between 70 and 90, although some critics would place the date of its composition in 120 or 150. The primitive condition of the liturgy and of the hierarchy described therein is an inducement to place the *Didache* as near as possible to the Apostolic times and to look upon it as the earliest known work of Christian antiquity."[1] Lightfoot states that "these indications point to the first or the beginning of the second century as the date of the work in its present form."[2] Vokes argues that *Didache* is later than the first Apology of S. Justin Martyr (A.D. 150–155), and records the judgment that "the *Didache* is almost certainly a work written between the years A.D. 155 and 250."[3]

5. Place of Composition

This likewise is a matter of conjecture. The circumstance that it is first quoted by Alexandrian writers has made some surmise that the

[1] *Manual of Patrology*, English trans. 1935, I, 44.
[2] *The Apostolic Fathers*, 1 vol. ed., 1891, p. 216.
[3] *Riddle of the Didache*, p. 86.

Didache was written in Egypt. However, the phrase about the grain from which the sacramental bread was produced being "scattered upon the mountains" (Chap. 9) would be a more natural usage in a hilly country such as Syria or Palestine, rather than in the flat valley of the Nile.

6. Commentary on "The Teaching of the Twelve Apostles"

Chapter 1

"There are two ways, one of life and one of death": The Moral Manual of *Didache* opens with "The Two Ways," the way of obedience and life, and of disobedience and death. If we may assume, as seems most reasonable, that this is a moral catechism for those who are being instructed for Holy Baptism, then *Didache* follows a logical course for a Church Order. Catechism leads to Baptism, and Baptism to prayer, fasting, the Eucharist, and to the office and discipline of the Christian Ministry. The Manual raises two closely allied spiritual and theological issues. Many commentators have observed that "The Two Ways" is Jewish in tone, so that it has been widely considered that parts of it were known to the Jews, and that what we have here is a Christian expansion and adaptation of an original Jewish "Two Ways." Then also the Manual is moralistic in approach. It instructs the catechumen, not, as some would have expected, in the Gospel of salvation by divine grace, declared through the crucified and risen divine Son, but in moral maxims supported by fear of punishment and hope of spiritual blessing. Thus such a writer as Dr. Torrance, supported in this particular instance by no less Catholic an authority than Dr. Kenneth Kirk, takes *Didache* severely to task for completely failing to comprehend the central point of the Christian Gospel.[1]

This compels us to consider what we should reasonably expect in a Christian catechism of this early period, working upon the assumption, which the present writer adopts, that *Didache* is probably early, and substantially orthodox. The fact has to be faced, whether modern theologians of Grace like it or no, that the missionary method of the primitive Church in a pagan environment was to preach the Law first,

[1] *Grace in the Apostolic Fathers*, p. 37.

and only after that the Gospel. Nor did the ancient Church in this make the clear distinction of many later theologians between the Mosaic Law, which is abolished for Christians, and the Moral Law, which is of eternal validity. It was indeed agreed that some of the ceremonial commandments of the Law of Moses were not to be taken literally by Christians, but the Church from the beginning accepted the whole Jewish Scriptures of its background as God's word to man, and treated the Old Testament as, among other things, a book of valid moral rules for the Christian life. It may be argued that our Lord Himself in principle made this approach, though He triumphantly avoided those errors of externalism and merit-mongering which tread all too easily in the footsteps of earnest moralists. In announcing the presence with men of the Kingdom, He called the multitude to repentance, and preached a lofty ethical standard in the tradition of the Hebrew prophets. To those from among His followers who had eyes to see, and apparently to them only, He declared the "messianic secret" that God's victory was to be by the strange method of the cursed death and wonderful resurrection of the divine Son. It is possible, therefore, that the author of the First Gospel is not false to the mind of his Master when he introduces the public preaching of Christ by collecting together a large part of the moral maxims known to him, and arranging them in the form of The Sermon on the Mount. This is plainly to treat the ethical precepts of Jesus as "the Christian Sinai," and some have objected that this is essentially unevangelical, for S. Paul had already expelled Sinai from the Christian terrain. We are not clear that this is a fair judgment upon the First Gospel, or a balanced judgment upon Paul. What we do observe, however, is that when S. Luke represents S. Paul himself, the Apostle of Grace, as preaching to pagans, either the rustic pagans of Lystra (Acts xiv, 14–18) or the cultured pagans of Athens (Acts xvii, 22–31) or a pagan governor (Acts xxiv, 25) he begins by preaching the Moral Law. Paul opens his case by talking, not specifically as a Christian, but as a Jew to pagans. He argues the unity, morality, and providence of God, the folly of idolatry, and divine judgment hanging over the licentiousness of paganism. Only with this foundation securely laid can the preacher declare the distinctive Christian message. Whether or no this is true to S. Paul in person, we know that this approach was, for good or ill, the missionary method of the ancient Church.

This is exactly what we find in *Didache*. The initial teaching of the catechumen is a moral, and in this sense a "Jewish," catechism. It is important to remember that it does not follow that this represents the whole of the instruction to be given to the catechumen before Holy Baptism. Indeed, the implication of *Didache* is probably the reverse. At the end of the opening Moral Manual we come to the Order for Baptism (chap. 7), and it is in the Triune Name. Thus the distinctive Christian Faith is plainly presupposed, but there is no exposition of it. The most likely supposition is that the inward mystery of the Faith is kept in reserve, just as it probably is also in the case of the Eucharist (see notes on chaps. 9, 10). The ancient Church was not like the modern, which commits everything to the printed page, and gives it the widest possible publicity, casting its pearls before swine in hope of winning some. The Church was then an underground Church, often a persecuted Church meeting in secret. What was expressly learned for initiation into the secret society, and what actually happened at initiation, was largely kept in sacred reserve, to be disclosed only to those who had shown themselves worthy to be initiated by their reliable conduct in preliminary training. Here we have a hint that the preliminary training of those interested in Christianity was, appropriately enough in a pagan background, moral rather than dogmatically "Christian."

However, though in this sense "The Two Ways" is moral and "Jewish," in another sense it is very distinctively Christian. It would appear that commentators have not always done justice to this side of the matter. The contrast between the arduous narrow way and "the primrose path to the everlasting bonfire" is so natural as a mode of moral exhortation that we are not surprised to find it in any context. In the Scriptural tradition it goes right back to the Mounts of Blessing and of Cursing of Deuteronomy xxvii–xxx, leading up to God's word: "I have set before you life and death, blessing and cursing: therefore choose life" (Deut. xxx, 19). Our Lord Himself used the method (cf. Luke vi, 20–26), for the Sermon on the Mount is itself a striking example of "The Two Ways" (particularly Matt. vii, 13, 14). S. Paul, likewise, gives lists of the contrasting "works of the flesh" and of "the Spirit," with their respective rewards (Gal. v, 16–25). What is of significance in this Moral Manual is not so much its undoubted similarity to its natural Jewish background, but rather the ample way in which this is filled out and adapted for Christian purposes by citation of distinctively Christian writing.

It is to be remembered that it is somewhat of an anachronism to speak at this time of New Testament Scripture. To the Christian "the Scriptures" proper were still the venerable Jewish Scriptures, as in the New Testament itself. The Apostolic Writings were indeed authoritative, but only in so far as they were the necessary substitute in the congregation for the personal presence and witness of an authoritative Apostle. Thus it is natural to find that in 1 Clement, a writing belonging quite probably to much the same period, almost all the quotations are from the Old Testament. The contrast of *Didache* herein is strong. The words of Jesus, chiefly from the Sermon on the Mount, are freely quoted as a guide to moral conduct, and there are also quotations of Acts, Romans, Hebrews, and Jude. Modern scholarship has rightly emphasized that the essential preaching (the so-called "kerygma") of the primitive Church was the message that the divine Son made man had died and risen for the salvation of believers. The "preaching" was not just the proclamation of the doctrine and ethics of Christ. However, this emphasis as to the character of original Christianity needs to be balanced by another. From the beginning Christ was regarded as the Master of disciples, and an essential part of discipleship was to mould one's life according to the teaching of the Master. The ethics of Christ are a part of the kerygma. It was for this reason, chiefly, that the parables and sayings of Christ were remembered and recorded: that they might be cited as authoritative guidance upon the path of life. Thus S. Paul himself always shows himself careful wherein he may discover some "word of the Lord," wherewith to determine with the highest degree of authority a given issue of Christian life and practice (for example, Acts xx, 35; 1 Cor. vii, 25). It is of great significance, therefore, that we have in *Didache* what are quite possibly the first quotations in Christian literature of S. Matthew's and S. Luke's Gospels.

It is to be noted, in conclusion, that "The Two Ways" also occurs in part at the end of the so-called Epistle of Barnabas (chaps. 18–20, see pp. 216-17). It is perhaps impossible to determine with certainty whether *Barnabas* has derived this material from *Didache*, or vice versa, or whether the two Christian works have derived it independently from a common Jewish source. All these possibilities have been maintained by various critics. The difficulty in the last-named view is that "The Two Ways" as recorded both in *Didache* and *Barnabas* apparently contains three very brief New Testament quotations (Acts iv, 32; Romans xii, 9; and Hebrews xiii, 7). This would hardly be the case if the two writings derived this document independently from a Jewish source. The difficulty in supposing that *Barnabas* derived "The Two Ways" from *Didache* is that the Jewish-sounding material is better and more systematically arranged in *Didache*. This makes *Barnabas* look like the first "rough draft." In particular, the *Didache's* impressive interpolation of sayings of Jesus to augment and Christianize the statement of the Jewish Law is not reproduced in *Barnabas*. It is hard to believe that in composing Christian works this matter, once introduced, would be left out again. The present writer thus inclines to the view that *Barnabas* adopted "The Two Ways" from a Jewish source, and that the writer of *Didache* took it over from him, greatly expanding and improving it (see p. 217). This would require the Epistle of Barnabas to be very early, if the usual early date for *Didache* be accepted. It is to be noted that some reliable scholars allow *Barnabas* to be early enough for this (see p. 201). F. E. Vokes, however, uses the dependence of *Didache* on *Barnabas* as an argument in support of his late date for *Didache*.[1] Book vii of the fourth century *Apostolic Constitutions* is an adaptation of the entire *Didache*.[2]

"The way of life": Compare Jeremiah xxi, 8.

"First of all, thou shalt love the God that made thee": S. Matthew xxii, 37, 39.

"And all things whatsoever thou wouldest not have befal thyself": Tobit iv, 15. The student will observe that the ancient Church used the Greek Old Testament, or Septuagint, and that therefore the Fathers quote as Scripture the books commonly known today as the Apocrypha.

"Bless them that curse you": S. Matthew v, 44, 46; S. Luke vi, 27, 28, 32, 33, 35.

"If any man give thee a blow": S. Matthew v, 39-42; S. Luke vi, 29-30.

"He shall not come out thence": S. Matthew v, 26.

"Let thine alms sweat into thine hands": It is not known whence

---

[1] *Riddle of the Didache*, pp. 27 ff.
[2] *Ibid.*, 20-1.

this somewhat prudential maxim is quoted. Some have condemned it as contrary to the Christian ideal of unselfish love, and it is opposed to the sense of S. Luke vi, 30–35, taken literally. However, it has much the same sense as "neither cast ye your pearls before swine," S. Matthew vii, 6. It is well possible that the writer of *Didache* regards this as a saying of Christ, and it is not impossible that he may be right.

Chapter 2

"And this is the second commandment": We have here the Decalogue (Exodus xx, 13–17), interestingly interpolated to suit Gentile conditions. The pagan sins of homosexuality, magic, abortion, and infanticide are appropriately added to the list of the acts which the Law needed to forbid to the Hebrews.

"Thou shalt not hate any man": Leviticus xix, 17–18.

Chapter 3

"Be not angry": In this passage there is a plain witness that the writer of *Didache* understands that obedience is to be inward as well as outward, in the evangelical spirit of S. Matthew v, 21–30.

"Be no dealer in omens": Leviticus xix, 26.

"The meek shall inherit the earth": Psalm xxxvii, 11; S. Matthew v, 5.

"Quiet . . . and fearing the words": Isaiah lxvi, 2.

Chapter 4

"Thou shalt remember him that speaketh unto thee the word of God": We observe here a very early quotation of Hebrews xiii, 7.

"For whensoever the lordship (ἡ κυριότης) [Lightfoot, p. 219] speaketh, there is the Lord": The sense of this is probably that the utterances of the spirit-filled prophets are to be respected as the voice of the Lord.

"Be not thou found holding out thy hands": Ecclesiasticus iv, 31.

"Shalt not say that anything is thine own": A very early quotation of Acts iv, 32.

"Thou shalt not command thy bondservant or thine handmaid in thy bitterness": It is to be noted that slavery is not forbidden, and the possibility is envisaged that a master and his slave may be members of the same Christian congregation. The Christian rule in the matter is that the slave is to be respected as a fellow Christian, and that the master is to be obeyed as an exercise in obedience to God. This answers substantially to the attitude of S. Paul in 1 Corinthians vii, 20–24 and Ephesians vi, 5–9. This standard had implicit within it the ultimate Christian repudiation of slavery as a sin against humanity, but the repudiation for long remained implicit. So long as the moral education of society had not advanced to the point when reasonable and humane men could be expected to see that the institution of slavery as such was an offence to God, the Christian duty in the matter consisted in being a Christian, brotherly, and humane master, and a Christian and respectful slave. This pointedly illustrates that Christian social morality is not so inseparably bound up with any particular social, economic, or political system, that there is specifically and exclusively "a Christian system."

"In church thou shalt confess thy transgressions": The Church holds the power of moral discipline. Public confession of faults is to be made there, and presumably proper penitential discipline administered.

Chapter 5

"Not cleaving to the good": This is usually considered to be a quotation of Romans xii, 9, and to be a very early reference to this Epistle.

Chapter 6

"For if thou art able to bear the whole yoke of the Lord": Some have strongly condemned this passage as radically unevangelical, and as betraying a lack of understanding of the essential principle of the Gospel. They have felt that any doctrine of a double standard of morality is inconsistent in principle with salvation by divine grace, and sanctification by the indwelling Spirit, because it answers to a morality which is man's work for God, not God's work in man and gift to man. Perhaps this is so in strictly logical theory. It is to be agreed in principle that man's action in salvation is not his own independent action, but is his free response to the initiative of God's grace, and the use he makes of God's grace. However, it is not possible to determine by strictly logical theory how much of the action in salvation is divine and how much human. The thing is a mystery, and the proportion doubtless varies with different individuals. To give the whole action to the divine initiative, and to make man purely passive in his salvation, is to embark upon the most precarious sort of predestinarian speculation. Yet if in the path of salvation man has some scope for responsive action, however small, it is not improper to exhort man to do his utmost in that action. Furthermore, the advice "to do as much as you can" so completely accords with the common experience of life that the giving of it is almost inevitable. Thus the maxim "If thou art not able, do that which thou art able," though it admittedly has a prudential rather than an evangelical flavour, is not necessarily and wholly to be condemned as proof positive that the writer of *Didache* misunderstands the gospel of grace. This is to overstate the case. After all, the teaching of S. Paul at certain points, and even of our Lord Himself, answers to the idea that some believers are called to a sterner standard than others (S. Matt. xix, 10–12, 21; I Cor. vii, 6–9; ix, 4–6, 15). We may regard this expression in *Didache* as inadequate, but we ought not to be too quick to accuse the writer of "legality" because he does not express himself so carefully upon this point as a later theologian might have done.

"Bear that which thou are able": Abstinence from food is an act of religious virtue, but is to be taken upon oneself in differing degree, according to the calling and ability of different individuals.

"Yet abstain by all means from meat sacrificed to idols": S. Paul's "law of liberty" in this matter was that the Christian should abstain from meat to idols not as a legal obligation, but as a gesture of charity toward the weak brother (I Cor. viii). We are not surprised to find that this rule has here hardened into a rigid prohibition. The Apostle's rule is admittedly the more exalted in spiritual principle, but the rule in *Didache* is practical and common sense in a Church of Gentile background, to which idolatry was very real.

Chapter 7

We now come to the opening of the second and more interesting section of *The Teaching of the Twelve Apostles*, namely, the Church Order for the Sacraments. It fittingly starts with regulations for the Holy

Baptism of the initiate, who presumably has been instructed in the foregoing catechism.

"Having first recited all these things": This can hardly be taken to mean that at the actual Baptism the whole of "The Two Ways" was to be recited. At the same time, as has been observed above, a distinctive Christian Baptism as opposed to a Jewish ceremonial washing, in which the Triune Name was used, logically presupposes some instruction in the Christian doctrine of salvation through the crucified and risen Son of God, and that the baptized should make confession of the same. This is not given here, the catechetical Manual being exclusively moral, not doctrinal. Perhaps the most reasonable supposition is that the Church of the *Didache* accounted the doctrinal confession, which was the distinctively Christian and most revered element, as too sacred to be written down, and thus possibly disclosed to the unbeliever. Certainly this idea was present in the ancient Church of a later period. Thus the primitive Creed was kept secret, and disclosed to the approved catechumen before his Baptism, that he might make due confession of the Faith. It is therefore quite possible that "these things" which are to be recited are simple doctrinal statements, which are not written in *Didache*. Indeed, Dr. J. N. D. Kelly, a recent authority writing upon the development of the Creed, states: "In the liturgies . . . to baptize in the name of the Father, etc., meant asking the questions 'Dost thou believe . . . ?' three times, and plunging the candidate in the water in three successive immersions. As the *Didache* too envisages a triple sprinkling, an interrogatory creed of this kind (whether confined to bare, unamplified questions about the three Persons, we cannot of course say) is almost certainly presupposed."[1] There is no reason to suppose that there was in the Church of this early period a fixed threefold baptismal Creed, professing faith in Father, Son, and Holy Spirit, similar to the Old Roman Creed, the precursor of the Apostles' Creed.[2] Yet the instinct to compose rhythmical recitations of the main facts of the Christian Faith, and for these to fall into a fixed form, was present in the Church from an early period. S. Paul's words in 1 Corinthians xv, 3, 4, may echo a primitive creed form. The writings of S. Justin Martyr (A.D. 150–155) and of S. Irenaeus and of Tertullian (end of the second century) contain many

[1] *Early Christian Creeds*, London, 1950, p. 66.
[2] The Old Roman Creed can be traced back to the end of the second century.

examples of such liturgical echoes. Thus we may reasonably suppose that in the baptismal rite described here the initiate recited not only a moral promise but also a confession of the Christian Faith, containing much of the contents of the later baptismal Creed, but not in a fixed form.

"In the name of the Father and of the Son and of the Holy Spirit": Cf. S. Matthew xxviii, 19. Some critical scholars have argued that originally in the New Testament period Baptism was in the Name of Jesus Christ alone, and that this primitive usage is called to mind by the wording of such passages as Acts ii, 38; viii, 37; x, 48. However, the Triune Name of God came into use very early, in time for the composition of the First Gospel. It is in use here, and answers to an early state of simple yet profound reflection upon the Christian belief. It has been realized that Christ was not just the Messiah of Jewish expectation. He is the divine Son, whose Name may be paralleled with the Name of the Creator-Father, and of the divine Spirit of prophecy.

"In living water": That is, in running water. Primitive Baptism was a threefold and substantial washing in water, though it would not appear that there was any special dogmatic emphasis that the immersion must be total. Rather do we find in this early document an interesting and divergent ritual emphasis. A Christian Baptism ought ideally to be in the river, in running water. This is a good example of the normal traditionalist and conservative character of religious ceremonial. The first and classic Baptism, which prefigures Christian Baptism, was in the river Jordan. Therefore river-baptism was the most fitting form.

"Then baptize in other water; and if thou art not able in cold, then in warm": Here is the parallel normal process at work, of convenient ecclesiastical adaptation. If there is no river available, it will suffice to go to standing water. A further concession, which we may surmise the writer of *Didache* regards as rather unworthy, is very revealing. If the initiate cannot stand cold water, then warm may be used. This seems to presuppose some form of indoor baptistry. Furthermore, it cannot have been easy for a company of simple Christians to muster a sufficient quantity of warm water for a Baptism by immersion. This would presuppose quite a developed Church building. Therefore we are not surprised to find that one concession has led to another. Baptism by a threefold pouring is known. It is possible that the demand for Holy

Baptism in warm water may bespeak an origin for *Didache* in a country where the weather was likely to be uncomfortably cold in the spring, Easter Eve being the usual time for baptisms in the first age of the Church. This would perhaps give preference to the mountains of Syria, rather than Egypt.

"Let him that baptizeth and him that is baptized fast, and any others also who are able": Fasting is a traditional Biblical discipline to enhance the earnestness and effect of prayer. This usage was naturally carried over into the Church.

Note: It is to be observed that the Baptism presupposed here is the "believer's Baptism" of an adult. For possible evidence of infant Baptism in this early period, see the *Acts of Polycarp*, ix, with notes (p. 172).

Chapter 8

"And let not your fastings be with the hypocrites": This is a less attractive but very human aspect of the Church. The instinct to be as different as possible from one's opponents is a deep-seated and very natural one, though quite irrational. The instinct of religious denominations to do or profess this, or to avoid doing or professing that, not on account of its intrinsic rightness or wrongness, but for the sake of being different from some opposed denomination, has been widely manifested in the Church. In modern Christendom it remains as perhaps the leading cause of continuing Church separation: the wall of institutional prejudice. This divisive impulse is seen at work here. Some have accounted *The Teaching of the Twelve Apostles* to be a very Jewish book. Nevertheless, the Christians are by now very definitely and consciously a body organized separately from the Synagogue. It is necessary to make good the claim that the Church, and not the Synagogue, is the true way. Perhaps there is competition between the two for support among that section of the pagan population which is sympathetic to a monotheistic "Jewish-type" religion. Perhaps there is memory of a time of bitterness at the actual separation. Therefore the Church of the *Didache*, though primitive and in this sense "Jewish," can also be anti-Jewish. The Jews are the "hypocrites," the professors of a false religion. The weekly fasts of Judaism are on the second and fifth days of the week (cf. S. Luke xviii, 12). Therefore the Christians must take care to fast on different days, on Wednesday and Friday. These days were the so-called "Stations" of the ancient Church, and the origin of the long Christian tradition of the Friday fast. (See Hermas, Parable v, 1, with note, page 250.) This fasting was not necessarily complete abstinence from food. It might be abstinence only for the first part of the day, or from meat or fruit or wine. We are, however, given no particulars here.

We may note in passing that this spirit of opposition to Jewish practices was doubtless responsible for the parallel movement of the day of Christian worship. The basic idea of a weekly Christian day of worship was clearly inspired by the tradition of the Jewish Sabbath, and by reverence for the Fourth Commandment. The first Jewish Christians kept two days of worship, the Sabbath with their fellow Jews, and the Lord's Day, the first day of the week, the anniversary of Christ's resurrection. The spirit of opposition acting upon this primitive situation would be sufficient to suppress the Jewish Sabbath in the increasingly Gentile Church, and to leave the Lord's Day alone.

"Neither pray ye as the hypocrites": S. Matthew vi, 5. However, our Lord's exhortation is given a new twist here! The hypocritical prayer which is forbidden is no longer an outward public show of false piety. It is the daily Jewish devotion. That it was necessary to make this prohibition is quite probably an indication that there was in the memory of the Church of the *Didache* the knowledge of a time when some Christians, perhaps of Jewish or proselyte antecedents, did use the traditional Jewish prayers for their Christian devotions.

"Thus pray ye": S. Matthew vi, 9–13. Most appropriately the Lord's Prayer is to be used three times a day in Christian devotion, in place of the Jewish prayers. It is to be noted that the prayer closes with the added customary Doxology.

Chapter 9

"But as touching the eucharistic thanksgiving, give ye thanks thus"; Περὶ δὲ τῆς εὐχαριστίας, οὕτω εὐχαριστήσατε (Lightfoot, p. 221): We come here to what is in many ways the most interesting, important, and mysterious part of *The Teaching of the Twelve Apostles*.

It is necessary, in introducing these next two chapters to the student, to give an outline of the origins of the Christian Eucharist.[1] It may come as a surprise to some that parts of this subject are a matter of real obscurity. It is agreed among orthodox Christians that the Eucharist is the central act of Christian worship, the Lord's own ordinance, and the most express mark of the existence in any place of the Christian Church. Surely, then, the origin of this rite "ought" to be most explicit in the New Testament, and in ancient Christian writings. The fact remains that it is not, yet the obscurity of much of the historical development of the Sacrament in no way detracts from its integrity and sanctity. It is to be remembered that the first believers had no idea that Christians of fifteen hundred and of nineteen hundred years later would be passionately interested in the course of events of their day. The Apostolic writers wrote to please themselves, not us, and in writing of the development of the Church addressed themselves to the interests and controversies of the day. Thus, for example, S. Paul has a great deal to say, and to say explicitly, about "the circumcision question" and "justification by faith." He mentions the Eucharist only occasionally, and then allusively and in passing, when dealing with other things. Yet this by no means indicates that in the first Church the doctrine of "justification by faith" was a matter of central and burning interest, and the Sacrament a peripheral interest. In fact, exactly the reverse was the case. S Paul, and also his opponents, and likewise the numerous "central" party, all took it for granted that the Eucharist was the Lord's ordinance, and the distinctive act of Christian worship. There was nothing to dispute about. The unchallenged prestige of the Sacrament is reflected in the paucity and obscurity of reference to it in the Epistles. On the other hand, "the circumcision question" is the background of a great deal of the New Testament, not so much because of its intrinsic importance to the mass of believers, but because it was an issue around which some Christians, who were in general agreement in fundamentals, happened to disagree. Thus a careful reading of our Lord's words of institution in the Gospels does not make it explicit beyond all shadow of doubt that our Lord intended to institute a permanent rite of perpetual obligation. The evangelists, in fact, seem regrettably careless, in view of later controversy! The real and substantial evidence of our Lord's intention

[1]"Eucharist" is the general theological name given to the rite instituted by our Lord at His Last Supper, in all the various ritual forms and theological complexions which it has borne in the Church.

is the manner in which it was taken for granted in the Church by all parties that He had in fact instituted the rite, and that it was the regular and distinctive act of Christian worship. It is this lack of controversy which alone makes possible the slight looseness of phrase in the Gospel accounts of the institution. Let the student, then, not be dismayed that we have to reconstruct the development of the Eucharist in the early Church from incomplete and indirect evidence.

First, the rite which our Lord instituted was a symbolical representation of, and participation in, "the night in which He was betrayed," rather than of Calvary. Later Christian thought has sometimes forgotten this, and tried to see in the Eucharist a symbol of the destruction of Christ's body upon the Cross. The sacrifice which accomplished man's salvation was a spiritual sacrifice of sinless obedience to the Father, offered by the divine Son as man. The climax of it was the prayer of Gethsemane, "not my will, but Thine, be done" (S. Luke xxii, 42). The physical death upon the Cross, and the bodily resurrection, have their importance as the outward marks that the sacrifice had actually taken place as an historic fact, and had prevailed. It was the inward spiritual sacrifice of perfect obedience, the spirit of Gethsemane, which made of Calvary not just one cruel execution among many, but the divine sacrifice for sin. Thus we appropriately find that the Eucharist is a solemn ritual reenactment of the Last Supper, from which Christ went to Gethsemane. Second, in line with this train of thought, we find that the Eucharist in New Testament times was a meal of Christian fellowship, of ordinary food, but marked by a special and distinctive grace of thanksgiving. The spiritual focus of the general meal of fellowship was the solemn ritual breaking of the bread and blessing of the cup, as Christ had done, with the recitation of His mysterious words of institution. The clearest evidence is that of S. Paul. He does not indeed expressly say that the words of institution are to be recited, but the way in which he impressively records in this context a composite and rhythmical assemblage of Christ's words at the Last Supper clearly has this implication (1 Cor. xi, 23–6). S. Justin Martyr's celebrated account of a Eucharist (c. A.D. 150–155) is exactly similar, in that the words of institution are recorded, and their recitation at the Eucharist plainly implied, but not explicitly stated.[1] So we find that when a clear account of eucharistic ritual first appears

[1] 1 *Apology*, lxvi.

to history in S. Hippolytus (end of the second century, but probably reflecting the usage of an earlier time), there is a recitation of the words of institution.[1]

The reason for the next stage of development we may surmise from the difficulties and irregularities hinted at in 1 Corinthians xi, 21. As the early pure simple-minded piety of the Church became a little tarnished and conventionalized, it became harder and harder in a gathering for general fellowship, which included "a good square meal," to preserve intact that atmosphere of dignity and spirituality which is clearly necessary for the celebration of the Lord's solemn thanksgiving. Thus the general meal was separated from the sacramental grace of thanksgiving. We then find in the Church the general meal of fellowship, the Agape, or "Love Feast," and, as a separate token meal, the purely sacramental act of worship of the Eucharist. This appears to be the position reflected in the famous letter of the Roman writer Pliny the Younger to the Emperor Trajan, which concerns Christian customs in Bithynia about A.D. 112, as viewed by a not entirely understanding pagan:[2] "On an appointed day they had been accustomed to meet before daybreak, and to recite a hymn antiphonally to Christ, as to a god, and to bind themselves by an oath [*sacramentum*]. . . . After the conclusion of this ceremony it was their custom to depart and meet again to take food; but it was ordinary and harmless food, and they had ceased this practice after my edict in which, in accordance with your orders, I had forbidden secret societies." The most natural construction to be placed upon this is that early in the morning on the Lord's Day the Christians met for a responsive order of service which could be sung, and which included some form of doctrinal confession of a distinctively Christian character. The essential part of this service was the *sacramentum*. To the Roman Pliny this would mean an oath, but to the Christians it would be a name for the Eucharist. Then, there being no day of rest on Sunday at this period, the Christians went to work, but in the evening they came together again for a less distinctively sacramental act of worship, namely, a fellowship meal of ordinary food. This would be the Agape.

---
[1] *Apostolic Tradition* of S. Hippolytus, iv, as edited by B. S. Easton, Cambridge, 1934, p. 36.
[2] Epistle X, xcvi. See Bettenson's *Documents of the Christian Church*, Oxford, 1950, pp. 4–5.

However, unlike the Eucharist, it was not an essential part of the life of the Church, and could be given up in time of persecution. Significantly, the Christians of Bithynia had apparently not admitted that in face of Pliny's edict they had given up the Eucharist also. The Love Feast gradually declined in Christian esteem, until it became more an act of charity to poor Christians than a means of grace. Finally it died out, or was suppressed.[1]

We must now consider how we may most intelligibly fit the Eucharist of *Didache* into this admittedly somewhat fragmentary background. First we must consider the positive side, the things which we have in chapters 9 and 10. (1) The rite is expressly called the Eucharist. (2) There is a regular rhythmical responsive prayer, such as could be sung. The repeated phrase "Thine is the glory for ever and ever" reads rather like a congregational response. (3) The first thanksgiving is for the messianic "rod out of the stem of Jesse" (Isaiah xi, 1), who has now been made known to the Church in the person of Jesus. This is a thoroughly Biblical conception. In particular S. John xv, 1 ff., points out Jesus as "the true Vine," that is, the true Christian fulfilment of Isaiah xi, 1, and other "vine prophecies," such as Psalm lxxx, 8–17. This very original and "messianic" thanksgiving is appropriately set in the archaic language of the first days of the Church. The word rendered "Son" in these prayers is παῖς (Lightfoot, pp. 221–2), which can also be rendered "child" or "servant," and is the word characteristically used of Jesus in the early speeches of Acts (cf. iv, 27). (4) The second thanksgiving, though a little less explicit, answers to the idea of Christ as "the Bread of Life," a clearly eucharistic notion (particularly S. John vi, 30–35, 48–58). (5) The third prayer is for the coming of the Kingdom, which will be marked by the gathering together of the People of God, the Church, into their divinely appointed unity. This answers to our Lord's own idea (S. Matthew viii, 11), which in turn echoes the many Old Testament passages where the exiled Israelites long for a return to their Promised Land, and associate this with the promised messianic deliverance (for example, Isaiah xliii, 5–9). We note particularly the striking phrase "as this broken bread was scattered upon the mountains." Many commentators have interpreted this naturally and literally, and deduced from it that the country where *Didache* first saw the light was a hilly land, where the

[1] S. Augustine, *Confessions*, Book vi, Chap. 2.

grain was sown upon the mountainside. This would point to Syria or Palestine rather than to Egypt. However, this phrase may well be a Scriptural rather than a geographical metaphor, and may echo the language of such a verse as Psalm lxxii, 16, "There shall be an handful of corn in the earth upon the top of the mountains." Such a verse might well be interpreted as a prophecy of the messianic Eucharist. It is noteworthy that this whole Psalm would be to the early Christians one of the most clearly "messianic" of all Psalms. A reference to it would fit perfectly in this messianic petition. We remember also that S. Paul teaches the idea that the unity of the sacramental bread is a figure of the unity of the Church (1 Cor. x, 17). (6) This chapter closes with a rubric that only the baptized are to partake of the Eucharist, upon the dominical sanction of S. Matthew vii, 6, "Give not that which is holy to the dogs."

Chapter 10

(7) The fourth thanksgiving is for the revelation of God, as the Father, and as the Son. To know the holy "Name" of God is a regular and classic Old Testament phrase for the reception of a revelation of the nature of God (for example, Exodus iii, 13–15; xxxiii, 12–23; xxxiv, 5–7). For the Christian this "knowledge and faith and immortality" has been made known through Jesus, the "Servant" ($\pi\alpha\hat{\iota}\varsigma$ Lightfoot, p. 221) of the Lord. (8) The fifth thanksgiving is "for our creation, preservation, and for all the blessings of this life," but above all for Christ, the "spiritual food and drink," partaken of in the Eucharist. (9) The sixth petition, closing the second group, is a parallel to the third, which closes the first group. It is a renewed prayer for the protection, perfecting, and gathering together of the Church, which will mark the coming of the promised Kingdom. This petition contains two New Testament allusions: "Perfect it in Thy love," 1 John iv, 18; "Gather it together from the four winds," S. Matthew xxiv, 31. (10) The more dignified style of a responsive prayer then breaks off, and place is given to a series of what appear to be ejaculatory prayers. However, the train of thought is still continuous, because it is the eschatological petition for the perfecting of the Church and the coming of the Kingdom which leads into the heightened eschatological fervour of these naïve exclamations. We may perhaps presume that they belong

to an earlier and freer form of the liturgy, before the development of the ampler and more theological responsive prayers, and to an earlier day of more enthusiastic adventist expectation in the Church. "Hosanna to the God of David": This is a very Jewish-sounding petition. We may well suppose that this goes back to the first Palestinian Church, and to simple believers who still hoped, despite the Lord's warning, that God would literally "restore the Kingdom to Israel" (Acts i, 6). Now presumably it has been partially "spiritualized." "Maran Atha": This phrase is still more manifestly primitive, being in Aramaic, the language of the original Palestinian Church. It remains in the vocabulary of a Greek-speaking Church, held by the tenacious power of a hallowed traditional usage, as a relic of a day when the Church worshipped in a different tongue. (Compare with this the Greek words "Kyrie eleison" remaining in the Latin Mass, and the Hebrew "Hallelujah" in English worship.) The phrase also occurs in I Corinthians xvi, 22. Aramaic scholars have debated the exact meaning of the words, and have construed them as either "The Lord has come" or "The Lord will come." It is, however, probably preferable to divide the letters differently, so as to read "Marana Tha," or "O Come! Our Lord!" Whatever be the exact translation, this phrase belongs to the first period of the Church, during which apparently most or all of the Christians cherished a vivid expectation of the almost immediate Second Advent of the Lord.

Two somewhat enigmatic phrases remain for comment. "And after ye are satisfied": The most natural sense of this is that the Eucharist of *Didache* is still, as in I Corinthians xi, a substantial meal, and not a purely token and symbolic meal. This would be a primitive feature. This construction is, however, not absolutely necessary. The worshippers might be "satisfied" in a purely spiritual sense. "But permit the prophets to offer thanksgiving [εὐχαριστεῖν, Lightfoot, p. 222] as much as they desire": At a later period the verb εὐχαριστεῖν could be used in the technical sense of "to celebrate." This would imply a claim that the Christian prophets were to be allowed to share in presiding at the Eucharist, together with the regularly ordained "presbyter-bishops." It would, however, be contrary to what else is known of the usage of the early Church to suppose that an unordained person would be allowed to preside at the Eucharist. It may reasonably be argued that the "presbyter-bishops" and the "prophets" were not mutually exclusive, and that the spirit of ecstatic prophecy might well descend upon some of the elders. A more natural reading of this clause, then, is that the regular "presbyter-bishops" who preside at the Eucharist are to permit the prophets, when under the influence of the Holy Spirit, to offer prayer, and presumably extemporaneous prayer, in addition to the customary liturgical prayers. This is clearly another relic of primitive usage. It is to be remembered that for many centuries after this time a good deal of liberty was allowed in the words used at the Eucharist.

In turning to the negative side we must now consider some things which we might expect to find in chapters 9 and 10, but which are not there. (1) In general, there is no particular association of these prayers with the thought of man's salvation by the sacrifice of Christ's sinless obedience, of His death and resurrection, or of a spiritual and sacramental communication to the worshippers of His body and blood. Most people would feel that this theme is essential to any adequate understanding of the Eucharist. Thus in pursuing the theme that *Didache* diverges sharply from the New Testament, and from the gospel of grace, Dr. Torrance remarks: "It is rather astonishing that there is not even mention of forgiveness in the Eucharistic prayer, while the sacrament does not appear to be related to the death of Christ. This fact seems to indicate the root difficulty: inability to grasp the evangelical message of the Cross."[1] (2) In particular, there is no recitation of our Lord's Words of Institution. All our other evidence, so far as it goes, indicates that this was the solemn and essential feature of the eucharistic liturgy. (3) It is not stated who is to preside at the Eucharist.

The usual constructions placed upon this perplexing evidence are: (1) These prayers answer to the very primitive usage, when the grace of thanksgiving, later separated as the Eucharist, and the meal of fellowship, later separated as the Agape, were still one act of worship. This may very well be the case, though there is no conclusive evidence. Two circumstances go to support this supposition. In the first place, it allows us to give a natural and literal sense to "after ye are satisfied." In the second place, it explains why there is in *Didache* no separate order for an Agape, which might have been expected in such a document. Nevertheless, this still does nothing to meet the difficulty that here is a Eucharist, albeit united with an Agape, where there is no

[1]*Grace in the Apostolic Fathers*, p. 40.

recital of the Words of Institution. (2) This is a Eucharist at which the Words of Institution were not recited, and where there was no clear reference to forgiveness of sins, and to a sacramental partaking of the body and blood of the Lord. If so, this is a very strange and eccentric Eucharist, and indeed a positively heretical Eucharist. Nor does it answer to what is known of the sacramental rites of heretical bodies. (3) Despite the opening statement that this is the liturgy for a Eucharist, chapters 9 and 10 of *Didache* do not describe a Eucharist. What we have here is the ritual for an Agape, apart from the Eucharist. The difficulty then arises why a Church Order should not contain the Order for the central act of Christian worship. The only feasible explanation is that the very brief and bare account in Chapter 14 represents the Eucharist of the Church of the *Didache*.[1] However, it is indeed strange that so full and dignified an account should be given of the admittedly nonessential ceremonial, and so inadequate an account of the essential.

We would suggest a fourth hypothesis, which appears most attractively to reduce all these elements to order. This is based upon the theory of liturgical and doctrinal reserve, which we have already suggested applies to the Catechetical Manual and to the Order for Holy Baptism.[2] It will be observed that the prayers of chapters 9 and 10 very adequately express what may be described as the supporting theology of the Eucharist, though not the theology of the Eucharist itself. We have Jesus presented as the Messiah, the True Vine of the heavenly wine. We have our Lord as the Bread of Life. We have a doctrine of Christ as the supreme revealer of the Father. We have the idea of the unity of the Church, expressed in the united Sacrament. We have the Advent hope, "until His coming again," implicit in the idea of a commemorative Sacrifice. But the sacrificial death of Christ, and the communication of its merits to the Church by the sacramental eating of His body and drinking of His blood, is conspicuous by its absence. The presence and adequacy of the supporting theology makes the absence of the central and essential theology all the more conspicuous, and renders it the harder to believe that in *Didache* we have the eccentric Eucharist of a Church which did not teach Christ's atoning Sacrifice. The prayers in *Didache* are like a portrait with the face cut out. The limbs are there, which make the presence of the face

---

[1] For this view see Vokes, *Riddle of the Didache*, p. 199.
[2] pp. 79-80.

intelligible. Yet the face, which is the focus of the personality of the whole subject, is absent. It is a reasonable supposition that the central formula of the Eucharist is not written in the *Didache* prayers. It is held in reserve, as too sacred to be written down. The Church is a secret society, and these are the Christian Mysteries. A certain amount may rightly be written down for the instruction of the sympathetic outsider, but the operative words and ritual action can only be disclosed to those who have definitely committed themselves to Christ and His Church, and who have been definitely initiated at Holy Baptism. Therefore, the supporting eucharistic theology is declared, while the central eucharistic theology is missing—but not because it is not known to the Church.

Other early Christian liturgies do indeed usually take the opposite course, and record the Words of Institution, but there is one highly significant support for the usage we seek to establish in *Didache*. One of the most important systematic treatments of these matters which has come down to us from the early centuries of the Church is the *Catechesis Mystagogica* of S. Cyril of Jerusalem (A.D. 348). He does not recount the Words of Institution, but this by no means involves that he did not know them. This hypothesis of reserve not only unifies the treatment in *Didache* of the Eucharist with that of the catechism and Holy Baptism. It accords with the rubric at the end of Chapter 9: "But let no one eat or drink of this eucharistic thanksgiving, but they that have been baptized into the name of the Lord." The catechumens are present for the first part of the prayers, and possibly for the Agape meal. They are then bidden to depart, as was certainly the custom of the later Church, as reflected in the Greek liturgy of the present day. Between the prayers of Chapter 9 and Chapter 10 the Words of Institution are then said, with the breaking of the bread and blessing of the cup, and the baptized communicate. It may well be that held in reserve at this point there is also some more distinctively christological doctrinal confession, and a more expressly "sacrificial" prayer. This would bring the liturgy into line with what is found in the *Apostolic Tradition* of S. Hippolytus, though one would suppose that in *Didache* these would be less theological and less elaborate than at this later period. After the close of the essential sacramental action, the more general prayers of Chapter 10 proceed.

Chapter 11

In the general introduction to *The Teaching of the Twelve Apostles* we have discussed the so-called "Charismatic Ministry" of the ancient Church, and its bearing upon the character of this document. In the next three chapters *Didache* takes up a most interesting discussion of the office, dignity, and discipline of Christian "prophets."

"If the teacher himself be perverted and teach a different doctrine . . . hear him not": This rule seems to be directed chiefly to the apparently itinerant "apostles," for the teacher is one who "comes." "These things" presumably include the baptismal and eucharistic ritual, and the prayers and fasts, as well as the teaching of the Moral Manual. An appeal is made to a fixed tradition of doctrine and worship. The idea of the Church as the possessor of an authentic and fixed tradition of truth, going back to the original Apostolic Church, is an important New Testament doctrine (S. Luke i, 1–4; xxi, 33; S. John xvi, 12–14; 1 Cor. xi, 23; xv, 3; Gal. i, 8; Eph. iv, 5, 13–15; 2 Pet. i, 16; Jude 3). *Didache* thus acknowledges an all-important conservative safeguard against innovation by those who claim to be prophets. If it is to be acknowledged as of God, the "Charismatic Ministry" must uphold and not destroy the established doctrine and worship of the Church. It was upon this ground that Montanism was rejected. The Church rightly or wrongly felt that Montanus claimed that his utterances were so far inspired by the Holy Spirit that they wielded an authority equal to Scripture. This claim, if made, can never be allowed.

"Apostles and prophets": First it is to be observed that both these words are used in a sense slightly different from that of the New Testament. In the New Testament the essential characteristic of an Apostle is that he is a witness of the resurrection; that is, he is an authenticating authority for the facts about Christ (Acts i, 21–2). However, the Apostles typically took up the work of itinerant preachers, so travelling evangelists in general can be more loosely described as Apostles (Acts xiv, 14). This latter sense is used in *Didache*. The essential characteristic of the "Apostle" is here his way of life. He is an itinerant. In the New Testament, furthermore, "prophecy" is in some sense the counterpart and complement of "speaking with tongues." It is preaching in an ordinarily intelligible manner. This at least appears to be the general sense of the leading passage, 1 Corinthians xiv, 1–25. In principle "prophecy" is open to all believers, and not alone to those who have a special "gift" like that of tongues. The Christian prophets have a voluntary control over their faculties, and so are amenable to discipline (verses 29–32). It is not precluded, however, that the inherently unaccountable and spontaneous "gift of tongues" may come upon either Apostle or prophet. However, in *Didache* it would appear that the characteristic of the Christian "prophet" is that he exercises "the Charismatic Ministry." Anyone, itinerant or no, ordained "presbyter-bishop" or no, who receives the gift of ecstatic "speaking in the Spirit" is a prophet.

"Let every apostle . . . be received as the Lord; . . . but if he abide three days, he is a false prophet": The presumption here is that the itinerant "Apostle" will in fact exercise the ecstatic gift of "prophecy." Naturally, if his "prophecy" is indeed the immediate work of the Holy Spirit, it is to be received as such. To him belongs the highest honour and authority. However, even the primitive Church of the *Didache* has had enough experience to teach it that there are grave possibilities of abuse in giving so high a dignity to an essentially wandering, spontaneous, unaccountable, and self-authenticating ministry. All too easily the Church may be imposed upon by impostors. Therefore there must be simple disciplinary tests even for divine "prophets." The first such test is that he must not batten for his living upon a single congregation. He must show his devotion to the Lord by maintaining the hardship of the itinerant life of poverty, and not stop for more than three days in one place. Thus change of circumstances has quaintly reversed our Lord's original discipline for His Apostles. They were not to be religious beggars (S. Luke x, 7). The Apostles of *Didache* were to demonstrate their sincerity by being just this!

"If he ask money, he is a false prophet": Here is another searching sanction for the wandering devotee to religious poverty.

"Any prophet speaking in the Spirit ye shall not try nor discern": There is an illegitimate and perilous test for the authenticity of an ecstatic prophet. It is believed that just as the Holy Spirit may possess some true Christian ecstatics, so demons may possess others, and work in them apparently similar phenomena. However, prophets in their ecstasy are not to be put to the test of exorcism, or the invoking of the Name of Jesus over them to cast out the supposedly evil spirit. To do this would bring risk of the horrid guilt of seeking to exorcise the Holy Spirit Himself. The Church of *Didache* assumes that this is "the unforgivable sin" of S. Mark iii, 28–30. This is clearly not the mind of our Lord, but it is not at all unlikely that this was the sense seen in this saying by the early Church, and provided the reason why it was remembered. The bishops of Phrygia did in fact put some of the Montanist prophetesses to this test of exorcism, to their natural great offence (Eusebius *H.E.*, V, xviii, 13).

"Only if he have the ways of the Lord": The discreet and pious test for true and false prophets is the moral test, the hardheaded and common-sense test of conduct.

"No prophet when he ordereth a table in the Spirit shall eat of it": The "table" referred to is presumably the Agape, because it is a meal such as might tempt a false prophet to greed. We observe that the prophet has some measure of authority in the Church to initiate an Agape.

"If he doeth not what he teacheth": A fitting test of true and false prophecy.

"He doeth ought as an outward mystery typical of the Church, and yet teacheth you not to do all that he himself doeth": The converse does not necessarily follow. A true prophet will himself do all that he commands the people to do, but the people are not to do all that the prophet does. As with the Old Testament prophets (for example, Ezekiel iv), the prophet may sometimes in his ecstasy perform strange symbolical actions for the instruction of the Church, which it would not be fitting for the people to copy.

"Give me silver or anything else": Another aspect of the test that the true prophet is disinterested.

Chapter 12

"That cometh in the name of the Lord": Compare Psalm cxviii, 26; S. Matthew xxi, 9; etc.

"If the comer is a traveller": The itinerant "Apostle" is not absolutely forbidden to forsake his calling of religious poverty and mendicancy. However, he must not accept the charity of the Church for more than three days. Otherwise he comes under the suspicion of being a false prophet who "is trafficking upon Christ." He must earn his living, and the Church may fittingly help to put him in the way of doing so. The implication of the next chapter appears to be that this rule applies to a probationary period only.

Chapter 13

"But every true prophet desiring to settle among you is worthy of his food": It is not expressly stated, but it appears to be implied that this case is the same as that of the travelling "Apostle" who wishes to settle. After a more prolonged period, during which the newcomer with the gift of the "Charismatic Ministry" has more thoroughly established his good standing with the local Church, by his continuance in a life of honest work, unselfishness, and disinterestedness, it may become an act of religious merit among the faithful to support him with their gifts.

"The workman is worthy of his food": S. Matthew x, 10.

"Give as the firstfruit to the prophets; for they are your chief-priests": The newcomer, being settled, is no longer a travelling "Apostle." He owes his permanent position in the Church to the circumstance that he faithfully and authentically exercises the "Charismatic Ministry." Presumably the Holy Spirit may choose anyone upon whom to bestow the "spiritual gifts," but there are in fact certain members of the congregation who more regularly and usually exercise this ministry, and they are properly designated "the prophets." At least in principle they are of the highest degree of honour of all Church functionaries. They are "chief priests." This is the logical and inescapable conclusion of any theology which allows that the authentic and approved "Charismatic Ministry" is the immediate operation of the Holy Spirit. The regular Ministry of the "presbyter-bishops" is, indeed, also the operation of the Spirit, but the Ministry of "gifts" is a more immediate operation.

"But if ye have not a prophet": Though the prophet is, at least in principle, chief in honour, he is not essential. He is the desired ornament of the Church, but there can be a duly constituted Church without him. It is not expressly stated what is essential, within the sphere of Christian Ministry, for the constitution of a genuine Church. However, the implication is not far away that this "regular" and essential, albeit humbler and less spectacular, Ministry is that of the "presbyter-bishops" and deacons mentioned in Chapter 15.

We may bring this subject to a fitting close by attempting a judgment upon the witness of *Didache* to the office and dignity of the "Charismatic Ministry" in the Church from which this document springs. We leave on one side the question as to whether other, and possibly more regular, orthodox, and sophisticated congregations would have given it less place. A first reading of *Didache* undoubtedly gives the impression that the so-called "Charismatic Ministry" is to be accorded primacy of repute and influence over the regular Ministry of bishops and deacons. The document has therefore been widely hailed as important evidence of an original situation in the Church, before the "Catholic" ministry of bishops, priests, and deacons rose to prominence. The present writer feels that this impression is not altogether correct, and that the case for the "Charismatic Ministry" in *Didache* can easily be overstated. Clearly there is a case to state. In the New Testament period there was a ministry of "gifts" which enjoyed a prominence it did not have in a later generation. *Didache*, whether it be very primitive or archaic or semi-Montanist, does reflect something of this proportion of Churchmanship. Nevertheless, it is also and equally a witness to the grave disciplinary difficulties attendant upon its function, even among those who in principle felt that it ought to be accorded the highest honour. *Didache* is in fact a witness to the circumstance that, as the Church developed and "found its feet," the regular Ministry of "presbyter-bishops" was bound to increase, and the Ministry of prophets in proportion to decrease. It is indeed well possible to argue that, just as S. Ignatius' strong argument and confident assumption that the ruling bishop is everywhere in control of the Church reflects in part his view of what *ought* to be, rather than what was, so it is here in *Didache*. The writer of *Didache* may dwell upon the dignity of "prophecy" at least in part because he knows quite well that even in his congregation the "Charismatic Ministry" was not what it had been in the first days. We are inclined to say: "Methinks he doth protest too much." In this sense it is possible that there is an element of archaism in *Didache*. Nothing is more common in the history of the Church than for writers on Church Order to be traditionalist in interest, and to be found legislating in terms of the generation which was swiftly passing, rather than of common custom. *The Teaching of the Twelve Apostles* may be an example.

Chapter 14

"On the Lord's own day"; κατὰ κυριακὴν δὲ Κυρίου (Lightfoot, p. 223). This is the original distinctively Christian name for the first day of the week, the weekly anniversary of Christ's resurrection (Rev. i, 10). S. Justin Martyr, however, in his early and valuable account of weekly Christian worship, can also allow the pagan name for the day, and say that the day of the Eucharist is "the day which is called the day of the Sun," ἣ τοῦ Ἡλίου λεγομένη ἡμέρα (1 *Apology*, lxvii).

"Break bread and give thanks": Here we have coupled together the two New Testament names for the Sacrament of the Lord's Supper, the "breaking of bread" (Acts ii, 42, 46; xx, 7), and the Eucharist, or "thanksgiving" (1 Cor. xi, 24; xiv, 16). Some writers, who deny that chapters 9 and 10 represent the Eucharist in *Didache*, confine the document's mention of the Sacrament to this brief chapter.[1] However, if it be allowed that chapters 9 and 10 give an account of the eucharistic ritual, this chapter is not wholly a repetition. In the context of the discussion of the Church's ministry, Chapter 14 appropriately adds two further points of discipline; namely, the proper day, and the due preparation in confession of sin, and moral discipline exercised by the Church.

"That your sacrifice may be pure": A note which is conspicuously absent in the prayers of chapters 9 and 10, as they stand, is here briefly mentioned. The Eucharist is the Christian Sacrifice, θυσία (Lightfoot, p. 223). This point is not expounded, and therefore a commentary on *Didache* hardly calls us to embark upon a general discussion of the Biblical doctrine of sacrifice. We may confine ourselves to a summary statement that the Biblical notion of sacrifice is neither that of the destruction of the animal as an alternative victim, in order to satiate the anger of the deity, nor is it a bribe offered to Him to appease Him. A sacrifice may be defined as "the divinely appointed means whereby God's people may offer themselves to Him in worship and obedient service, by means of a symbolic offering, and also the means by which man, being accepted by God in his sacrifice, may have fellowship with God." The Eucharist is "the Christian Sacrifice."

"In every place . . . wonderful among the nations": Malachi i, 11, 14. The main incentive among the early Christians for describing

---

[1]Vokes, *Riddle of the Didache*, p. 199.

the Eucharist as a sacrifice was not a consciously held theory about the meaning of sacrifice. It was the strong instinct to find in the Old Testament a "type" or spiritual anticipation of every part of the Christian religion. This often led the Church into exegesis which today would be dismissed as unscientific or unhistorical. At a deeper level of spirituality, however, the ancient Church was right. This theology of "types" indicated the spiritual continuity of the Church of the New Covenant with the Church of the Old, though at a higher level of revelation. Malachi i, 11, 14, is one of the favourite texts in use among the Fathers to indicate the wonderful spread of the Christian religion among the Gentiles, and in this context the Eucharist, the focus of Christian worship, is naturally "the pure sacrifice" of this prophecy.

Chapter 15

"Appoint for yourselves"; χειροτονήσατε (Lightfoot, p. 224), *elect*, as in a Greek city. This is hardly to be taken as implying that the "presbyter-bishops" and deacons were simply elected by the congregation, and appointed without laying on of hands. There is no evidence for any such custom in the ancient Church. What the phrase does probably indicate is simply that in the Church of the *Didache* the principle is still a living reality that the bishop is to be "elected" with the consent of, and by the Spirit-guided acclamation of, the general body of the faithful. It is a common mistake to import into the ancient "election" of the bishop the associations of modern representative democracy. The theory of the ancient Church was emphatically not that "power resides in the people," that the initiative for the appointment of officers comes from the general membership, and that the minister is the deputy of the congregation. Very much the reverse: the power to make a bishop, and the power wielded by the bishop, was seen as divine power. He was God's gift to the flock, a ruling "father-in-God." The initiative for his appointment came from the Holy Spirit. Yet by what instrument did the Holy Spirit operate, save by the consensus of the whole body of the faithful? Thus the "election" was not seen as the counting of votes to determine the will of man. It was much more akin to the Quaker "taking the sense of the meeting," to determine a divine guidance by the general consensus of the spiritually-minded and prayerful people. Those "elected" in this way would certainly be ordained to their office by laying on of hands by those who were "presbyter-bishops" before them. It may perhaps seem strange to some that in a book which gives so much instruction about some points of Church ritual and discipline nothing is said more explicitly about the manner of appointment of the bishops and deacons. This is in marked contrast to the detailed instructions given regarding the honour to be paid to the "Charismatic Ministry," and also regarding the careful safeguards to be observed in relation to it. The implication probably is that the office and repute of the "prophets" was to some degree an occasion of controversy in the Church, while the position of the bishops and deacons was secure and accepted on all sides, and could be passed over in relative silence.

"Bishops and deacons": This is the same phrase as in Philippians i, 1, and the same usage as found in the Epistle of S. Clement of Rome (see pp. 49–50). There are only two ranks of regular local ministers, not the threefold ministry of "bishops, priests, and deacons" of the later Church. The ruling bishop has not yet been clearly differentiated from the body of presbyters, and therefore the ministry of *Didache* consists of a body of "presbyter-bishops," assisted by deacons. The same test is to be applied to these as to the "prophets": they are to be unselfish and disinterested.

"Despise them not": This does not necessarily carry the implication that some in the Church exalted the "prophets" at the expense of the repute and power of the bishops. It is a general pious exhortation. There is no trace of the exaltation of charismatic prophecy in the Churches known to S. Clement, but he writes to enforce the same necessary plea.

"Prophets and teachers": It is a little puzzling that the teachers in the Church appear to be bracketed with the charismatic prophets rather than with the regular bishops. This arrangement answers to the New Testament usage, where "prophecy" is preaching, rather than to the charismatic prophecy characteristic of *Didache*.

"The Gospel": We have passed away from the New Testament usage, natural to a time when "the New Testament" was not yet written. There "the Gospel" is the Christian message. Here it is a book, containing a record of the teaching of Jesus.

Chapter 16

Didache appropriately closes with an Epilogue, being an apocalyptic exhortation to faithfulness, framed in language derived from the Gospels. This is therefore both a "Jewish" and a highly Christian passage.

"Be watchful": S. Matthew xxv, 13; S. Luke xii, 35, 40.

"If ye be not perfected at the last season": To the writer of *Didache* the present is "the last time," when the Church expectantly awaits the Second Advent of Christ, and the Judgment.

"False prophets and corrupters shall be multiplied": S. Matthew xxiv, 11, 24.

"They shall hate one another": S. Matthew xxiv, 10.

"And then the world-deceiver shall appear": S. Matthew xxiv, 24.

"They that endure": S. Matthew xxiv, 13.

"By the Curse Himself": Christ died the death marked out by the Law of Moses as an excommunicate and cursed death (Deut. xxi, 23). Thus Christ made Himself one with man in his dark disgrace, and in this sense was "made to be sin" (2 Cor. v, 21). This does not involve that God the Father laid a curse on our Lord.

"And then shall the signs appear": S. Matthew xxiv, 30. It will be observed that the signs have been given a fuller description than in the Gospels.

"A resurrection of the dead; yet not of all": The writer of *Didache*, like the generality of the Church of the first centuries, was a pre-millenarian, and held that the Second Advent of Christ would bring the Resurrection of the righteous only, so that they might take part in the earthly Rule of the Saints. The resurrection of the wicked, and the Last Judgment, would take place only after this. This doctrine arises from a very literal rendering of Revelation xx, 1-7.

"The Lord shall come and all His saints with Him": Zechariah xiv, 5.

"Then shall the world see the Lord coming upon the clouds of heaven": S. Matthew xxiv, 30.

IV The Epistles of S. Ignatius of Antioch

1. The Writer

An introduction to these Epistles must open with a word about the writer, because one of the most valuable things they have to bring to us is a vivid picture of his personality. In this the Epistles differ from most of the writings we have to consider, which say little or nothing about their authors. There are not many figures in the post-Apostolic Church of which it is possible to paint a character study, but of Ignatius even the critical Dr. Torrance allows: "Of all the early Fathers it is the figure of Ignatius which comes nearest the apostolic picture as we find it in the New Testament. His was a robust character grounded in a passionate faith and in an invincible loyalty to his Lord. His Christianity is not the tepid persuasion of his successors in the second century, which clings simply to tradition and ethical knowledge as the important elements; it is centred wholly round the Person of Christ who still lives on in the church fellowship."[1] Schaff writes: "Ignatius stands out in history as the ideal of a Catholic martyr. . . . Clement shows the calmness, dignity, and governmental wisdom of the Roman character. Ignatius glows with the fire and impetuosity of the Greek and Syrian temper, which carries him beyond the bounds of sobriety. He was a very uncommon man, and made a powerful impression upon his age. He is the incarnation, as it were of the three closely connected ideas: the glory of martyrdom, the omnipotence of episcopacy, and the hatred of heresy and schism."[2]

With regard to this lack of "sobriety," the modern reader will find one trait in the character of S. Ignatius which is most offensive to conventional modern taste. He looks forward to his death. To us this seems regrettably "otherworldly" and morbid. To make things worse, he looks forward with keen anticipation to a death by horrid torture. To the modern mind this is not a mark of exceptional sanctity, but of

[1]*Grace in the Apostolic Fathers*, p. 56.
[2]Quoted in *Nicene and Post-Nicene Fathers*, Vol. I, p. 167, col. 2.

psychological disorder. We are reminded that modern humane but worldly society would send not a few of the historic saints and heroes of the Faith to the clinic and the mental home rather than to the arena, though whether this would be a more or a less merciful form of misjudgment we leave the reader to determine for himself. However, as we consider the striking contrast between the calm and judicious dignity of Clement of Rome and the "fire" which pious fancy has often discerned in the very name Ignatius, we must make allowance for the difference in occasion and purpose of the two writings. S. Clement wrote to adjust the discipline of the Church. S. Ignatius writes to bestow a Confessor's blessing and exhortation upon the faithful who had ministered to him. He knows that he is already condemned to be thrown to the beasts, and that the authorities are taking the trouble to conduct him to Rome in order to augment the number of victims "butchered to make a Roman holiday." Our physically comfortable though mentally uncomfortable age does not find it easy to understand the psychology of martyrdom, in which men may find mental comfort amidst physical torment. Yet it is manifest that a man who by "screwing his courage to the sticking place" has resolved to die for his Lord, fortified by the faith that the horrid awaiting death is the crown of discipleship and the gate of heaven, does not and cannot look upon life with that balanced and sober judgment proper to "peaceful homes and healthful days." It is idle to blame him for a heightened nervous tension, for were his psychological condition normal he would not dare to die. And once he has dared, he must be judged by the standards proper to his condition. S. Ignatius says some things which jar upon our taste, but he is not morbid or unbalanced any more than is the bizarre book of the Revelation, which speaks from the same condition. He is simply a man waiting to be thrown to the lions, who fortifies his resolution by the only method possible to a man in that strange situation.

Though there is an admirably clear picture of his personality, not very much is known for certain about the life of Ignatius. Most of the information we have is derived from the Epistles, which are not autobiographical. Eusebius says that S. Ignatius was the second Bishop of Antioch, Evodius being the first.[1] This account may reasonably be accepted, for if Eusebius were recording a pious legend it would doubt-

[1] *H.E.*, III, xxii. Cf. Ep. to Romans, 9, to Smyrneans, 11, to Polycarp, 7.

less have made the famous martyr the first bishop, thus giving him personal contact with the Apostles. Eusebius can also call S. Peter the first Bishop of Antioch, which would make Ignatius the third, and in this passage gives a date for the beginning of his episcopate which works out at about A.D. 69.[1] We know that S. Peter was active at Antioch in the first period of the Church, and before he went to Rome (Galatians ii, 11). It rather begs the question whether there was at this early period at Antioch a "bishop," that is, a single ruling bishop of the later pattern. While the great S. Peter was there in person, he would naturally be a predominating influence at Antioch, though whether Galatians makes him a "ruler" is a moot point. It would be interesting to have an account from the party opposed to S. Paul! Following him, there was presumably a period when the Church of Antioch was ruled by a body of joint "presbyter-bishops," like other Churches. Evodius may have been an outstanding figure among these. Clearly Ignatius himself is a good example of the outstanding type of "presbyter-bishop" who would become a ruling single bishop, and who in his person would call into being the institution of the ruling bishop. We can see both that there was a succession of Apostolic office in the Church, and that S. Ignatius was very near to the Apostles in this succession, and also that later Church writers naturally enough read the customs of their own time back into the history of the early decades of the Church.

Eusebius also informs us in his *Chronicle* that S. Ignatius began his episcopate during the 212th Olympiad (that is, A.D. 69-72), and was martyred in the tenth year of the Emperor Trajan (A.D. 107).[2] These dates are very generally accepted by scholars. Nor is there any need to doubt the strong and early tradition, and the supposition of the Epistles themselves, that Ignatius met his death at Rome. The occasion would quite possibly be the gladiatorial games, exceptionally prolonged and extensive, by which Trajan celebrated the end of his military campaign in Dacia, in the year 107. No fewer than 10,000 gladiators perished, and 11,000 wild beasts, which gives a grim but very practical reason why the administration should have gone to the trouble and expense of bringing a prisoner like Ignatius to Rome for his execution.

[1] *H.E.*, III, xxxvi, 2.
[2] *Chronicle*, ed. Schöne, ii, 152, 158, 162.

2. Date of the Epistles: Their Relation to the Development of Episcopacy

The Epistles were written immediately before the martyrdom of S. Ignatius. Harnack, and some others, have rejected the early date of A.D. 107, following Eusebius, and have preferred to place the writing of the Epistles later, say in the time of the Emperor Hadrian (A.D. 117-138). The chief reason for this judgment is the somewhat subjective one that there could not have been a well-developed, accepted, and universal system of a single ruling bishop in each Church, as presupposed by Ignatius, as early as A.D. 107. This is only twelve years later than the usually accepted date of the Epistle of Clement, which knows only the rule of a body of "presbyter-bishops." A somewhat later date gives more time for the evolution of Church polity. It appears doubtful whether this argument is to be upheld, and the usual early date rejected. In the first place, the development of the single ruling bishop admittedly took place quickly, and much can happen even in twelve years in the early, fluid, and formative days of an institution. In the second place, there may not be so much discrepancy between Clement and Ignatius as at first sight appears. The circumstance that Ignatius can write as he does with confidence in the existence and acceptance of episcopacy in the Churches of Syria and Asia Minor is reliable evidence that this polity did then exist in those parts. It does not follow from this that the evolution of the Church was complete, and that episcopacy was in existence everywhere by A.D. 107, though it was at this very period doubtless rapidly extending itself.

The circumstance that S. Ignatius so strongly presses the exclusive claims and universality of episcopacy is a double-edged weapon. It may indicate that these claims still needed to be pressed in some quarters, though not in Asia Minor. Ignatius may know that the polity to which he is accustomed, and which he plainly regards as the only legitimate one, is not in fact in existence in some places. He is using his prestige as a Confessor to advance the institution of the single ruling bishop. When he writes ahead to the Church at Rome, S. Ignatius is suspiciously silent about the bishop. We may surmise that possibly he knows that, very regrettably, there is in point of fact no single bishop at Rome, though there certainly "ought" to be. Possibly there was not at this time a single ruling bishop at Corinth, being also in Europe, the other Church of which we have evidence in Clement. It is quite natural to suppose that the evolution of Church polity would go forward more rapidly in Asia Minor than elsewhere, for we do know that Christianity first flourished, and Christians became a numerous section of the population, in these parts. By contrast, the prudent and judicial Church in Rome has ever been a conservative one. It would be natural if the polity characteristic of an earlier decade had lingered for a little there. The impulse behind the rise of episcopacy would doubtless be the instinct of veneration for leading presbyters, working together with the experience that bodies of equal "presbyter-bishops" were apt to be divided by quarrels, once the hand of the first Apostles was removed. Possibly in Rome, with her gift of government, the body of primitive "presbyter-bishops" managed to avoid the need of a single head longer than elsewhere. In all events, S. Ignatius is witness to the rapid and early spread of the polity of one ruling bishop in each city Church, assisted by presbyters and deacons (the threefold traditional Catholic Ministry).

3. Writing and Order of the Epistles

At the time of writing S. Ignatius is being taken by ten brutal guards ("ten leopards") from Antioch to Troas, and thence by sea to Greece. Probably the party went by sea to Attalia, and then overland to Troas, because there are no letters to places he would have visited during the earlier part of a completely overland journey. It would seem that at Laodicea, where there was a choice of route, the guards selected the northern road through Philadelphia, Sardis, and Smyrna, missing Tralles, Magnesia, and Ephesus, which lay on the southern road. It is clear that at each place which he visited along the road the confessor-bishop was honoured and ministered to by the local Christians, and received their bishops. Messengers go to the three Churches missed on the southern route, and they send deputations headed by their bishops to meet Ignatius at Smyrna, to encourage him, and to receive his blessing. So from Smyrna he writes, in somewhat rough and ungrammatical Greek, a first group of letters to Churches which he had not visited, to Ephesus, Magnesia, and Tralles, and one ahead to the Church at Rome, telling them not to seek his release.

There is then a second group, written from Troas before embarkation, to Churches and to a friend whom he had visited on the journey, to Philadelphia, to Smyrna, and to S. Polycarp. Eusebius mentions the Epistles in this rational order, which he had perhaps worked out for himself. In this order they will be treated of here. The Greek MS of the Epistles puts them in a different order: Smyrna, Polycarp, Ephesians, Magnesians, Philadelphians, Trallians, Romans. Perhaps this is the order in which Polycarp collected them at the time, so that he might send them to the Philippians, in response to their request for letters and information about the end of the martyr (Ep. to Philippians, 13).

4. Manuscript Sources and Number of the Epistles

(i) The seven genuine Epistles of S. Ignatius have come to us traditionally in the so-called Long Recension. This consists of the seven Epistles, with interpolations, alterations, and omissions, together with six other pseudonymous Epistles, entitled the Epistle of Mary of Cassobola to S. Ignatius, and the Epistles of Ignatius to Mary, to the Tarsians, the Philippians, the Antiochenes, and to Hero, a deacon of Antioch. These spurious Epistles have been made up on the basis of the genuine ones, and the whole appears to have been the work of a semiheretical writer of the fourth century. The purpose of this pious forgery would be to bring the prestige of this ancient and venerated martyr to the support of the views of the forger. It was the work of Lightfoot in 1885 which finally established the distinction between the true and false Epistles, and the genuine text of the former, bringing much controversy substantially to an end. The Long Recension occurs in Greek MS, and there is also an old Latin version of this, which is not to be regarded as an independent authority.

(ii) Scientific study of Ignatius goes back to the discovery and publication of the so-called Short Recension, that is, of MSS containing only Epistles now regarded as genuine. The famous Medicean Greek MS at Florence was first published by Voss in 1646. This contains the text of only six Epistles, being incomplete at the end, and omitting Romans. The primitive Greek text of Romans has, however, been established from another important source. This Epistle was at an early date incorporated into the Antiochene Acts of Martyrdom of S. Ignatius, which has come down in several not very satisfactory ancient MSS. A Latin version of the Short Recension was made in England, probably by the great English mediaeval scholar Robert Grosseteste, Bishop of Lincoln (1250), or by his circle. This represents a purer text than the Greek, but is of the same family of manuscripts as the Medicean. In 1644 Archbishop Ussher published six of these Epistles, rejecting Romans. Dom Ruinart later published the text of the latter. There is also part of an ancient Syriac version of this Recension, with a complete Armenian version made from the Syriac, and a Coptic fragment.

5. Commentary on the Epistles of S. Ignatius of Antioch

I. To the Ephesians

"Ignatius, who is also Theophorus": Legend has been busy with this second name, and has taken it in two senses. (i) It has been translated in the passive " borne of God." This is the basis for the legend that Ignatius was the child taken by Christ into His arms (S. Mark ix, 36). (ii) Or it can be taken in the active, "bearer of God." This is the basis of the story that after his martyrdom the name of Christ was found written in gold on his heart.

"Unto her which hath been blessed": We have here a Christian expansion of the conventional greeting at the opening of a Greek letter, in a manner similar to that familiar in the New Testament Epistles. Though there is no express citation, both the language and the thought are reminiscent of S. Paul.

1. The general reminiscence of Pauline language continues to be very plain in this passage also, particularly in the phrase "fighting with wild beasts in Rome," which is doubtless an adaptation of 1 Corinthians xv, 32, and an appropriate remark to address to Ephesus.

"I might have power to be a disciple": We are introduced to one of the characteristic thoughts of these Epistles, which occurs again and again. The essence of discipleship is to suffer with Christ (S. Mark viii, 34, etc.), and therefore the seal that one has indeed consummated discipleship is to come to the martyr's death.

"Onesimus": The characteristic figure of these Epistles, the ruling bishop and Father-in-God, here makes his first appearance. Onesimus is the Bishop of Ephesus, who has led the deputation representing the whole Church; to which salutation this Epistle is the response.

"Blessed is He that granted unto you . . . to have such a bishop": The bishop is the gift of God to the Church.

2. "My fellow-servant Burrhus, who by the will of God is your deacon . . . submitting yourselves to your bishop and presbytery": We here have the three orders of ministry, bishop, presbyters, and deacons, distinctly named. It is to be observed that the government of the Church is in the hand of the bishop, acting with the presbytery. The office of deacon is a divine calling, but not to government.

"Crocus": He presumably has brought a gift. Euplus and Fronto are the names of the remainder of the deputation.

"Perfectly joined together in one submission . . . sanctified in all things": The principle of sanctity is unity in the Church, and the principle of unity is obedience to the bishop and presbyters. This is the thought characteristic of S. Ignatius, and is constantly reiterated. There is here a characteristic difference of proportion in theological thought, as compared to S. Paul, with whom we instinctively compare S. Ignatius. To Paul, sanctification is the work of the Spirit, who provides the atmosphere of the life "in Christ" and "in the Spirit," and the Spirit operates in the Church. To Ignatius sanctification is worked by incorporation into the Church, where the Spirit operates. There is a similarity in fundamental principle, but a significant difference in order and proportion. We would not say that the Church is in point of fact more prominent in the religion of Ignatius than it was in S. Paul, but the fact is presented in a more pointed way. As in the case of S. Clement, we find ourselves in the generation which found that the contest for the Faith largely consisted in the vindication of the discipline of the Church.

3. "I am not yet perfected [ἀπήρτισμαι, Lightfoot, p. 106] in Jesus Christ. Now I am beginning to be a disciple": The due goal of Christian discipleship is martyrdom.

"Jesus Christ also . . . is the mind [γνώμη, Lightfoot, p. 106] of the Father, even as the bishops . . . are in the mind of Jesus Christ": This is the essential thought of such passages as 1 Corinthians ii and Ephesians vi, 18–19. The mystery of the mind of God is an "open secret" in

Christ, and the revelation in Christ is declared by the Church. Significantly, while to the Apostle it is himself who is the declarer of the mystery, to Ignatius it is the bishop.

"Settled in the farthest parts of the earth": There is an element of rhetoric in this. S. Ignatius does indeed speak as though all Churches had bishops, but he need not be taken too literally, as meaning that there are bishops in every part of the world.

4. "Attuned to the bishop, even as its strings to a lyre.... And do ye, each and all, form yourselves into a chorus": In a rhetorical and rather high-flown passage the unity of the Church is likened to harmony in music. The principle of unity, both among presbytery and people, is obedience to the bishop.

5. "If any one be not within the precinct of the altar [ἐντὸς τοῦ θυσιαστηρίου, Lightfoot, p. 106] he lacketh the bread [of God]. For, if the prayer of one and another hath so great force, how much more that of the bishop and of the whole Church." Every believer, and every group of believers, can pray with power. There is thus a priestly character inhering in the whole body of the Church (1 Pet. ii, 9). The priestly principle is not limited exclusively to the ordained Ministry. However, it is the disciplined and ordered prayer of the whole corporate body of the Church which is the most prevailing prayer, which is Christian prayer in the fullest and proper sense of the word. And the eminent mark of this prayer incorporate is that it is led by the bishop. In fact, the supreme prayer of the Church, in which prayer comes to its full power, and the Church is most fully and truly the Church, is the Eucharist. The eminent mark of a Eucharist celebrated in due and proper order is that it is presided over by the bishop. Those, and only those, who are in fellowship with the Church incorporate, presided over in due order by the bishop, have a share in the Christian altar, and partake of the bread of God. This is not to say that the body of believers is spiritually dependent upon, and spiritually inferior to, the bishop. This is an impious form of argument, based on sinful human emulation, condemned by S. Paul in 1 Corinthians xii, 14-21. The bishop is an absolutely essential limb of the body, for his presence and presidency enshrine the principle of discipline and unity. Yet what is accomplished at the Christian altar is by no means something done to or for the congregation by the bishop. It is done by God through the whole body of the Church, as and when that corporate principle is

duly expressed by the presidency of the bishop, in his presbytery. Such, we submit, is the way in which it is likely that S. Ignatius would have expounded this important passage.

"Be careful not to resist the bishop, that by our submission we may give ourselves to God." The door into all Christian virtue is humility, because a man must greatly feel his utter need of what God can do for him before he will yield himself up to God, for God to do for him what only God can do (S. Mark ii, 17). The earthly lesson in humility is submission to the discipline of the Christian fellowship, symbolized in the person of the bishop. Conversely, self-sufficient and self-opinionated pride, which causes folk to forsake the disciplined fellowship, is eminently the sin which separates man from God.

"God resisteth the proud": Proverbs iii, 34; James iv, 6; 1 Peter v, 5.

6. "And in proportion as a man seeth that his bishop is silent, let him fear him the more": Obedience is to be willing, not constrained. The bishop is a Father-in-God, not a master; the obedience due to him is that of a son, not a servant. Perhaps there is here a quiet hint to the bishops also that they are to exercise their rule by self-effacing moral persuasion, not "as being lords over God's heritage."

"We ought to regard the bishop as the Lord Himself": A later writer, of a day when the traditional form of the doctrine of Apostolical Succession had been developed, would have said that the bishop is the representative of the Apostles. S. Ignatius does not argue like this. To him the bishop is the representative of Christ. (Cf. Ep. to Magnesians, 6.)

7. "Some are wont of malicious guile to hawk about the Name": This is the first warning against false teachers, who are already troubling the Church. For the end of their own advancement they are trying to press the claims of their own special teachings. The fact that these were teachers of heretical doctrine regarding the Person of Christ is implied by the way in which Ignatius promptly passes to a statement of orthodox doctrine.

"There is only one physician . . . Jesus Christ our Lord": In this most interesting and important passage we have one of the earliest statements of the doctrine of the Incarnation. The doctrine of the Two Natures, as later defined, is implicit, though it is not stated in the more precise terms of later orthodoxy. We are reminded that an ancient Father is not necessarily to be regarded as heretical because he expresses himself in loose terms, which a later century would regard as heretical.

The essence of orthodoxy is in the underlying spiritual intention of the doctrine, not in the bare form of words. The early Fathers are to be judged in light of their intention. Thus in the development of doctrine it is possible for the same intention to be expressed less precisely in one generation, and more precisely in a later generation. To read the conditions of the later time into the earlier is a common anachronism. "Son of Mary and Son of God": From the Blessed Virgin the incarnate Christ derived His human nature. His divine nature is His own, by virtue of His eternal Sonship. "Generate and ingenerate": The human nature was "generate," being born of the Virgin Mary. The divine nature was "ingenerate," says Ignatius, for it existed before the Incarnation. Later orthodoxy would have pronounced that the divine Son is eternally begotten of the Father. "First passible and then impassible": The incarnate Christ as man could suffer. The risen, ascended, and glorified Christ can suffer no more, and so is impassible.

8. "They that are of the flesh": Compare Romans viii, 5.

"Nay, even those things which ye do after the flesh [κατὰ σάρκα, Lightfoot, p. 107] are spiritual": Despite the allusion to S. Paul's characteristic contrast of "flesh" and "spirit" in the passage above, we are left with a suspicion that Ignatius is using "flesh" in a slightly different and more usual sense. To Paul the "flesh" is "human nature in rebellion against God," so that it is a contradiction in terms to speak of doing things which are "spiritual" while men are still "after the flesh." What Ignatius seems to mean is that the Ephesian Christians are spiritual, that is, they live in obedience to Christ, while they are still living in their bodies of flesh and blood. This answers to an antithesis between "the bodily" and "the spiritual," as though it were the physical organism which is the enemy of the higher life. This is not New Testament thought.

9. "Ye are stones of a temple": This quaint and rather naïve simile is perhaps the echo of a primitive sermon. It is not very fruitful to discuss the orthodoxy of the details!

10. "Pray ye also without ceasing for the rest of mankind, for there is in them a hope of repentance": This is the opening of a noble and truly Christian passage in Ignatius. The gospel of divine grace is an universal one. Universal, therefore, is the duty of prayer "for all sorts and conditions of men."

"Permit them to take lessons at least from your works": There is likewise a duty of universal charity towards wrongdoers and persecutors. Not all are called to the consummation of martyrdom, but all are called to the spirit of martyrdom.

"Stedfast in the faith": Colossians i, 23.

11. "These are the last times": This is one of the most familiar of ancient Christian themes. Most of the Fathers of the first centuries believed that the Second Advent of the Lord was very near.

"For either let us fear the wrath which is to come or let us love the grace which now is": Here is a truly Christian view of grace. It is the undeserved mercy of God, opened in Christ, to which the proper response is the love which renders willing obedience. It is the counterpart of "the wrath," which is the inevitable nemesis which comes upon the disobedient in a world ruled by a moral God. "Wrath" and "grace" represent the two complementary ways in which the God of holy love deals with sinners, the lower and preparatory way, the higher and Christian. If man will not obey for the higher reason, then he must for the lower (S. Matt. xviii, 23–35).

12. "I am in peril, ye are established": In view of the situation of Ignatius the prisoner, this looks like an appropriate and moving allusion to S. Paul's magnificent irony in 1 Corinthians iv, 8–13. It shows that while Christians were liable at all times to persecution, and had no legal security, they were not all in peril all the time.

"Ye are the high-road of those that are on their way to die unto God": Doubtless the pious custom of ministering to victims on their way to suffering, so as to receive a Confessor's blessing, was a regular one, in the case of Churches which literally were on the highroad to Rome. There were others travelling with Ignatius in this party.

"Ye are associates in the mysteries"; συμμύσται (Lightfoot, p. 109): The "mystery" is the revelation of God in Christ, that is, the Gospel. Ignatius means that those who have dared to show their Christain solidarity with condemned victims would have been owned by S. Paul himself as "fellowlabourers in the Gospel" (Phil. iv, 3; 1 Thess. iii, 2). To stir them up Ignatius goes on to remind the Ephesian Christians how often the Apostle mentions their forefathers in his writings.

"In whose foot-steps I would fain be found treading": Ignatius might well have claimed that in a more especial sense he himself was admitted with S. Paul to this solidarity of the Communion of Saints.

Like the Apostle he was going as "a prisoner of Jesus" to Rome. Yet the martyr is modest, and makes his claim in the form of an aspiration.

13. "Meet together more frequently for thanksgiving [εἰς εὐχαριστίαν, Lightfoot, p. 109], to God and for His glory. For when ye meet together frequently, the powers of Satan are cast down": The Eucharist is the prevailing prayer, which destroys the power of Satan. The custom of the ancient Church was to celebrate it each Lord's Day, and we need not suppose that Ignatius advocates a more frequent Eucharist. What he means is that every Christian must be regular.

14. "Faith is the beginning and love is the end": S. Ignatius shows that he has a real grasp of the Gospel. It is not that man summons up love to God, and so comes to fidelity and obedience. He has to begin as a humbled and undone sinner, putting his trust in what God has done for him in Christ. That love which works obedience is then the gift of God to such. Thus faith and good works are united, for "No man professing faith sinneth."

"The tree is manifest from its fruit": S. Matthew xii, 33.

15. "One teacher, who spake and it came to pass": Psalm xxxiii, 9.

"Even the things which He hath done in silence are worthy of the Father": The mental association of the eloquent silence of the believer who lives the Gospel leads Ignatius into a most interesting doctrinal section to this Epistle, in which he expounds the idea of divine revelation. He is on the same ground as S. Paul, who had taught the doctrine of the "mystery" of the Gospel. God is beyond the power of the mind of man to scan. That which He has done for man's salvation is so wonderful and unexpected that the intellect neither of human nor of superhuman beings could have reached up to it (1 Cor. ii, 8-9). But what man could never have searched out, God has now made known, so that the secret is an "open secret." This is the "mystery" of the Gospel (1 Cor. ii, 7; Eph. iii, 3, 9, 10). The doctrine of the "mystery" conveys the idea that the Gospel is a revelation.[1] That it is known is due to the grace of God, not to the wisdom of man. S. Ignatius follows this with his doctrine of the "silence" of God, a silence from which God in due time spoke the facts of the Faith.

"He that truly possesseth the word of Jesus is able also to hearken

---

[1]However, in later Christian nomenclature the Christian "Mysteries" were the Sacraments.

unto His silence": The sense of this seems to be that those who receive the revelation in Christ are able to understand the mystery of God.

16. "Shall not inherit the kingdom of God": 1 Corinthians vi, 9, 10; Galatians v, 21.

"How much more if a man through evil doctrine corrupt the faith of God": The heretic in the Church has less excuse and more guilt than the worldly adulterer. "The faith" is here the body of orthodox doctrine, the "mystery" in fact (cf. Gal. i, 23; Jude 3). This is a different sense from "faith" as trust, as in Chapter 14. It does not make for the clearest theological thought that the one word has to be used in two distinct senses, but it is an old usage, going back to the New Testament itself, and must therefore be accepted.

17. "For this cause the Lord received ointment on His head": Such a statement, which makes a modern critical exegete smile, is characteristic of much ancient exposition, which was dominated by the doctrine of Scripture "types." Just as many events in the Old Testament were believed to have "hidden meanings" which were portrayals beforehand of Christian truths, so many events in the life of Christ Himself were interpreted as mysterious symbols of parts of the Christian Faith.

"Receiving the knowledge of God . . . knowing the gift of grace": The notion of revelation is one aspect of the general notion of grace. "Canst thou by searching find out God?" (Job xi, 7). The answer is, "No: not by man's own faculties." Man can only search out truth about God because God has first, by His own gracious initiative, willed to make Himself known. And this gracious revelation is made supremely in Jesus Christ, as Ignatius here observes.

18. "My spirit is made an offscouring for the Cross": This very Pauline passage is manifestly a reminiscence of 1 Corinthians iv, 10–13.

"Where is the wise? Where is the disputer?": 1 Corinthians i, 20.

"Our God, Jesus the Christ": Notice how Jesus Christ is called "our God."

"Of the seed of David but also of the Holy Ghost": Here are brought together the two opposite doctrinal interests of the ancient Church, regarding the birth of Christ. The first was the doctrine that Jesus was the Messiah, fulfiller of the Jewish hopes, the "rod from the stem of Jesse," and born in Bethlehem, "the city of David" (cf. Heb. vii, 14).

This is the presupposition of the genealogies of S. Matthew i, 1–16, and S. Luke iii, 23–38. The second was the doctrine that Christ was born of a virgin by direct divine interposition. The only way in which these two can be completely harmonized is by the supposition that the Blessed Virgin herself was likewise of Davidic descent. If we could see into the mind of the early Church, we should probably find that it was not a matter of the first importance to assert that Christ's physical body was literally descended from David. It was sufficient that He should symbolically be "of the house of David." The Messiah of common expectation was looked to to come from Heaven, so he would be a "Son of David" in a symbolic sense. It is somewhat otherwise with the doctrine of the Virgin Birth. Critical scholars have often advanced theories that this doctrine is unhistorical, and that it was put about in the ancient Church by the influence of pious imagination, in response to various doctrinal presuppositions of the early Christians.[1] Actually the reverse would seem to be the case. Naturally enough, first in possession of the field was the doctrine that Jesus was the Messiah, the Christ "of the house of David." The doctrine of the Virgin Birth was known at first only to some, and by no means all Christians, and gradually spread.[2] It is natural to find that this was so, for the miracle of the Virgin Birth was by the nature of things, and unlike the Resurrection, a private miracle, known at first only to one or two. The point is, belief in this miracle made its way in the ancient Church not because of, but in spite of, doctrinal presuppositions. The doctrine that Jesus was "the son of David," which was awkward to square with it, was there first! Therefore we may draw the conclusion that the doctrine of the Virgin Birth was believed not because it suited pious imagination to do so, but because it was believed to be the fact by people who could know more about it than anyone can today. In this

[1] Particularly, the argument has been, first, that the doctrine was believed because it allowed Isaiah vii, 14 (LXX) to be interpreted as one of the most striking of all "prophecies of Christ" (though there is no evidence that this text was regarded as a prophecy of the birth of the Messiah before the event of our Lord's birth; i.e., the Virgin Birth was believed in as an event first, and the text interpreted as a "prophecy" afterward, not vice versa); and also, in the second place, that the Christians thought that virginity was spiritually a more exalted state than matrimony and childbearing (though there is no such notion in their Old Testament Scriptures).

[2] Thus S. Luke, though himself believing in the Virgin Birth, has apparently incorporated into his Gospel certain primitive narratives coming from circles which were content to describe Joseph as the father of Jesus (S. Luke ii, 27, 41, 48).

matter S. Ignatius has his place as the first in Christian writing, outside the New Testament, who emphasized the importance of the Virgin Birth as a Christian doctrine. Unfortunately he does not go on to make it explicit what spiritual significance he saw in our Lord's miraculous birth. The most likely supposition is that his doctrine would have been based upon the idea of Scripture "types," or of analogy between the Old Testament and the New. Eve, the typical mother of the human race, while still a virgin disobeyed God, and became a channel of death to the race (Genesis iii, 1–21). A mark of the reversal of this fatal process was that at the call of God the Blessed Virgin obeyed, and yielding herself up to God, became the historic instrument of the Incarnation, and so the channel of life into the world (S. Luke i, 38). This analogy of "types" between Eve and the Blessed Virgin was probably the Church's first form of theological treatment of this subject. This, at least, is what first appears in the work of S. Irenaeus, at the end of the century.[1]

"Was baptized that by His passion He might cleanse water": The connection and significance of this passage may not be at first apparent to the reader, but it is very revealing for the theology of the ancient Church. The principle of Christ's saving life and death was that of "making Himself one with man," or "identification." By being born as man, the divine Son made Himself one with the human race in its shame and weakness, so that as man He might fight and conquer the spiritual foes of man, in His life of sinless obedience to the Father, and might declare the divine grace by taking upon Himself a share of the human lot. Our Lord's baptism by John in Jordan (S. Matt. iii, 13–17) was His first decisive public act of this self-identification with His people. In the day when the awakened among the Jews were declaring their repentance, in preparation for the coming Day of the Lord, Christ who had no sin of which to repent went with them, that He might be fully one with the People of God, both in its fallen condition and its aspiration. Thus the baptism in Jordan, which was the "type" prefiguring that Holy Baptism which was the rite of incorporation into the Church, answered to the principle which eventually took Christ to Gethsemane, and to the Cross. It spoke of self-identification with man in his shame and suffering. The converse is also true. The effect of

[1] *Adv. Haer.*, III, xxii, 4; V, xix, 1.

Christ's victory of sinless obedience at this price of suffering, and of His gracious call to man, comes to the Church by self-identification with Christ. The believer is to make himself one with Christ by accepting Him as Lord, in trust and obedience, by taking upon him His name and sign, by joining His People the Church, and thus by taking an open stand as a Christian before the world. This way of life necessarily involves self-denial, probably the bearing of contempt and hardship, and possibly physical martyrdom. And the spiritual fruit of this painful self-identification with Christ is to share in His strange new spring of victorious resurrection life. Thus Christian discipleship involves "dying with Christ," that is, self-denial and divine obedience such as took Christ to the Cross, in order to "live with Him" (S. Mark viii, 34–8). The outward operative sacramental mark of this costly "making oneself one with Christ," alike in His Cross and His Crown, was Holy Baptism, the rite of union with the Church ordained by the Lord, in succession to that baptism in Jordan of Himself and probably of many of His Apostles. Thus Baptism answers to the principle of the Cross, and of the disciple's "Cross-bearing." It is a sacrament of "dying with Christ," in order to "rise with Him to new life" (Rom. vi, 3–6). This is a way of saying that Church membership is the way of that suffering which leads to moral triumph. We do not go so far as to claim that S. Ignatius would have put all this theology into these precise terms, which are in part the result of later Christian reflection upon the nature of the Christian life. Nevertheless, this is the plain implication, though perhaps as yet the incompletely drawn-out implication, of what he writes here. The Baptism and the Passion of the Lord answer to one and the same spiritual principle, at different stages of divine revelation. The Baptism of the believer into the Church likewise answers to the spiritual principle of the Passion. Thus Ignatius can metaphorically say that the fruit of Christ's Baptism and Passion was the preparation of the Church's water of Holy Baptism.

19. "Three mysteries to be cried aloud—the which were wrought in the silence of God." Ignatius lists three salient doctrines of the divine revelation: the Virgin Birth, the Incarnation, and the Atonement. These are wonders foreordained in the mysterious counsels of God, too marvellous even for satanic intelligences to look into, and now made known to man and proclaimed by the Church. Doubtless, if he had thought more carefully, S. Ignatius would have added the Resurrection to the list, for he goes on to treat of "the abolishing of death" by the end of the chapter.

"A star shone forth in the heaven above all the stars": Here we may read an interesting and revealing early Christian exposition of the theme of the Epiphany star (S. Matt. ii, 2, 9–10). The Incarnation marked the overthrow of the reign of those malign powers which ruled men from the stars, holding the superstitious in the iron chains of Fate. The coming of Christ released mankind from the debasing fears of astrology and magic. Thus Ignatius can boast that "the ancient kingdom was pulled down." This is a thoroughly Pauline idea (1 Cor. ii, 6–8; Gal. iv, 3; Eph. vi, 12; Col. ii, 15). So Justin Martyr also can write, "He was made man also . . . for the destruction of the demons."[1] It was an old Christian fancy that at the time of Christ's Nativity the pagan oracles for a time stood dumb.

"Newness of life": Romans vi, 4.

20. "My second tract": No such second Epistle is known.

"The new man Jesus Christ . . . faith . . . love . . . in His passion and resurrection": A clearly Pauline and evangelical passage.

"Especially if the Lord should reveal aught to me": S. Ignatius could at times receive the gift of tongues, and make prophetic utterances in the Church (cf. Ep. to Philadelphians, 7).

"In grace": The primary meaning of this word is "the unmerited favour of God." It expresses the fundamental Christian idea that God loves and forgives man not at all because he deserves it, but because it is His will to love and forgive. It conveys the doctrine that man's salvation is by the divine initiative. This is the more usual New Testament sense (e.g., Eph. ii, 5). There is, however, a secondary and derived meaning, which has become very usual in later theology. Grace is also the saving power of God, exerting this initiative (2 Cor. xii, 9). This is the sense we have here.

"In one faith": Faith here is not trust, but the body of sound doctrine, as in Ephesians iv, 5.

"Who after the flesh was of David's race, who is Son of Man and Son of God": In days when it had been forgotten in the Church that "Son of Man" was a title for the Messiah (S. Mark xiv, 62), it was often considered that this title indicated the human nature of Christ, as "Son of God" indicated His divine nature. This is what we expect

[1] *2 Apol.*, vi.

when the two are coupled. Ignatius does not make his view explicit here, but the manner in which he leads to the title "Son of Man" from a clearly messianic phrase may indicate that he was aware of the original New Testament sense.

"Breaking one bread, which is the medicine of immortality (φάρμακον ἀθανασίας) and the antidote that we should not die (ἀντίδοτος τοῦ μὴ ἀποθανεῖν) [Lightfoot, p. 111], but live for ever in Jesus Christ." This is one of the most celebrated passages in the Epistles, and has been the subject of some critical discussion. Many have felt that we here see sacramental doctrine taking a wrong turning. The phrase suggests to some that the grace which is brought to man in the eucharistic means of grace is thought of as a quasi-physical entity inhering in the consecrated elements, which is introduced into man by the act of communion, almost after the manner of a "spiritual inoculation." Such a doctrine, it is rightly felt, would represent grace not as a personal divine influence, but as a "spiritual electricity" flowing down a sacramental wire, which is to obscure the fact that the Real Presence of Christ in the Eucharist is the presence of a personal Lord with His Church, not the presence of an invisible "thing." Any movement in this direction would be indeed a serious impoverishment of Christian thought, and one step in the fatal descent which can degrade the Sacraments into magic. We believe, however, that it is a too severe judgment upon Ignatius to see this in the present passage. We have here not a piece of considered systematic theology, but a flight of religious rhetoric. It is a vivid poetic metaphor, perhaps suggested to the mind of Ignatius by what he has been writing above on the dissolution of magic. He boldly ventures to suggest that the Eucharist is the true and spiritual equivalent to the unclean magic potions of paganism, which are now vanishing away before Christ. This is perhaps a daring thing to say, and it can be misunderstood. Nevertheless, in itself the comparison is an apt one, and the metaphor a vivid expression of the truth. Any objection which may be raised to it occurs because the language of Ignatius might be misunderstood in a material sense by unspiritually minded persons in a later age, rather than on account of what he himself here says.

21. "Those whom . . . ye sent to Smyrna": That is, the deputation sent from Ephesus to meet S. Ignatius as he passed through Smyrna.

"Polycarp": The Bishop of Smyrna, whom Ignatius met there (see

Ep. to Magnesians, 15). An account of him is given in introducing the Epistle of S. Polycarp, pp. 153-7.

II. To the Magnesians

"Theophorus": See note on p. 107.

"Magnesia on the Maeander": The name of the mineral magnesia is derived from this town, and the verb "to meander" from the winding course of this river.

1. "Union of the flesh and of the spirit which are Jesus Christ's": This somewhat enigmatic phrase would appear to reflect the conception of the Church as the Body of Christ. The believers form the visible part of this Body. They are, as it were, the flesh of Christ's body. The invisible part of the Body is the Holy Spirit, who is the Spirit of Christ. Ignatius prays that the believers may be fully indwelt by the Spirit, and so united both to one another and to Christ.

2. "Subject to the bishop as unto the grace of God and to the presbytery as unto the law of Jesus Christ": It is curious to find "grace" and "law" put in parallel to each other. This is in contrast to the Pauline usage, where the two so often appear as opposites (for example, Gal. v, 4). We have to admit that the Apostle could hardly have written this! Nevertheless, we observe that it is the law of Christ which is the law of love, to which the Christian is subject. This is no so different from being subject to grace. However, Ignatius retains the general idea that "grace" is a higher state that "law," for the one corresponds to the rule of the bishop, who is the higher officer, the other to the rule of the presbytery, which is of lower rank.

3. "The youth of your bishop": The Magnesians seem to have departed from the rule of 1 Timothy iii, 6.

"Yet not to him, but to the Father": The bishop is here described as the representative of God the Father in the Church. See note on Chapter 6.

"Not with the flesh": That is, not with his fellow humans.

4. "They do not assemble themselves lawfully": A company of Christians meeting apart from the rule of the bishop is not in proper order. These disorderly brethren have the bishop's name on their lips. This may be a veiled reference to a schismatical bishop in Magnesia.

Perhaps one of the old "presbyter-bishops" was leading a faction, and claiming to be a bishop, though he is not recognized as such by the orthodox party.

5. "Life and death are set before us together": Compare Deuteronomy xxx, 19.

"To his own place": Acts i, 25.

"There are two coinages, the one of God and the other of the world": This may be a reference to the Jewish custom of having a special Temple coinage for the payment of religious dues, so as to avoid bringing the normal Roman money, with its idolatrous inscriptions, into the Temple. This in turn might imply an allusion, quite appropriate in this context, to Christ's comment upon the said Roman money (S. Matt. xxii, 17–21).

"We accept to die unto His passion": S. Mark viii, 34–5.

6. "The bishop presiding after the likeness of God, and the presbyters after the likeness of the council of the Apostles, with the deacons." Here is a very clear witness to the threefold ministry of bishop, priests, and deacons. There is the highest doctrine of the spiritual foundation of the Ministry. The hierarchy is the earthly copy of the government which exists in heaven (so also Chap. 7). Nevertheless, it is not the later doctrine of Apostolical Succession, which would place the bishop in the position of the Apostles.

7. "The Lord did nothing without the Father": John v, 19; xii, 50.

8. "Strange doctrines . . . antiquated fables . . . Judaism": The heresy or schism at Magnesia was clearly some form of Ebionism (see also Chaps. 9, 10). The Ebionites were the unduly conservative Christians, descendants of the "circumcision party" of S. Paul's day, who tried to keep Christianity in its original position within Judaism.[1] Hence they are rebuked as "antiquated." The marks of Ebionism were an insistance that Christians ought to keep the whole Mosaic Law literally, and a tendency to regard our Lord simply as a "messianic" prophet, upon whom the Spirit descended.

"If we live after the manner of Judaism, we avow that we have not received grace": This is the position S. Paul so forcefully stated in the Epistle to the Galatians. Insistence that literal obedience to the whole Law of Moses is essential to salvation carries with it the implication

[1] Eusebius, *H.E.*, III, xxvii.

that salvation is not by divine grace (Gal. v, 1–4). It is to be observed that this is an extreme statement of the Pauline position, which is balanced by other parts of Paul's teaching and example. He did not condemn the keeping of the Jewish Law as wrong, but only the enforcement of circumcision upon Gentile Christians as essential to salvation. The Church at large has rightly followed the moderate rather than the extreme Pauline attitude; and the somewhat bitter attitude toward the Mosaic Law reflected in the impetuous Epistle to the Galatians does not represent by itself the central and balanced position of orthodox Christianity. We observe, however, that when confronted by Ebionite heresy, S. Ignatius can show sympathy with S. Paul's plea.

"For the divine prophets lived according to Jesus Christ": The prophets and heroes of Israel were the spiritual ancestors of the Church, which is the New Israel. They were therefore "Christians before the time," and were not properly part of "Judaism," that is, the Jewish religion considered as opposed to Christianity. A mark of this is that these "Christians before the time" were in their own day persecuted by their unbelieving fellow countrymen.

"Being inspired by His grace": The ancient prophets of Israel indeed lived by Christian grace, and not by the religion of Jewish legality.

"His Son, who is His word that proceeded from silence"; λόγος ἀπὸ σιγῆς προελθών (Lightfoot, p. 114). Here is another striking statement of the doctrine of the "mystery" (see on Ep. to Ephesians, 15). The revealer of the secret nature and counsel of God is the divine Word (Logos), who is also the Son (S. John i, 1).

9. "No longer observing sabbaths but fashioning their lives after the Lord's day [κατὰ κυριακὴν ζῶντες; Lightfoot, p. 114], on which our life also arose through Him": A mark of Ebionite heresy was to keep the Jewish Sabbath. The condition of opposition between Christianity and Judaism is now such that the keeping of the Sabbath is no longer to be regarded as a permissible Jewish custom. Christians must make a point of not keeping the Sabbath.[1] Ignatius teaches that to keep exclusively to the Lord's Day, the distinctive Christian day of worship, and anniversary of Christ's rising from the dead, is a mark of sharing in Christ's risen life.

"Which some men deny": This clause would appear to apply to the

---
[1] See also *Didache*, Chap. 8, with notes.

doctrines of Christ's resurrection, and that His death was an atonement, for the heretics would hardly deny that Christ died. These doctrines are part of the "mystery," that is, the divine revelation which summons man to belief.

"And for this cause He whom they rightly awaited, when He came, raised them from the dead": This passage interestingly expresses the deep Christian conviction that the saving work of Christ extends backward in time to those righteous and faithful men who were "Christians before the time." This is the natural and fitting consequence of the fundamental doctrine that the Church is the new and true Israel of God, continuous with the old, and the due heir of all the promises declared in ancient time to those Jews who were "Israelites indeed." The ancient prophets, who have been so long awaiting Christ, have already been raised to a new dignity of spiritual life, so that presumably they now dwell in the same sphere as departed Christian saints. This is the noble doctrine which the Church has traditionally seen in the somewhat enigmatic 1 Peter iii, 19–20, and expressed in the clause of the Creed, "He descended into hell."

10. "For if He should imitate us according to our deeds, we are lost": Ignatius clearly sees that acceptance with the God of holy love cannot be by the merit of frail and sinful men. Our Christian discipleship is dependent on grace.

"It is monstrous to talk of Jesus Christ, and to practise Judaism": S. Ignatius does not say in so many words that the wrong of those who would seek salvation by "practising Judaism" (the Ebionite Christians) is that their system presupposes salvation by the merit of human good works in keeping the Mosaic Law, with the consequence that they have inadequate views on salvation by grace. Yet quite probably this very "Pauline" thought is not far away, in the rhetoric of this passage.

"For Christianity did not believe in Judaism": This is a somewhat enigmatic phrase. It is again rhetoric, not systematic theology. The sense would appear to be that Christianity comprises within itself everything that was good in Judaism, but that Judaism does not comprise Christianity.

"Every tongue . . . was gathered together": Isaiah lxvi, 18.

11. "Be ye fully persuaded concerning the birth and the passion and the resurrection": Ignatius fittingly closes his warning against heresy by strongly affirming the strictly historical character of the work of

Christ. One would have expected that this affirmation would have been called forth by opposition to Gnostic and Docetic heresy, rather than to Judaizing error. It reminds us that we cannot be too sure of every detail of the circumstances. Possibly this passage reflects the natural reaction of S. Ignatius to confront any form of heresy by reciting the baptismal confession of faith, irrespective of whether it exactly fits the error in question. Although we cannot deduce a definite early creed-form from this passage, it reads very much as though Ignatius has one in mind.

12. "The righteous man is a self-accuser": Proverbs xviii, 17.

13. "Prosper in all things whatsoever ye do": Psalm i, 3.

"Be obedient to the bishop and to one another": Compare 1 Peter v, 5.

"That there may be union both of flesh and of spirit": See Chapter 1, with note.

14. "Remember also the church which is in Syria": That is, Antioch, now for a time bereft of its bishop, and presumably suffering persecution.

15. "Whence also I write to you": Evidence that the place of meeting of the deputations, and the place of writing of the first group of Epistles, was Smyrna.

III. To the Trallians

"Theophorus": See note on Epistle to Ephesians (p. 107).

1. "Your godly benevolence": Polybius the bishop, and the deputation from Tralles, had brought a gift.

2. "Do nothing without the bishop": A characteristic phrase of Ignatius (see Ep. to Philadelphians, 7, with note, pp. 133-4).

"Be ye obedient also to the presbytery": The bishop is not a solitary ruler in the Church.

"Deacons of the mysteries . . . not deacons of meats and drinks": "The mysteries" in Ignatius are not the Sacraments, as in much Christian literature, but the revelation of God. It would not seem, therefore, that this is a reference to the deacons assisting at the Eucharist. The deacons had charge of the Church's charity, a very important function when a congregation might have Confessors in prison to help. Ignatius points out that they are not just servants of bodily charity, but of the Gospel.

3. "Respect the deacons as Jesus Christ": This is a reminder to us that the language of Ignatius is often rhetorical, not always consistent systematic theology. In this passage the deacons are likened to Christ, and the presbyters, though in a superior office, to the Apostles.

"The presbyters as the college of the Apostles": See Epistle to Magnesians, 6, with note, p. 121.

"Apart from these there is not even the name of a church": The due order of the threefold ministry is essential to the constitution of the Church.

"I might write more sharply on his behalf": Possibly some of the Trallians were not so obedient to their bishop as S. Ignatius thought they ought to be. He reminds them, though gently, of his authority as a Confessor.

4. "For though I desire to suffer, yet I know not whether I am worthy": Compare Epistle to Romans, 4–6. Here is the mind of the martyr. He does not count it a misfortune that he must suffer, but a privilege.

5. "I am in bonds and can comprehend heavenly things": S. Ignatius is a Confessor of the Faith, and is being admitted to discipleship in its truest sense. He can therefore claim that he has been granted special revelations and visions (see Ep. to Philadelphians, 7, with note, p. 133). Yet it would not be right to declare these things to the spiritually immature (cf. 2 Cor. xii, 1–4).

"Arrays of the angels and the musterings of the principalities": The conflict of the martyr with temptation and pain is only a pale earthly copy of the real spiritual conflict which is now being joined between the celestial servants of God and the demonic powers which rule from the stars (Eph. vi, 12).

"I myself am not yet by reason of this a disciple": The innate modesty of the Confessor fittingly comes out in this remark. He has received visions from God and honours from the Church, but he knows that he is assailed by fear within, and he cannot feel sure that he will stand firm even to the martyr's death until the dreadful moment has actually come (See Ep. to Romans, 7, with note, p. 131). So he will not dare to claim that he is yet fully and truly a disciple.

6. We gather from Chapter 9 that the particularly poisonous heresy against which warning is here given was of a Docetic character. Presumably, therefore, some incipient Gnostic heresy had broken out at Tralles, as in the Church addressed in 1 John iv, 2–3. The developed Gnostic systems had not, however, formed at this time.

7. The bishop and Apostolic Ministry is a safeguard of orthodoxy, as well as a guarantee of discipline and unity. This doctrinal aspect of Church authority was especially important as the early Church faced Gnostic heresy, for it was characteristic of Gnosticism that it could claim to accept the Scriptures and Creeds, yet it was skilled to interpret them in ways which took away the accepted sense. Therefore pressure of controversy drove the Church to find in her Ministry an organ capable of giving an authoritative interpretation of Scripture.

8. "In faith which is the flesh of the Lord, and in love which is the blood of Jesus Christ": The primary reference here is doubtless to the circumstance that the Gnostic-type heresy denied that our Lord had a true body of flesh and blood, and that He truly suffered. This doctrine answered to the presupposition that the material had no part in the purposes of God, and that the work of the Saviour was to bring a secret teaching from Heaven, not to make an atoning sacrifice. However, the Church was quick to observe that, although the Gnostics had various sacramental rites, they were really inconsistent in this.[1] The sacramental principle, in which it is affirmed that God uses material means as the covenanted channels of His spiritual grace, answers to the doctrine that our Lord's coming into this world was a real Incarnation, and His death upon the Cross a real redemption. Possibly S. Ignatius has this in mind, so that his mention of the flesh and blood of the Lord has a secondary reference to the Eucharist. To partake of this is a guarantee of the true faith in the Incarnation, and a bond of love.

"Woe unto him": Isaiah lii, 5.

9. "Who was of the race of David, who was the Son of Mary": See Epistle to Ephesians, 18.

"Who was truly born and ate and drank": This doctrinal passage, one of the most important in Ignatius, is strongly anti-Docetic in character. It plainly affirms the real bodily character of every part of

---

[1] Thus Irenaeus, *Adv. Haer.*, IV, xviii, 4–5; V, ii, 2.

our Lord's earthly career. It prefigures the main line of defence which the Church made against Gnostic heresy; namely, that the Gospel record concerning the life of Christ, and the statements of the Creed concerning the same, were to be taken seriously as factual history, and not "spiritualized" away into allegories of theological ideas. We have no reason to suppose that there was a developed Creed in fixed form in the Church known to Ignatius, but clearly events are moving in that direction. He is here quoting a primitive and unformed precursor of the later baptismal creeds.

"In the sight of those in heaven and those on earth and those under the earth": The most likely sense in which this is to be taken is that God's victory of the Cross was won in the presence of His spiritual foes alike of the heavenly, the earthly, and the infernal spheres. The first class were the "principalities and powers" which crucified Christ, and are now overthrown (1 Cor. ii, 8; Col. ii, 14–15). The second class was the unholy throng on Calvary, while the third was "the strong man" whom Christ has now bound, so that He might "spoil his goods," and release from Hades the awaiting spirits of the righteous who were "Christians before the time."

10. "That He suffered only in semblance": The Docetists, who teach that Christ suffered only in semblance, are themselves Christians only in semblance. If their doctrine were true, there would be no point in seeking by a martyr's death to be one with a martyred Christ. S. Ignatius' faith would then be in vain.

11. "Branches of the Cross, and their fruit imperishable": This interesting rhetorical metaphor is a union of the idea of Calvary and of the Parable of the True Vine (S. John xv, 1–8). The Cross, being of wood, is a tree, and has branches and fruit. The test of those who are true and fruitful branches of the Vine is that they accept the true bodily sufferings of Christ, and the discipleship of martyrdom presupposed by union with the Crucified.

12. "Pray ye also for me . . . reprobate": See Epistle to Romans, Chap. 7, with note, p. 131.

13. We observe the strong sense of corporate unity between the Christian congregations in different places.

"For I am still in peril": His martyrdom may yet fail to come about.

IV. To the Romans

This moving and human Epistle was, like that of S. Paul to the Romans, written ahead to a Church which the writer had yet to visit, in order to prepare his way.

"Theophorus": See Epistle to Ephesians, with note, p. 107.

"Even unto her that hath the presidency (ἥτις καὶ προκάθηται) [Lightfoot, p. 120], in the country of the region of the Romans": This Epistle opens with an unusually ceremonious salutation, as does S. Paul himself. Clearly from the earliest times the Church in Rome enjoyed an outstanding degree of dignity. S. Ignatius hints at two reasons for this. Two of the most outstanding Apostles had been martyred in Rome (Chap. 4), while the Church in Rome was the only one in Italy, and indeed in the whole West, which could claim this foundation in Apostolic blood. Another reason for the prestige of Rome is implied in the contents of the Epistle. The Roman Christians, being at the imperial capital, had facilities not open to others for underground communication with officials in the bureaucracy who might be susceptible to a bribe, or even secretly sympathetic to Christianity. The Church in Rome was a good one to know, and enjoy the favour of, if one was in trouble with the authorities and wanted lenient treatment! The purpose of writing this Epistle is to make sure that the Roman Christians will not exercise this kind of "influence," and by misplaced kindness deprive Ignatius of his crown. It is possibly most significant that the greeting in this case makes no mention of the bishop at Rome, in striking contrast to the salutations addressed to the Asian Churches. This is the more pointed because Ignatius mentions the martyrdom of Peter and Paul at Rome (Chap. 4), and asks the Church in Rome to pray for his home Church in Syria, now bereft of its bishop. Either or both of these contexts would by association quite fittingly have called forth some greeting to the Bishop of Rome. Possibly, therefore, S. Ignatius knew that in point of fact, and contrary to all his convictions of how a Church ought to be governed, there was no single ruling bishop at Rome. This might also explain why this Epistle, unlike the others, does not salute the presbyters and deacons at Rome either. The question of Church polity at Rome was perhaps so painful to this writer that he prefers to pass it over in discreet and diplomatic silence!

1. "For I dread your very love": The purpose of the Epistle is most pointedly declared. Ignatius has an arduous destiny before him, which will take all his resolution to fulfil. The Romans' kindness and effective good offices may well make it more arduous.

2. "I would not have you to be men-pleasers": Ignatius does not wish for the dubious arts of diplomacy to be exerted in his behalf. It will be more to the glory of God if the Romans allow him to suffer, in the way God has called.

"For, if ye be silent and leave me alone, I am a word of God; but if ye desire my flesh, then shall I be again a mere cry": A memorable and eloquent phrase, which sums up the whole ancient Christian attitude to missionary propaganda. The conversion of the world was the work of God, through His faithful witnesses. Their sole qualification was their faithfulness, their preparedness to be used by God according to His counsel. Human talents, exerted in the arts of persuasion, would never suffice. Thus even a preacher of commanding personality like Ignatius, if he be guided by counsels of human wisdom, is a mere "voice crying in the wilderness." If in obedience to God's plan his physical voice is silenced for ever in death, he becomes a prevailing word from God, and a testimony to the divine Logos. Thus if the Roman Christians remain silent, and drop no word in his behalf, Ignatius will be enabled to utter God's Word in the arena.

3. "So that I may not only say it but also desire it; that I may not only be called a Christian, but also found one": To the modern reader, S. Ignatius may seem to display an overheightened confidence in his destiny to suffer. However, he is not foolhardy or filled with bravado. He knows that he has a daunting ordeal before him. Though he is not afraid, he is a wise man, and has a healthy fear of being found afraid when the dreadful moment comes. He expresses this with great poignancy and realism in Chapter 7. Those who come through the awaiting ordeal are the real Christians.

"Nothing visible is good": Divorced from its context this phrase might indicate that the material is that which is opposed to the spiritual, the false doctrine which lay at the bottom of the Docetic heresy. Clearly, Ignatius does not intend this, and his rhetoric is not to be taken too literally. What he means by this aphorism is explained in the next phrase. We have already seen in the previous chapter that when the martyr's voice is stilled in death, "he being dead yet speaketh." The supreme example of this principle is Christ Himself, who, "being in the Father," that is to say, having ascended into glory and being no longer seen of man, is in spiritual effect "more plainly visible." The work of the Gospel, then, is not of human resource, but of divine.

"Christianity is a thing of might, whensoever it is hated by the world": This is the acid test of the above principle. When Christianity is persecuted it is seen in its true colours, and prevails (S. Matt. v, 10–12).

4. "Let me be given to the wild beasts": The general commentary upon this and the next chapter is given in our introduction, pp. 101–2.

"So that I may not, when I am fallen asleep, be burdensome to any one": To the early Christians the crowning wickedness of the persecutor was that sometimes the bodies of the victims were not returned to their friends for due burial, but were, as here, consumed by the beasts, or burned, and the ashes deliberately thrown into the river. This was often viewed as a greater horror than the torments in which the Christians had seen their comrades perish. This view, which to the conventional modern mind may appear wrongheaded to the point of perversity, ultimately goes back to the primitive feeling that it was above all necessary for the bodies of the dead to be duly disposed of, or else their ghosts might return and trouble the living. How deep is this instinct in the human heart may be seen from the circumstance that even in the most secularized and sophisticated circles of modern society, where infants are not baptized, and civil marriage commonly resorted to, it is still rare to find a body buried without some form of religious ceremony. There was in those times the strongest moral pressure upon the Church to seek if possible to recover the bodies of the martyrs, and to give them honourable burial. In times of persecution this might well be a risky duty to perform, and doubtless the executioners often looked for a bribe as a perquisite to their gory office. In his self-immolation Ignatius will spare the Roman Christians any burden.

"Peter and Paul": He speaks of them as the Apostolic governors of the Roman Church, and himself as one who is asking a courtesy.

5. "Who only wax worse when they are kindly treated": Perhaps this, endured for many weeks, is as severe a test of Christian devotion as a few hours of waiting at the arena.

"Yet am I not hereby justified": 1 Corinthians iv, 4. Real spiritual insight is displayed by the making of this observation in this context. Satan has many devices, and every spiritual state has its own besetting temptation. The temptation of the martyr is that of self-righteousness. He knows that he is showing outstanding devotion, beyond his fellows, and it is easy for him to be persuaded that this sets up a claim upon God for His good will. S. Ignatius has the insight to see that this is a vain delusion, and to quote S. Paul, the supreme exemplar of this principle, in his support.

"Refusing to touch them through fear": For an actual example of this, see "The Passion of SS. Perpetua and Felicitas" xix.[1] To the naturalist this might be the outcome of the unwonted tumult of the arena, to the believer a divine providence.

6. "Neither the kingdoms of this world": Compare S. Mark viii, 36.

"The pangs of a new birth are upon me": Holy Baptism is the sacrament of the new birth, but in the case of an unbaptized catechumen who died as a martyr the Church accounted him to have been incorporated into the Church by "the baptism of blood." In like manner, other baptized martyrs could look upon their bloodshedding as a sort of second baptism.[2] S. Ignatius doubtless has this in mind, in his metaphor of martyrdom as a "new birth."

"Do not hinder me from living": Compare S. Mark viii, 35.

"Permit me to be an imitator of the passion of my God": The martyr's death is the supreme act of identification with his Lord.

7. "Even though I myself, when I am with you, should beseech you, obey me not": This is a very human picture. He is fully persuaded what is his real mind, but is healthily aware of his frailty. The courage of a Cranmer, who dares to die a horrible death after long and painful hesitation, is perhaps of a higher order than the more appealing courage of a man of spirit, who goes to suffer in apparent cheerfulness.

"Only water living in me, saying within me, Come to the Father": The principle of Holy Baptism is that of self-identification with Christ, to suffer with Him so as to triumph with Him (see Ep. to Ephesians, 18, with note, pp. 116–17). Therefore one who has been baptized can look to martyrdom as the consummation of his baptism.

[1] *Acts of the Early Martyrs*, trans. by E. C. E. Owen, p. 90.
[2] *Ibid.*, p. 91.

"I desire the bread of God": The other Gospel sacrament, the Eucharist, expresses the same principle of self-identification with Christ, to suffer with Him so as to triumph with Him. Therefore one going to martyrdom desires to receive the Eucharist, as the most fitting preparation.

9. "Jesus Christ alone shall be its bishop—He and your love": Ignatius invites the Romans to pray for his own distressed Church of Antioch. A faithful Church bereft of its bishop is not out of Order, like a rebellious group meeting apart from the bishop. They are ruled immediately by the supreme Head, Jesus Christ, and supported by the solidarity of the Catholic Church.

"Being the very last of them and an untimely birth": Compare 1 Corinthians xv, 8, 9. We see here the great bishop's modesty. As he enrolls himself among the august company of the bishops, he does so as S. Paul did among the company of the Apostles. His name is indeed there, but only just.

10. "Now I write . . . by the hand of the Ephesians": It would appear that the letter is to be taken ahead to Rome by Ephesian friends. Probably the Crocus mentioned is the same as the man named in Epistle to Ephesians, 2. He seems to have been an Ephesian Christian already known in Rome.

We have already observed that S. Ignatius significantly does not salute the bishop and presbyters (p. 128).

"The 9th before the Kalends of September": That is, August 24th, probably in the year A.D. 107.

V. To the Philadelphians

"Theophorus": See Epistle to Ephesians, with note, p. 107.

1. We have here the ideal of a Christian bishop. He is to rule by love. He has divine authority, but he is not an authoritarian.

2. Unity under the bishop is the key to orthodoxy.

3. "He doth not inherit the kingdom of God": 1 Corinthians vi, 9.

4. "Be ye careful therefore to observe one eucharist": For this is the eminent mark of that unity under the bishop which is the key to orthodoxy.

5. "Yea, and we love the prophets also . . . having faith they were saved in the unity of Jesus Christ": These are not the prophets (preachers) of the New Testament Church, nor the "charismatic" prophets of *Didache* (see pp. 92–6). They are the counterpart of the Apostles under the Old Covenant, that is, the spiritual leaders and heroes of Israel. These all lived by faith (Rom. iv, 1–16; Heb. xi, 13), and so were "Christians before the time," and, being the true Israel, were by anticipation a part of the Church.

6. "But if any one propound Judaism unto you, hear him not": The heresy which threatens the Church at Philadelphia is that of Ebionism, as at Magnesia (Ep. to Magnesians, 8, 9, 10, with notes, pp. 121–3). This may be the error hinted at in Revelation iii, 9.

"It is better to hear Christianity from a man who is circumcised than Judaism from one uncircumcised": The mere fact of being circumcised is not an objection in a teacher. One can have a Hebrew Christian of true doctrine, for were not the prophets such? An Ebionite or Judaizing Christian is however to be rejected. It would almost seem as though these particular Judaizing heretics were physically uncircumcised, for the connection would hardly allow "uncircumcised" to be used here in a metaphorical sense.

7. "It knoweth whence it cometh and where it goeth": S. John iii, 8.

"I cried out when I was among you; I spake with a loud voice, with God's own voice": We think of S. Ignatius as a chief pillar of the Catholic Ministry and of episcopal discipline in the Church, and the idea of him exercising "the Charismatic Ministry" may appear strange to some. However, we see from this passage that he was able and willing to claim, as was S. Paul (1 Cor. xiv, 18), that on occasion the Spirit came upon him, so that he spoke "with God's own voice." It would not appear from this account that Ignatius "spoke with tongues" in the sense of uttering unintelligible words, but he did speak in some degree with the voice of religious ecstasy. He is emphatic in his claim that what he said was not premeditated, nor adapted to the circumstances of the Church by human wisdom. It was a spontaneous utterance, to be regarded as a work of immediate divine inspiration. Thus, "I learned it not from flesh of man; it was the preaching of the Spirit."

"Give ye heed to the bishop and the presbytery and deacons . . . Do nothing without the bishop": Thus S. Ignatius' most celebrated and characteristic phrase was spoken in the exercise of a "prophetic"

Ministry! The scene at Philadelphia is symbolical of what was happening in the Church at large. The less formal and disciplined forms of Ministry which existed in the primitive Church were at this time abdicating in favour of the regular and disciplined Catholic Ministry of bishops, priests, and deacons. Nor was this to be regarded as the decay of the work of the Spirit in the Church, though possibly some thought so then, as some do now. To Ignatius this change of emphasis in the Lord's ministry was itself the guidance and work of the Spirit.

8. "Now the Lord forgiveth all men when they repent, if repenting they return to the unity of God and to the council of the bishop": Here S. Ignatius clearly sets out the sound position regarding the forgiveness of sin. In principle God freely forgives the penitent sinner. Yet how is this divine forgiveness to be mediated to men, and assured to men? It is by ecclesiastical discipline, which alone is the outward sign of the inward grace. Those who are indeed penitent will be found to return to the unity of the people of God, the mark of which is to Ignatius obedience to the bishop.

"If I find it not in the charters ($\dot{\epsilon}\nu$ $\tau o\hat{i}s$ $\dot{a}\rho\chi\epsilon i o\iota s$) [Lightfoot, p. 126] I believe it not in the Gospel": The meaning of this somewhat enigmatic phrase has been much discussed. The most natural sense seems to be that the "charters" are the Old Testament Scriptures, for this agrees with the circumstance that the disturbing faction at Philadelphia were Judaizers. In the first days of the Church the authoritative Scriptures were the Old Testament. Conservative Judaizing Christians would cling to this position, and insist that the essential primary authority for all Christian doctrine was the Jewish Scripture. The Apostolic Writings were of authority, but were only secondary to the ancient Scriptures. It was not enough for a position to be substantiated from New Testament texts alone. It is to be observed that "the Gospel" is here a book.

"And when I said to them, It is written, they answered me, That is the question": This was the controversial impasse. It was the accepted orthodox position, advanced by Ignatius, that the prophets had foretold Christ, and that therefore Christian doctrine could be substantiated from the Old Testament. Yet the Judaizers did not agree with the official exegesis. We may suppose that in particular they did not agree that certain Jewish ceremonial commandments were not to be taken literally by Christians.

"My charter is Jesus Christ . . . His cross and His death and His resurrection, and faith through Him; wherein I desire to be justified": (δικαιωθῆναι; Lightfoot, p. 126). The falsity in the doctrine of the Judaizers, with its unduly conservative Old Testament literalism, was that it obscured the doctrine of salvation by the death and resurrection of Christ, and of justification by faith in Him. This classic Pauline position seems to be implied by this answer of S. Ignatius to the Judaizers, for it speaks of the Cross, and of justification. The Christian position is that the Old Testament is to be interpreted as a prophecy of the death and resurrection of Jesus Christ, and of the life of faith. The foundation of all is the Lord, and not literal Jewish legalism.

9. "The priests likewise were good, but better is the High-priest . . . to Him alone are committed the hidden things of God": S. Ignatius proceeds to discuss more explicitly the relation of the religion of the Old Israel to that of the New. Reaction against Judaic heresy does not hurry him into anti-Judaic heresy such as Gnosticism, which in general sought to sever the link between Christianity and Judaism. The priests and prophets of Israel were "good," and "beloved," and yet they were not the best. They were preparatory. It is noteworthy that Ignatius here chooses for our Lord the title of "High-priest," which is characteristic of the Epistle to the Hebrews, the classic Scriptural treatment of this theme. Christ alone is the bringer of the "mystery," the revelation, out of the silence of God (see Ep. to Ephesians, 15, 19, with notes, p. 113, p. 117).

"He Himself being the door—through which Abraham and Isaac and Jacob enter in": See Epistle to Magnesians, 8, 9, with notes, p. 122, p. 123.

"But the Gospel hath a singular preeminence in the advent of the Saviour. . . . For the beloved Prophets in their preaching pointed to Him; but the Gospel is the completion of immortality": Here then is the judicious and central Catholic answer alike to Judaic heresy on the one hand, and anti-Judaic heresy on the other. The Old Covenant has an essential place in the Christian system as a preparation for and promise of the New. The Old and the New are one continuous whole. Yet the New is better than the Old, in that it is the fulfilment of the preparation, and the actual possession of that which aforetime was promised. Irenaeus has exactly the same idea. "What then did the Lord bring to us by His advent? . . . know ye that He brought all novelty, by bringing Himself who had been announced."[1] It is to be observed that modern Old Testament scholarship has not changed the substance of this essential Christian position, though it has revolutionized the intellectual presentation of it. We no longer think of the prophets as possessing supernatural knowledge of future detailed events, yet the religion of Israel remains in the most proper sense the spiritual promise of the Christian faith.

"All things together are good, if ye believe through love": S. Ignatius fittingly summarizes the discussion. Christians are saved, not by Jewish legality, but by "the faith that works by love," yet the Old Covenant and its Scriptures are wholly good and from God, if read with the eye of Christian faith.

10. "It hath been reported to me that the Church which is in Antioch of Syria hath peace . . . it is becoming for you . . . to appoint a deacon to go thither . . . that he may congratulate them when they are assembled together": It would appear from this that better news has come through about the Church at Antioch, and that persecution has now ceased (Cf. Ep. to Magnesians, 14, Romans 9, with notes, p. 124, p. 132). They will presumably therefore in due course meet together to elect another bishop, to take the place of the martyr. It is fitting that so many Churches as possible should take notice of this event, by sending a delegation of good will. S. Ignatius is clearly zealous that the Church should express its Catholic unity through the outward discipline of mutual visits. It is sometimes asked: "Did the ancient Church have authoritarian government, or were the local congregations originally independent in polity?" The answer is "Neither," for this is a false antithesis. The local Churches were clearly not "independent." They were possessed of a strong sense of belonging to a universal disciplined body. Yet this corporate discipline was exercised by outward means less elaborately hierarchical, less formal, and less legal, than those which came into use in later times. Some will regret this inevitable historic development, but everyone who appreciates the genius of the first Church will surely have to agree that, Christianity being what it was, it was inevitable, necessary, and right that the Church should develop an adequate outward and visible expression of the fundamental principle of world-wide corporate ecclesiastical discipline.

[1] *Adv. Haer.*, IV, xxxiv, 1.

11. The Epistle closes with a greeting.

VI. To the Smyrnaeans

"Theophorus": See Epistle to Ephesians, p. 107.

1. "Ye are established in faith"; ἐν πίστει (Lightfoot, p. 127): It is not clear from the context whether this is "the Faith," that is, the right doctrine, or "faith," that is, trust. The fact that Ignatius moves into another doctrinal passage, reminiscent of the Creed, suggests the former. The circumstance that those having this faith are "firmly grounded in love" suggests the latter. This credal statement is again strongly anti-Docetic, so presumably any heresy which is to be guarded against in this Church is of the incipient Gnostic type, as at Tralles (Ep. to Trallians, 9, with note; see pp. 126–7).

"Of the race of David . . . truly born of a virgin": See Epistle to Ephesians, 18, with note, pp. 114–6.

"That all righteousness might be fulfilled": S. Matthew iii, 15.

"He might set up an ensign": Isaiah v, 26; xlix, 22.

2. "He raised Himself"; ἀνέστησεν ἑαυτόν (Lightfoot, p. 128): A curious phrase, for the Scripture says that "God raised Him from the dead" (Acts ii, 32).

"Being themselves mere semblance": See Epistle to Trallians, 10, with note, p. 127.

3. "Lay hold and handle me, and see that I am not a demon without body": This is not an exact quotation of any text in the New Testament, though it conveys the sense of S. Luke xxiv, 39. It is therefore probably a quotation from some lost apocryphal Gospel.

"He both ate with them and drank with them as one in the flesh, though spiritually He was united with the Father": Compare S. Luke xxiv, 41–3. This is not precise theological language, but we cannot say that we know any more today concerning the mysterious subject of our Lord's resurrection body.

4. "Only pray ye for them": Heretics are to be loved, but avoided.

"This indeed is difficult": That is, for heretics to repent, though we might also add that it is equally difficult to love those whom one on principle avoids.

"Then also am I a prisoner in semblance": The principle that discipleship consists in martyrdom answers to the fact that Christ really suffered in the flesh, to accomplish our salvation.

"Only let it be in the name of Jesus Christ, so that we may suffer together with Him": It is not suffering as such which is beneficial. Possibly Ignatius knows that some heretics have also suffered as martyrs, and has their unprofitable case in mind. That suffering which is the token of identification with Christ alone brings spiritual victory.

5. "They have not been persuaded by the prophecies nor by the law of Moses": This would be apt to the case of an incipient Gnostic heresy, for Gnosticism was normally a deviation from Christianity in the direction of paganism, and was consequently anti-Judaic. It would cut the tie between Christianity and the Old Testament.

6. "Even the heavenly beings . . . if they believe not in the blood of Christ, judgment awaiteth them also": The angels, though glorious, are creatures, and are therefore mutable. They continue in a state of grace by faith in the Crucified, even as men do.

"He that receiveth let him receive": S. Matthew xix, 12.

"Mark ye those who hold strange doctrine touching the grace of Jesus Christ . . . They have no care for love": This was a very common charge for the orthodox to make against the heretic, not always justified by the facts. We need not take too literally all that Ignatius says. Nevertheless, a Gnostic-type heresy does fit into this picture. Gnosticism taught salvation by attainment to superior knowledge, and this implies a denial of salvation by grace. It formed inner circles of select disciples, and looked down upon the ordinary simple and literal believers as an inferior grade of Christians. This might well give rise to the charge that they neglected the underprivileged.

"They abstain from eucharist": So far as we can judge, the usual aim of Gnostics was to form an inner circle within the Church, until they were expelled. There may well, however, have been places where Docetic heretics abstained from the usual eucharistic worship. The separated Gnostic sects certainly had rites analogous to the Christian sacraments, though it would appear theologically somewhat inconsistent for them to do so (see Ep. to Trallians, 8, with note, p. 126). Naturally, Ignatius could not regard these sectarian rites as eucharists at all.

"They allow not that the eucharist is the flesh of our Saviour": The student is warned against trying to find in the ancient Fathers of the

Church eucharistic doctrines analogous to those characteristic of the various modern Christian communions. Just as other doctrines are not always stated in the precise terms of later orthodox formulations, though the underlying spiritual intention may be the same, so here. The doctrine of the sacraments has often been the subject of controversy, and sometimes of unseemly controversy in attempts to define the mysterious. The result is that later thought has propounded exact theories, acceptance of which has often been treated as a salient mark of sound Churchmanship. These formulations are not found in the ancient Church. Thus when we compare ancient with modern views it is easier to say what such an one as S. Ignatius would not accept, were he alive today, than to say what he would accept! Ignatius is certainly not to be understood as teaching that the body and blood of Christ are present in the Eucharist in any manner such as modern scientific thought would describe as "physical" or "material." Whatever ignorant believers, the record of whose views has perished, may have thought, this view is not found in writers of the ancient Church. It was, however, possible for some of the ancient Fathers, speaking as they did from a background of Greek philosophy, and particularly if they were influenced by Stoic thought, to define "spirit" as though it were a kind of very attenuated quasi-matter, which could have shape and location, though one could not see or feel it in the ordinary sense of the word. No modern thinker would speak of "spirit" in this way, but if this presupposition be allowed, it becomes possible to speak of the presence of the "spiritual" body and blood of the Lord in the Eucharist in a more "material" and spatial way than modern doctrines would allow, and yet the presence would not be regarded as "physical" in the modern sense of the word.

S. Ignatius does not inform us whether he thinks in this way. Nor is the later doctrine of Transubstantiation here, based as it is upon a subtle Scholastic distinction between the "substance" of an object, which is the ground of its existence, and yet is in the modern sense of the word "nonphysical," and the "accidents," which represent more or less what modern thought would describe as "the chemical and physical properties" of the object. This distinction, and this mode of expounding the Real Presence of Christ in the Sacrament, was unknown at this time. Yet we are bound to affirm that S. Ignatius teaches what a later generation would have called "the Real Presence" of

Christ in the Eucharist. The appointed means by which believers receive their share of the spiritual fruits of the death and resurrection of Christ is inseparably associated with the breaking of the bread and blessing of the cup, and the actual eating and drinking of the same. The modern "liberal" idea that the Sacrament is essentially a vivid psychological reminder of the death of Christ, and of His great love, which takes the modern Church back in thought and imagination to Calvary, would hardly have seemed a sacramental doctrine at all to the ancient Church, or to Ignatius. It is to be noted that the flesh of Christ which is partaken of in the Eucharist is the resurrection flesh. This precludes gross and materialistic ideas, but answers to the affirmation of Christian experience, that to partake of the Eucharist is the supreme and covenanted means by which the Church apprehends the presence of the Risen Christ in the midst.

7. "Give heed to the Prophets, and especially to the Gospel": Here is the happy mean between Judaizing and anti-Judaizing heresy. The Old Testament Prophets are an essential witness to the death and resurrection of Christ. That they foresaw the strange event is to Ignatius a proof that the strange event was indeed the work of God. Yet the Four Gospels are the supreme witness to these things.

8. "Do ye all follow your bishop, as Jesus Christ followed the Father": Here is yet another strong statement of the threefold Ministry. There is possibly another aspect of the doctrine that the form and discipline of the Church on earth is a figure of spiritual principles which obtain in the sphere of God. Christ became our Saviour through a life of obedience to the Father (Heb. v, 7–8). Man partakes of the fruit of this sacrifice of obedience by his discipline of obedience in the Church.

"Let that be held a valid eucharist ($\beta\epsilon\beta\alpha\iota\alpha$ $\epsilon\upsilon\chi\alpha\rho\iota\sigma\tau\iota\alpha$) [Lightfoot, p. 129], which is under the bishop or one to whom he shall have committed it": The first stage of Order would appear to be that the company of "presbyter-bishops" jointly celebrated the Eucharist. Naturally, on any particular occasion one of the company would have to perform the act of consecration, supported by the others, but he would not be regarded as having a different order from the others, nor need we suppose that the same "presbyter-bishop" celebrated on every occasion. It must be admitted that there is a strong element of supposition in this, resting upon the circumstance that the original "presbyter-bishops" appear to have been a single order. There is no more positive historical record of the existence of such a eucharistic order. However, the instinct to seek the spiritual leadership of a single Father-in-God, who should be the figure of the presence of Christ in His Church, elevated one "presbyter-bishop" to be the permanent and acknowledged president of the remainder. The orders of bishop and of presbyter therefore diverge. It would not follow that the presbyters would cease to consecrate the Eucharist, but it would come to be regarded that when they did so they acted as the representatives of the bishop. This is the position we have here. A further important stage of this episcopal delegation of powers took place when the original city church became associated with an increasing number of outlying country Churches. The bishop then could not always be at each, so presbyters had to consecrate the Eucharist regularly. Here is the germ of a "diocese," spreading outward from the original foundation. It does not appear from the Epistle whether there was in fact more than one congregation under the presidency of the bishop of Smyrna.

"Even as where Jesus may be, there is the universal Church"; ἡ καθολικὴ ἐκκλησία (Lightfoot, p. 129): This passage is notable in Christian literature, as the first appearance known to us of the phrase "the Catholic Church." It is not surprising to find the word, as the whole drift of Ignatius' arguments about the Church imply the idea. To him the guarantee of orthodoxy and the token of Christian love is the sense of disciplined corporate solidarity uniting all the local congregations in every place, of which solidarity the bishop is the symbol and instrument. Thus the word "Catholic" advanced by natural stages from its primary geographical sense to its secondary theological sense. The faith of the Church everywhere is the true Faith, as opposed to the endless variety of local heresy. To many modern ears the proposition that "wherever the Lord is, there is the true Church" means that any company of Christ-loving people, who live by faith in Him, and who are aware of the presence of the Spirit in their midst, constitute thereby "a true Church," irrespective of their Church Order. Clearly this view is very far from the intention of S. Ignatius, and of other ancient Fathers, when they make such statements. The idea that a company of Christians can create a ministerial Order *de novo*, and of their own devisal, is a distinctively modern one, and is the outcome of the increasing proliferation of denominations within Protestantism.

The classic Reformers would have joined with the ancient Church in repudiating this notion. The Reformers claimed that they were restoring the ancient succession of the Ministry to its original and authentic form, not starting a new ministry. In the ancient Church it is always presupposed that due ministerial and sacramental Order is observed in the constitution of the Church.

"It is not lawful apart from the bishop either to baptize or to hold a love-feast": It is not said that the bishop must preside personally at these rites, but that they must be subject to his spiritual jurisdiction. The question is raised by this passage as to whether the Agape is here spoken of as separate from the Eucharist. If the sense is to bring out a contrast between the Eucharist and noneucharistic ceremonies which are also under the bishop, then we have three rites mentioned. The Eucharist and Agape are separate. On the whole, this seems to be the more natural sense. However, some commentators read the coupling of Baptism with the Agape as an indication that the latter is also regarded as a Sacrament. This would answer to the supposition that the Eucharist and Agape are still united in the Church at Smyrna.

9. It is very strongly enforced that the rule of the bishop is a token of the rule of God.

10. "Philo and Agathopus": See Epistle to Philadelphians, 11.

11. "It is meet that your church should appoint ... an ambassador": See Epistle to Philadelphians, 10, with notes, p. 136.

12. "Which was both carnal and spiritual"; σαρκικῇ τε καὶ πνευματικῇ (Lightfoot, p. 131): To Ignatius it is important to affirm that the death and resurrection of Christ were real bodily events, but they are of significance to the Christian faith because they were the tokens and agents in this world of a spiritual victory over man's spiritual foes, wrought out by God as man for man.

13. "And the virgins who are called widows": The "widows" in the ancient Church were partway toward a religious order. They were needy widows who received a charitable allowance from the Church, and were expected in return to live a chaste life of regular worship in the Church.

VII. To S. Polycarp

"Who is also Theophorus": See Epistle to Ephesians, with note, p. 107.

"Polycarp who is bishop of the church of the Smyrnaeans": For a note on this very distinguished figure, see the introduction to the Epistle of S. Polycarp, pp. 153–7.

2. "If thou lovest good scholars, this is not thankworthy in thee": Or rather, "disciples," "followers," μαθητάς (Lightfoot, p. 132). This is not an animadversion against Christian learning, but an exhortation not to shun difficult pastoral tasks. The bishop is to go to the awkward, and not confine his attention to those who respond to his lead. It brings the life of the ancient Church very near to us, to overhear one Apostolic man finding it fitting to give such advice to another.

"Be thou prudent as the serpent in all things, and guileless always as the dove": S. Matthew x, 16.

3. "The Impalpable, the Impassible, who suffered for our sake": God is defined after the Greek manner, rather than the Biblical, but Ignatius is, as always, firm on the Incarnation. Here is the paradox of the Incarnation. God has no body, and cannot suffer, yet in Christ, the divine Son incarnate, He suffered for us.

4. "Widows": See Epistle to Smyrnaeans, 13, with note, p. 142.

"Let meetings be held more frequently"; συναγωγαί (Lightfoot, p. 132).

"Despise not slaves": Slaves are brethren in the Church, and must be honoured as such, and treated humanely, but there was little notion in the ancient Church that the social institution of slavery as such was wrong. See *Didache*, Chapter 4, with notes, pp. 76–7.

"Let them serve the more faithfully": Compare Ephesians vi, 5–7.

"Let them not desire to be set free at the public cost"; ἀπὸ τοῦ κοινοῦ (Lightfoot, p. 132): That is, by subscription from among the membership of the Church. To do this was often regarded as a pious custom. Ignatius takes a very "conservative" line in discouraging this, and more so than his master, S. Paul (see 1 Cor. vii, 20–23).

5. "My sister . . . my brothers": That is, the Christians, this being the common mode of address one toward another (Acts ix, 17; xxi, 20; 1 Corinthians vi, 6; ix, 5).

"As the Lord loved the Church": Ephesians v, 29.

"If any one is able to abide in chastity to the honour of the flesh of the Lord, let him so abide without boasting": Although marriage is an honourable estate, and conjugal love a type of the love which unites the Church to Christ, yet Ignatius appears to hold, following S. Paul in 1 Corinthians vii, 7-9, that to be unmarried is in principle the higher state. This was a noteworthy deviation of Christian morality from its original Jewish pattern, and was largely due to the common Christian expectation that Christ would come for the Judgment in the immediate future (1 Corinthians vii, 25-31). There was also the influence of the somewhat enigmatic "word of the Lord" in S. Matthew xix, 12, which to the ancient Christians, at any rate, appeared to exalt celibacy. We observe that the Christian's own body is a part of the Body of Christ, so that a discipline which exalts it exalts "the flesh of the Lord." This conveys to us in what a vivid and realistic sense the early Christians felt that they were "members incorporate in the mystical body of thy Son." This was much more than a poetic metaphor, as so often today (cf. 1 Corinthians vi, 15-17).

"If he boast, he is lost; and if it be known beyond the bishop, he is polluted": Long and sad experience in the Church shows that the besetting sin of those who give themselves to strict disciplines, such as celibacy, is self-righteousness, and trust in the merit of one's own good works. Ignatius is well aware of this. It is interesting to observe that the bishop, as the chief pastor of the flock, is to guard his people against this fault, and provision is apparently made for private moral counsel between bishop and people. This is the first beginning of confession and penitential discipline, following S. Matthew xviii, 17 (which, whatever it originally meant upon our Lord's lips, was clearly applied by the first Christians to the Church).

"To unite themselves with the consent of the bishop": We have here the first hint of the appearance of a distinctive Christian marriage ceremony. For an early view of the Christian marriage law, see *The Shepherd*, Precept iv, 1, with note, p. 236.

6. "Give ye heed to the bishop": This letter, therefore, is not a purely personal one. The presupposition is that, like the letter addressed to the Church, it will be read to the whole congregation. This Epistle is, in fact, not Ignatius' advice to a friendly bishop, but his counsel to pastors in general. The continuation of the chapter makes this plain.

"Please the Captain in whose army ye serve": Compare 2 Timothy ii, 4.

"Let your baptism abide with you as your shield": Here we have a variant upon S. Paul's "whole armour of God" (Eph. vi, 11).

7. "Seeing that the church which is in Antioch of Syria hath peace": See Epistle to Philadelphians, 10, with note, p. 136.

"To call together a godly council": Clearly, the ideal Ignatian bishop rules by consultation and persuasion, as did the greatest of the Apostles themselves (Acts xv, 23–9), "neither as being lords over God's heritage" (1 Pet. v, 3). It is pleasing to find that S. Ignatius is an exponent of episcopacy, but not of "prelacy," which has done so much to hide the merits of episcopacy from the eyes of some.

"A Christian hath no authority over himself, but giveth his time to God": To make the journey from Smyrna to Antioch would be a considerable sacrifice of time and money, in a Church with no paid clergy, and presumably little by way of "travelling expenses."

8. "Thou shalt write to the Churches in front": Ignatius finds that embarkation will prevent him from writing more letters ahead. He therefore asks Polycarp to do this for him, so that the Churches of Greece and Italy which lie upon his route may have warning. He wishes for them to have full opportunity of receiving a Confessor's blessing. This is not a mark of egotism. There was a genuine feeling in the ancient Church that a Confessor had something of special spiritual value to bestow.

6. Summary of the Theological Thought and Church-Principles of S. Ignatius

Theologically speaking, Ignatius is the outstanding personality of the somewhat obscure but very formative age of the Church which immediately succeeded the New Testament period. It may be of value to the student, therefore, to close our study of him by gathering together, and by rendering into the terms of modern theology, his system of belief and churchmanship. In doing this it is first necessary to call to mind that Ignatius was not what we today would call a systematic theologian, at least, not in his surviving works. The main purpose of his writing is devotional and hortatory, to bring a Confessor's blessing to the faithful. His second purpose is controversial, to warn against heresy and schism. Therefore, what he has to say about belief is commonly said in passing, and he is not careful to make every utterance logically consistent with every other, while he passes many points over in a measure of ambiguity or silence. Nevertheless, S. Ignatius shows an active and constructive mind, and has the authentic genius of a theologian. A great advance in theology can be seen in him.

This brings us to another consideration calling for caution in judgment. On the one hand, Ignatius does not speak simply for himself. He is not like some modern theologians, who would found everything they write upon their own personal learning and conviction, and form their own system apart from the accepted teaching of the Church. He has a great sense that his business is to express the corporate voice of the Church. By and large we may accept that this is what he does. However, though we may treat him as representative of the Church of his time, we may also safely assume that he is more formed and conscious in his opinions, and more vocal in expressing them, than the majority of his fellows. The majority would be more conservative and more confused than he, though substantially agreeing with him. Developments of thought and Church polity which were only in process of arising are seen clearly developed in him. As a man of outstanding personality, and a constructive leader, he is a little ahead of his age, as well as representative of it. With these provisos in mind we may seek to reconstruct his system, so as to obtain as clear a view as we may of the life and thought of the post-Apostolic Church.

With regard to the doctrine of God, S. Ignatius is substantially in the position of the New Testament. God the Father can be defined in terms associated with Greek philosophy, but He is also very decidedly the God of the Old Testament. God the Son is affirmed to be divine in the proper sense of the word. He is the preexistent creative Word, or Logos, the Agent by which the Father makes known to man the mysterious divine counsel of salvation. God the Spirit is the inspirer of the Prophets, and in particular the Agent of the Incarnation, but His divine Person is not dealt with so clearly as that of the Son.

With the doctrine of the Incarnation we come to the "Mystery"; that is, to the divine self-revelation of things so wonderful that neither angels nor men could have brought them out of the great silence of

God, but which God has now fully made known, so that they are plainly declared to all men through the Church and her Scriptures. God entered the world, and joined the spiritual to the material, by the Incarnation of the divine Son. A miraculous birth of the Blessed Virgin, by the influence of the Holy Spirit, is strongly emphasized as the means by which the union of divine and human natures took place. Christ's birth as man, of the House of David, is a guarantee that His human nature was real. It is vitally important to Ignatius to affirm, against the Docetic heresy of an incipient Gnostic system, that Christ was capable of genuine human suffering, because the mystery of human redemption depends upon His suffering and rising again as man and for man. The saving significance of the Cross and Resurrection is essentially that it marks the mightiest attack of, and final overthrow of, the demons. Degrading pagan magic has now lost its hold on the lives of the faithful. The effect of this historic saving work extends backward in time to the saints of the Old Testament, who were, in effect, "Christians before the time." Now that the anticipation of their faith is rewarded, and their redemption fully consummated, they are in the proper sense part of the Church. The same is true of the angels, who likewise hold their positions in bliss by virtue of faith in Christ.

However, though the Church of the New Testament is one continuous People of God with the Church of the Old Testament, conservative Judaizing Christians who would keep the Church imprisoned within the ceremonial provisions of the Law of Moses, taken literally, are to be disowned as heretics. Some of these claim that the orthodox position regarding Christ is not borne out from the Old Testament Scripture, and is therefore false. Ignatius disagrees, and affirms strongly that the Old Testament does bear full witness to Christ, but also that the new revelation in Christ is an independent spiritual authority. Already the important facts about Christ are being collected together into an incipient Creed. Ignatius' citations of the Old Testament are somewhat sparing compared with some writers of this time, but he is in no doubt about its authority as the Scripture. Nor is it his manner to quote New Testament writings very frequently, but he is in no doubt as to the eminent authority of the Gospels. He cites the sayings of our Lord as an authority, and is extensively based upon S. Paul. We have a few Pauline quotations, 1 Corinthians being by far the favourite Epistle, and numerous allusions, often very apt and showing real understanding of the Apostle. The emphasis of S. Ignatius upon a particular form of Church polity as essential to the Christian faith may be new, as compared to S. Paul, but his witness to salvation by grace is to be defended as substantially Pauline.

There is in these Epistles a vigorous conception of the Church as a world-wide, united, and unifying community of God's People. S. Ignatius is the first writer known to us to use the word "catholic" in a technical sense to express this idea. The catholicity of the Church in every place is to be outwardly expressed and safeguarded by a regular discipline of authoritative and brotherly visits of deputations from one local congregation to another. Thus, though there is no centralized administrative control within the Church, its polity is not "independent," but firmly "connexional." The nexus and operative symbol of this connexionalism is the intercourse of one bishop with another. The heavenly dispensation of the sovereign Father, and of the divine Son who declares Him through the Spirit, is symbolized on earth in this divinely appointed ecclesiastical polity in the Church. Corresponding to the sovereign Father is the one ruling bishop in each Church. The presbyters, who support the bishop, also have their place of honour, together with the assisting deacons. The company of presbyters corresponds spiritually to the Apostles, who surrounded Christ. Thus the traditional threefold ministerial Order of the Church is present in the writings of Ignatius, and is vindicated on the highest theological grounds as a part of the essential Christian faith. However, S. Ignatius plainly does not know of the later form of the doctrine of Apostolical Succession, which pronounced the bishop to be the successor and spiritual representative of the Apostles.

The office of the bishop, supported by the presbytery, is to serve as a focus for the unity of the Church, and to safeguard orthodoxy. Obedience to the bishop is a salutary exercise, for it spiritually corresponds to that human obedience of the incarnate Son to the Father, which was the accomplishment of our salvation. The bishop also celebrates the sacraments of Holy Baptism and the Eucharist, presides at the Agape, and can bless marriages. He can, however, delegate authority to do these things to the presbyters. Thus for S. Ignatius the government of the Church is authoritative, in the sense that the bishop is a ruler representing God, and not the delegate of a Church meeting which has elected him. However, this rule is not properly authoritarian, for it is presupposed that the bishop acts by a measure of consultation with, and with the good will of, the presbytery, the diaconate, and the body of the faithful. The assumption throughout is that the whole Church is under the guidance of the Spirit, so no question arises of one man imposing his will upon another. Thus the polity envisaged by Ignatius is neither "prelatical" nor "democratic," to import anachronistically into the discussion two terms derived from the thought of later times. Rather is the ideal held up of a benevolent patriarch presiding over a family under God. The "prophetic" Ministry of spontaneous utterance under the immediate guidance of the Spirit, so prominent in the New Testament, has fallen into the background of the time of these Epistles. S. Ignatius does appear to claim that on at least one occasion he himself had exercised this prophetic office, but significantly he used it to advance the spiritual claims of the regular episcopal Ministry.

The assumption is made throughout that this episcopal polity exists throughout the Church. On the one hand it is clear that S. Ignatius could not have argued as he does were not ruling bishops an established and accepted feature of the Churches with which he had to do. He is to be accepted as a reliable witness to the firm establishment of primitive "monepiscopacy" in Syria and Asia Minor by the beginning of the second century. On the other hand, some commentators feel that the constraint he is under to press the exclusive claims of this polity indicate by implication that Ignatius knows that in point of fact there are some Christians who do not fully acknowledge the claims of this Ministry, and perhaps even that there are some local congregations where it does not exist. The leading case in point is that of the Church at Rome. He greets no bishop there, and this may quite well indicate that he knows that, despite his ecclesiastical theories, there continues at conservative Rome the old form of government by a body of substantially equal "presbyter-bishops," so that there is in fact no single ruling bishop. Nevertheless, the Church in Rome is addressed as a Church of outstanding prestige, and two reasons which contributed to the growth of this prestige are clearly indicated. It was the scene of the two outstanding Apostolic martyrdoms, of S. Peter and of S. Paul. It was also the Church of the imperial city, some of whose members might, if asked, exercise backstairs influence with Roman officials to secure a merciful judgment upon accused Christians.

There is an universal priesthood of all believers, in the sense that to the whole body of the faithful, and to every individual in it, belongs the privilege of prevailing prayer to God. However, the prayer of the Church is only seen in its completeness and full power when it is the disciplined prayer of the whole united company, under the leadership of the bishop and presbyters. The focus of this united prayer is to be found in the sacraments of Holy Baptism and the Eucharist, which are only rightly celebrated in a spirit of unity, and under the authority of the bishop. Apart from this Ministry and sacramental system the Church does not exist, and man has no saving contact with God. Ignatius expounds both Gospel Sacraments as rites which correspond to the principle of the Cross. Each is to be understood as a symbolic representation of Christ's human life of sinless obedience to the Father, of the sufferings and death which this entailed, and of the victory over evil which was wrought out thereby, and witnessed to in the resurrection and ascension. In consequence, to partake in the sacraments is the operative symbol whereby the Church makes herself one with the Lord as He obeys, suffers, and rises again, and is the means whereby the faithful take their share of that which was accomplished in Christ crucified and risen. Holy Baptism is the initiation into the life of "bearing the Cross" with Christ, so as to "wear the crown." The Eucharist is the continued renewal of the same, to the spiritual sustenance of the faithful. S. Ignatius teaches that this spiritual sustenance is operatively received in the reception of the Eucharist, so that to eat with faith that bread and drink that cup is to receive the body and blood of the Lord. This is expounded in various metaphors, particularly as "the bread of God," and (more rhetorically, perhaps) as "the medicine of immortality."

The practical principle of life issuing from this identification with Christ in the Church is humble submission to God and to His ordinances, which works mutual forbearance, discipline, and unity in brotherhood. Social distinctions are of no account within the fellowship. Regarding those who are without, Ignatius enjoins that there is a duty of prayer for the enemies of the truth, but they are not to be received into familiarity. A very distinctive Ignatian emphasis is that real and full discipleship begins only when the believer is called actually to suffer with Christ and for Christ. The Christian Confessor is the true disciple and the ornament of the Church, and is able to bring a blessing with him to the Church, wherever he goes. The actual martyr's death, though a dreadful thing, and not to be embarked upon in any spirit of bravado, is to be welcomed as the Christian's crown of perfection. It provides God's most prevailing witness to the truth of the Gospel. Yet Ignatius would have it remembered that the Christian does not earn his salvation by his own merit as a Confessor or Martyr. He is saved by grace, through faith in Christ crucified, the spiritual fruit of which is "the faith that works by love." In conclusion, S. Ignatius sees the Church as expectantly waiting for the early Second Advent of Christ, and the Last Judgment, though he says little in detail about the millenarian hope of the ancient Church.

This summary suffices to indicate that S. Ignatius reproduces with substantial integrity the vital religion of the New Testament. It is the more tribute to his powers that he does this without deliberately setting out so to do. An Epistle like that of S. Paul to the Romans is a letter only in literary form. Actually, it is the considered theological statement of a position. The Epistles of Ignatius are real personal letters addressed to the immediate occasion, more to be compared to Galatians or Corinthians. Yet in passing, and while his attention is centred elsewhere, Ignatius shows his grasp of the whole Christian system. This is surely evidence that in the Churches from which Ignatius speaks, the religion of the New Testament was rapidly being developed into a clearly formulated system of doctrine. It is not all expressed in the precise language of later orthodoxy, for there were many lessons yet to be learned, yet the underlying intention is there. Thus S. Ignatius is a most valuable dogmatic link between the sources of dogma in the Bible, and the later Catholic theologians.

It is idle to deny that at one important point there is a distinct difference of emphasis between the New Testament and S. Ignatius. The New Testament is filled with a commanding sense of the Church, but it says very little that is explicit about the Ministry, and ecclesiastical discipline. This element is memorably prominent in S. Ignatius. We come here to a fundamental matter of judgment. Some writers approach Church history with the presupposition that a vital concern for the visible polity and discipline of the Church is prima-facie evidence of a decline of spirituality, and a movement of Christianity away from the things which really matter. The assumption is that in the sphere of Church polity the informal and the spiritual are virtually names for the same thing. This view, which would have astonished almost everyone in the ancient Church, has become widespread today in semisecularized circles because it suits the prejudices of those who desire an excuse for not taking up the yoke of Christ. It is an invidious business to criticize Christ Himself, or His exalted ethics, but "organized Christianity" is more vulnerable. Yet criticism of the Church has very much the same ease-giving practical effect as has rejection of Christ. Those who profess to reserve their admiration for a supposed original nonecclesiastical Christianity will certainly not take kindly to Ignatius! He will be to them an evident token of the decline of Christianity. However, those who take a more realistic view of the situation will remember that the Church was now a rapidly extending and fundamentally Gentile organization, no longer protected by the Jewish "hedge of the Law." If the spirit was to be preserved, it was of paramount necessity that the living Body be provided with a firmer skeleton. This we see happening in the Epistles of S. Ignatius. That it was happening is a mark that the Spirit's providential guidance of the Church was not failing.

V Literature Concerning S. Polycarp of Smyrna

1. Historical Note on S. Polycarp

Polycarp of Smyrna was without doubt one of the most venerated figures in the Church of the post-Apostolic period. His surviving Epistle does not seem to show him a man of the calibre of S. Ignatius, but the stirring eyewitness account of his martyrdom displays him as a man of real force of character. We may perhaps see a warning in this against passing too facile a judgment upon any of these ancient figures, simply on account of that part of their writings which the accident of history has preserved for us. The great veneration which was felt by the ancient Church for S. Polycarp arose eminently from the circumstance that as a young man he had known some of the first great Apostles, and other eyewitnesses of Christ, and also that he survived to a great age. We have already observed in the Introduction (pp. 3-4) that the first authorities for the Gospel were the Apostolic eyewitnesses of the Resurrection, and that the Apostolic writings made their way into the Church in the first place only as the substitute for the personal presence of one who had known the Lord. Polycarp must to a unique degree have represented in the Church of his day that precious but passing order of living witnesses to the Apostles, before the witness to Christ had become exclusively that of a book.

It is almost universally accepted that S. Polycarp was martyred in A.D. 155 or 156. He was then at least eighty-six years old.[1] He must in consequence have been born about A.D. 70, or a little before. Living in Asia Minor, he would therefore as a lad enjoy a good chance of meeting many elderly surviving Christians of the first generation, for he was a Christian from his youth. In particular, a strong and reliable tradition associates Polycarp with S. John, who lived to a great age in Asia Minor. S. Irenaeus, who was born in Asia Minor, was able to say, writing toward the end of the second century, that he clearly carried from his own young days a recollection of the impressive appearance and teaching of the venerable Polycarp. The information is contained

[1] *Martyrdom of S. Polycarp*, Chap. 9.

in that part of Irenaeus' Epistle to Florinus which is preserved by Eusebius.[1] It opens with a most enigmatic passage: "For when I was a boy, I saw thee in lower Asia with Polycarp, moving in splendour in the royal court (ἐν τῇ βασιλικῇ αὐλῇ), and endeavouring to gain his approbation." One difficulty is that no court which could properly be called "royal" or "imperial" is known to have been held in Asia Minor in this period. A greater difficulty is that of supposing that in days when the Christians were illegal, unpopular, and frequently persecuted, an outstanding Christian leader like Polycarp, and a man of most uncompromising principles, could have moved with any degree of regularity and publicity in official Roman circles. Possibly, therefore, Irenaeus uses "royal" in a purely metaphorical sense of the formal assembly of some important local Church (cf. 1 Pet. ii, 9). The letter to Florinus continues: "I am able to describe the very place in which the blessed Polycarp sat as he discoursed, and his goings out and his comings in, and the manner of his life, and his physical appearance, and his discourses to the people, and the accounts which he gave of the intercourse with John and with the others who had seen the Lord. . . . These things being told me by the mercy of God, I listened to them attentively, noting them down, not on paper, but in my heart. . . . And I am able to bear witness before God that if that blessed and apostolic presbyter had heard any such things [that is, as the error of Florinus] he would have cried out, and stopped his ears, and as was his custom, would have exclaimed, 'O good God, unto what times hast thou spared me that I should endure such these things?' And he would have fled from the place where, sitting or standing, he had heard such words." We may perhaps wish that Irenaeus had taken up a little less of his precious space in saying how sure he was of these things, and a little more in giving us the facts! However, the picture is clear enough in essentials.

We see S. Polycarp as a venerable and impressive presbyter, who owed his repute not alone to his personal character, but even more, to his unique memory of the first Apostles. He is the regular teacher, and in point of fact the governor, of the Church where he lives. In policy he is a strong traditionalist, quick to sense and to repel any "modern" heresy creeping in to contaminate the original faith of the Apostolic Church. In fact, he perfectly represents the process by which out of

[1] H.E., V, xx, 5-7.

the company of "presbyter-bishops" one became a ruling bishop. We are not surprised, therefore, to find that Irenaeus says that Polycarp was "appointed by Apostles in Asia Bishop of the Church of Smyrna."[1] To a certain extent S. Irenaeus is very naturally reading back into this early period the conditions which obtained in his own day, and assumes that Polycarp was appointed a single ruling bishop. However, it is well possible that, if S. John lived to a great age in Asia Minor, and if S. Polycarp were appointed presbyter at an early age, he may have been put in office by an Apostle in person. And in that office he could in his latter years be fittingly described by Ignatius as "the bishop of Smyrna."[2] No neat theological doctrine of how the ministry of the Church "ought" to have been founded and maintained can ever be demonstrated historically, for we are so very, very far from possessing the necessary records of all the officers in all the Churches. Yet the evidence, so far as it goes, appears decisively to uphold the general principle of a governing Christian Ministry going back in succession to the Apostolic circle, in which Ministry the office of a single governing bishop for each principal local Church rapidly appeared, probably first in Asia. The history of this contentious matter is obscure, but a fair reading of such evidence as there is appears to support neither the strict upholders of the later doctrine of "Apostolic Succession" nor those who have objected to this doctrine!

There is one other historical episode recorded of S. Polycarp, apart from what we shall learn in his single surviving Epistle,[3] and the account of his martyrdom. This is well worthy of mention, for the pleasing incident most fittingly sets forth in action the Catholic discipline and the Catholic charity of the ancient Church. It is recorded by Eusebius from an otherwise lost letter of Irenaeus to Victor of Rome, who was bishop there about A.D. 189–198.[4] There had been a long-standing disagreement in the Church regarding the proper day for the celebration of Easter. Some Churches, particularly in Asia Minor, maintained that the festival of Christ's Resurrection was to be held on a day calculated from the time of the Jewish Passover, as it fell

[1] *Adv. Haer.*, III, iii, 4.
[2] Ep. of Ignatius to Polycarp, salutation.
[3] He apparently wrote other letters, which are lost (Eusebius, *H.E.*, V, xx, 8). Irenaeus, however, who should have been in a position to know, mentions only one, *Adv. Haer.*, III, iii, 4.
[4] *H.E.*, V, xxiv, 12–17.

in each year, whatever be the day of the week. These so-called Quartodecimans (from the Latin word for "fourteenth") celebrated Easter on the 14th day of the Jewish (lunar) month Nisan. The majority of Churches, however, held that Easter must always fall on a Sunday, being the day of Christ's Resurrection, even at the expense of departure from the Passover season. There seem to have been various attempts to accomplish this, and yet withal to preserve in the Church the memory of the fact that the Christian Paschal season originated in the Passover, the Jewish festival of the spring full moon. In particular, the Church in Rome developed the custom of keeping Easter on the first Sunday after the full moon which succeeded the spring equinox, or which fell upon that day (March 21st).[1] This eventually became the universal custom, being one of the canons of the Council of Nicaea, A.D. 325, and gives us our present variable date of Easter. The Quartodeciman question may seem to the modern mind a trifling and unworthy ground for widespread controversy in the Church, until we remember that it was an issue left over from, and related to, the great controversy which had faced the Church in her first days, namely, the degree to which Christianity was free to diverge from Judaism. The issues which divide modern Christians from one another often have as much, and as little, theological weight as this!

However, Victor attempted to constrain the Churches of Asia Minor to conform to the Roman and general usage by excommunicating them (or as some read the account, by threatening to do so), and by calling on other Churches to do the same. Though Irenaeus approved of the Roman date of Easter, he wrote to Victor to rebuke him for his overbearing conduct, and in doing so cited the happier precedent of Anicetus, one of the Roman bishop's predecessors: "And when the blessed Polycarp was at Rome in the time of Anicetus[2] . . . they immediately made peace with one another, not caring to quarrel over this matter. For neither could Anicetus persuade Polycarp not to

---

[1] Thus if the full moon fell on the spring equinox, and the next day was a Sunday, Easter would be celebrated on its earliest possible date, March 22nd. If the full moon happened to come one day before the equinox, the necessity to wait for a whole lunar month before beginning to count for the Sunday could take Easter to its latest possible date, namely, April 25th.

[2] This must have been shortly before the martyrdom, because Anicetus became Bishop of Rome about A.D. 155, while Polycarp was probably put to death in this or the next year.

observe what he had always observed with John the disciple of our Lord . . . neither could Polycarp persuade Anicetus to observe it, as he said that he ought to follow the customs of the presbyters that had preceded him. But though matters were in this shape, they joined in the communion together, and Anicetus conceded the administration of the Eucharist in the Church to Polycarp, manifestly as a mark of respect" (16, 17). Though we know relatively little about S. Polycarp, the centuries which have gone by have not lessened this respect. He was a great and heroic man, if not an original and constructive thinker.

2. The Epistle of S. Polycarp to the Philippians

The writing of this letter is intimately connected with the Epistles and the martyrdom of S. Ignatius. It was written so soon after this event that Polycarp has not yet heard for certain what happened to Ignatius at Rome (Chap. 13). The Epistle must therefore be dated about A.D. 107 (see p. 103). It is worthy of note that a long series of critics have found an inconsistency between this statement and that in Chapter 9. It is claimed that in this earlier chapter Polycarp speaks of "the blessed Ignatius" and his companions as though they were long enshrined in popular esteem as martyrs. The most recent and learned treatment of this important critical theme is that of P. N. Harrison, who argues strongly that there were really two Epistles of S. Polycarp. The first was a very short one, being represented by Chapter 13 and possibly 14 of the traditional Epistle. This was written very shortly after S. Ignatius had passed through Smyrna on his way to Rome, and perhaps while he was still on the journey. Some decades later, when the esteem of Ignatius was firmly fixed in the Church, and Polycarp himself had come to a position of great repute, he wrote another and longer Epistle, exhorting the Church in face of the spiritual perils which increasingly surrounded it at that period.[1] Then when S. Polycarp himself was dramatically martyred, and a pious interest in his deeds and letters was aroused, his two Epistles to Philippi were recorded, but became mistakenly united in copying the manuscript.[2]

[1] P. N. Harrison, *Polycarp's Two Epistles to the Philippians*, Cambridge, 1936, p. 15, *et passim.*
[2] *Ibid.*, p. 16.

One's judgment is that the evidence for such an inconsistency of timing between Chapters 9 and 13 is not conclusive. At the time of writing Chapter 13, Polycarp could very reasonably assume that Ignatius and his companions had in fact been martyred, even though he had yet to learn the details. He might very reasonably therefore describe them as already "blessed," and companions in heaven with the Lord and the Apostles. Chapter 13 as it stands does not appear to preclude that the writer had knowledge that Ignatius had met his death, but only indicates that he had not a full and edifying account, as is given in the *Martyrdom*. Another difficulty is that, if at the death of Polycarp a deliberate attempt was made to collect memorials of him, it is hard to see why the other lost Epistles mentioned by Eusebius were not also preserved.

Whatever be the truth of this matter, it is certain that the Church at Philippi had recently escorted on their way, and ministered to, certain Confessors, including Ignatius. He had apparently exhorted them, like other Churches which he visited, to write to his own Church at Antioch, in order to salute them on the occasion of the cessation of persecution. The Philippian Christians in turn wrote to Polycarp asking him to forward their letter to Antioch, and requesting him to send to them such of S. Ignatius' letters as were in his possession. This shows the early interest in the circulation of copies of Epistles. The Philippians also wish for an exhortation from the Bishop of Smyrna, and this Epistle is Polycarp's reply. It is more conventional and less stirring than the Ignatian Epistles, and by contrast is notable for its large number of varied Scriptural quotations, particularly from the New Testament. This is a warning that the relative paucity of express New Testament quotations in Ignatius by no means constitutes evidence that these books were not known and revered in the circle whence Ignatius wrote. The difference is not more than a preference of style, for Polycarp wrote from the same circle, and is full of New Testament references. It is also interesting that a writer who must perhaps more than any other man of his time have had his mind stored with information about Christ based directly upon personal and oral tradition, should so gladly have recourse to the Apostolic writings. He certainly looks to S. Paul and S. Peter as authorities to be quoted. The quotations from the Gospels are short, and are of striking words such as would be likely to be remembered in the Church in a fixed traditional form. It is less clear, therefore, that these are quotations from written Gospels rather than independent reproductions of the oral tradition which lies behind the Gospels.

Another aspect of this subject is that the relatively short Epistle of Polycarp is a very early and valuable witness to the use of a large part of the writings which now compose the canon of the New Testament. He was a man who knew many leading Christians of the generation which produced much of the New Testament, and he quotes S. Matthew, S. Mark, S. Luke, Acts, Romans, 1 and 2 Corinthians, Galatians, Ephesians, Philippians, 2 Thessalonians, 1 and 2 Timothy, Hebrews, 1 Peter, and 1 John. The chief matter of interest herein to New Testament critics is the early use of the Pastoral Epistles, and in particular the numerous citations of 1 Peter. Many feel that this usage ill accords with some modern critical theories, which deny the Apostolic authorship of the Pastoral Epistles, and 1 Peter, and which place their composition too late for quotation in a work composed at the very beginning of the second century. This is an incentive for finding a later date for the bulk of the Epistle of Polycarp.[1] However, we observe that he does not attach names to these writings. Thus while this Epistle provides very early evidence of the use of 1 Peter as an authoritative "Apostolic Writing," it does not provide evidence as to whether it was indeed written by S. Peter. Polycarp's silence does not indicate that he doubted it, however, for he quotes several undoubtedly Pauline Epistles without giving any name either. We really cannot say what he thought.

3. Sources of the Epistle

There are nine ancient Greek manuscripts of the first nine chapters, which then run without a break into Chapter 5 of the Epistle of Barnabas. Clearly all these must belong to the same family, and go back to an original in which mutilated copies of Polycarp and Barnabas were incorrectly joined together in copying. Nearly the whole of Chapter 13 is also given in Greek, in Eusebius, *H.E.*, III,xxx vi, 13-15. There is also an ancient Latin version of the whole, which does not

[1] Cf. P. N. Harrison, *Polycarp's Two Epistles to the Philippians*, pp. 4-7, 285-310.

follow the original very literally, contained in nine main MSS, and also some fragments of Chapter 12 in Syriac.

4. Commentary on the Epistle of S. Polycarp to the Philippians

"Polycarp and the presbyters that are with him": This is a significantly different form of greeting, as compared with that which opens S. Clement to the Corinthians. Here the clergy write, there the Church.

1. "Ye received the followers of the true love": It appears that Ignatius was in fact one of a party being taken to Rome to suffer for the Name. Quite possibly there were other prisoners as well, to swell the number for the Games.

"Your faith which was famed from primitive times": The extensive mention of the Philippian Church in Acts, and the currency of S. Paul's Epistle, would account for this.

"Whom God raised, having loosed the pangs of Hades": Acts ii, 24.

"On whom, though ye saw Him not": 1 Peter i, 8.

"By grace ye are saved, not of works": Ephesians ii, 8, 9.

2. "Wherefore gird up your loins": 1 Peter i, 13.

"Serve God in fear": Psalm ii, 11.

"Ye have believed on Him that raised our Lord": 1 Peter i, 21.

"Unto whom all things were made subject": Possibly an allusion to Philippians ii, 10–11.

"Judge of quick and dead": Acts x, 42.

"He that raised him from the dead will raise us also": 2 Corinthians iv, 14.

"If we do His will . . . and love the things which He loved": In isolation this passage has a moralistic sound, but it is not intended to deny the doctrine that salvation is by grace (see Chap. 1). Christ is also our Saviour (Intro.), He died and rose for us (9), and "endured to face even death for our sins" (1). Nevertheless, there is a moralist tone in the general body of exhortation. However, we may see from the *Martyrdom* that S. Polycarp was a man of great devotion to his Lord, one who clearly lived by faith. This only illustrates how difficult it is to judge of the evangelical experience of the Fathers from their less than exact phraseology.

"Not rendering evil for evil or railing for railing": 1 Peter iii, 9.

"But remembering the words which the Lord spake, as He taught; Judge not": S. Matthew vii, 1, 2, and S. Luke vi, 36-8, conflated. It is arguable that we have here oral tradition of these well-known words, largely independent of the written Gospels. They must have been known by heart by the early Christians, and recited in a fixed customary form. It is significant that they are introduced with the solemn formula "as He taught" (compare Acts xx, 35). There is not yet a New Testament Scripture, to be quoted in like manner to the Old. The writings of the Apostles are cited as an authority, but the words of the Lord Himself as a special authority. We are not far from the sense of the formula "as it is written," which introduces Scripture.

"Blessed are the poor": S. Matthew v, 3 and 10 united.

3. "Paul, who when he came among you ... when he was absent, wrote a letter unto you": Polycarp appropriately reminds the Philippians of their glorious Apostolic foundation, and the reflected glory of the Epistle.

"The faith"; "Love toward God and Christ and toward our neighbour": The faith here is a body of doctrine; but the evangelical principle that Christianity is more than the acceptance of a doctrine, that it is God's gift of love, is not forgotten.

"Which is the mother of us all": Galatians iv, 26. It is a little curious that in the present context S. Polycarp does not quote from Philippians.

4. "But the love of money ... neither can we carry anything out": 1 Timothy vi, 7, 10.

"Our widows": The "order" of widows had a duty to join regularly in the prayers of the Church, in return for a charitable allowance.

5. "God is not mocked": Galatians vi, 7.

"A minister of all": S. Mark ix, 35.

"For if we be well pleasing to Him in this present world, we shall receive the future world also": Compare S. Matthew xxv, 34 ff.

"We shall reign with Him": 2 Timothy ii, 12.

"If indeed we have faith"; $\epsilon \mathring{\iota} \gamma \epsilon \ \pi\iota\sigma\tau\epsilon\mathring{\upsilon}o\mu\epsilon\nu$ (Lightfoot, p. 170): Here we have a witness to salvation by faith.

"Lust warreth against the Spirit": Galatians v, 17.

"Neither whoremongers ... shall inherit the kingdom of God": 1 Corinthians vi, 9, 10.

"Submitting yourselves to the presbyters and deacons": No bishop is mentioned, in a context where this might be expected. This may be an accident, but quite possibly as at Rome, so here also at Philippi (likewise a European Church), there is not as yet a ruling bishop.

6. "Turning back the sheep that are gone astray": Ezekiel xxxiv, 4. This, which is one of the very few Old Testament quotations in the Epistle, is most appropriately drawn from one of the great "pastoral" passages of the prophets.

"Providing always for that which is honourable": 2 Corinthians viii, 21.

"We must all stand at the judgment-seat of Christ": Romans xiv, 10–12.

"Them that bear the name of the Lord in hypocrisy": There is a rumour of heresy at Philippi also. As S. Polycarp goes on to warn against Docetism, presumably this heresy was incipient Gnosticism.

7. "Every one who shall not confess that Jesus Christ is come in the flesh, is antichrist": 1 John iv, 2, 3. This is the leading New Testament passage directed against a definite doctrinal heresy, presumably also of a Gnostic character.

"Not confess the testimony of the Cross . . . neither resurrection nor judgment": Docetic Gnosticism was based upon the assumption, quite alien to the genius of the Bible, that material existence is the enemy of God. This assumption condemned the Christian doctrine of the Cross, because by definition the Divine could not have genuine contact with the man Jesus, who suffered in a body of flesh and blood. Similarly, Gnosticism condemned the Biblical doctrines of the General Resurrection and Last Judgment, because it was felt that the divine triumph could only take place in some celestial sphere, and certainly not within the confines of this lower material world, which by definition could have no part in the purposes of the supreme God.

"Let us turn unto the word which was delivered us from the beginning": Polycarp quite correctly affirms that these Gnostic doctrines were semipagan importations into the original and authentic Biblical "faith once committed to the saints," which spoke very plainly of God's saving action in the material world.

"Sober unto prayer": 1 Peter iv, 7.

"Bring us not into temptation": S. Matthew vi, 13.

"The spirit indeed is willing": S. Matthew xxvi, 41.

8. "Took up our sins in His own body upon the tree": 1 Peter ii, 22-4.

"For our sakes He endured all things, that we might live in Him. Let us therefore become imitators of His endurance." Some have felt that Polycarp quotes evangelical texts without really entering into their meaning. We would hesitate to accept this adverse judgment. He makes his own one of the greatest of New Testament passages on the Cross, and then says that the Christian is to "live in Him." This surely means that to be a Christian consists in self-identification with Christ in His victorious struggle with sin upon the Cross, and in His Resurrection victory. To "become imitators of His endurance" is much more than to seek bravely to follow the example of His heroism. It is to walk through suffering in company with a victorious Lord.

9. "Zosimus and Rufus": We are given the names of two other of the party of martyrs.

"Ran not in vain": Philippians ii, 16. The Philippians' own Epistle is here quoted. The slightness of the quotation warns us to beware of arguments from silence, in deciding what books were known to different writers. One would have presumed that had S. Polycarp wished to quote the Epistle to the Philippians to the Church to which it was originally addressed, he would have taken pleasure in doing so very pointedly, as S. Clement does when writing to the Corinthians (Ep. to Corinthians, 47). In fact Polycarp barely quotes Philippians, and yet shows that he knows it.

"Loved not the present world": 2 Timothy iv, 10.

10. Note: We now come to the part of the Epistle which is preserved only in the Latin.

"Being firm in the faith and immovable": 1 Corinthians xv, 58.

"In love of the brotherhood": 1 Peter ii, 17.

"Forestalling one another in the gentleness of the Lord": Romans xii, 10.

"When ye are able to do good": Proverbs iii, 28.

"Pitifulness delivereth from death": Tobit iv, 10.

"Be all subject one to another": 1 Peter v, 5.

"Having your conversation": 1 Peter, ii. 12

"Woe to him": Isaiah lii, 5; compare Ignatius, Epistle to Trallians, 8.

11. "Valens": It would appear from the nature of the warning given that Valens and his wife had fallen into some act of dishonesty, and that he had been removed from the office of presbyter.

"Covetousness . . . he shall be defiled by idolatry": Compare Colossians iii, 5.

"Know not the judgment of the Lord": Jeremiah v, 4.

"Nay, know we not, that the saints shall judge the world": 1 Corinthians, vi, 2.

"Who were his letters": Compare 2 Corinthians iii, 2.

"For he boasteth of you in the churches": 2 Thessalonians i, 4.

"Hold not such as enemies": 2 Thessalonians iii, 15.

12. "In the sacred writings"; *in sacris literis* (Lightfoot, p. 172): This phrase could well include the Apostolic writings and Gospels, as well as the Old Testament Scripture.

"Be ye angry and sin not": Psalm iv, 4.

"Let not the sun set on your wrath": Ephesians iv, 26. The interesting question is: Does Polycarp intend to include Ephesians as well as Psalms as "in these scriptures"? *his scripturis* (Lightfoot, p. 173). At this time the Apostolic writings were venerated as a spiritual authority, but not looked upon as "Scripture" in the proper sense of the word.

"The God and Father of our Lord Jesus Christ": We have here the typical Pauline title for God the Father; see Romans xv, 6; 2 Corinthians i, 3; xi, 31; Ephesians i, 3.

"The eternal High-priest . . . Jesus Christ": And fittingly to match the above we have the doctrine of the Person of Christ characteristic of Hebrews (v, 5, etc.).

"Faith and truth": This is the confession of the distinctive Christian doctrine of God in Christ, alluded to above. This confession is to bear fruit in "all gentleness . . . etc."

"That raised Him from the dead": Galatians i, 1.

"Pray for all the saints": Ephesians vi, 18.

"Pray also for kings": 1 Timothy ii, 2. The Church, though persecuted, is loyal to the imperial government (cf. Rom. xiii, 1–7).

"For them that persecute you": S. Matthew v, 44.

"Enemies of the cross": Philippians iii, 18. See note on Chapter 9.

"Manifest among all men": 1 Timothy iv, 15.

13. "We see from this chapter that the Philippian Christians had asked S. Polycarp to see to the forwarding to Antioch of their own

letter of greeting. See Introduction, p. 106, and Ignatius, Epistle to Philadelphians, 10, with note, p. 136.

"The letters of Ignatius . . . we send to you": We observe that Polycarp himself made the first collection of copies of these precious writings. It is no accident that they were valued and preserved in the Church.

"If ye have any sure tidings, certify us": Polycarp, therefore, has not had a full report of what had happened at the martyrdom of his late guest. This dates the Epistle of Polycarp very shortly after the Ignatian Epistles, about A.D. 107.

14. "His sister": That is, his wife, being a Christian (cf. 1 Cor. ix, 5).

5. The Epistle of the Smyrnaeans on the Martyrdom of S. Polycarp

From the ancient Church come many "Acts" of the Martyrs, some of which are most moving reading. These accounts of the confessions, the tortures, and the deaths of these heroic witnesses often open to us invaluable insight into the Christian devotion and spiritual experience of early believers. This is a side of Christianity not always adequately represented in the theological and hortatory works of the Fathers. The existence of these "Martyrdoms" therefore enables us to form a more balanced judgment as to what it meant to be a Christian disciple, in the view of the early Christians. These books also sometimes record important historical information. The student will not be surprised to find that, human nature being what it is, these "Acts" are often marred by a tendency to expatiate upon gory details of physical tortures. Nor is it surprising to find, in view of the mentality of the times, that stories of prodigies were multiplied and improved upon, in recounting the deaths of the heroes and heroines of the Faith. The ancient world was as anxious to see the miraculous hand of God in unusual and remarkable events as we are to explain things away in terms of natural causes! The Epistle of the Church of the Smyrnaeans on the martyrdom of their aged Bishop Polycarp is the earliest, and one of the most valuable, of these "Acts" of the Martyrs. It tells a magnificent story magnificently, and is furthermore notably restrained regarding gory details and wonder stories. As we read sympathetically, we may gain a real view of the hope by which the Christians lived during some of the most formative days of the Church.

Many "Acts" of ancient martyrs are spurious or interpolated, and therefore it is natural that there should have been much discussion of the authenticity of the present document. Reliable critics, however, regard it as genuine beyond dispute, apart perhaps from one or two small added touches of the miraculous in the story. The Epistle of the Gallican Churches regarding the persecution there,[1] which was written about A.D. 177, and also the writer Lucian (c. A.D. 165) both seem to echo its language. This is evidence that it was extant and in circulation at the appropriate time. Furthermore, Eusebius paraphrases nearly the whole of it, stating it to be the earliest story of a martyrdom with which he was acquainted.[2] We may therefore accept the Epistle as a reliable eyewitness account of the scene in the arena, written within perhaps a year of the event.

6. Sources of the Epistle

The authority for the text resides chiefly in five ancient Greek manuscripts, going back to the tenth to thirteenth centuries. Of these, the Moscow MS of the thirteenth century is accounted the most valuable, and has a slightly different ending. However, the extracts found in Eusebius are the earliest authority. There are numerous Latin MSS of a version which goes back to Rufinus' translation of Eusebius (A.D. 403).

7. Commentary on the Martyrdom of S. Polycarp

"Philomelium, and all the brotherhoods of the holy and universal Church"; τῆς ἁγίας καὶ καθολικῆς ἐκκλησίας παροικίαις (Lightfoot, p. 189): The martyrdom of S. Polycarp presumably took place at Smyrna, though we cannot be sure. Possibly the Church at Philomelium has written, in expression of Catholic solidarity, to the Church

---
[1] Recorded in Eusebius, *H.E.*, V, i–iii.
[2] *H.E.*, IV, xv.

at Smyrna for particulars. However, the Epistle was intended for wider and for general circulation (see Chapter 20). In this passage we come for the first time to the fuller traditional title of the Church, "the Holy Catholic Church." Compare Ignatius, Epistle to Smyrnaeans, 8, with note, p. 141.

1. "Those that suffered martyrdom": There were a number of Smyrnaean martyrs at this time, of whom the venerable bishop was chief.

"Who stayed the persecution, having as it were set his seal upon it . . . for he lingered . . . to the end that we too might be imitators of him": The attitude here is clearly that an outbreak of persecution, though the work of wicked men, is by no means the miscarriage of God's plan for the Church, but its consummation. The bishop was preserved that he might give firm leadership until the allotted number of the martyrs had suffered, and then, last of all, he suffered himself. It was then the good pleasure of God to protect His Church, and bring the persecution to an end.

"Martyrdom which is comformable to the Gospel": Compare S. Mark viii, 35. This is the same idea that is so prominent in the Ignatian Epistles. Confessorship and martyrdom are the very principle of discipleship.

"For it is the office of true and steadfast love, not only to desire that oneself be saved, but all the brethren also": Here is indeed an inversion of the world's standard! Love is shown not so much in securing that one's fellows escape the persecution, but that they hold firm, and suffer unto salvation.

"Not looking to that which concerneth ourselves": Philippians ii, 4.

2. "It behoveth us . . . to assign to God the power over all things": So that the martyrdom of Polycarp is not a mark of the limitation of God's ruling power.

"None of them uttered a cry or groan, thus showing to us all that at that hour the martyrs of Christ being tortured were absent from the flesh": It is very hard for modern Christians, without experience, to speak with sympathy of the peculiar psychology of martyrdom (see p. 102). Some Christian men, including some of the greatest bravery, have reacted to ghastly torture in the natural way. Others have at times displayed a fortitude beyond anything which could be expected of the human frame. Presumably such sufferers have been carried out of themselves almost into an ecstasy by the crisis of their heightened faith. Some today would explain this away in psychological terms, and doubtless it has a psychological background, but the ancient Church was surely nearer to the truth in accounting this superhuman heroism a mark of the special grace of God.

"The Lord was standing by and conversing with them": Here is the profoundest truth of the matter. The eye of faith can see that in the suffering and triumph of the Church, which is the Body of Christ, Christ is Himself continuing His own suffering and triumph, and fulfilling the salvation of the world (cf. Col. i, 24).

"Purchasing at the cost of one hour a release from eternal punishment": It is an idle and unsympathetic judgment to see here a doctrine of salvation by human merit, not by divine grace. The fortitude of the martyr is eminently a work of divine grace.

"Which neither ear hath heard": Isaiah lxiv, 4; 1 Corinthians ii, 9.

3. "He verily prevailed against all": The victory of the martyr is not a mere victory of human courage over pain. It is the victory of God over Satan.

"Bade him have pity on his youth": The Roman magistrate was no sadist, though there were doubtless many in the crowd. He saw himself as an upright and humane man carrying out the necessary but most unpleasant duty of ridding the city of those whose perverted and impious worship was felt to be imperilling the very fabric of society, by offending the gods who brought "fortune" to the state.

"Marvelling at the bravery ... of the people of God": Or, as the more cynical would account it, stung to fury by the irrational bravado of Germanicus.

"Away with the atheists": That is, the Christians, who would not take part in the traditional community religion on which the welfare of the city was held to depend.

4. "He it was who had forced himself and some others to come forward of their own free will." It was not unknown in time of persecution for some enthusiasts to bring notice to themselves as Christians, so as to prompt their arrest, and secure the crown of martyrdom.

"Persuaded to swear the oath and to offer incense": That is, to swear the oath adjuring Christ (see Chapter 9) and to burn incense at the altar of the Genius of the Emperor, in token of loyalty.

"We praise not those who deliver themselves up, since the Gospel doth not so teach us": Compare S. Matthew x, 23. Responsible Christian leadership did not encourage would-be victims to court martyrdom, for this was felt to be an impious interference with God's providence. The Christian was to suffer when and in the way that God brought it upon him, not in accordance with his own will. He was to endure by the grace of God, not vaingloriously in the strength of human courage.

5. "The greater part persuaded him to withdraw": It was not felt to be inconsistent with the calling of the martyr to save onself if one honourably could. The Smyrnaean Christians naturally try to protect their venerable bishop, and he accedes, though he is prepared to die.

"He falleth into a trance": To a modern student of psychology nothing would be more natural than that a bishop whose mind was filled with such prayers and such expectations should dream such a dream. To the eye of ancient simple faith, however, it was a revelation vouchsafed from God. Both views are doubtless correct. Actually, however, the sign was not literally fulfilled (15, 16).

6. "The very persons who betrayed him were people of his own household": Compare Psalm xli, 9. The writers of this story were quick to see, and to make the most of, any parallels between the sufferings of S. Polycarp and the passion of his Lord. The first of these is, that he was betrayed by one of his own. Some have supposed that these farms were part of Polycarp's patrimony, he being therefore a man of position and substance, and that these lads were his household slaves (cf. Ignatius, Ep. to Polycarp, 4, with note, p. 143). This may well be so, but one cannot be too definite. If Polycarp were betrayed by someone who was about him there would be the strongest tendency to represent him as part of Polycarp's "household."

"Who chanced to have the very name, being called Herod": The captain of police happened to have a most apt name for one sent to arrest a martyr. We are only sorry, for the story's sake, that it was not Pilate!

7. "On the Friday"; $τῇ$ $παρασκευῇ$ (Lightfoot, p. 191): That is, "on the Preparation," that is, the day before the Jewish Sabbath. It is interesting to find these Gentile Christians describing the day in terms of the Jewish calendar (compare S. John xix, 14). The reason is not

far to seek: they are pointing out a further parallel with the sufferings of Christ.

"As against a robber": S. Matthew xxvi, 55.

"In an upper chamber": This too may be intended as a parallel to the Upper Room of Christ's Supper.

"The will of God be done": Acts xxi, 14.

"He stood up and prayed": Christian prayer was at this time offered standing, in the Jewish manner. We have little information as to what sort of prayer would be offered by a Christian of this period on a more or less private occasion, and how far it would be extemporaneous. Most probably it would largely be based on Scriptural and synagogue models. An example of an extended prayer of the early period may be found in Clement, Epistle to Corinthians, 58–61.

8. "All the universal Church throughout the world"; πάσης τῆς κατὰ τὴν οἰκουμένην καθολικῆς ἐκκλησίας (Lightfoot, p. 192).

"They seated him on an ass": This would be the most natural and utilitarian thing to do, but to the eye of faith another "sign."

"It being a high Sabbath": This day would not be of religious significance to the magistrate, or the Smyrnaean population, or directly to the Christians. It is not quite clear why this should be mentioned, but possibly it reflects the idea that the old Sabbath was a "type" of the Christian's rest, to which Polycarp was going (compare Heb. iv, 3–10). Incidentally, the circumstance that the day was a Sabbath does not seem to have prevented the Jews from being active in the arena (Chapter 13). It is, however, likely that the Christian writers exaggerated the part played in the execution by the Jews.

"What harm is there in saying, Caesar is Lord (Κύριος Καῖσαρ) [Lightfoot, p. 192], and offering incense?": Here in a single phrase is the tragic impasse of the Christian in a pagan world. To the Roman constable the formula suggested was an ordinary declaration of civic allegiance and citizenship. To Polycarp it was an impious parallel to the first Christian creed, "Jesus Christ is Lord" (compare Phil. ii, 11), followed by idolatry.

"He bruised his shin, as he got down from the carriage": This is the sort of unobtrusive detail which speaks of a first-hand eyewitness account, not a pious reconstruction.

9. "Be strong, Polycarp, and play the man": It is an excess of scepticism to say that this voice is a later pious fiction, simply because we do not understand the psychology of such occurrences!

"The proconsul enquired whether he were the man": We here have a much abbreviated account of the normal Roman proceedings of a legal trial before the proconsul, or Roman magistrate. Again the humane purpose of the proceedings is to secure the welfare of the state by obtaining the repentance of Christians. They are not seeking victims to sate their cruelty, as sometimes happened when the mob got out of hand.

"Swear by the genius of Caesar": That is, by the presiding spirit of the imperial family, considered as the embodiment of the state.

"Away with the atheists": The Roman administration in general was tolerant, and respected the traditional forms of worship offered to all recognized national, tribal, and city gods, so long as the citizens in question would profess the Roman allegiance in due form. This attitude was natural in a world where it was universally and deeply felt that the due propitiation of local divinities was essential if the respective provinces and cities were to enjoy good fortune, good harvest, freedom from plague and calamity, and the like. The Jews were a "hard case" before this law, because they unaccountably refused to give respect to any worship other than their own. However, their own religion did just pass muster as a legal religion, for it was ancient and associated with a recognizable national group. The tragedy of Christianity was that it did not fit in anywhere to the conventional pattern. It was new. It was exclusive. It appeared in the guise of a secret society engaged in most improperly drawing people away from their ancestral cults, to the great detriment of the state. Therefore the natural and conventional judgment was that Christians were "atheists" and "haters of the human race." The populace did not understand Christianity, and therefore hastened to believe the worst about it, but they dimly sensed that it was a revolutionary movement, and in this they were right. To confirm these suspicions, the Christians refused to take the ordinary oath of allegiance to Caesar! What could be more natural than persecution? Even today, and in countries with a long tradition of civil liberty and religious tolerance, most people find it hard to extend toleration to groups which actively express opinions which are directly subversive to the whole conventional basis of society.

"Looked upon the whole multitude of lawless heathen": And made one of the famous answers of Christian history.

"Forescore and six years have I been His servant": Many have viewed this even more memorable saying as the first evidence for the custom of Infant Baptism in the Church. S. Polycarp says that he has been a Christian for eighty-six years. The question is, Does this presuppose that he had been baptized eighty-six years previously? In this case he must surely have been an infant, or at least a young child. It would not appear that we have evidence sufficient for any certain judgment. On the one hand, it would be quite foreign to the thought and usage of the ancient Church to allow that one could be in any proper sense of the word a Christian without Baptism. On the other, it is difficult definitely to exclude the possibility that Polycarp is speaking less precisely than this, and that he is only saying that he has been "a servant of Christ" all his life in the more general sense that he was brought up as a Christian in a Christian home. Nothing may be intended either way as to when he was baptized. After all Polycarp was making his confession before a persecuting tribunal, not appearing before a catechism class!

10. "The proconsul said, 'Prevail upon the people' ": The magistrate has the law to administer, and must do his duty, but the incentive for the persecution is clearly with the brutal and ignorant mob. What makes it hard for the magistrate to give reasonable treatment to the venerable bishop is the necessity of quieting the multitude. Possibly the writers see here a parallel to the case of Christ.

"We have been taught to render, as is meet, to princes and authorities appointed by God such honour as does us no harm": The Christians accept the doctrine that Caesar's government exists by divine providence, and that it is the duty of a Christian to be a loyal and dutiful subject (Rom. xiii, 1–7; 1 Pet. ii, 13–17).

12. "Polycarp hath confessed himself to be a Christian": It was not always clear whether the Christians suffered for "the Name," that is, for being Christians, or on account of the "crimes" which they were supposed as Christians to have committed. Naturally the former was the greater glory (1 Pet. iv, 12–16). It appears that Polycarp suffered for "the Name."

"Asiarch": The particular local title of the Roman magistrate, compare Acts xix, 31.

"Since he had brought the sports to a close": The gladiatorial so-called "Games" were held in honour of some event or anniversary, and while they were going on, criminals condemned to die might be used as the victims. At other times criminals would be given a normal civic execution, and this is what is now to happen.

13. "The crowds forthwith collecting": The enthusiasm for this shocking business was clearly with the mob. We surmise that the magistrates and police are not finding it easy to keep order. One reason for judicial executions was to forestall or prevent lynchings of Christians.

"The Jews more especially assisting in this with zeal, as is their wont": See also 17, 18. This is not necessarily a fair comment upon the situation, being made by critics hostile to the Jews. Undoubtedly there were occasions when the Jews instigated persecution of the Christians, and there were two very natural reasons for this, based upon the Jews' own position as an unpopular and defenceless minority. The first was to provide a scapegoat alternative to themselves, so that when the mob was working up to a pogrom its fury might expend itself in another direction. The second was to show to the mob that they themselves had no connection with the still more unpopular Christians. However, this most unhappy relationship between Jews and Christians did not always obtain. Thus at very much the same period S. Justin Martyr at Ephesus wrote his *Dialogue with Trypho* on the basis that courteous scholarly controversy could exist between Jew and Christian, and that one may hope to win Jews to Christianity by reasonable argument.

14. "O Lord God Almighty": We cannot too readily presume that this noble prayer gives the actual words used by S. Polycarp on this occasion, in view of the custom of ancient historians to compose speeches to put into the mouth of their characters on significant occasions. We may have a memory of the actual words used, or perhaps, what is just as interesting, the Church's view of what was a suitable and representative prayer for this occasion. The two salient theological points of the Martyr's prayer are: (i) His suffering is a continuation of the redeeming sufferings of Christ, as He suffers and triumphs in His Body, the Church ("a rich and acceptable sacrifice, as Thou didst prepare and reveal it beforehand"), and (ii) Polycarp's death works his immediate admission to the Church in heaven, as it triumphs over evil through these sufferings ("the whole race of the righteous, who live in Thy presence . . . that I might receive a portion among the number of martyrs").

"The cup of Christ": Our Lord's own metaphor for martyrdom. Compare S. Mark x, 38–9; S. Matthew xxvi, 39, 42.

"Unto resurrection of eternal life": S. John v, 29.

"Both of soul and of body, in the incorruptibility (ἐν ἀφθαρσίᾳ) [Lightfoot, p. 195] of the Holy Spirit": Greek theologians of a later period, who in their thinking were less exclusively Biblical, and who were in part moulded by the presuppositions of Greek philosophical thought, frequently and characteristically use the word "incorruptibility" of Christian salvation. The term answers to the notion that "spirit" is a sort of celestial essence derived from the being of the unchanging and incorruptible God, which was brought down to earth by the "initial contact" of our Lord's Incarnation, and was thence diffused into the body of believers. Man's salvation, therefore, is a change of metaphysical substance rather than of moral will, whereby he is rendered capable of surviving the dissolution of death. However, "incorruptibility" is also a New Testament word, and was used by S. Paul in 1 Corinthians xv, 42, 50, 52–4. It is here an expression for the traditional Jewish expectation of the resurrection of the body, with the added connotation that the resurrection-body is no mere resuscitated body of frail flesh and blood, but a glorified resurrection-body like our Lord's, appropriate to the Kingdom's triumph. We prefer to think that Polycarp uses the word "incorruptibility" in this early, Biblical, and less philosophical sense, speaking as he here is of the resurrection of the body.

15. "We saw a marvel": Compared to what is found in this class of literature as a whole, here is a relatively restrained prodigy for the accompaniment of the death of a holy martyr. The whole question is a difficult one for the modern mind. The simple unreflecting attitude that "miracles do not happen, and therefore any story containing a miracle must be a legend" will hardly commend itself to the thoughtful Christian mind. It involves the unspoken assumption that there is no God in control of the processes of "natural law," and that things cannot happen in the realm of nature which are startlingly and significantly outside our normal expectation and understanding. At the same time, while we discount the anti-supernaturalistic bias of the modern mind, we have to take account of the pro-supernaturalistic bias of ancient piety. We cannot doubt that there are many events in sacred history recorded in terms of sheer miracle which, if they could have been seen by a modern critical observer, would have been described as very remarkable but quite "natural" occurrences, because of the difference in the eye of the beholder and his manner of expression. But this does not involve that the remarkable event did not happen, or that it was not remarkable in spiritual significance. Then in addition there is the undoubted tendency of "wonder stories" to grow in the telling. However, we do not have here a long-accumulating and frankly unhistorical pious legend. It is an eyewitness account, and a substantially sober narrative. We can never know exactly what happened, and why it proved impossible to burn S. Polycarp alive, but it would seem that there was some unusual occurrence, which the faithful delighted to describe as a sign worked by God. Perhaps the language they used is partly inspired by such Scriptures as Isaiah lxiii, 2, and Daniel iii, 25–7.

"A loaf in the oven": These odd words are usually considered to be an interpolation.

16. "A dove and": These words are also usually considered to be an addition to the original account, possibly made in the fifth century *Life of Polycarp* falsely ascribed to Pionius (see p. 177). The symbolism, however, is manifest. The dove is the sign of the Holy Spirit, Who had rested in so eminent a manner upon the Martyr (compare S. Luke iii, 22).

"A quantity of blood, so that it extinguished the fire": Clearly this event is recounted as a prodigy, and, if any such event actually took place, it must have grown in the telling. Possibly the fuel would not burn up rapidly, which would give a reason why the magistrate in mercy ordered the lingering Polycarp to be killed, and possibly blood then extinguished a relatively small fire. But this is to look upon all with the critical eye of barely suppressed unbelief in the supernatural. The Church at Smyrna was in a more devout mood!

"An apostolic and prophetic teacher in our own time": The Church had not yet got used to thinking of its history in terms of centuries. Time was felt to be moving speedily toward the Second Coming. Already the first heroic and Apostolic generation was relatively speaking a long way away, and was an elect company in an age of its own. It was therefore accounted a matter of congratulation that the Church of a more mundane age should have produced a figure to be compared to the Apostles.

17. "Managed that not even his poor body should be taken away by us": For a note on Christian sentiment in this matter, see Ignatius, Epistle to Romans 4, p. 130.

"When we were about to take it from the fire": It must have taken no little courage to show this measure of public sympathy with the Christian cause, after such persecution, and before such an audience. It shows also that the representatives of the Christians were protected to some extent in their task by the general public feeling that the bodies even of the criminal dead should be duly disposed of.

"For Him, being the Son of God, we adore, but the martyrs as disciples": Great as was the admiration of the Church for the saints, the Smyrnaeans utterly disown any devotion which would take away from those divine honours to be paid to the Saviour. They can never forsake Him for other heroes.

18. "Burnt him after their custom": The Greeks practised both burial and cremation for the disposal of the dead. Though cremation was not banned in the ancient Church, in general the Christians followed the Jewish custom of burial.

"And so we afterwards took up his bones which are more valuable than precious stones . . . to celebrate the birth-day of his martyrdom": Here we see the natural and humble beginnings of a number of customs which later became a prominent part of Christian devotion. We have: (i) veneration of the relics of a Saint; (ii) a Eucharist on the anniversary of his martyrdom, which is the origin of a saint's day;[1] (iii) the Eucharist is celebrated, where possible, upon the site of the martyrdom, or the grave of the martyr. When in later times the Christians could build public churches, they did so on these traditional sites. This is the origin of the dedication of a church to a patron saint.

"For the commemoration of those that have already fought in the contest, and for the training and preparation of those that shall do so hereafter": These aspects of Christian worship were from the beginning especially associated with the doctrine of the fellowship of the Church Militant here on earth with the Church Triumphant.

[1] Compare Tertullian, *de Corona*, 3.

19. "It was after the pattern of the Gospel of Christ": The most fitting epitaph for a great man.

"He rejoiceth in company with the Apostles": Again we have the strong sense of the Communion of Saints.

20. "Marcianus": He is the bearer of the Epistle, and witness to its authenticity. Euarestus is the scribe, writing on behalf of the Church of Smyrna.

"Send the letter . . . to the brethren which are farther off": Thus from the beginning it was the intention that such Epistles should be circulated and copied.

"Who maketh election from His own servants": God chooses some of His servants for the honour of martyrdom.

21. This date, calculated in the Greek and also in the Roman manner, is February 23rd. The year is unfortunately not stated, but must be about A.D. 155 or 156, which would agree with the data given.

"To whom be the glory": This is the same doxology as occurs at the end of 1 Clement 63. It may have been copied, or may have been a conventional ending.

22. "We bid you God speed . . . kingdom of Jesus Christ": This greeting is a manifest addition to the work as originally written, and is omitted by the Moscow MS and the Latin.

"This account Gaius copied": We have an interesting account of the successive copyings of the Epistle, from S. Irenaeus to Gaius, to Socrates, and finally to Pionius. A man named Pionius who was a devotee of S. Polycarp is known to have been martyred under Decius (A.D. 250), and he may be the same. There is a fifth century *Life of Polycarp*, incorporating this Epistle, and full of wonder stories, which falsely claims to be by the martyr Pionius.

The Moscow MS has a fuller account of the descent of the Epistle, replenished with details about Polycarp drawn from the writings of S. Irenaeus.

VI Homilies and Hortatory Literature

i. The Second Epistle of S. Clement and the Epistle of Barnabas

1. Introduction

Included among the writings of the Apostolic Fathers are three works given to ethical and devotional exhortation, largely upon the basis of an exposition of Scripture. In them we find, if not actual sermons, at least echoes of the material and the approach of the common Christian preaching of the second century. Here we are introduced to a leading difference between this literature and the Epistles of S. Clement, S. Ignatius, and S. Polycarp. The Epistles are the work of outstanding personalities, of differing gifts indeed, but all alike great men. By contrast, we venture the judgment that this hortatory literature represents the common Christian preaching of the time. The Christians of the period were mostly folk of humble rank and little education, meeting in an obscure room in the lower quarters of the town. They counted in their number a few outstanding leaders, but for the more part they were, as S. Paul himself observed, "not many wise, not many mighty." Furthermore, the Christians of the post-Apostolic period had no great incentive to write. Their own practical needs in Gospel preaching were met, and more than met, in the Apostolic writings they already possessed, which we now call the New Testament Scripture. They had no great interest in writing historical records for posterity, because for the more part they expected the Second Advent of Christ, and the end of history, to take place within a relatively short time. They could not know how interested we would be in their activities in the development of the Church! Furthermore, the intellectual task of conquering for Christ the culture and learning of the day had hardly swum into their ken, though this phase was soon to come. For a variety of reasons, therefore, the Church of this period was neither a Church richly endowed with genius, nor a writing Church. The student must therefore be prepared to find that the literature we are now to study often moves at a disappointingly commonplace level.

That it is largely commonplace by no means involves, however, that it is either unimportant or uninteresting. If it is valuable to know something of the mind of a Paul or an Ignatius, it is at least as important for the understanding of the Church and the Christian life to know something of the mind of the more ordinary people, in their thousands. This is also more difficult to find out, for in every phase of history the few exceptional people are apt to be more vocal than the undistinguished multitude. It is most revealing to us to discover that that which to us seems second-rate was highly valued in the primitive Church. If the history of thought represents the difficult attempt to step into the mind of another age, here we have valuable material. The discovery that that which to us seems uninteresting was then found very interesting is itself important evidence! It is significant that no one in the ancient Church thought of the writings of S. Ignatius or the Acts of S. Polycarp as suitable candidates for inclusion in the canon of New Testament Scripture, even though these men were greatly revered as Saints of the Church. By contrast, the Epistle of Barnabas and *The Shepherd* of Hermas were apparently two of the strongest among the finally unsuccessful candidates. Many responsible figures in the Church thought of them almost as Scripture. We would prefer Ignatius or Polycarp, while most modern readers will be devoutly thankful that Barnabas and Hermas are not in the Bible! It is important for us to consider why many in the first days of Christianity showed a different preference.

In our general introduction to the Apostolic Fathers we have already approached the problem of the alleged decline in spirituality of the post-Apostolic Church (see pp. 9–16). Many have felt that Christian Phariseeism swiftly invaded the Catholic Church, so that the authentic and Pauline principle of salvation by divine grace was increasingly lost in Christian "legality." This charge is in part answered, we feel, by the affirmation that the more extreme statements of S. Paul are not the sole and sufficient guide in the matter of grace, and in part by the observation that to force typical post-Reformation issues upon the ancient Fathers savours of theological anachronism. In part, however, the charge has to be candidly admitted. There is some force in the case that in the period after the New Testament there was a certain decline of spirituality in some quarters, and that not all writers show the clearest understanding of "the pure word of general grace." That some have overstated this case does not require that defenders of the integrity of the piety and doctrine of the ancient Catholic Church should seek to maintain that there is no case to state, along this line.

Not all the Christians of this second period of the Church were heroes like Polycarp, accomplished theologians like Ignatius, or judicious ecclesiastical statesmen like Clement! As today, there were many well-intentioned folk, faithful according to their light, but whose light was rather dim. The Church therefore did not march forward from victory unto victory with even tread, nor did her Lord ever promise that she should. After the first creative Apostolic period the Church, as it were, paused for breath. Some would even say her footsteps faltered a little. Then she rallied her powers, or the Lord rallied them in her, and she marched on. That this was possible was the true fulfillment of the promise to the Church. In the period of which we write, the institutions and discipline of the Church were being rapidly developed, but in the main it was not a time of penetrating thought on spiritual or theological issues. And it is in this hortatory literature, answering as it does so largely to the failings and needs, the hopes and fears, of the more commonplace class of Christian disciple, that any symptom of faltering spiritual footsteps is likely to be diagnosed. We see then a reason why somewhat second-rate books like Barnabas and Hermas were so widely and deeply reverenced. They met a clamant need—not the highest need of the human spirit, perhaps, but a common and pressing need. And if Christianity is to be truly "catholic" it has to cater for the lower levels of the spiritual life as well as the higher, yet without confusing the two. So often the just rebuke of the Master is: "This ye ought to have done, and not to have left the other undone."

2. The So-Called Second Epistle of S. Clement to the Corinthians

This work has been traditionally ascribed to S. Clement because it follows immediately after the genuine Epistle in all three of the MS sources, and is here apparently ascribed to him. The internal evidence of style and content, however, lead critical scholars to a confident judgment that this is a later work, by a different and unknown author. The allusions to the Games, in the manner of S. Paul writing to the Corinthians (1 Corinthians ix, 24–7), in Chapter 7 may provide an indication that this work was addressed to Corinth, and might explain its association with the genuine Epistle. However, this is not an epistle, but a sermon, as is indicated by echoes of the spoken address in Chapters 19 and 20: "Therefore, brothers and sisters . . ." Lightfoot dates this work about A.D. 120–140, which would make it the earliest Christian homily extant. It was known and quoted by the Fathers of the fourth century, but not stated by them to be by S. Clement. It is chiefly a moral discourse, being a call to repentance, love, and good works, of a lofty tone but a rather tedious and repetitive character. There are a considerable number of quotations both from the Old and New Testaments, and some from apocryphal writings.

3. Commentary on the Homily

1. "We ought not to think mean things ($\mu\iota\kappa\rho\grave{\alpha}$ $\phi\rho o\nu\epsilon\hat{\iota}\nu$ ['small things,' 'unworthy things,' Lightfoot, p. 43]) of our Salvation": It is most noteworthy that this moral homily starts with a firm doctrinal statement. It is manifestly not the work of an active, constructive mind like Ignatius, and the statement is bare and very simple. Nevertheless, the substance is there. Jesus Christ is affirmed to be a divine Saviour, and the Judge of all: "we ought to think of Jesus Christ, as of God, as of the Judge of quick and dead." Man was helpless in sin, and his salvation is by divine grace: "we had no hope of salvation, save that which came from Him. . . . What recompense then shall be given unto Him? or what fruit worthy of His own gift to us? And how many mercies do we owe to Him!" This unmerited and unmeritable salvation was the work of divine mercy: "For He had mercy on us, and in His compassion saved us"; and was accomplished by the divine sufferings and death: "how many things Christ endured to suffer for our sake." There are admittedly passages in this discourse which, if taken in isolation, present a somewhat bare moralism. It is not fair to the sense of the homilist to take them thus in isolation. His present emphasis is moral exhortation to good works, but he understands the gospel of salvation, and it is always there in the background. The beginning of

Christianity is to have an adequate Creed, and not "to think unworthy things" of Christ.

"We who were blinded in our understanding, and worshipped stocks and stones": Compare Romans i, 21–3. The New Testament writers are aware that they have been saved from the self-righteousness of exclusive moral Phariseeism. This Gentile preacher is aware that he and his brethren have been saved from the gross superstition and uncleanness of pagan idolatry. S. Paul could say to his Corinthian converts, "And such were some of you" (1 Cor. vi, 11). This writer, perhaps in the same community, would have said, "And such were some of *us*."

2. "Rejoice, thou barren that bearest not": Isaiah liv, 1.

"For our Church was barren . . . Our people seemed desolate and forsaken": The sense here is not absolutely plain because the speaker's mind moves between two ideas, both of which are natural to a Gentile Christian. He is familiar with the doctrine that the Church is the New and True Israel of God, so that the true Israelites of old were the spiritual ancestors of the Gentile Christians (Chap. 13). Nevertheless, he cannot forget that under the Old Covenant the race to which he belonged was entirely outside the promises of God, so that the prophecy just quoted comes with special force to him. When for the first time he says "our Church" ($\dot{\epsilon}\kappa\kappa\lambda\eta\sigma\acute{\iota}\alpha$, Lightfoot, p. 44), he is probably thinking chiefly of Israel, which before the coming of Christ had not received the power to convert the Gentiles to herself. When for the second time he says "our people" ($\lambda\alpha\grave{o}s$, Lightfoot, p. 44), the word used by the Greek Bible for the ancient People of God is employed, so this thought is still close to hand. However, the contrast is made that "we have become more than those who seemed to have God." The Gentile Church has now outgrown not only the Jewish Christian community, but the whole Jewish nation. This would make "our people" the former pagan ancestors of the preacher and his congregation.

"I came not to call the righteous, but sinners": S. Matthew ix, 13; S. Mark ii, 17.

"So also Christ willed to save the things which were perishing": Here again is the doctrine of salvation by divine grace.

"And He saved many" ($\H{\epsilon}\sigma\omega\sigma\epsilon\nu\ \pi o\lambda\lambda o\acute{\upsilon}s$, Lightfoot, p. 44): This may quite possibly be an echo of our Lord's words "a ransom for many" (S. Mark x, 45), which again is usually considered to be our Lord's own echo of Isaiah liii, 11–12.

3. "First of all, that we, who are living, do not sacrifice to these dead gods": The fitting and necessary human response to divine grace made known in Christ is confession of Christian discipleship, and the first great mark of this discipleship is the avoidance of idolatry. The less stable and understanding members of a Gentile Church needed constantly to be reminded, as Jewish Christians did not, that the "gods many and lords many" which were worshipped all round them did not really exist (cf. 1 Cor. viii, 5, 6). It was hard not to feel the pull of the subconscious group mind, steeped in idolatry from time immemorial. To make it harder, if the dreadful prospect of persecution opened, the one avenue of safety was a relatively small and simple compromise with idolatry, to swear "by the genius of Caesar" (cf. *Martyrdom of S. Polycarp*, 9). Avoidance of idolatry was thus a very important matter, and is given pride of place. The sanction introduced here is a simple one. Heirs of eternal life do not worship dead gods.

"Whoso confesseth Me, Him will I confess before the Father": S. Matthew x, 32; S. Luke xii, 8. These words of our Lord had a very pointed application to a Gentile Church living in a pagan city. They were referred to the matter of idolatry, which could be literally "a matter of life and death."

"Honour Him with our lips": S. Mark vii, 12; xii, 20.

"This people honoureth Me with their lips": Isaiah xxix, 13.

4. "Not every one that saith unto me, Lord": S. Matthew vii, 21.

"Let us confess Him in our works": The second great mark of discipleship is the living of a righteous life, preserving the spirit of brotherhood in the Church.

"The Lord said, Though ye be gathered together with me in my bosom": It is not known whence this quotation comes, but presumably it is from some apocryphal Gospel purporting to contain "words of the Lord."

5. "For the Lord saith, Ye shall be as lambs . . . into the gehenna of fire": This again is presumably a quotation from an apocryphal Gospel, perhaps the same as that cited above. The quotations are typical of those ascribed to Christ in the known apocryphal Gospels, being recognizable authentic words of Jesus which have been worked

over and "improved upon" by the less discriminating among the ancient Christians.

6. "No servant can serve two masters": S. Matthew vi, 24.

"For what advantage is it": S. Matthew xvi, 26; S. Mark viii, 36; S. Luke xvi, 13.

"Now this age and the future (οὗτος ὁ αἰὼν καὶ ὁ μέλλων) [Lightfoot, p. 45] are two enemies": We have here a genuine passage of original Hebraic Christianity, with the contest between good and evil portrayed as the contrast between the present evil age when Satan rules, and the promised age of God's Kingdom.

"And the scripture also saith in Ezekiel": Ezekiel xiv, 14, 18. We have here a very good example of primitive Christian usage, of the time before the Apostolic writings were regarded as canonical Scripture. The Epistles are quoted with no solemn introductory formula. They are authoritative because they are the substitute for the personal presence in the Church of an Apostle. The words of Christ from the Gospels are commonly introduced with such a formula as "the Lord saith." They are a higher authority than the Apostles, being the personal voice of God through His incarnate Son. And when we come to an Old Testament quotation, it is introduced solemnly as "Scripture." This is the continuation in the Church of the original Jewish tradition. An Old Testament text is fully authoritative in a somewhat different way: it is canonical Scripture cited from a holy and venerable book. It has not yet been discussed in the Church which of these three authorities is to be preferred in case of an apparent discrepancy. It is taken with the confidence of an unspoken assumption that they are bound to be at one, all alike being parts of the revelation of God.

"We cannot therefore be friends of the two": Compare S. James iv, 4.

"With what confidence shall we, if we keep not our baptism pure and undefiled, enter into the kingdom of God?": The doctrine of the two Ages brings the homilist to consider the beginning and the end of the Christian life. Answering to the grace of God's purpose, and the initiative of His grace in providing the saving work of Christ (Chap. 1), there is Holy Baptism, which admits the believer pure and undefiled into the Church. It is the Christian conviction that this has washed away the guilt of previous sin. This is what God has first done for man. Yet man has much to do in response to God's initiative (Chaps. 3, 4).

He must use the grace given, and live in accordance with his Baptism. It was indeed a widespread opinion in the Church, in its early and rigorous days, that grievous sin after Baptism could not be forgiven, or at least, that this was almost impossible (cf. Heb. vi, 4–6, and *The Shepherd*, Precept iv, 3, with note, pp. 237–8). The present homilist does not say anything explicit on this point.

"Or who shall be our Advocate ($παράκλητος$) [Lightfoot, p. 46], unless we be found having holy and righteous works?" Christ is the Advocate, who by dissolving the guilt and breaking the power of sin has opened the door for man to come to God (1 John ii, 1, 2). This is the believer's first acceptance by God, freely, by His act of grace. But there is no such free acceptance at the last. In the coming Age of God, which brings the Judgment, those are accepted who have used the grace of God to bring forth the fruits of a righteous character. By what they are and have done they stand or fall (S. Matthew vii, 22, 23; xxv, 31–46). The work of Christ will in that day be of no assistance to careless and compromised Christians, who have long trifled with the offered grace of God. Much acrimonious discussion in the later Church about "faith and works" would have been saved if this distinction between man's first and last acceptance by God had always been clearly kept in mind, the first "by faith alone," the second by good works, which are the fruit of faith. This ancient writer is not an accomplished theologian, and does not express himself very explicitly, but he understands the heart of the matter.

7. "So then, my brethren, let us contend, knowing that the contest is nigh at hand": It would appear likely that this passage is based upon 1 Corinthians ix, 24–7, and 2 Timothy iv, 7, 8, though we cannot be sure, for the simile is a very natural one. Many have seen this use of 1 Corinthians as an indication that perhaps this homily was addressed to Corinth. This is less certain.

"Them that have not kept the seal": That is, the seal of Holy Baptism.

"Their worm shall not die": Isaiah lxvi, 24.

8. "For we are clay under the craftsman's hand": Compare Jeremiah xviii, 1–6.

"Let us repent with our whole heart": In view of what the homilist says in his opening chapter regarding divine grace, we may reasonably assume that had he been questioned upon this point he would have agreed that man repents in response to the drawing of grace, and not simply by his own resolve.

"For after we have departed out of the world, we can no more make confession there, or repent any more": It is to be agreed that this, the orthodox Christian position, is in agreement with the general tenor of the New Testament, and with our Lord's attitude to sin and judgment. However, it is difficult to substantiate from any explicit text, for Hebrews x, 26–31, is concerned with the impossibility of restoration after apostasy, rather than after death.

"If ye kept not that which is little": Compare S. Matthew xxv, 21; S. Luke xvi, 10–11.

9. "And let not any one of you say that this flesh is not judged, neither riseth again." So little information is given about this heresy that it is difficult to judge precisely what it was. A denial of the bodily resurrection, and of a judgment upon earth, is a denial of the distinctly Hebraic tradition within Christianity. It therefore speaks of an anti-Judaic deviation, under the influence of the presuppositions of Greek thought regarding the antithesis between the material and the spiritual. As Gnosticism was the great example of such a deviation, the doctrine condemned here may be some form of Gnosticism.

"Guard the flesh as a temple of God": Compare 1 Corinthians vi, 19.

"In like manner as ye were called in the flesh, ye shall come also in the flesh": That is to say, man's body is to rise to judgment, and the body is to be saved.

"The Lord who saved us, being first spirit, then became flesh, and so called us": This is not a very theologically expert presentation of the doctrine of the Incarnation, but it suffices to make an important theological point. The great overthrow of Gnostic and Docetic doctrines, which denied that the saving purpose of God extended to the material, is the basic Christian doctrine of the Incarnation. If God united Himself with flesh and blood, He is interested in the salvation of flesh and blood.

"These are My brethren": S. Matthew, xii, 50.

10. "For they know not how great torment": Compare S. Luke xvi, 25.

11. "For the word of prophecy also saith": It is not known whence this strange "prophecy" is quoted. Interestingly enough, it is also cited in Clement, Epistle to Corinthians, 23. (For note, see p. 40.)

"Faithful is he that promised": Hebrews x, 23.

"If therefore we shall have wrought righteousness in the sight of God, we shall enter into His kingdom": Taken in isolation, this sentence admittedly betrays a lack of understanding for the conception of salvation by grace. However, it is not to be taken in isolation.

"Ear hath not heard nor eye seen": 1 Corinthians ii, 9.

12. "Let us therefore await the kingdom . . . since we know not the day of God's appearing." It is to be observed that the "Kingdom of God" here is not the present Kingdom which our Lord announced as brought by His own presence (S. Mark i, 15; S. Luke xvii, 20). It is the expected millennial Kingdom.

"When the two shall be one": It is not known whence this strange "word of the Lord" is derived, but presumably it is from some apocryphal Gospel. It is quite typical of the supposed words of Christ as they are recorded in the known apocryphal Gospels, for these are usually garbled versions of recognizable sayings of Jesus from the canonical Gospels. Thus in the present instance, the phrase "the outside as the inside" may go back to S. Matthew xxiii, 25. The exposition given, as referring to soul and body, would be in a sense an adaptation of our Lord's meaning.

"And by the male with the female, neither male nor female, He meaneth this; that a brother seeing a sister should have no thought of her as of a female": This again may represent a primitive Christian attempt to expound a meaning from our Lord's enigmatic but fascinating saying regarding the coming Kingdom, recorded in S. Mark xii, 25. The "brother" and the "sister" refer to male and female Christians in general. Taken strictly, this passage of the homily would appear to uphold the ascetic standard that celibacy is a higher spiritual state than marriage (cf. 1 Cor. vii, 7-9, 26-35). This construction is not necessary, however, and the intention may be no more than a strongly worded statement that the Christians, who are presumably mostly married, are not to exchange "adulterous" glances at one another (cf. S. Matt. v, 27-9). It is a plea for inward as well as outward chastity. This would be quite in agreement with the context.

13. "Let us desire to please . . . those men that are without, by our righteousness": Compare 1 Peter ii, 12.

"Every way My Name is blasphemed among all the Gentiles": Isaiah lii, 5.

"For the Gentiles, when they heard from our mouth the oracles of God": It is noteworthy that a Gentile Church can speak of the surrounding unbelievers, of the same race as themselves by natural descent, as "Gentiles." This is the doctrine of the Church as "the New Israel."

"For when they hear from us that God saith, It is no thank unto you, if ye love them that love you": S. Luke vi, 32, 35. We notice that the homilist has no hesitation in introducing words of our Lord with the formula "God saith" (cf. Chap. 1). He then takes a somewhat "realistic" view of the level of morality of some professing Christians, and makes a just rebuke to such.

14. "We shall be of the first Church, which is spiritual, which was created before the sun and the moon": This striking saying leads us into the most interesting and valuable theological passage of the homily. We have here a development of the type of thought regarding the Church pioneered in the Epistle to the Ephesians. The Church is much more than a "this-worldly" society, existing for the practical purpose of mutual support and cooperation in living the Christian life. The ideal Church exists from eternity in the mind of God (cf. Eph. i, 4, 5; iii, 5, 6).

"The Church existeth not now for the first time, but hath been from the beginning: for she was spiritual, as our Jesus also was spiritual, but was manifested in the last days": At the appointed time the earthly Church was called into being by God to demonstrate to mankind the nature of the preexistent heavenly Church (Eph. iii, 9–11). This is manifestly a process analogous to the Incarnation of our Lord.

"The living Church is the body of Christ . . . Now the Church, being spiritual, was manifested in the flesh of Christ": The Church, which is the New Israel, found its historical start in the Person of Christ, who was Himself the first Man in the Church. The visible organization of Christians which has grown up from that point is the manifestation in the life of the world of the eternal divine plan, and of the Spirit of Christ. Its growth is an Incarnation-like growth, and the Church is the Body of Christ, "for this flesh is the counterpart and copy of the spirit."

"My house was made a den of robbers": Jeremiah vii, 11. To be of the visible organization does not guarantee that one is of the spiritual Body. This was observed by Jeremiah of the Old Israel. Some Israelites after the flesh were not "Israelites indeed." The homilist's implication is that the same can be sadly true of the New Israel.

"The Church is the body of Christ": 1 Corinthians xii, 27; Ephesians i, 23.

"God made man, male and female": Genesis i, 27.

"The male is Christ and the female is the Church": The divinely ordained union of the first man and first woman is a Scripture-type of the union of the spiritual Christ with His earthly members into the Church, which is His Body (Eph. v, 25–32).

"The Books and the Apostles (τὰ βιβλία καὶ οἱ ἀπόστολοι) [Lightfoot, p. 50] plainly declare": Here we have most plainly displayed the primitive Christian classification of holy books.[1] Two of the three classes of Christian writings are mentioned. There are first the fully authoritative canonical Scriptures, that is, the Hebrew Scriptures. Then there are the writings of the Apostles, which though noncanonical are authoritative in another way: they represent the Apostles, the first witnesses to the facts of the Gospel. These two classes are mentioned here because they are to be regarded as witnessing to the Church, which is the doctrine under discussion. (We have examples, from Genesis and Ephesians, of the kind of Old Testament and New Testament witness to the Church which the homilist has in mind.) Not mentioned in this context is the third class of writing, namely, the record of the words of the Lord Himself. This is another aspect of "the voice of God."

"If any of us guard her [the Church] in the flesh and defile her not, he shall receive her again in the Holy Spirit. . . . No man therefore, when he hath defiled the copy, shall receive the original for his portion": Those, and only those, who as earthly members of the Church have lived conformably to their character as members of the Body of Christ will be found part of the perfect Church, in the day of the outpouring of the Spirit. And this glorious Church of the millennial Kingdom is none other than the supreme manifestation of the original Church, which preexisted in the mind of God. The true Christian will receive both the end and the beginning, for the beginning and the end are the same.

[1] Cf. Ignatius, Ep. to Philadelphians, 8, with note, p. 134.

"This therefore is what He meaneth, brethren; Guard ye the flesh": Presumably this also is intended as a word of the Lord, and is a quotation from some apocryphal Gospel.

"He that hath dealt wantonly with the flesh hath dealt wantonly with the Church. Such an one therefore shall not partake of the spirit, which is Christ": Compare 1 Corinthians vi, 15. Those whose lives defile and scandalize the Church are separated from the true Body of Christ, which is another way of saying that they are separated from Christ.

"The spirit, which is Christ": The homilist has been entrapped into this theologically inexact phrase by his desire to bring out the parallel "flesh" and "spirit" in man, and in the Church.

The homilist has not always been much esteemed as a theologian. However, we have in this chapter the substance of as able a piece of Christian theology as any in the Apostolic Fathers, though it suffers somewhat by the confused order of presentation, and various inexactitudes.

"Those things which the Lord hath prepared": 1 Corinthians ii, 9.

15. "For it is no mean reward": Compare Ezekiel iii, 21.

"Let us therefore abide in the things which we believed, in righteousness and holiness, that we may with boldness ask of God": "To believe" is here largely personal trust, and not acceptance of a body of doctrine.

"Whiles thou art still speaking": Isaiah lviii, 9.

"For this word is the token of a great promise": Answering to faith as trust in God, we come to a passage declaring the grace of God.

"He is more ready to give": Compare S. Matthew vi, 8.

16. "While we still have One that receiveth us": Compare Chapter 6, with note, p. 185.

"If we conquer our soul . . . we shall be partakers of the mercy of Jesus": This is a somewhat legal-sounding phrase. However, it refers to man's acceptance at the Judgment, not his initial forgiveness. See Chapter 6, with note, p. 186.

"As a burning oven": Malachi iv, 1.

"The powers of the heavens shall melt": Isaiah xxxiv, 4.

"Fasting is better than prayer, but almsgiving than both": Compare S. Matthew xxiii, 14, 23.

"Love covereth a multitude of sins": Proverbs x, 12; 1 Peter iv, 8.

"Almsgiving lifteth off the burden of sin": A suspiciously "legal" statement!

17. "How much more is it wrong": Compare 2 Peter ii, 20–22.

"While we are admonished by the presbyters": This leaves us asking: Was there no bishop in this Church, as the chief pastor? Or was the routine pastoral work already completely in the hand of the presbyters, with the bishop behind the scenes as a supervisor?

"But coming hither more frequently": This is clearly in the style of a spoken address in the Christian congregation, and is perhaps the first example on record of the preacher telling his congregation that they ought to come and hear his good advice more regularly!

"I come to gather together all the nations, tribes, and languages. . . . And the unbelievers shall see His glory": Isaiah lxvi, 18.

"He speaketh of the day of His appearing ($τῆς\ ἐπιφανείας\ αὐτοῦ$) [Lightfoot, p. 52] . . . They see the kingdom of the world given to Jesus": Here is the strong Advent hope of the ancient Church (S. Mark xiv, 62; S. John v, 22; 1 Cor. xv, 25; Phil. ii, 11; Rev. xix, 11–16).

"Thou wast, and we knew it not": Compare S. Matthew xxv, 44.

"Their worm shall not die": Isaiah lxvi, 24.

"How that they are punished . . . shall give glory to God": This is not a very gracious or evangelical note, though it has been a common enough theme in Christian preaching (cf. Rev. xviii, 20, 21).

18. "Being an utter sinner and not yet escaped from temptation . . . while I fear the judgment to come": This is perhaps not the highest level of Christian confidence and assurance to which the believer may be admitted,[1] but it has a measure of Scriptural warrant (1 Tim. i, 15; S. Matt. vi, 13; xxiv, 44).

19. "Therefore, brothers and sisters . . . I read to you an exhortation": The spoken style is again manifest here.

"We are darkened in our understanding": Ephesians iv, 18.

"That we may be saved unto the end": Compare S. Matthew x, 22.

"They may endure affliction for a short time": Compare Hebrews xi, 35; xii, 11.

"With the fathers": This may refer to the saints of the Old Covenant, but it may just as well refer to the Apostles and first heroes of the

---

[1] T. F. Torrance, *Grace in the Apostolic Fathers*, p. 132.

Christian faith, who are now far enough away in time to be looked back upon with distant veneration.

20. "We are contending in the lists of a living God": 1 Corinthians ix, 24–7.

"No righteous man hath reaped fruit quickly": Compare James v, 7–8.

4. The Epistle of Barnabas

Character and Purpose of the Epistle

The position of Old Testament Scripture in the Christian system was a matter of great importance, and of some difficulty, to the ancient Church. The so-called Epistle of Barnabas is a book of homiletical exposition of the Old Testament, addressed to this problem. No difficulty was felt in the first days of the Jewish-Christian Church, when most Christians were Jews by race, or at least by adopted religious background. The tradition of the ancient Scriptures as the authoritative book of God was handed on to the Church without question. The Church explained her status as the New and True Israel of God, and the rightful heir of these ancient promises. A general reading of the Apostolic Fathers indicates how near was the Church of this period to the usage of the New Testament, wherein "the Scriptures" are the Old Testament. To these writers a saying of Christ is "a word from God," and the writings of the Apostles are a precious substitute for the authoritative witness of an Apostle in person, but canonical Scripture is the Old Testament. The proof of Christian doctrine from the Old Testament is a very important part of their activity, and their writings are for the most part full of quotations from the Law and the Prophets.

However, as soon as predominantly Gentile Churches appeared, with no deeply ingrained tradition of veneration for the Jewish Scriptures, difficulty began to be felt. The more extreme Gentile deviationists, such as Marcion, and most Gnostics, wished to cut the link between the Church and her Jewish background, in token of which they would repudiate the Old Testament Scriptures. These lapsed into heresy, and separated from the Church. The rise of a heresy, however, is usually the symptom of the existence of some genuine difficulty, and for every one who lapses into heresy there is another, among those who remain faithful to the Church and substantially orthodox, whose thinking bears the mark of the same interests as engender heresy when developed to a more extreme degree. Thus there were not a few orthodox, who gladly accepted the Old Testament as authoritative Christian Scripture, who yet found many perplexities in the book. Christian teaching quoted certain Old Testament Commandments, for example, the Decalogue, as a binding sanction obliging the Christian to do certain things. Yet it was manifest that there were many other things which were apparently equally commanded by God of old times, which the Church did not in fact carry out, for example, the Temple sacrifices. It had to be explained why there was one rule for one part of the Law, and another for another! Furthermore, it was accepted that the Law and Prophets prepared the way for Christ, and spoke of Him. Yet a discriminating reader with a background of Gentile culture could not but feel that there were some customs and ceremonies enjoined in the Scriptures which appeared odd, grotesque, or even downright repulsive. Even more, there were some actions praised, and even some impulses attributed to God Himself, which could not but be condemned by Christian morals. Here indeed was a grave perplexity.

The opening article of the Creed is a memorial to the circumstance that the first great doctrinal attack upon Christianity was made by those who would repudiate the Old Testament Scriptures, and with them, the God of the Old Covenant. The answer was strongly to affirm the unity of the creator-God of the Old Testament with the God of Christian grace of the New, and likewise the sanctity of the Hebrew Scriptures. The ancient Fathers of the Church do not usually give much conscious and reasoned explanation why they so tenaciously adopt this attitude to the Old Testament. Rather are they in the position of traditionalists, supporting the existing position in the Church against innovators, upon the plea that it is traditional. However, reasons can be divined. There was first a more superficial reason, which was doubtless the strongest incentive in the majority of conventional minds. This was the desire to retain in the Church's hand the powerful propagandist and apologetic weapon of the "argument from prophecy." We live in an age of modernity, with an itch for innovation. The modern man instinctively assumes that the latest book is the most authoritative, an attitude of mind engendered by the swift progress of scientific research. It is hard for us to take our minds back into the ancient world, where men venerated ancient and mysterious books precisely because they were mysterious and ancient. The Church possessed books apparently written before the works of the classic Greek philosophers, and therefore very wise. In these books there were passages which could be interpreted as forecasts of many of the events of the life of Christ, including some which were so unexpected (for example, the Virgin Birth) that the wisest of men could not possibly have guessed at them many centuries beforehand. That these events actually came about proved the divine inspiration of the Old Testament, and the presumption of the divine inspiration of Scripture in turn gave authority to the Christian doctrine supported from it. This mode of argument was of great appeal in the ancient Church, and has traditionally been one of the chief apologistic Christian weapons, even though it is perhaps hard for us to feel its full force today. It is hardly surprising that the ancient Fathers did not want this weapon struck from their hands by a repudiation of the Old Testament.

There was also a reason of profound and lasting theological principle for clinging to the Old Testament, and for affirming the spiritual continuity of the Old and the New Israel. Naturally, this only finds expression in the more accomplished theologians of the ancient Church, but it was doubtless felt as a dim instinct in wider circles. There is in Hebrew religion a view of God as the Living God, a personal and active God who is in intimate and ruling contact with the world He has made, and who is a righteous God of holy love and inflexible morality. This doctrine of God is different in many important respects from the common presuppositions about the nature of God held by the Gentile culture of the day, and derived from classic Greek philosophy. God did not leave Himself without a witness among the Greeks, and there is much of truth about God to be found in the best of their philosophy. The wisest Christians have not repudiated Greek thought. Its intellectual apparatus has fittingly been employed as a means of communication, to expound the basic Biblical Christian doctrine. Nevertheless, the substance of the Christian faith has remained Biblical and Hebraic, and heresy has always followed when the presuppositions of Gentile philosophy about God and the world have been admitted into the basic substance of the faith, as distinct from its intellectual presentation. The first great Gentile deviation was Gnosticism, which was a rendering of Christianity wholly garbled and vitiated by being based upon the Hellenic assumption that the Supreme God is the remote, unmoved, impersonal, and unknowable Absolute, who by definition cannot possibly have direct contact with the material universe. The answer to this heresy was made by such an one as S. Irenaeus, who with deep insight made appeal from the remote Supreme of "philosophy falsely so-called" to the Living God of the prophets.[1] Long experience shows that the only adequate basis for the specific Christian doctrines of the divine Son and Spirit, the Incarnation, and the Atonement, is the God of the Old Testament. It is the devotional reading of the spacious poetry of the prophets, and the long tradition of worship from the Psalms, which alone enables people to think and feel about God in such a way as to make intelligible the Gospel of redemption by a divine sacrifice of suffering. The ancient Church may not have said much about this, but its members felt it, and clung to the Old Testament. We may be indeed grateful that curious and obscurantist arguments regarding "the proof from prophecy" were overruled by God to the preservation in the Church of the precious and irreplaceable heritage of Hebrew religious devotion.

We must return, however, to the ancient Church, and the twin master propositions of the sanctity of the Hebrew Scriptures, and the essential spiritual continuity of the Old and the New Israel. The Fathers were left to solve the manifest "Old Testament difficulties" as best they could, and, be it well observed, without the invaluable assistance of the typically modern and evolutionary doctrine of "progressive revelation," which can allow that some doctrinal and ethical positions in the Old Testament are imperfect and temporary, and are yet authentically from "the God and Father of our Lord Jesus Christ." They were also without the light which modern scientific historical and linguistic study has cast upon innumerable Old Testament passages which to the ancient Church presented themselves as the more obscure windings of "the dark wood of prophecy." The only way out for Christian antiquity was by recourse to allegorism and typology. This method had already been pioneered to explain away intellectual and

---

[1] Cf. Lawson, *Biblical Theology of S. Irenaeus*, pp. 122–129, and refs. given there.

ethical difficulties in the venerable Greek classics, and, by an intellectualist Jew such as Philo, to commend the Hebrew Scriptures to thoughtful people. The method as applied by the Church to Scripture was as follows. In addition to the ordinary historical surface meaning of a narrative, and any moral lesson which might be learned directly from it, there was also probably a hidden parable of spiritual truth to be discerned by the eye of Christian faith. This third sense of Scripture, which might have little or nothing to do with the plain historical sense, was accounted to be the highest and real significance of the Bible. Thus the story of Abraham's intended sacrifice of Isaac was an historical narrative in the first place, and a moral lesson to the faithful of obedience in the second. But supremely it was a "type of Christ." It was a mysterious foreshadowing of the sacrifice of God's Son and God's Lamb upon that same mountain centuries later. The whole of the Old Testament was worked over in this way, and the ancient Church with a little ingenuity proved most resourceful in extracting an edifying Christian message from even the most unpromising of passages. Thus in treating of the sordid story of the incest of Lot's daughters, S. Irenaeus quotes with approval the advice of one of the Elders before him that in such Scriptures one "should search for a type, for not one of those things which have been set down in Scripture without being condemned is without significance."[1]

The great creative pioneer in this line of thought is to be found in the New Testament itself: the Epistle to the Hebrews. Because this work of genius is so absorbed in interest with the Old Testament a superficial reading has suggested to every age that it must have been written to Hebrew Christians, hence the traditional title. Actually, however, it is to be viewed as one of the more Hellenic parts of the New Testament. It is to be understood as an attempt to show Christians whose general mental presuppositions were those of secular Greek philosophy how they might understand and appreciate as a Christian book the traditional Jewish Scriptures of the Church. The familiar Platonic doctrine of "Ideas" held that the authentic and perfect original of everything which is good, beautiful, and true exists eternally in the mind of God. That which is good, beautiful, and true in this lower material world, and in human experience, is derived from the heavenly original. The earthly virtue is the imperfect and passing

[1] *Adv. Haer.*, IV, xxxi, 1–2. Cf. Lawson, *Biblical Theology of S. Irenaeus*, pp. 82–6, 94–6.

shadow of the heavenly Idea, in which the virtue has its perfect and eternal existence. This Platonic doctrine of Ideas is used in Hebrews with great spiritual insight and grace of argument to state the relationship between the religion of the Old and the New Covenants. The Old Covenant had institutions which were on the one hand divinely ordained, and yet on the other, were largely external, ceremonial, and temporary. This was the shadowy earthly copy of religion, drawing its existence from the perfect and spiritual heavenly Idea of religion. The New Covenant, with its prevailing spiritual sacrifice of Christ's sinless obedience to the Father, and its inward spiritual "Law written upon the heart" (of which Jeremiah had dreamed), was as it were the authentic heavenly religion itself come down to earth. The Ideal religion which had always existed in the mind of God was now made known on earth in the person of the divine Son incarnate. Thus in a masterly way the relationship between the Old and New Testaments is established. They are alike the work of the one true God, and the New is the spiritual continuation of the Old. The validity and majesty of the Old Covenant are vindicated as a preparation for Christ, yet the superior majesty and validity of the New are abundantly vindicated.

The antique and quaint *Epistle of Barnabas* is not at first sight a very intelligible or attractive book. It is to be understood as an attempt to do the same as the Epistle to the Hebrews, and for the same motives. It is an essay in allegory and typology, in order to vindicate the Old Testament as a Christian book. *Barnabas* is a sort of "poor relation" to Hebrews. The two have a distinct family likeness, but, while Hebrews is a work of imperishable genius and artistry, *Barnabas* writes at a much lower level of intellectual ability and good sense. He can write very sound theology at times, but exegesis, in which he delights, always confuses him! Nevertheless, like some other second-rate works, the Epistle made a wide appeal in the ancient Church, and was reverenced by some of the greatest writers among the Fathers. This may be in part because, through some circumstance of which we have no knowledge, the name of the Apostle Barnabas became attached to it, so that it was regarded as an "Apostolic writing." Indeed, the fact that it occurs, together with *The Shepherd*, as an appendix following the Revelation of S. John in Codex Sinaiticus, seems to indicate that some schools of thought regarded it as a candidate for the canon of Scripture. We may be profoundly grateful that the Church was more wisely guided, and that the New Testament has escaped the inclusion in it of some of *Barnabas*' curious exegesis and fantastic natural history! However, this work cannot properly be called apocryphal, as nowhere in the text does it claim to be by S. Barnabas, and the author does not write in the person of another.

Much may be learned of the mind of the ancient Church from this Epistle, which is really not a letter but an expository discourse. It represents in its own rather blundering way the central, orthodox, and Catholic position of "a war on two fronts" regarding the Old Testament. It is both strongly anti-Judaic in tone, and also, rather paradoxically, is written against the type of anti-Judaic heretic who would abandon the Old Testament as unworthy to be regarded as Christian Scripture. The writer is aware that some have taken offence at the Old Testament because they have taken it all literally, and have perceived that there are in it things which, if taken literally, are an offence to the Christian. Therefore the offence is to be abated by insisting that the Old Testament is not to be taken literally! The dignity of the Old Testament as Christian Scripture is vindicated by departing from the historical sense, and by resorting to allegorical exegesis. The error of *Barnabas*, in contrast to the method of the Epistle to the Hebrews before him, and of the great allegoristic exegetes who came after, is that he goes too far in stating his case. He teaches not only that the Christian is not bound literally to observe all the commandments and institutions of the Jewish Law, but that they were never meant by God to be taken literally. Thus, for example, the old Jews were in error in actually building a Temple at Jerusalem, because the narratives relative to it are allegories of theological truth! This is a cardinal lapse of historical understanding.

It is not known where the Epistle was written. Allegorical exegesis prevailed widely in the Church, and is found in the New Testament itself. However, this school of exposition first flourished in the Church of Alexandria, and it is by Alexandrian writers that *Barnabas* is first quoted. At the close of the second century the great Clement of Alexandria cites it frequently, and ascribes the Epistle to "the Apostle," or "the prophet Barnabas," and states that this was the Barnabas who preached with S. Paul.[1] Thus this work was quite possibly written in Alexandria, and may perhaps be regarded as the humble and rather

[1] *Miscellanies*, II, 6, 7, 15, 18, 20; V, 10; VI, 8.

crude beginning of the Church's earliest school of "scientific" or intellectualist theologians. It is a far cry from this rather confused soul to the mighty Origen, the master of philosophical theology in the ancient Church. However, if the writer of this Epistle is indeed in some sense the founder of that school, the title of an "Apostolic Father" can hardly be denied him. If not a great Father of the Church, he was perhaps a father of great things.

5. Date of the Epistle of Barnabas

The most difficult problem associated with this Epistle is the date, which still seems to remain quite uncertain. The most various hypotheses have been advanced. The work apparently alludes to the first destruction of Jerusalem under Titus in A.D. 70 (Chap. 16, with note, p. 215). It must therefore be later than this date. However, the argument of the Epistle is such that it has been widely assumed that the second destruction of the city under Hadrian in A.D. 132 could hardly have escaped mention, if this event had already taken place. As it is not mentioned, the work is generally assumed to be earlier than this date, though an argument from silence is always dangerous. Many scholars have attempted to calculate a more exact date, within these limits, on the basis of which Roman emperors may be referred to in the exposition of Daniel vii, 7, in Chapter 4. However, it is very difficult to make any arrangement of emperors to fit in exactly, and the whole matter is most speculative (see p. 204). There is also the important question of the relation of the Epistle to *Didache*, which has already been touched upon in introducing "The Two Ways" in *Didache* (see pp. 74-5). The passage *Barnabas* 18-20 contains a large part of the matter of *Didache* 1-6, though with an inferior and less orderly arrangement. There is, however, at least one substantial passage which is so nearly word for word in the two that literary dependence may be regarded as established (*Didache* 5 from "persecutors of good men," and *Barnabas* 20, second half). The present author prefers to regard *Barnabas* as the source used in *Didache*, rather than vice versa. This would bring the Epistle to an early date unless, as with F. E. Vokes, the writing of *Didache* itself is placed considerably later than is usual.[1]

[1] *Riddle of the Didache*, p. 210, etc.

However, it must be admitted that the whole matter is most uncertain. The great authority of Lightfoot places it early, between A.D. 70 and 79. This would be just early enough to allow it to be used as a source for *Didache*. In relation to this, however, there is in Chapter 15 what appears to be a quotation of 2 Peter iii, 8, "Behold, the day of the Lord shall be as a thousand years." If the critics' usual late date for 2 Peter be accepted, *Barnabas* would have to be placed much later than Lightfoot's date. However, quite possibly both *Barnabas* and 2 Peter quote this saying from some common source, so that the question of dependence may not arise. It is a striking saying which would be likely to be remembered, and to have wide currency in the Church in the generation when the Christians were beginning to become perplexed at the continued delay of the expected Second Advent. As is natural to the subject of the Epistle, there are numerous Old Testament quotations. A number of sayings of Jesus are quoted, apparently from S. Matthew, but they are so brief that it could be argued that they may arise from the remembered oral tradition of the words of the Lord. There is also a possible though not indisputable allusion to Acts and to Romans. Thus little may be deduced with certainty from quotations regarding the date of writing, save that the evidence would well accord with the early date.

6. Sources of the Text

The MS sources of this Epistle are: (*a*) the Codex Siniaticus, where it occurs at the end of the New Testament, together with *The Shepherd of Hermas*; (*b*) the Constantinopolitan MS published by Bryennios, where it occurs with the other works listed on p. 63 ; (*c*) a series of nine Greek MSS where the text runs on without a break from the broken end of the Epistle of S. Polycarp, the first four and a half chapters of *Barnabas* also being missing; (*d*) fairly long quotations in Clement of Alexandria; (*e*) a Latin version of the ninth century, with the last four chapters missing.

7. Commentary on the Epistle of Barnabas

1. "So innate is the grace of the spiritual gift that ye have received";

οὕτως ἔμφυτον τῆς δορεᾶς πνευματικῆς χάριν εἰλήφατε (Lightfoot, p. 243). T. F. Torrance observes that χάρις ἔμφυτος is an Hellenistic usage, largely corresponding to the later idea of *gratia infusa*.[1] This is not the primary idea of grace as the lovingkindness, the undeserved favour, of God (Eph. ii, 5). It is the derived idea of grace as the action of God communicating itself to man, an influence in his life (Col. iii, 16).

"For great faith and love dwelleth in you through the hope of the life which is His": We observe the traditional virtues of faith, hope, and love linked together, as in 1 Corinthians xiii, 13. It would appear that "faith" here is loving personal trust, and not "the Faith," that is, a body of doctrine.

"That alone with your faith ye might have your knowledge"; γνῶσις (Lightfoot, p. 243). The writer has a strong doctrine of knowledge, gnosis. It is here the counterpart and complement of faith, or trust in God. It is that true understanding of the Old Testament which enables it to be read as a Christian book, which knowledge will save the believer from many errors.

"For the Lord made known to us by His prophets things past and present, giving us likewise the firstfruits of the taste of things future": Here is the introduction of the theme of the Epistle, the nature and place of Old Testament prophecy.

"We ought to offer a richer and higher offering to the fear of Him": Clearly this is not a servile fear which leads only to the religion of stern duty. In this greeting there is a strong sense of love for God and joy in God.

2. "Seeing then that the days are evil, and that the Active One himself has the authority": See also 4, 21. This is the common ancient Christian attitude. This age is the age when Satan rules, and the troubles of the times are a mark that the Lord is soon coming to bring the promised Age of God.

"The aids of our faith then are fear and patience": Compare 2 Corinthians vii, 1.

"Wisdom, understanding, science, knowledge"; σοφία, σύνεσις, ἐπιστήμη, γνῶσις (Lightfoot, p. 244). According to *Barnabas*, this true Christian gnosis, which is the theme of his Epistle, is an understanding that under the Old Covenant God did not require the

---
[1] *Grace in the Apostolic Fathers*, p. 108.

ceremonial religion of the Jews. We see this demonstrated from the great prophetic utterance he significantly chooses, with which to open his argument.

"What to me is the multitude of your sacrifices": Isaiah i, 11–13. We are here introduced to the genuine difficulty under which *Barnabas* labours. His imperfect understanding of the nature of the prophetic utterance does not permit him to grasp that when a Hebrew prophet says, "I desire mercy and not sacrifice," it is a vivid poetic way of saying, "Sacrifice is good, but it is not a substitute for mercy, which I desire still more." To a certain extent it is both historically and spiritually legitimate to quote the prophets to the effect that the ceremonial Law is by no means the highest aspect of religion. But it is a mistake to quote them as *Barnabas* does here, taking their rhetoric literally, in order to support the idea that through the prophets God forbade the Temple sacrifices, and other Jewish institutions.

"That the new law of our Lord Jesus Christ, being free from the yoke of constraint, might have its oblation not made with human hands": The doctrine that the Gospel is "the New Law" is characteristic of *Barnabas*, and is common in later Fathers. This is one of those phrases which is legitimate or illegitimate, according to what is meant by it. It can mean that Christianity is regarded as a purified and more ethical form of legal religion, in fact, a sort of Christianized religion of pharisaic merit. This is a dangerous perversion. But it can just as well represent the parallel which exists between the Old and New Israel. If the religion of the Old Israel was the old Law, then the religion of the New Israel is the New Law, without any necessary denial of the doctrine of salvation by grace. We do not therefore condemn *Barnabas* for the use of this phrase, but we look narrowly at his usage. He clearly means here that the abolition of "the yoke of constraint" of literal obedience to the Jewish Law had left the way open for the spiritual sacrifice of Christ, which is the sacrifice of the New Covenant.

"Did I command your fathers": Jeremiah vii, 22, 23.
"Let none of you bear a grudge": Zechariah viii, 17.
"The sacrifice unto God is a broken heart": Psalm li, 19. It is not clear whence the latter part is quoted.

3. "Wherefore fast ye for me": Isaiah lviii, 4–10.
"That we might not as novices shipwreck ourselves upon their

law": Some naïve Christians are making shipwreck of their faith through the assumption that literal obedience is required to the Jewish Law. Those possessing the true Christian gnosis which is the subject of this Epistle will see that the prophets have repudiated this idea. The way is open for the doctrine that the Old Testament is to be expounded allegorically.

4. "Let us therefore flee altogether from all the works of lawlessness ... to consort with sinners": *Barnabas* is aware, as was S. Paul, that an assertion that the Christian religion is spiritual, not legal, leaves one open to the charge of antinomianism. Before he goes further in his attempt after a spiritual rendering of Christianity he will rebut this charge in advance. To this end he appeals to the fear of the coming Last Judgment. This is, so far as it goes, a legitimate ground of ethical appeal, though by no means the highest.

"The last offence is at hand": The time when the power of evil in the world will be fully revealed, preliminary to its overthrow, is at hand (e.g., 2 Thess. ii, 3-12). Therefore the Christians must especially guard against temptation.

"Which the scripture speaketh, as Enoch saith": The apocryphal Book of Enoch is referred to and apparently called "scripture," οὗ γέγραπται (Lightfoot, p. 245). See also Chapter 16, with note, p. 216.

"Ten reigns shall reign upon the earth": Daniel vii, 24. The assumption has been widely made that *Barnabas* sees some current arrangement of Roman imperial affairs as a literal fulfilment of this prophecy, and a mark that the End is nigh. This is of course a somewhat precarious assumption to make, for we do not know how far the writer took Daniel literally. However, he may be doing so, for it is a very common mental quirk of a certain type of expositor to allow secondary and applied allegorical meanings to every part of Scripture save apocalyptic, which alone, it is insisted, must be interpreted literally. Bishop Lightfoot (p. 240) gives a summary of the contradictory calculations of various scholars, and himself prefers to count Vespasian as the tenth king, while the three kings who are to be humiliated before the power of evil are Vespasian and his two sons Titus and Domitian, whom Vespasian associated with himself as joint emperors. This is the basis for placing the writing of *Barnabas* early, in the reign of Vespasian (A.D. 70–79).

"In like manner Daniel speaketh . . . And I saw the fourth beast": Daniel vii, 7–8. This "little horn," which is presumably the same as the "little kings," and is a symbol of Antichrist, may be a reference to the current rumour that Nero would presently reappear to displace the Flavian dynasty.

"Saying that our covenant remains to them also. Ours it is, but they lost it in this way for ever, when Moses had just received it": Those referred to are the Jews, and their claim to be the People of the Covenant is sharply disowned. *Barnabas* advances the strange and unhistorical position that God annulled the Old Covenant with the Jews almost as soon as the Law was given to Moses. This is part of the characteristic theory that the whole of the Jewish understanding of religion was radically in error.

"And Moses was in the mountain": Exodus xxxiv, 28, and then xxxi, 18.

"Moses, Moses, come down quickly": Exodus xxxii, 7; Deuteronomy ix, 12.

"And their covenant was broken in pieces, that the covenant of the beloved Jesus might be sealed unto our hearts in the hope which springeth from faith in Him": This is a rather curious rendering of the theme of Hebrews x, 9. However, *Barnabas* clearly teaches that the New Covenant is founded on faith in Christ.

"These last days": The present day, which shows the release of the power of lawlessness, is a time of hope and also of special temptation.

"Do not stand apart by yourselves, as if ye were already justified"; δεδικαιωμένοι (Lightfoot, p. 246). This is the characteristic Pauline word, but is not used in the characteristic Pauline sense. The reference is not to the Christian's initial justification at conversion, which is by faith (see above), but to his final justification at the expected Day of Judgment, which is by the love and good works brought forth by faith. *Barnabas* teaches that the guarantee of perseverance in those good works through the present time of distress is faithful continuance with the Church.

"Woe unto them that are wise": Isaiah v, 21.

"Let us strive to keep His commandments": This exhortation to good works, in view of the coming Judgment, has a somewhat "legal" air. There are two sides to *Barnabas*. When he speaks of Christ, he speaks of salvation by grace, through faith. When he gives moral exhortation, he appears to call on men to save themselves by their own efforts. It is never easy to keep the due emphasis upon "faith" and upon "good works" in proper balance, and this writer is not the most expert of theologians. We may perhaps assume that his intentions are sometimes better than this mode of expression, taken literally.

"As the scripture saith (ὡς γέγραπται) [Lightfoot, p. 247], many called but few chosen": S. Matthew xxii, 14. It is not the regular usage of *Barnabas* or of the other writers of this period to speak of the words of Jesus as "Scripture," γραφή, though they are fully authoritative for faith and morals. Possibly we may here render the phrase more generally as "it is written."

5. "For to this end the Lord endured. . . . He was wounded for our transgressions": Isaiah liii, 5. There is a clear statement of the atoning death of Christ here, though the Church has not yet arrived at the stage of constructing the later theological theories to explain how the atonement works. The significant fact is that Isaiah liii can be quoted as referring to the death of Christ, yet without any mention of the substitutionary theology which more modern theologians have found there. This exposition is quite in the manner of the ancient Fathers.[1]

"Not unjustly is the net spread for the birds": Proverbs i, 17.

"Unto whom God said . . . Let us make man": Genesis i, 26. The "us" is in fact the outcome of the circumstance that the Hebrew word for God used here is plural in grammatical form, though singular in sense. To a long tradition of ancient exegetes, however, the apparent "conversation" within the Godhead is a "prophecy" of the Trinity.

"How then did He endure?": The statement of the doctrine of the divinity of the preexistent Son leads into a simple but thoroughly Biblical presentation of the doctrine of the atonement. Christ's death and resurrection were the divine victory over death, the power which held men in bondage (Rom. v, 21; 1 Cor. xv, 20-22). This is the fulfilment of prophecy, and the foundation of the New Israel.

"He came not to call the righteous but sinners": S. Matthew ix, 13.

"Forasmuch as when they look upon the sun . . . they cannot face its rays": The purpose of the Incarnation was so to veil the glory of the divine Son as to enable frail man to comprehend Him (Ex. xxxiii, 20; S. John i, 18).

[1] Cf. Irenaeus, *Demonstration*, 69.

"That He might sum up (ἀνακεφαλαιώσῃ) [Lightfoot, p. 248][1] the complete tale of their sins": S. Mark xii, 1-9. Christ brings judgment, as well as the revelation of salvation.

"When they shall smite their own shepherd": Zechariah xiii, 7; S. Matthew xxvi, 31.

"Spare My soul from the sword": Psalm xxii, 20; xxii, 16.

"Behold I have given My back to stripes": Isaiah l, 6, 7.

6. "Who is he that disputeth with Me?": Isaiah l, 8, 9.

"Behold I will put into the foundations": Isaiah xxviii, 16.

"And He set Me as a hard rock": Isaiah l, 7.

"The stone which the builders rejected": Psalm cxviii, 22, 24.

"The assembly of evil-doers gathered about me": Psalm xxii, 16; cxviii, 12; xxii, 18.

"Woe unto their soul": Isaiah iii, 9, 10.

"Behold, these things saith the Lord God": Exodus xxxiii, 1, 3.

"For the prophet speaketh a parable concerning the Lord": This difficult chapter, with its catena of Old Testament quotations in the unfamiliar guise of the Septuagint, is an example of the allegorical method of interpreting Scripture. It is full of "secret things," which require "wisdom" to understand!

"He made us to be a new type (τύπον) [Lightfoot, p. 249] . . . as if He were re-creating us": The redeemed are a new imprint of the Image of God. They are a new birth and a new creation of the race.

"Let us make man": Genesis i, 26, 28.

"Behold I make the last things as the first": This is possibly intended to be a quotation of S. Matthew xx, 16.

"Enter into a land": Exodus xxxiii, 1-3.

"Behold, saith the Lord": Ezekiel xi, 19; xxxvi, 26.

"For wherein shall I appear": Psalm xlii, 2; xxii, 22.

"Because the child is first kept alive by honey, and then by milk": This is possibly a reference to the custom in the ancient Church of giving milk and honey to the newly baptized (cf. 1 Pet. ii, 2). It does not mean that children were baptized, but that the newly baptized were children in the Faith.

"And let them increase": Genesis i, 28.

7. "If then the Son of God": The writer of *Barnabas* reveals, or

---

[1] Cf. Ephesians i, 10; Irenaeus, *Adv. Haer.*, V, xiv, 1.

betrays, his mentality here. He starts with a clear statement of the doctrine of atonement by the sufferings of the divine Son. When he seeks to support the doctrine by an allegorical treatment of the sacrifices in Leviticus, expanded by curious quotations from apocryphal books, his argument becomes more and more obscure!

"Whosoever shall not observe the fast": Leviticus xxiii, 29.

"He was in His own person about to offer the vessel of His Spirit a sacrifice for our sins, that the type also which was given in Isaac . . . should be fulfilled": The meaning of this possibly is that Christ's Spirit dwelt in His body. The offering of His body was therefore the means of the offering of His Spirit as a sacrifice of obedience (cf. Heb. ix, 14). The intended sacrifice of Isaac, being a sacrifice of obedience, was a "type" of this atoning sacrifice of Christ.

"And let them eat of the goat": There follow two quotations from an unknown "prophecy," but the argument is not easy to follow.

"Take two goats": Leviticus xvi, 7, 9, and then 8. The argument here returns abruptly to Leviticus, and *Barnabas* attempts a parallel between the Scapegoat and the Crucified, not very successfully.

"And do ye all spit upon it": Here is another unknown quotation, but it looks as though it were some attempt to expand the narrative of Leviticus.

"The branch that is called Rachia"; ῥαχία (Lightfoot, p. 251).[1] We have no knowledge of this reference.

"The one for the altar, and the other accursed": Leviticus xvi, 8. The imagery by now is very confused, but the writer errs at a deeper level than in choice of imagery. In Leviticus the Scapegoat, which bore the sins of the people, was the animal which was *not* sacrificed. The driving of it out was a symbol that the people were putting away their sins, in order that they might be fit to offer the sacrifice of the pure goat. Thus the ritual of the Scapegoat does not bear out the imagery of Christ dying "under a curse." However, *Barnabas* is so anxious to see the humiliation and rejection of the Scapegoat as a "type" of Christ that he forgets this!

"Wearing the long scarlet robe about His flesh. . . . Is not this He . . . ": This would appear to be an allusion to Revelation i, 7, and xix, 13, though the scarlet robe may be the one worn by our Lord at His mockery (S. Matthew xxvii, 28).

[1] An emendation for C. Sinaiticus ῥαχήλ, and Constantinopolitan MS ῥαχή.

"The goats shall be fair and alike": Another unknown quotation. The argument which follows is equally obscure.

8. "The commandment is given to Israel": This passage is probably an allusion to Numbers xix, 1–10, but the details are strangely worked out, and we do not know who the "three children" are.

"The children who sprinkle are they that preached unto us ... being twelve in number": The natural sense is that these "sprinklers" of the virtue of the Crucified are the twelve Apostles, the foundation of the Church which is the New Israel (cf. S. Matt. xix, 28). It is therefore puzzling that the children are three! Presumably the idea is that the Christian Ministry corresponds to the Patriarchs as well as to the Apostles.

"Then there is the placing the wool on the tree": As the narrative from Numbers does not supply these and following details, they are presumably from some early expansion or apocryphal book, and it is hard to expound them.

9. "How that it is our heart which He circumcised": *Barnabas* opens what is clearly one of his most cherished themes; namely, that the Church has done right in abandoning circumcision, and interpreting the Old Testament commandments of the same in an allegorical sense. We start appropriately with Old Testament passages which may be interpreted as authority for a "spiritual" view of circumcision.

"With the hearing of the ears they listened unto Me": Psalm xviii, 44.

"They that are afar off": Isaiah xxxiii, 13.

"Be ye circumcised in your hearts": Jeremiah iv, 4.

"Who is it that desireth to live": Psalm xxxiv, 12–13.

"Hear, O heavens": Isaiah i, 2.

"Hear the word of the Lord": Isaiah i, 10.

"Hear, O my children": Isaiah xl, 3.

"But they transgressed, for an evil angel taught them cleverness": The Jews had been deceived, and sinned, in practising circumcision literally.

"Thus saith the Lord ... sow not upon thorns": Jeremiah iv, 3, 4.

"Be ye circumcised in the hardness of your heart": Deuteronomy x, 16.

"Behold, saith the Lord, all the Gentiles are uncircumcised": Jeremiah ix, 26.

"In truth the people hath been circumcised for a seal": *Barnabas* disowns the argument that physical circumcision is a spiritual thing, because it is a symbol. Syrians, Arabians, and Egyptians also practice the rite, and, says the writer, it can have no divine significance for these.

"Abraham, who first appointed circumcision, looked forward in the spirit unto Jesus": The key point of the argument is to show that in the case of Abraham himself, the originator of circumcision, the ceremony was a "spiritual" thing.

"And Abraham circumcised of his household eighteen males and three hundred": Genesis xiv, 14; xvii, 23. We come now to the most ingenious of *Barnabas*' "types of Christ." The passage is most instructive for the mentality of the ancient Church, for it shows how by the employment of allegorical exegesis crumbs of Christian truth could be picked up in the most unlikely parts of the Old Testament, while texts the surface meaning of which was offensive could have their literal sense explained away. There is a great deal of exposition comparable to this to be found in some of the Fathers. Its use was one of the main factors which rendered so necessary the development of the authority of the Church as a guide to the interpretation of Scripture, as these methods were so subjective. In Greek, letters of the alphabet are used for numerals. Iota stands for 10, eta for 8, and tau for 300, making 318. Iota and eta are also the first two letters of the name "Jesus" in Greek, so these two numerals stand for our Lord. Tau is *T*-shaped in form, and so stands for the Cross, thus:

$$I \quad T \quad H \quad \text{or} \quad \underset{\text{on the Cross.}}{\text{I T H}} = \text{Jesus } (I H \Sigma O Y \Sigma)$$
10 300 8

So a passage which at first sight looks like an argument for physical circumcision is really a mysterious "ordinance of three letters" speaking of Christ crucified, and of salvation by faith.

"And because the cross in the *T* was to have grace"; ὅτι δὲ ὁ σταυρὸς ἐν τῷ *T* ἤμελλεν ἔχειν τὴν χάριν (Lightfoot, p. 253). Torrance rightly observes that the best reading for this difficult phrase is to give χάριν ἔχειν the ordinary secular sense current at the time, and render it "to find acknowledgment."[1] Thus the principle of Christ and the Cross finds acknowledgment in the incident, and the three numerals associated with it.

"No man ever learnt from me a more genuine word": This strange piece of exposition is clearly *Barnabas'* tour de force!

10. "Ye shall not eat swine": Leviticus xi, 7, 10, 13-15; Deuteronomy xiv, 8, 10, 12-14.

"And I will lay as a covenant upon this people My ordinances": Deuteronomy iv, 10, 13.

"It is not a commandment of God that they should not bite with their teeth, but Moses spake it in spirit": In exposition of the Law of unclean meats, we come to the characteristic assertion that the commandments were never intended by God to be taken literally, but were from the beginning an allegory of Christian truth. This strangely unhistorical argument is decorated with some very strange natural history!

"Neither shalt thou eat eagle" Leviticus xi, 13-15; Deuteronomy xiv, 12-14.

"And thou shalt not eat lamphrey nor polypus nor cuttle fish. . . . Neither shalt thou eat the hyena": Here are two more quotations from an unknown source, but it would appear to be some form of expansion upon the Jewish Law.

"Thou shalt not eat the hare": Leviticus xi, 5.

"Blessed is the man": Psalm i, 1.

"Ye shall eat everything that divideth the hoof and cheweth the cud": Leviticus xi, 3; Deuteronomy xiv, 6.

11. "Concerning water and the cross": This chapter reminds us again that the author of the Epistle is a better theologian than an exegete. There is a strange irony in this, for he obviously prides himself upon his superior skill in expounding Scripture! Here is a sound Scriptural theological argument, showing that the Sacrament of Holy Baptism is the symbol of dying and rising again with Christ, and answers to the principle of the Cross (see Ignatius, Ep. to Ephesians, 18, with note, pp. 116-17). It is, however, supported by numerous prooftexts, which in our eyes do not seem to prove very much.

"Be astonished, O heaven": Jeremiah ii, 12, 13, and Isaiah xvi, 1, 2.

[1] *Grace in the Apostolic Fathers*, p. 109.

"I will go before thee": Isaiah xlv, 2, 3; xxxiii, 16-18; and Psalm i, 3-6.

"He pointed out the water and the cross at the same time": There is a clear doctrine of Christian regeneration here. Those who put their trust in God's divine victory in the Cross, and in token thereof are baptized, receive the gift of faith and love, and are used in God's service for the conversion of others.

"And the land of Jacob was praised above the whole earth": An uncertain quotation.

"And there was a river streaming": Ezekiel xlvii, 1, 7, 12.

"And whosoever shall eat of these shall live for ever": John vi, 51.

12. "Another prophet who saith: And when shall these things be accomplished?": 4 Esdras v, 5. We observe that the Apocrypha is cited as Scripture, in the manner of the ancient Church.

"And He saith again in Moses": The narrative of Exodus xvii, 8-16, is treated as a type of salvation by faith in the Crucified, who stretched forth His hands. This is a familiar theme in the Fathers (cf. Justin Martyr, *Dialogue*, 90).

"The whole day long have I stretched out My hands": Isaiah lxv, 2.

"Ye shall not have a molten or a carved image for your God": Deuteronomy xxvii, 15. We may make an interesting comparison here with S. John iii, 14-15. The Evangelist and *Barnabas* employ the same basic method. The brazen serpent is a "type of Christ." The Gospel, with its restrained detail, just serving to convey the idea, strikes us as dignified symbolism. *Barnabas*, with his ingenious wealth of detail, to us appears fantastic.

"Jesus the son of Nun": Jesus is the Greek form of the Hebrew name Joshua.

"Take a book in thy hands": Exodus xvii, 14.

"Not a son of man, but the Son of God": As used by our Lord, "Son of Man" is a title of the Messiah (S. Mark xiv, 62). *Barnabas*, however, in line with common later Christian exposition, takes the phrase to denote Christ's human nature.

"Since then men will say that Christ is the son of David": It is clearly in the interest of *Barnabas* to demonstrate that the Christian Christ is not the military Messiah of Jewish expectation. He therefore fittingly quotes the text used by our Lord in disowning the proposition that He was "the Son of David," that is, the restorer of the military power of the traditional ruling house of Judah.

"The Lord said unto my Lord": Psalm cx, 1; compare S. Matthew xxii, 44.

"The Lord said unto my Christ the Lord": Isaiah xlv, 1.

"See how David calleth Him Lord, and calleth Him not Son": Compare S. Matthew xxii, 45.

13. "Let us see whether this people or the first people hath the inheritance": There follows a series of texts from Genesis, Exodus, and Isaiah to demonstrate that the New Israel of the Church is the true heir of the promises of the Old Covenant, and not the Jews.

"And Isaac prayed": Genesis xxv, 21–3.

"Behold, the Lord hath not bereft me": Genesis xlviii, 11, 9.

"And Jacob crossed his hands": Genesis xlviii, 14, 18, 19. Here are three Scripture precedents for the principle that there are two Peoples, and that the second shall take the place of the first in the divine blessing. Thus the Church has taken the place of the Jews.

"Behold I have made thee, Abraham": Genesis xvii, 5; compare Romans iv, 11.

14. "As regards the covenant . . . let us see whether He had actually given it": It is characteristic of the unhistorical theory of *Barnabas* that the Old Covenant never actually came into force, on account of the deep error of the Jewish nation. Texts are now cited to illustrate this point.

"And Moses was fasting": Exodus xxiv, 18; xxxi, 18.

"Moses, Moses, come down quickly": Exodus xxxii, 7, 8, 19.

"Moses received them being a servant, but the Lord himself gave them to us . . . having endured patiently for our sakes": *Barnabas* rightly observes a valid distinction between the giving of the Law under Moses, and the giving of the New Law by Christ. The first was God's law adapted to the status of a servant; the second was a direct divine gift, the fruit of the Atonement. This is made plain in the passage which follows, which speaks clearly of redemption by Christ's death.

"I the Lord thy God called thee": Isaiah xlii, 6, 7.

"Behold, I have set thee": Isaiah xlix, 6, 7; lxi, 1, 2.

15. "Moreover concerning the sabbath": *Barnabas* proceeds with his anti-Judaic argument by a characteristic denial that the Old Testament Scriptures which speak of the Sabbath require the keeping of the weekly Jewish day of rest. Rather are they to be understood as prophecies of the "promised rest" of the millennial Kingdom.

"And ye shall hallow the sabbath": Exodus xx, 8; Psalm xxiv, 4.

"If My sons observe the sabbath": Jeremiah xvii, 24.

"And God made the works of His hands": Genesis ii, 2.

"Behold, the day of the Lord shall be as a thousand years": This very interesting quotation seems to be from 2 Peter iii, 8. Its relation to the date of the Epistle has been discussed in the introduction, p. 201. The use of this phrase in 2 Peter marks the beginning of a painful realization in the early Church that the Second Advent of Christ, which so many had overenthusiastically expected to be very soon, was being delayed, and would perhaps only occur in the uncertain future. The argument that the Creation would last six "days," each of a thousand years, placed the end of history sufficiently far ahead in the future as to tone down the adventist expectation of the Church, without utterly repudiating it. At the end of the sixth day, that is, at a destined but perhaps distant and unknown date, Christ would come (cf. S. Mark xiii, 32–7). The seventh day would be the millennial Kingdom. *Barnabas* adopts this position in the passage following, but with this addition: he uses this doctrine as a basis for denial that the "day of God" mentioned in the Old Testament was ever anything but the millennial Kingdom.

"His Son shall come, and shall abolish the time of the Lawless One, and shall judge the ungodly, and shall change the sun": It is noteworthy that *Barnabas* would appear to be a premillenarian. He writes as though the Advent of the Lord, the destruction of the power of Satan, and the judgment of the ungodly would take place before the 1000-year Kingdom. (By contrast, compare the arrangement of Revelation xx, 1–8.)

"Then and not till then shall we truly rest and hallow it, when we shall ourselves be able to do so after being justified (δικαιωθέντες) [Lightfoot, p. 261] and receiving the promise": This is a curious mixture of Pauline and non-Pauline doctrine. In the first place, it plainly teaches salvation by grace. A man cannot keep the true Sabbath of God until he has been justified, and has received the promise, even though he has a pure heart. But the justification which is spoken of is that which takes place finally, at the Second Advent and Judgment. This is not S. Paul's usage. Thus, in fact, full salvation is removed to the future Kingdom, and all that the believer has now is the hope of salvation. This is a considerable toning down of the Christian expectation, as reflected in the New Testament, though it would pass with most people as "a common-sense attitude."

"Your new moons and your sabbaths I cannot away with": Isaiah i, 13.

"The eighth day which is the beginning of another world": After the millennial "Sabbath rest," there is to be the final glorious divine order with a new creation (cf. Rev. xxi, 1). This is the eighth day. The Christians keep the Lord's Day, that is, the day after the Sabbath, on which Christ rose from the dead, as a day of rejoicing, in anticipation of this promised "eighth day" of glory.

16. "Likewise concerning the temple": As with circumcision, the law of meats, and the Sabbath, so it is with the Temple! God's commandments regarding its building were intended solely as a parable of spiritual truth, and the Jews deeply erred in taking them literally, so as to construct the actual Temple at Jerusalem.

"Who hath measured the heaven with a span": Isaiah xl, 12. This is quoted, not inappropriately, in rebuke of those who would put their trust in the possession of a sacred building.

"Behold they that pulled down this temple themselves shall build it": Isaiah xlix, 17.

"Because they went to war it was pulled down by their enemies. Now also the very servants of their enemies shall build it up": This is a most perplexing passage, and has been the centre of much learned speculation. The destruction of the Temple referred to here is preferably taken to be that under Titus, A.D. 70. If the writer knew of the second destruction under Hadrian, A.D. 132, it is considered likely from the nature of the argument that both destructions would be referred to. This dates the Epistle between A.D. 70 and 132. Efforts have been made to find some occasion when the Jews might have had reason to expect that the agents of the Romans would assist in the rebuilding of the Temple, but there is no evidence forthcoming. It can be argued that the hostile attitude of *Barnabas* to the existence of an actual Temple would forbid him to speak of the prospect of its rebuilding, but this point is not conclusive, because in any case it is the building of an unfaithful Jewish Temple which is here under discussion. *Barnabas* may have disapproved of the event he was expecting! However, the Temple which is to be rebuilt may be intended for the spiritual Temple of the Church, which was certainly being built by the Gentiles, who were the enemies of the Jews and the destroyers of the Temple (cf. S. Luke xxi, 24). In favour of this second interpretation is the circumstance that the chapter continues the theme of the building of the spiritual Temple of God. However, *Barnabas* does not make his meaning very plain!

"For the scripture saith; And it shall be": Enoch lxxxix, 56, 66. It is interesting to note that the apocryphal book of Enoch is here quoted, apparently as "Scripture" (cf. Jude 14).

"And it shall come to pass": Daniel ix, 24.

"I find then that there is a temple": It is singular how regularly *Barnabas*, the self-appointed and self-confident exegete, writes his best passages of theology when now and again he disentangles himself from his tortuous and unhistorical exposition. We have another example here. The rest of the chapter is a beautiful treatment of the catholic and evangelical theme that the Church, which is the corporate company of the regenerate who live by faith in Christ, is the true spiritual Temple of God. This Temple is indwelt by Christ.

17. "For if I should write to you concerning things immediate or future, ye would not understand them": We can well believe this! *Barnabas* is a little condescending.

18. "There are two ways": We now pass by a somewhat abrupt transition to a section of the Epistle which has rather the appearance of being an afterthought. It has little connection with the foregoing chapters, and argues in an entirely different way. Chapters 1 to 17 are the Jewish Law twisted into an anti-Judaic sense by allegoristic exegesis. Here we have a very Jewish-sounding section, which takes the moral commandments of the Old Testament in a plain, literal sense. Chapters 18–20 are in fact a version of "The Two Ways," the moral catechism with which *Didache* opens.[1] There has naturally been much discussion of the relation between these passages in *Barnabas* and in *Didache*. As we have already observed, there is sufficient word-for-word correspondence reasonably to establish real literary dependence.[2] In

[1] See p. 71.
[2] See p. 200.

introducing "The Two Ways" as it occurs in *Didache*, we have inclined to the view that *Barnabas* is the source used for *Didache*, and not vice versa.¹ One other thing remains to be added to this discussion, in light of our consideration of the teaching of the Epistle. On the face of it, it would not look as though "The Two Ways" was composed by the writer of *Barnabas*. The difference in outlook is too great. So great is the contrast, in fact, that it is somewhat surprising that this writer was attracted to the document. The likelihood therefore is that the original material was a Jewish or Jewish-Christian tract. *Barnabas* incorporated this as a moral Epilogue to his main exegetical section. The writer of *Didache* shortly afterward took it over from him, rearranging the material in a better and more logical order, and making the tract longer and much more distinctively Christian by considerable interpolation of New Testament writings, particularly the sayings of Jesus.

For a general introduction to "The Two Ways," it will suffice to refer to the notes on *Didache*.²

19. "Thou shalt love Him that made thee, thou shalt fear Him": Compare Deuteronomy vi, 5, 13.

"Thou shalt not commit adultery": Exodus xx, 14.

"Quiet . . . fearing the words": Isaiah lxvi, 2.

"Thou shalt not take the name of the Lord in vain": Exodus xx, 7.

"Thou shalt not say that anything is thine own": Acts iv, 32.

"Be not thou found holding out thy hands": Ecclesiasticus iv, 31.

"Every one that speaketh unto thee the word of the Lord": Hebrews xiii, 7.

20. "But the way of the Black One is crooked": We observe that *Didache* eliminates Barnabas' vivid references to a personal Devil.

"Cleaving to the good"; Romans xii, 9.

21. "For he that doeth these things shall be glorified in the kingdom of God": Taken by itself, this phrase has a very "legal" sound. There are a number of passages, however, in the Epistle which lead us with confidence to claim that the writer had some degree of understanding of salvation by grace, redemption by the Cross, and the faith that works by love.

¹See pp. 74–5.
²See pp. 75–8.

"The day is at hand, in which everything shall be destroyed together with the Evil One": See Chapter 15, with note, p. 214.

"The Lord is at hand and His reward": Isaiah xl, 10; Revelation xxii, 12.

VII Homilies and Hortatory Literature

ii. "The Shepherd" of Hermas

1. Character of the Writing

This most interesting though not altogether inspiring book is a tract on the moral discipline of the Christian life, and on the ecclesiastical discipline of erring Church members. It is the work of one Hermas, who shows himself to be a serious-minded though rather pedestrian and prudential puritan moralist, deeply concerned at what he feels to be the laxity of the Roman Church of his day (though he was rejected by Tertullian in his Montanist days as not severe enough: *De Pudicitia*, 10). It is impossible to judge from what Hermas says whether the Roman Christians of the time were in fact inclined to easygoing and worldly standards of life. He may well be too severe upon them, for his concern is with the delinquents. However, it can hardly be disputed that the book does not belong to the most heroic strain of Christian discipleship. It has none of the majesty of 1 Clement, the passion of S. Ignatius, or the ordered and competent theology of the writer to Diognetus. *The Shepherd* comes as a reminder that all sorts were required to make the Church, then as now. We need to be reminded that the Church of that day is not necessarily to be condemned because there are things in this work which need to be called in question. Many critical scholars have been unduly severe in their judgment upon the religion of Hermas.

The impulse which led to the writing of this book was apparently the deliverance of Hermas from a temptation to commit adultery (Vision 1, i). The writer, therefore, was an all too "human" saint. Throughout he deals with questions of moral and ecclesiastical discipline from the humbled and salutary point of view of one who knows that he needs to receive and endure discipline. He is not content simply to lay down the law for other and frailer mortals. Nor is Hermas' home an idyllic one. His wife has to be rebuked for being a gossip, while of his children we read that "they have got the name of betrayers of parents" (Vision 2, ii). Some have taken this to mean that the children had informed against Hermas in some time of persecution, though this most unworthy action seemingly had not led to the most disastrous consequences. However, Hermas writes as one who had made and then lost some money, and was spiritually the better for his loss. This could conceivably be connected with some outbreak of persecution, which was by no means always official legal action carrying the penalty of death. Nevertheless, Hermas does not write as one who had been greatly delivered from great sin. He is no Augustine, either in the heights or the depths. He is a good, well-meaning, but ordinary man.

Much the same appears to be true of the Church of which he writes. Hermas has a good hope that most of its members will persevere to final salvation, but he certainly has no "rose-coloured-spectacles" view of them. The main fault they need to be guarded from is worldliness and undue absorption in daily business, and to a less extent from incontinence.

The medium of the teaching is a series of Visions and Parables, for the most part recognizably built up from New Testament themes. There are a few Old Testament and very many New Testament allusions, but few of them are express citations. *The Shepherd* is therefore a very Scriptural book, at least in form and intention. These reminiscences of the Bible are sufficient to show that Hermas knew the Four Gospels, the Epistles to the Romans, 1 and 2 Corinthians, Ephesians, Hebrews, and 1 and 2 Peter, and also the Revelation of S. John.[1] However, Hermas characterizes himself, in that his favourite Scriptural source is the Epistle of S. James, to which *The Shepherd* has a very similar tone. Some of Hermas' Parables are spun out to a great length of skilfully interlocking yet rather prosaic detail. This considerably reduces the effect, when they are compared with the New Testament originals. The character and style of these moralizing homilies, and the manifest acceptance they enjoyed in the ancient Church, is a valuable piece of contributory evidence in a most important issue. Many critics

---

[1]For a thorough treatment of this topic see C. Taylor, *The Witness of Hermas to the Four Gospels* (Cambridge, 1892). Not all his numerous parallels are close enough to be convincing, but he clearly demonstrates the main point that Hermas accepted four, and only four, Gospels.

have maintained that the representation in the Gospels of our Lord's life, character, and teaching was largely brought to birth from the "group mind" of the ancient Church, and is therefore not reliably historical. Here is a piece of evidence to rebut this charge. In *The Shepherd* we have, as it were, a demonstration of the tastes and inclinations of this same "group mind." If the Gospel portrait of Christ had been framed as some have maintained, it would doubtless have been in this pious and well-intentioned but unimaginative and uncreative style, a very different thing from the awesome and mysterious Figure we actually have.

The problem must now be faced why *The Shepherd* was so popular and respected in the early Church. The book is found in general circulation alike in the Eastern and Western Church soon after the middle of the second century, and at this time it had already been translated into Latin. It was one of the strongest of all unsuccessful candidates for admission to the canon of the New Testament. It is quoted as in some special sense inspired, and as quasi-Scripture, by such influential Doctors of the Church as S. Irenaeus, Clement of Alexandria, and Origen, and by Tertullian in his pre-Montanist period. Of particular importance is the evidence of Irenaeus, because this writer is so central in his conservatism, and so orthodox. In *Adversus Haereses*, IV, xx, 2, he writes: "Truly, then, the scripture (γραφή) declared, which says, 'First of all believe that there is one God . . .' " There then follows a citation of Hermas, Mandate 1. The use of the word γραφή is not absolutely conclusive, as it can mean "writing," but the context in S. Irenaeus makes the construction "Scripture" highly likely, as the quotation is incorporated with a number of other Scriptural citations. Eusebius, who reproduces this passage, certainly takes Irenaeus in this sense (*H.E.*, V, viii, 7). We judge that the same characteristic which makes the book unattractive to many modern students brought it respect in the ancient Church. *The Shepherd* is a pioneer manual of penitential discipline, and would be of manifest value to a Church in which as time went on the Penitential System became an increasingly prominent feature.

The background here is the sad human problem of "sin in believers." Even the Church of the so-called "early pure centuries" contained many members who were Christians not so much by dominating and heroic conviction as by upbringing and general good will. These could not all be trusted to run the straight race in that spirit of Christian liberty commended by S. Paul. Many needed the assisting crutch of ecclesiastical discipline. Those who had compromised the Faith had to be put out of communion, and could only be readmitted after they had pledged the sincerity and stability of their penitence by willingness to undergo punishment and humiliation. Some theological purists will maintain that this recourse to penitential discipline marked the sad fall of the Church from Gospel principles, and represents the invasion of Christianity by that "legality" and Christian Phariseeism which the great Apostle had particularly sought to expel. Be that as it may, the "weaker brethren" were there, and had to be cared for by the faithful pastor as best he could. That to which Hermas points is not the highest ideal of the life of adult spiritual liberty, but it was a practical necessity in the Church, as it still is. This book answered to a pressing practical need, and is most appropriately called *The Shepherd*. We cannot call it a visionary book. Rather has Hermas written a manual for the humdrum working pastor as he goes about necessary duties among somewhat unpromising human material. The historic Church owes more than can be told to those who have carried out these duties, even though the administration of penance is beset by many spiritual "occupational hazards" both to priest and to people. Therefore we may judge that *The Shepherd* has a rightful place among the Apostolic Fathers, though not the most exalted place.

It must be remembered, however, that Hermas is by no means an external Christian. He well realizes that God requires willing obedience from the heart, and looks upon the thought as well as the deed. Yet he has a great confidence that voluntary self-punishment and humiliation can purify the heart, and can discipline man to that obedience in which God delights. Here we come to an issue upon which sincere believers are divided, for there have been many in the Church all down the centuries who have found that their own spiritual experience has corresponded to the attitude of Hermas. Yet there are other outstanding men of God who have notably found it otherwise. They have laboured after a heart filled with loving obedience to God in the paths of ecclesiastical discipline, and found, not bread, but a stone. And then God has suddenly come to them in a more immediate and seemingly unaccountable act of divine grace. Those whose thought is moulded chiefly by this type of experience will find Hermas insufficient. The tragedy is that the Church should at times have been divided, and its fellowship of mutual instruction and upbuilding in these things impoverished, by disputes in this matter.

The fact surely is that both forms of Christian experience are to be looked upon as ways in which God deals with the human soul, in different cases, so that there is truth on both sides. Thus when Hermas writes of "penitence" it can often with almost complete justice be rendered "penance," much in the later sense of the word. He teaches that the amount of voluntary punishment to be undergone is proportioned to various sins, and that the due measure of penitential punishment can in some sense make amends for sin in the sight of God. (However, it must be borne in mind that Hermas teaches that God gives the desire thus to make amends, and that man requires God's grace if he is to do so.) We are not surprised, therefore, to find that such a writer as T. F. Torrance, writing from a strongly "Reformed" position, can say: "Behind all this Hermas has a general outlook which is not very Christian. Hermas represents the beginning of what has been known in Church history as 'paganism baptized into Christianity.' Already there are germs of many a later Roman Catholic doctrine."[1] There is material to support this case, but in general Torrance's judgment is far too extreme and severe. It deprecates too much Hermas' doctrine of grace, and savours perhaps of the assumption that if a Patristic doctrine of grace is not stated with that clarity of terminology developed by Reformation controversy the doctrine in question is inadequate. By contrast, Roman Catholic writers naturally find Hermas much more weighty and attractive as a theologian, because *The Shepherd* is to them so important a stage toward the development of the later doctrines of Penance, the Merit of Good Works, and of Purgatory. Possibly some of these err too far in the other direction.

Nevertheless, though popular and useful in the Church of the Fathers, it was with justice that *The Shepherd* did not come finally to be included in the canon of Scripture. Essentially it belongs to the passing outward forms of Christian religion, not to the fixed Apostolic principles. Thus the Muratorian Canon says of it: "Therefore it ought also to be read; but it cannot be read publicly in the Church to the people, either among the Prophets . . . or among the Apostles."[2]

[1] *Grace in the Apostolic Fathers*, p. 112; cf. p. 121, etc.
[2] Bettenson, *Documents*, pp. 41–2.

Eusebius likewise places it "among the rejected writings" (ἐν τοῖς νόθοις, H.E., III, xxv, 4). He says of it: "It should be observed that this too has been disputed by some, and on their account cannot be placed among the acknowledged books; while by others it is considered quite indispensable, especially to those who need instruction in the elements of the faith. Hence, as we know, it has been publicly read in Churches" (III, iii, 6).

2. Authorship and Date

The two questions are connected. Eusebius (H.E., III, iii, 6) records that some had ascribed the writing of *The Shepherd* to the Hermas mentioned by S. Paul in Romans xvi, 14. Origen, in his Commentary on this passage, gives this as his personal opinion only, though he does not write as though he were certain. If such had been the general received opinion in the ancient Church, the book could hardly have escaped a place in the Canon as "Apostolic," while Eusebius records that Apostolic authorship was sufficiently in dispute that the work could not be received. Modern scholars do not support this early date of writing. The only other piece of information is that given in the Muratorian Canon, which is usually given a date about A.D. 180–200. "But *The Shepherd* was written very recently in our time by Hermas, in the city of Rome, when his brother, Bishop Pius, was sitting in the chair of the Church of Rome." This statement is also attended by some perplexity, which is made the worse in that we have only a translation in barbarous Latin, and cannot be sure what was the original Greek of the document. If this statement be accepted, as it is by many competent scholars, *The Shepherd* was written during the episcopate of Pius I (c. A.D. 140–155). The main difficulty here is that the admittedly not very explicit references by Hermas to the Christian Ministry (Vision ii, 4; iii, 5, 9; Parable ix, 27) give the distinct impression that the Church at Rome was at this time governed by a body of "presbyter-bishops," and not by a single ruling bishop. This would continue the primitive form of Ministry for quite a long period of time in Rome, and ill accords with the tradition of early bishops there. The effect would be to make Pius I at most a "presiding presbyter" after the apparent manner of S. Clement of Rome, but hardly a "bishop," and still less a pope. Certainly the interest of *The Shepherd* in somewhat humdrum disciplinary details answers to this somewhat later period, when the first heroic pioneer Church had had a little space to settle down into an established community, and had to face the problems of communal self-preservation. The Church was indeed a community from the beginning, and in the New Testament period had to face the problems of discipline. It is the somewhat pedestrian approach of the book to this subject, rather than its penitential aim, which separates it from the post-Apostolic age.

Another difficulty about the date given above is the instruction in Vision ii, 4, to send a copy of the work to "Clement," and so "Clement shall send to the foreign cities, for this is his duty." This certainly reads as though Clement were a bishop, or at least a "presiding presbyter." Some have therefore assumed that S. Clement of Rome is intended, and place *The Shepherd* back to A.D. 90–100. The main attraction of this is that it agrees with the internal evidence, such as it is, about the development of the Ministry at Rome. It would be pleasing to feel that in Rome at the end of the first century we have the antetype not only of an archbishop, in Clement, but also of the harassed but careful curate and father-confessor in Hermas. This date would involve regarding the information given in the Muratorian fragment as incorrect. Quite possibly, however, some otherwise entirely unknown Clement may be intended, or Hermas may even have adopted the device of fathering his writing onto a revered figure of "the great days of old," in hope of increasing its authority.

The scene of the book is quite plainly Rome, where Hermas lives, and the vicinity. Parable ix is, however, placed in the mountainous district of Arcadia, and some have surmised on this account that this was where he grew up, whence he was sold as a slave to the Roman Christian lady Rhoda by his former master (Vision i).

3. Manuscript Sources[1]

(*a*) The first quarter of the work, and some fragments, occur in Greek at the end of the Biblical Codex Sinaiticus, following the Epistle

---

[1] There is a new critical text of *The Shepherd*, with commentary, edited by M. Whittaker, Berlin, 1956.

of Barnabas. (b) The fourteenth century Mount Athos MS continues up to Parable ix, Chapter 30, and so is the sole Greek authority for a long section of the text. (c) There are about twenty copies extant of the Old Latin version, and also a fourteenth century copy of another Latin version. These give a virtually complete text. (d) An Ethiopic version was discovered in 1847, and appears to represent a purer original than the Athos MS.

4. Outline

In view of the length and complicated plan of *The Shepherd* it may be useful to give an introductory outline of the contents.

(i) In introduction to the work proper there is a series of five Visions, which come to Hermas at different occasions. In the first two of these Visions a Woman, representing the Church, reminds him of his own duty of penitence and growth in holiness, and also of his duty to correct his family. There follow two Visions representing the Church as she undergoes the discipline of penitence and growth in holiness. In the fifth Vision, which is dignified by the title of a Revelation, the Shepherd, who is also the Angel of Repentance, appears, and brings to Hermas a series of messages. This introductory part of the book contains the historical and biographical allusions.

(ii) There follows a series of twelve Mandates, or moral Precepts, delivered by the Angel of Repentance in exhortation to various virtues and duties.

(iii) The longest part of the work consists in a series of ten Parables or Similitudes, delivered by the Angel of Repentance to Hermas. These further elaborate the theory of penitential humiliation and punishment, as a means to growth in grace. These Parables are adaptations of New Testament themes, and are highly Scriptural in their allusions, though containing few direct quotations. We may doubtless see in these homilies interesting reflections of early expository preaching from the New Testament.

5. Commentary on "The Shepherd"

Vision 1

1. It would seem that Hermas was born in slavery, and that he was a Greek, judging by his name. One gathers from his independent status and actions that his Christian mistress Rhoda had set him free, or enabled him to buy his freedom, probably because he was a fellow Christian. Though Christianity did not absolutely ban slavery, to free slaves was a common and laudable act of Christian charity (see 1 Cor. vii, 20–23).

"I began to love her as a sister": That is, as a fellow Christian. Presumably after some years of freedom, dwelling in another place, Hermas became associated with Rhoda in the life of the Church at Rome.

"I merely reflected on this and nothing more": Clearly Hermas "doth protest too much." For all his pious self-defence, it would seem that Hermas, a married man with a family, was tempted to more than "Platonic" love. However, it does not appear that he fell. There is no evidence that he committed adultery. He certainly does not write of penitence like an Augustine, by grace greatly delivered from great sin. Nevertheless, this is apparently the incident which moved the mind of Hermas toward the problems of moral discipline, and of the expiation of sin.

Cumae: near Rome, the spot traditionally associated with the ancient Roman prophetess, the Sybil (cf. Vision ii, 4).

"The desire after evil entered into thine heart": There are two sides to the morality and spirituality of Hermas. When he writes of the expiation of sin by punishment he not infrequently strikes an external and unevangelical tone, which can easily create an impression both unfavourable and not altogether true to his real mind. Here the teaching is that sin is inward as well as outward, and that God requires willing obedience from the heart (see also Parable ix, 28). The reference is to S. Matthew v, 28.

"His repute stands stedfast in the heavens": It is surely a blemish in Hermas that he can speak of a man's "repute" before God (see also Parable ix, 28).

"Propitiated"; εὐκατάλλακτον ἔχει (Lightfoot, p. 298): The word used here in the Greek answers to καταλλαγή, "reconciliation," not to ἱλαστήριον, "propitiation," though there is in fact no important difference in the New Testament sense of the two terms.

"They that claim for themselves this present world, and boast in its riches": To Hermas the chief snare of the saints is the mundane temptation of worldliness. (See also Parables i and ix, 30, 31).

2. "Propitiate"; ἐξιλάσομαι (Lightfoot, p. 298): The verb used here corresponds to ἱλαστήριον.

"An aged lady": This lady is later disclosed to be the Church (Vision ii, 4).

3. "But out of fondness for thy children": The next fault of Hermas is that he has spoiled his children.

"Be attentive, and hear the glories of God": The moral exhortation is enforced by a vision of the majesty of God, described in Old Testament language.

Vision 2

2. "Now that this day has been set as a limit . . . repentance for the righteous hath an end": The expression of Hermas upon this point is not quite consistent, even though it is his central theme. The general subject of the book is the repentance and forgiveness of believers. In Mandate iv, 3, a Christian is allowed the possibility of only one restoration after a serious fall from grace. Here there seems to be none. The general sense here is the familiar apocalyptic theme that men are called to recognize that they are living in the times of Judgment, and are summoned to special strictness of life. Those that have the clearer Christian light, particularly as witnessed to by Hermas, have no excuse for continuing in sin (cf. S. John xv, 22).

"For the Gentiles there is repentance until the last day": The "Gentiles" are the non-Christians, those outside the Church, which is the Israel of God. For the uninstructed there is the excuse of ignorance, and for the unbaptized there is the open door of salvation until the end, which is presumed to be near.

"The rulers of the Church": It appears that the government of the Church at Rome is by a presbytery, not a ruling bishop, but the statement is not quite explicit. (See also Chap. 4, Vision iii, 9; Parable ix, 27.)

"The great tribulation that cometh": Hermas, like the generality of

Christian writers in the early period, believed that he was living in "the last days," and accepted the usual eschatological scheme of a final tribulation of wickedness, leading to the Advent of Christ (S. Mark xiii, 3–13).

3. "Thy simplicity and thy great continence": The notion that one virtue can make up for another fault appeals to most unreflecting minds as a common-sense idea, but it is really quite inconsistent with the Christian principle of salvation by divine grace. It represents the opposite to the position laid down in the previous chapter, that those having the clearest light partake of the severest judgment. Hermas is not a very deep or systematic thinker, and complete consistency is not to be expected of him, though he is systematic in the complicated structure of his book.

Maximus: We have no idea who Maximus was, but he was in danger of falling into serious post-baptismal sin for a second time, and so of forfeiting all hope of further forgiveness (see Mandate iv, 3).

Eldad and Modat: The writing from which this citation comes is not otherwise known. It was presumably a Jewish work.

4. "A youth": This youth is later revealed to be The Shepherd, the Angel of Repentance, under another form (Revelation v).

"I say, 'The Sybil' ": This is natural, seeing that the place is Cumae (see 1).

"She was created before all things": This is a development of the thought of Ephesians iii, 9–11, where the ideal Church has existed from the ages in the mind of God.

"The Elders": Clement; there appears to be no ruling bishop mentioned, in a context where this would be natural, unless Clement be the Bishop of Rome (see Intro. 2).

Grapte: This is apparently the woman to whom was entrusted the instruction of the widows and orphans.

Vision 3

2. "Therefore to them belongs the right side of the Holiness . . . to all who shall suffer for the Name": As in the thought of S. Ignatius, and of the writer to Diognetus, so here; the martyrs are the essential Christian disciples.

"Dost thou not see a great tower?": The same theme of the Church as a tower is repeated to much greater detail in Parable ix. It is an elaboration of such passages as 1 Corinthians iii, 9–15; Ephesians ii, 20–22; and 1 Peter ii, 5–8.

3. "The tower is builded upon waters": Perhaps an allusion to Psalm xxiv, 2.

"Your life is saved and shall be saved by water": Entrance to the Church is by "the water" of Holy Baptism (see 1 Pet. iii, 20).

4. There is a very prominent doctrine of angels in Hermas. In Parable v, 6, they are described as subordinate fellow-workers with Christ in His saving work.

5. "The stones that are squared and white, and that fit together in their joints, these are the apostles and bishops": See Ephesians ii, 20, and Revelation xxi, 14.

"Their office of bishop and teacher and deacon": In a context like this, concerning the apostolic foundation of the Church, it is hard to see that Hermas could have accidentally failed to mention the presbyters, if by this time the bishop had become a separate office at Rome. There is presumably still a twofold Ministry of "presbyter-bishops" and deacons, as in Philippians i, 1.

"Some of them already fallen on sleep": This sentiment sounds "early," like the reference to the Ministry above. It is still a matter worthy of comment that many of the Apostolic successors are dead. Thus the Apostles are not yet viewed as distant historic figures.

"But if the building shall be finished, they have no more any place": When the Church is finished the number of the elect is made up, "and then cometh the End" (8). This is not the later speculative doctrine that a fixed number of the elect were predestined to be saved, but the simple New Testament conviction that God's plan of salvation is no mere divine afterthought, contingent upon man's disobedience. It is the sovereign outworking of a wise and age-long purpose (Eph. iii, 11; Rev. xiii, 8; xvii, 8). See also Chapter 8, and Parable ix, 32.

6. "These are they that have faith, but have also riches of this world": There is a strong and characteristic fear of riches in Hermas, which plainly echoes the teaching of our Lord in the Gospels, and also S. James. The allusions here are to such passages as S. Matt. xix, 21; S. Mark iv, 17–19; James ii, 5, and so on.

"When thou hadst riches, thou wast useless": It would appear from this that Hermas, the freedman, had prospered to some extent, and then suffered misfortune.

7. "Thus thinking that they can find a better way": These rejected stones presumably represent heretics.

"Yet they shall be fitted into another place much more humble": The symbolism here is confused, for theologically speaking there cannot be more than one Church. The finally penitent are either in or out of the one Tower.

8. "The first of them . . . is called Faith": It is a sound evangelical note to put faith first, to teach that faith is the source of the virtues, and that man is saved by faith. It is characteristic of Hermas, however, to put continence before love in the scale of virtues. He is an exponent of the severe and semiascetic virtues of self-denial, rather than the spontaneous and "human" virtues of affection.

9. "Their moaning shall go up unto the Lord": Compare S. James v, 4.

"Rulers of the Church": This answers to a presbytery, rather than a bishop.

"Lest these divisions of yours deprive you of your life": Compare Galatians v, 15, 10–13.

10–13. This involved allegory of the Church, as a woman appearing three times with increasing youth and beauty, is not very appropriate in its outworking. The spiritual decay of Hermas is the cause of the Church appearing aged and feeble. His repentance and growth in grace rejuvenates the Church. There is indeed a sense in which the unworthiness of members makes the Church appear unworthy, but the thought of Hermas is somewhat superficial at this point. It is man which suffers the infirmity, not the ideal Church.

10. "A young man": We later find that this young man is a form of "The Shepherd" (Revelation v, 1).

11. "Cast not your cares on the Lord": Compare Psalm lv, 22; 1 Peter v, 7.

13. "For the couch hath four feet and standeth firmly; for the world too is upheld by means of four elements"; στοιχεία (Lightfoot, p. 314): These "elements" are the constituent principles of the universe (cf. Ep. to Diognetus, 8), or the superhuman beings which exercise control over the world (cf. Gal. iv, 9). The four feet of the "couch" (see also 10) are most probably an allegory of the Four Gospels, which are the support of the Church. We are guided to this somewhat obscure result by the accident that S. Irenaeus, who used *The Shepherd*, and reverenced it almost, but not quite as Scripture (Eusebius, *H.E.*, V, viii, 7), takes up the same idea, but makes it more explicit. Indeed, it is more than likely that at this point Irenaeus has based himself upon Hermas.[1] He argues that "since there are four zones of the world in which we live, and four universal winds (or "spirits," τέσσερα καθολικὰ πνεύματα)[2] it is fitting that the Church should have four pillars" (*Adv. Haer.*, III, xi, 8). These pillars are the four canonical Gospels. We are left wondering how many more of the artful Hermas' "hidden meanings" might be detected in some of the multitudinous but apparently insignificant details of his allegories had we more to guide us in this way concerning the mind and teaching methods of the ancient Church. We are at least given a valuable glimpse of the mentality of Hermas.

Vision 4

1. The fourth Vision is a short Apocalypse, which reflects the common Christian sense of living in "The Last Times." We are not surprised to find that this passage is packed with allusions to New Testament writings, and one to Daniel. The scene is set out in the country on the Campanian Way. The power of evil presents itself in the familiar apocalyptic guise of a monster. Hermas is comforted, significantly enough, by another appearance of the Church, this time younger and more beautiful than ever in the form of a virgin bride.

"Can it be that cattle are coming?": The genius of Hermas is a little too prosaic and earthy to tell an apocalyptic vision well.

"Put on the faith of the Lord": Compare Ephesians vi, 13, 16.

"Four colours": These nearly but not quite, correspond to the colours of the four horses of Revelation vi, 2–5, but in the reverse order.

2. "A virgin arrayed as if she were going forth from a bride-chamber . . . it was the Church": Compare Ephesians v, 23–32; Revelation xxi, 2.

---

[1] C. Taylor, *Hermas and the Four Gospels*, Cambridge, 1892, pp. 5–18.
[2] Translated in the Latin, *quatuor principales spiritus*. See Lawson, *The Biblical Theology of S. Irenaeus*, London, 1948, pp. 43–4.

HOMILIES AND HORTATORY LITERATURE 233

"Cast thy care upon God": Compare Psalm lv, 22; 1 Peter v, 7. This allusion occurs twice.

"Saved by nothing else but by His . . . Name": Compare Acts iv, 12. We here have another view of Hermas' doctrine of salvation by faith in Christ.

"Shut its mouth": Daniel vi, 22.

"Escaped a great tribulation by reason of thy faith": Compare Hebrews xi, 33.

"Better for them that they had not been born": S. Matthew xxvi, 24; S. Mark xiv, 21.

3. "This world must perish by fire": Compare 2 Peter iii, 10, 12.

"Gold is tested by the fire": Compare 1 Peter i, 7.

"Ye that pass through the fire will be purified by it": Compare 1 Corinthians iii, 12–13.

Revelation 5

The final Vision is dignified by the name of a "Revelation"; Ἀποκάλυψις (Lightfoot, p. 317), and marks the more decisive appearance of "The Shepherd," who is "The Angel of Repentance." He introduces the main matter of the book.

"Dost thou not recognize me?": It is hard to resist the thought that quite possibly "The Shepherd" is a veiled representation of our Lord. He is the Good Shepherd of S. John x, 11–16. It is impossible to be sure, for the identification is nowhere made explicit, and there are some objections of real weight. In the first place, "The Shepherd" is described as "sent by the most holy angel," which is admittedly a curious phrase to use of Christ. Yet as we have seen, the language of Hermas is often confused and theologically inexact. In the second place, "The Shepherd" speaks about "The Lord," as though He were another than Himself. However, "The Lord" may simply mean "God." Finally, "The Shepherd" is described as an "angel," which would be a serious infraction of later orthodoxy. This is a less weighty objection, for Hermas is a sufficiently vague theologian in his doctrine of the Person of Christ to render this expression quite possible. Furthermore, Isaiah lxiii, 1–10, was to the ancient Church a leading Old Testament "prophecy of Christ," and verse 9 speaks of the suffering of "the angel of God's presence." Traditional exegesis would certainly apply this to Christ.

Reasons for maintaining that "The Shepherd" is Christ, or at least a type of Christ, are as follows: (*a*) In view of the general style and treatment of this work we would almost expect Hermas to prefer a veiled reference to Christ. (*b*) The book is substantially a Christian one in spirit, despite its sometimes confused doctrine of the Person of Christ, and inconsistencies of phraseology in the matter of salvation by divine grace. Yet it contains extraordinarily few explicit mentions of the name of Christ. This encourages us to look for a veiled reference. (*c*) If "The Shepherd" is indeed Christ, then the work is a much more consistent whole. (*d*) In this Revelation "The Shepherd" is introduced by Hermas in a manner reminiscent of the appearance of Christ in glory to S. John in Revelation i, 13–17: "there entered a man glorious in his visage . . . with a white skin wrapped about him." Like John, Hermas is overwhelmed with distress when he recognizes the Visitor, is reassured, and bidden to write commandments from God. (*e*) "The Shepherd" is the Shepherd of the Church, which is the Flock of God. This is a prominent theme in Hermas. It is derived ultimately from the Old Testament (Isa. xl, 11; Zech. xiii, 7; and so on). It was used by our Lord Himself (S. Matt. x, 16; S. Mark vi, 34; xiv, 27; S. Luke xii, 32). It is expounded by the Apostles (S. John x, 11–16; 1 Pet. ii, 25; v, 2, 4). (*f*) "The Shepherd" gives to Hermas a series of Christian commandments of divine authority, beginning with Christ's first and great Commandment of the Law. (*g*) He teaches Hermas in a series of Parables which are plainly in the main adaptations of the Gospel Parables. (*h*) The Visitor is described as "the Shepherd, unto whom thou wast delivered." He is the master of Hermas. This language becomes most appropriate, if "The Shepherd" be allowed to be a figure of Christ. (*i*) That "The Shepherd" is called "the Angel of Repentance" is not an objection to this identification. He is not the same as "the angel of punishment" of Parable vi, 3. The Gospels themselves introduce the call to repentance as one of the fundamental elements of the message of Jesus (S. Mark i, 15).

"I recognized him as being the same, to whom I was delivered": The reference is not very plain, but presumably this is "the young man" of Vision ii, 4, and Vision iii, 10. In each case he appears as the interpreter of a mysterious revelation.

"If then ye . . . do them with a pure heart, ye shall receive from the Lord all things that he promised you": This again is an inexact and deficient statement, judged from the standpoint of a strict doctrine of salvation by grace. God's blessing is not properly a reward for obedience. Nevertheless, obedience is a condition for continuing in God's blessing, and Hermas probably here means just this.

Precept 1

The Precepts of the Shepherd start fittingly with the first and great Commandment of the Law. The passage alludes to Genesis i, 1; Deuteronomy vi, 4, 14; S. Mark xii, 28–31, and so on. This is the one passage in Hermas expressly quoted by Irenaeus, and called "Scripture" (*Adv. Haer.*, IV, xx, 2): but see note on Vision iii, 13.[1]

Precept 2

"Speak evil of no man . . . Give to all": In Precept 2 Hermas is exhorted to truthfulness and avoidance of gossip, and to almsgiving. The passage is largely dependent on S. James.

"Slander is evil": Compare James iv, 11.

"It is a restless demon": Compare James iii, 5, 8.

"And thy heart pure and undefiled": Compare James i, 27.

"Keep this commandment . . . that thine own repentance . . . may be found to be sincere": This is the characteristic thought of the administrator of penitential discipline. The virtue of obedience is that it is the mark of sincere penitence.

Precept 3

"I always lived deceitfully . . . and no man ever contradicted me, and confidence was placed in my word": An exhortation to truthfulness convicts Hermas of deep untruthfulness in his past business life, which had apparently not been found out. His financial misfortune must have been due to some other cause. He is to make amends by future integrity in business, which can make good for what he has done in the past, and secure eternal life for himself. This is the penitential attitude to life.

"The Lord, Who dwelleth in thee": Compare 1 John ii, 27.

[1] See Lawson, *Biblical Theology of S. Irenaeus*, pp. 50–51, for a discussion.

"And brief grief to the Spirit which is holy and true": Compare Eph. iv, 30.

Precept 4

1. "Remember thine own wife always": In an exhortation to sexual purity, Hermas is forcibly reminded by the Shepherd of his former occasion of weakness.

"Sir, if a man that has a wife": There appropriately follows from this one of the most important sections of the moral teaching of Hermas, in which he gives us invaluable information as to the early Christian doctrine of marriage. Marriage is for life (see also Chap. 4). A Christian who has put away his wife on account of repeated and unrepentant adultery, lest he condone and fail to punish her sin, is not to marry again. He is to leave open the possibility of eventual penitence in his erring partner, and is then to be reunited to her. If he definitely divorces her so as to remarry, he commits adultery. The implication is plain. In order to punish an erring partner the Christian may have recourse to the provisions of Roman law, and be legally separated from his wife. But he cannot be spiritually separated from her in the sight of God.

"He likewise committeth adultery": Our Lord's own words in S. Matthew xix, 9, are appropriately cited in support of this position.

2. "For the man that hath sinned understandeth that he hath done evil . . . Thou seeest then that repentance is great understanding": "Repentance" in this passage plainly has much of the sense of "Penance." Punishment is to be undergone voluntarily as a mark of penitence, and this will purge the soul. This is an important passage for the understanding of Hermas. Certainly there is a tension between this doctrine of Penance and Hermas' conception of salvation by grace. Many scholars have strongly felt that this is a sign that Hermas is insecure in his doctrine of grace, and that he really does not understand the Gospel. This appears to be an unduly severe judgment. Hermas does not always express himself very accurately, and he is inexpert as a theologian. However, his underlying intention is correct, for there surely is in the Christian scheme a place both for salvation by divine grace and also for moral and ecclesiastical discipline as a means of grace.

3. "I have heard from certain teachers that there is no other repentance, save that which took place when we went down into the water": The rigorous position that, while Holy Baptism freely remits all previous sin, there is no place for repentance and remission of sin for the lapsed believer, was held by at least some teachers in the early Church (see Heb. vi, 4–7). This was a natural position for those who emphasized the New Testament doctrine that Baptism, inward and outward, by the Holy Spirit and by the water, was an actual incorporation into Christ in His death and resurrection, and was a decisive death to the old life and a rebirth to the new life in Christ (see Rom. vi, 3–6). However, this is looking at the matter from the point of view of an ideal theological principle. Hebrews discusses post-Baptismal sin in terms of some great fault, such as would in effect involve apostasy from Christ. A complete forsaking of Christ, strangely and grievously following a complete and devoted self-identification with Him, is manifestly the ultimate sin. However, it is obvious that Hermas is discussing another problem, different from that of Hebrews, and of those "certain teachers" who adopt the position of Hebrews. He is interested in the discipline of frail but well-meaning believers. The faults he has in mind are chiefly those of worldliness, avarice, gossip, and lustful thoughts. Manifestly it is an impossible position that all baptized believers who have been guilty of these are lost souls, for there can never have been more than a few of such perfect believers, even in the heroic Apostolic period. Hermas well illustrates the mind of the Church as it moves away from the ideal theological principle to the necessary practical task of discipline within the Church, as she has existed as an historical institution. The Church rightly decided that it was possible to restore believers who had compromised the Faith, provided that by their conduct they showed that they were sincerely penitent. This is the sense of the clause in the Apostles' Creed: "I believe in the forgiveness of sins." Hermas shows a very guarded movement away from original "ideal" rigorism to later penitential practice. He is nervous lest the baptized presume upon the goodness of God in the restoration of lapsed believers, and he can allow his readers to hope for one restoration, but not more.

"But if he sin off-hand and repent, repentance is unprofitable": This one restoration is open only for those who have become entangled in the minor faults of frail humanity (as was presumably the case with

Hermas himself). There is apparently no place of repentance for those who have sinned "with a high hand," or in crimes that involve definite apostasy (see also Parable vi, 1, 2; ix, 19, 26).

"For he shall live with difficulty": The normal channel of restoration through penitential discipline is not open to the highhanded apostate, yet Hermas apparently cannot forbear to hope that God will have some way of receiving them, though it is arduous and not to be counted on (see also Parable ix, 26).

"The Lord then, being very compassionate, had pity on His handiwork . . . and to me was given the authority over this repentance": The provision of an opportunity for repentance, and of Baptism as the seal of the new life, is a mark of the divine grace. This answers to Hermas' underlying doctrine of salvation by grace. The context makes it natural to suppose that "the Lord" is the Creator, not the incarnate Christ, which in turn supports the idea that "the Shepherd," who is here speaking, is Christ Himself. It is natural to have it stated that Christ has been given divine authority over penitence.

"Thou shalt be saved . . . as many as shall do these things": Here again is the opposite side to Hermas' doctrine of salvation. Salvation is to be sought in penitence (and perhaps "Penance") as a means of grace. This statement is not intended to deny salvation by grace, which is affirmed in the present context, but Hermas does not teach "salvation by grace alone."

4. "He sinneth not, but if he remain single, he investeth himself with more exceeding honour": The doctrine that for a widow or widower to marry again is legitimate, but that to remain unmarried is the more excellent way for a Christian, is derived from 1 Corinthians vii, 26–40. The difference is, however, that S. Paul is avowedly legislating for the short period of tribulation before the Coming of the Lord (v. 26), while Hermas is applying the principal generally. Hermas indeed believes himself to be living in "the last times," but it appears likely that he writes as he does here because he feels that marriage is by way of a concession to human frailty, rather than a thing excellent in itself.

Precept 5

1. 2. "Be thou long-suffering and understanding. . . . For the Lord

dwelleth in long-suffering, but the devil in angry temper. . . . Long-suffering is great and strong": We have here an exhortation to patient endurance, and a warning against its opposite, hasty bad temper, in a passage reminiscent of S. James.

1. "The Holy Spirit that abideth in thee shall be pure, not being darkened by another evil spirit": It is characteristic of Hermas that he is vague in his conception of the Holy Spirit. The Spirit is here written of almost as though He were merely the higher side of man's natural faculties, rather than an empowering and indwelling divine Presence. (See also Chap. 2, and Precept x, 1, 2, 3, and Precept xi.) This failing was not uncommon in the ancient Church and is still with us. A possible reason for this is that in the first days "the Spirit" was eminently associated in the Christian mind with "charismatic" prophecy, as in the Acts of the Apostles. As this phenomenon died down, many were left in the Church with an insecure grasp of the conception of a personal Holy Spirit.

"For they all were justified by the most holy angel"; ἐδικαιώθησαν γὰρ πάντες (Lightfoot, p. 324). This very difficult statement makes sense, in conformity with established Christian doctrine, if it be allowed that "the most holy Angel" (who is here apparently speaking) is Christ Himself, the Shepherd.

2. "And for no cause whatever the man or the woman is embittered": It is to be observed how often Hermas argues on a very human and somewhat mundane level, concerning the common small failings of Christians. That there were many such at this time is a salutary corrective to romantic views of "the early pure days" of the Church. It also shows how natural and practical was that disciplinary and "penitential" attitude toward growth in grace, which some have found unevangelical in Hermas.

"But angry temper is in the first place foolish": Compare S. James i, 13-15.

"Unstable in all his actions": Compare S. James i, 8.

Precept 6

1. "Whosoever shall turn unto the Lord with his whole heart": Compare Jeremiah xxiv, 7.

2. This renewed exhortation to constancy and contentment, and

against quick temper, worldliness, and sensuality, in the guise of a parable of "the angel of righteousness" and "the angel of wickedness" which dwell in man, is reminiscent of S. James iii, 13–iv, 7.

Precept 7

"Fear the Lord and keep His commandments": What is said in this exhortation regarding the fear of God, as an incentive to obedience, is true so far as it goes, but it would have been more profoundly true had something also been said about the love of God as a motive.

"This is the fear wherewith thou oughtest to be afraid . . . for, if thou fear the Lord, thou shalt be master over the devil": This is the thought of our Lord in S. Luke xii, 4–5.

"Because every creature feareth the Lord, but not every one keepeth His commandments": This is a typical carelessness in presentation, for Hermas now uses "the fear of God" in a different sense from the above. By "the fear of God" he here means that all creation is subject to God's sovereignty, though all do not render Him moral obedience.

Precept 8

"What kinds of wickedness are they from which we must be temperate and abstain": We have an exhortation to abstinence first from fleshly, and then from spiritual, sins.

"Theft, falsehood, deprivation, avarice . . . refrain from all these things, that thou mayest live unto God": Compare 1 Corinthians vi, 9.

"First of all there is faith, fear of the Lord, love, concord": It is good that faith comes first in this list. Some will account it less good that fear of the Lord comes before love. It is dangerous to read too much significance into the order of words here, particularly with such an unsystematic writer as Hermas. For example, it might be objected that in Galatians v, 22, S. Paul himself puts faith after, and not before, the moral virtues of joy, peace, long-suffering, gentleness, goodness. Nevertheless, we may judge from the context that "love" here is not love toward God, which is the source of moral virtue, but love toward man, which is a moral virtue itself derived from faith and the fear of the Lord. This is not an unsound position.

"To minister to widows, to visit the orphans": Compare James i, 27.

Precept 9

"Remove from thyself a doubtful mind": Compare Ecclesiasticus xii, 13. The exhortation is to unwavering faith in prayer.

"How can I ask a thing of the Lord . . . seeing I have committed so many sins against Him? . . . Turn to the Lord with thy whole heart, and thou shalt know His exceeding compassion": Here is a clear declaration of the principle of divine grace.

"Turn to the Lord with thy whole heart": Compare Jeremiah xxiv, 7.

"Cleanse thy heart from all the vanities of this life": On the surface this denies the principle of grace, but Hermas can hardly intend this, in view of the general tenor of the chapter. The statement reflects his confidence in penance as a means of grace.

"Nothing wavering": Compare James i, 6.

"Put on faith": Compare Ephesians vi, 16.

"Trust God that thou wilt receive all thy petitions": Compare S. Mark xi, 24.

"For assuredly it is by reason . . . of some transgression, of which thou art ignorant, that thou receivest thy petition so tardily": S. Paul gives a more seeing answer to this problem (2 Cor. xii, 8, 9).

"Cease not to make thy soul's petition": Compare S. Luke xviii, 1–8.

"Faith is from above from the Lord": This is a clear enunciation of the principle of divine grace. Man comes to have faith primarily through the initiative of a gracious God (cf. Acts xiv, 27; 1 Cor. xii, 3).

Precept 10

1. "Perceivest not that sorrow is more evil than all the spirits" Hermas is exhorted to cheerfulness ($\dot{\iota}\lambda\alpha\rho\acute{o}\tau\eta s$, Lightfoot, pp. 333–4), as a quality pleasing to and concordant with the indwelling Spirit. This is not the most usual note among moralists. A clue to the thought of Hermas is perhaps given by the quotation of Psalm civ, 15, in Precept 12, iii, where it is taught that obedience to the commandments of God will "gladden the heart of man." Hermas feels that the converse is true. A glad heart before God leads to obedience. This is perhaps a somewhat dim glimpse of "the faith that works by love." Hermas is trying to say that obedience is made possible by a delight in God, which admits the Spirit to dwell in the heart.

"Crushes out the Holy Spirit": Again we see the characteristic vagueness of the doctrine of the Holy Spirit. He is spoken of almost as though He were the higher aspect of man's own spiritual faculties.

"Mixed up in business affairs": This characteristic emphasis of Hermas is here clearly based upon a reminiscence of S. Mark iv, 18–19.

"As good vineyards": Compare Isaiah v, 6.

2. "Grief at this entereth into the man, and grieveth the Holy Spirit, and crusheth it out": Compare Ephesians iv, 30. Hermas teaches that trifling with temptation produces frustration, bitterness, and despair, and this separates man from the influence of the Holy Spirit. This is true enough, but it will be observed that this again is the converse of the proposition with which the Precept starts; namely, that a heart rejoicing before God can obey. The general intention is fairly clear, but the expression confused.

3. "The intercession of a sad man hath never at any time power to ascend to the altar of God": Here a substantially true principle is pressed to a misleading and superficial application, contrary to the witness of Christ (cf. S. Luke xxii, 41–4; Heb. v, 7).

Precept 11

"Men seated on a couch, and another man seated on a chair": This Precept expounds the contrast between the official teachers of the Church and the self-appointed, self-opinionated, and self-seeking heretical teacher. The symbolism of men seated on a couch is curious. The first thought which emerges is that there are several of these, seated together. The orthodox teaching of the Church's officers is collective, and therefore authoritative. On the other hand, the heretic has seated himself by himself in the chair of the Teacher, and is making the pretension of being himself a sufficient authority. In line with this, "he prophesieth to them in corners." Any heretical teacher would be open to this charge of religious individualism, and of forming his own conventicle, but the figure here is perhaps best filled by a Gnostic, on account of this charge of secret teaching. Possibly, again, "the couch" on which the Presbyters sit is intended by Hermas to be the secure and four-legged one on which the Church sits in Vision iii, 13. The teachers of the Church base themselves upon the admitted and approved Four Gospels, not upon a private "tradition," like the Gnostics. However, if there is here a defence of the fourfold character of the true Gospel tradition, the polemic would equally suit the case of Marcion, who accepted but a single Gospel.

"Having no power of a divine Spirit in himself": It is not quite certain whether Hermas intends to represent the heretical teacher as having the prophetic gift of a delusive "charismatic" ministry. The passage "that man is emptied, and the earthly spirit fleeth from him in fear, and that man is struck dumb" would agree with this construction, but does not make it necessary. The "striking dumb" may only mean that in the Church the heretic is ashamed to go on teaching. The other references seem to indicate the contrary. The spirit of the heretical teacher "speaketh not at all, unless it be consulted," and the heretic requires a fee, "and if he receiveth not, he prophesieth not." This sounds like a Gnostic teacher with his secret charms, rather than a true ecstatic. It is to be noted, however, that ecstatic prophecy did occur among some Gnostic devotees.

"For no Spirit given of God needeth to be consulted": By contrast, the true Christian prophecy is under the direct guidance of the Holy Spirit, and is therefore unbidden and spontaneous.

"When then the man who hath the divine Spirit cometh into an assembly of righteous men . . . intercession is made to God by the gathering of those men . . . and the man, being filled with the Holy Spirit, speaketh to the multitude": The true Christian prophet is a modest man who, unlike the heretic, "holdeth himself inferior to all men." He utters his oracle under the collective discipline of the prayers of the whole Church. It is most interesting that the disciplinarian Hermas can find this room in the Church for the authority of prophecy, but it is significant that the criterion of true and orthodox prophecy is its amenity to collective ecclesiastical discipline.

"Because it is from above": Compare S. James iii, 17.

"The spirit which speaketh according to the desires of men is earthly": Compare S. James iii, 15.

"The Spirit which is from above": S. James iii, 17.

"The angel of the prophetic Spirit": We observe again in this chapter the characteristic vagueness of doctrine concerning the Holy Spirit, who is here called an "angel." However, this does not necessarily preclude the idea of His divinity, for "the Angel of Repentance" is quite possibly Christ. (See note on Revelation 5.)

"Take a squirt of water . . . The hail is a very small grain": Very pedestrian parables!

Precept 12

The theme of the last of the Precepts is "the good fight of faith." This, the climax of the Precepts of "the Shepherd" to Hermas, is in some ways perhaps the most interesting part of the whole work. The charge which has often been laid against Hermas is that he is not a genuine Christian moralist, but a mere moralist, who looks upon Christianity as a self-imposed system of moral duties by which a man is to earn the favour of God. He has but a dim conception of redemption in Christ, and of salvation by divine grace. It has to be admitted that a tendency to slip into Christian Phariseeism of this sort has ever been the besetting weakness of systems of penitential discipline, necessary and legitimate though they may be for many purposes. This weakness has to be guarded against in the Church by a constant and counterbalancing emphasis that the valuable means of grace which God has provided in the Church are only means, and that man is to trust for his salvation in the divine grace which he may receive through the means, and not simply in his own diligence in the use of the means. It is important to determine whether Hermas is indeed overtaken by weakness at this point. If, as some have maintained, Hermas is found to have based himself upon a fundamental misunderstanding of the Christian Gospel, the admission is a very damaging one, in view of the prestige of this work in the ancient Church, and the illustrious names of those who bestowed their favour upon it. It has seemed to some that the writing and wide acceptance of this book is a token of the weakness of the ancient Church in regard to some of the very principles of the Faith.

This is the issue which has now to be faced in this twelfth Precept, which is in a sense the turning point of the whole work. It is the climax of the Shepherd's commandments, and leads into his hortatory sermons of application, or "Parables." Hitherto we have come upon certain isolated sayings which appear not to accord well with the doctrine of grace, in that they speak of "faith" as though it were man's action, or put "fear" or "continence" where one would expect love (see pp. 229, 231, 235, 240). We now encounter a more outspoken statement in this direction, which looks forward to several others in the succeeding Parables. On the other hand, the twelfth Precept also contains some strong counterbalancing considerations, which require carefully to be weighed.

Before we proceed to the examination of the two sets of material, two cautions are to be urged. The first is the standing danger of theological anachronism in the reading of all these ancient writings. It is useless to suspect heresy at every point where the expression is not so clear as it would have been had it been framed in the light of later doctrinal controversy and definition. The case in point is that Hermas is by no means to be condemned as "a mere moralist" because he does not state the doctrine of salvation by grace with the clarity, consistency, and severity of post-Reformation divines. The second caution is that the interest of Hermas is plainly in moral discipline, not in theology. This is a legitimate and valuable interest, but it has to be admitted that in not a few matters he is an inexpert and confused theologian, who we may suspect does not do full doctrinal justice to the Church for which he speaks. It is perhaps just to give him the benefit of the doubt in some issues where the fault of his theology may be in his manner of expression rather than in his real intention.

1. "Remove from thyself all evil desire." The theologian of grace will object that this is precisely what man cannot do, and that this statement displays the weakness of Hermas.

"For the evil desire is wild": Compare S. James iii, 2 ff.

"These men then it hands over to death": Compare S. James i, 15.

2. "Before all is desire for the wife or husband of another." The characteristic morals of Hermas.

"Ye must therefore abstain from the evil desires." See below.

"But do thou clothe thyself in the desire of righteousness." See below.

"If the evil desire shall see thee armed with the fear of God . . . it shall flee far from thee": Compare S. James iv, 7. See below.

3. "Practising these thou shalt be well-pleasing as a servant of God." See below.

"If thou set it before thyself that they can be kept, thou wilt easily keep them, and they will not be hard."

In these passages containing a number of parallels to S. James,

Hermas is exhorted to remove from himself all evil desire, which brings death to the servants of God. Particularly mentioned are adulterous desire and desire for luxury. Those who abstain, and clothe themselves in righteousness, will "live unto God," and be "well-pleasing" to Him as His servants. These commandments admittedly appear very hard, but Hermas is reassured that they will become easy if a sufficiently single-minded moral effort be made. On the face of it this is very far from the doctrine of salvation by divine grace, and is unsatisfactory as a statement of Christian principles of morality. This impression is seconded by such passages in the succeeding Parables as V, 1, 3, where contrary to our Lord's words in S. Luke xvii, 10, it is stated that "if thou do any good thing outside the commandment of God, thou shalt win for thyself more exceeding glory": Parable VII, where it is taught that simple repentance does not produce divine forgiveness, and Parables VIII, 11; IX, 33; and X, 4. Such then is the evidence to support the charge that Hermas does not appreciate the guilt and power of sin, and that he teaches a religion of human effort and human merit, not of God's grace in redemption. The case clearly has weight.

3. "These commandments . . . are able to gladden the heart of the man who is able to observe them": Compare Psalm civ, 15.

4. 5. 6. "He began to speak more kindly to me, and he saith . . . 'Perceivest thou not the glory of God'." See below.

"The man that hath the Lord in his heart can master all these commandments." See below.

"For I will be with you, I, the angel of repentance, who have the mastery over him." See below.

"He cannot . . . overmaster the servants of God, who set their hope on him with their whole heart." See below.

"As many then as are complete in the faith oppose him mightily." See below.

"Fear not the devil; for I was sent . . . to be with you who repent with your whole heart, and to strengthen you in the faith."

It has not always been adequately noticed that in the second part of this admittedly difficult Precept there is a strong doctrine of grace, and of salvation through faith in Christ. However, it is not expressed as explicitly as one would wish. When Hermas naturally is confounded at the prospect of having to obey God's strict commandments he is reassured by the Shepherd that "the man that hath the Lord in his heart can master all these commandments." This conveys something of the conception of an indwelling Lord, who is the bringer of grace. Moreover, if it be allowed, as probably it may, that "the Shepherd" is in reality a guise for Christ Himself, then this suggestion is greatly strengthened. (However, see Parable IX, 7, and note.) "The Shepherd" forthwith goes on to declare Himself as the one who has conquered Satan, so that those who have Him with them need not fear the power of the Adversary. "The Angel of Repentance" is to us a misleading title, which leads the mind away to the thought of "the Shepherd" as a mere taskmaster of penitential discipline. Actually, He is the one who makes repentance possible, because He is the conqueror of Satan. "For I will be with you, I, the Angel of Repentance, who have the mastery over him." The Good Shepherd at a great price protects the flock from the destroyer (S. John x, 11, 12). This is Christ's own thought of Himself as "the Strong Man," who, in token of the coming of the Kingdom, has bound Satan and released his prisoners (S. Matt. xii, 28–9; S. Luke xi, 20–22, and so on). Here surely is a true reflection of one of the great original themes of the teaching of our Lord. In the background is the conception of salvation by faith in Christ, a Christ who once conquered the adversary, and who now in the Spirit can come to dwell in the hearts of those who trust Him.

This side of the doctrine of Hermas is likewise seconded by a number of important references in the succeeding Parables. Salvation is by divine grace, "that thou mayest see the abundant compassion of the Lord, how great and glorious it is, and He has given His Spirit to those that are worthy of repentance" (Parable VIII, 6). Repentance is something which God "gives" to those in whom He sees a sincere desire to turn from evil (see also VIII, 9). Parable IX, 14, speaks of the compassion of God who "sent forth the Angel of Repentance to us that had sinned against Him, and refreshed our spirit, and, when we were already ruined and had no hope of life, restored our life." Of the Virgins representing virtues, of whom the first in order is "Faith," we read, "it is impossible that these commandements be kept without the help of these Virgins" (Parable X, 3). This side of the case has weight too. Hermas is not always clear, and he is certainly not consistent throughout. In passages where he is concerned to emphasize the value of the penitential means of grace, he is sometimes guilty of improper phrases regarding grace, but it is quite unjust to him to declare that he has an entirely inadequate and sub-Christian doctrine of salvation by grace.

4. "Therefore do you, who are empty and fickle in the faith, set your Lord in your heart, and ye shall perceive that nothing is easier than these commandments, nor sweeter, nor more gentle." In light of the above discussion we may perhaps venture the judgment that the intention of Hermas in this passage is to invite men to open their hearts to a "faith-union" with the indwelling victorious Christ, who can bring to man the power of glad and spontaneous obedience to the commandments of God. This is "the faith that works by love" (see also Parable I, V, 4; VI, 1; IX, 24).

5. "If then ye resist him, he will be vanquished": Compare S. James iv, 7.

6. "If ye turn unto the Lord with your whole heart, and work righteousness the remaining days of your life . . . He will give healing to your former sins, and ye shall have power to master the works of the devil." In light of the context we may interpret this as much more than a call to self-reformation.

"Who is able . . . to save and to destroy": One of the rare verbal quotations of Scripture in Hermas, of S. James iv, 12.

Parable 1

This is a parable of the Christian's heavenly citizenship, in closely Scriptural terms. The Christian is to eschew "laying up treasures upon earth," and the folly of Dives. He is to live as "a stranger and a pilgrim," always ready to leave this world for his real home (see also Vision I, Parables IV, IX, 30, 31).

"Ye who are servants of God, are dwelling in a foreign land": Compare Hebrews xi, 13–14. We have the same thought in Epistle to Diognetus, v.

"Why do ye here prepare fields?": Compare S. Matthew vi, 21; S. James iv, 13–14.

"When thou art cast out by him, what wilt thou do with thy field and thy house?": Compare S. Luke xii, 20.

"As dwelling in a strange land": Compare 1 Peter ii, 11.

"Instead of fields buy ye souls": Compare S. Matthew vi, 20.

"Visit widows and orphans": Compare S. James i, 27.
"Spend your riches and your displays . . . on fields and houses of this kind": Compare S. Mark x, 29–30; S. Luke xvi, 9.

Parable 2

We have here an interesting parable, most revealing of the mind of Hermas. There is cooperation between the strong elm, standing for the rich man in the Church, and the fruitful vine, standing for the poor man. The rich man, who is presumed to be poor in the things of the spirit, can of his charity relieve and support the poor man, who is rich in faith. The poor man can in his turn enrich the wealthy by his prayers. So the fellowship of believers in the Church yields a characteristic exhortation to charity and prayer (see also Parable V, 3).

"Distracted about his riches": Compare S. Mark iv, 19.

"Even that which he giveth is small and weak and hath not power above": The presumably larger gift of a prayerless rich man is not valuable before God, who looks on the heart. Compare S. Mark xii, 41–4.

"He shall be able to obtain a reward with God": This is not strictly the idea that charitable giving purchases religious merit, but the profounder idea of the spiritual solidarity of the Church, which is the body of Christ. Different members have different gifts, and can bless one another.

"The poor man is rich in intercession": This is the theme of S. James ii, 5, and reflects the Old Testament conception that the poor are the righteous, who are well-pleasing to God (cf. S. Luke vi, 20).

"His intercession hath great power with God": Compare S. James v, 16.

"Blessed are the rich, who understand also that they are enriched from the Lord": This paradoxical conclusion, which brings the Parable to an apt climax, possibly reflects the thought of 1 Chronicles xxix, 14–15, a passage on the theme of pilgrimage treated of in the preceding Parable.

Parable 3

A short parable with the moral "Judge nothing before the time," because the difference between the righteous and the unrighteous is not yet apparent. (Cf. the parable of the Wheat and Tares, S. Matt. xiii, 24–30.)

Parable 4

This parable is a continuation of the theme of 1 and 3, and is a warning against worldliness, in view of the coming Judgment.

"Then they that serve God shall be made manifest": Compare S. Matthew xiii, 43.

"But the Gentiles and the sinners": Observe that sinners are "Gentiles"; that is, the Church is "the true Israel."

"Abstain from overmuch business, and thou shalt never fall into any sin." A characteristic touch with Hermas, though many moralists have affirmed the opposite!

Parable 5

We now come to an interesting but theologically very obscure parable, obviously based upon our Lord's great parable of the Unthankful Husbandmen (S. Mark xii, 1–9). The parable, however, is adapted and introduced as one concerning fasting. In Hermas' parable a slave is left by his master to care for a vineyard. He greatly exceeds in service what he is bound to do, and is rewarded by being made a joint-heir with the master's son. It is significant for the future that the discipline of fasting is here connected with the basic idea of "works of supererogation."

1. "A station": That is, the primitive Christian weekly fast on Wednesday and Friday; compare *Didache*, viii.

"Ye know not how to fast unto the Lord . . . But fast thou such a fast as this, do no wickedness in thy life": Compare Isaiah lviii, 5–7.

2. "So he called his beloved son, who was his heir": Compare S. Mark xii, 6–7.

"I desire to make him joint-heir with my son": It will be remembered that S. Paul himself can describe the believer as a "joint-heir with Christ," Rom. viii, 17. This phrase, therefore, does not necessarily imply confusion between humanity and divinity.

3. "But if thou do any good thing outside the commandment of God, thou shalt win for thyself more exceeding glory": Hermas

ventures upon more than dubious ground here, for it is surely unfitting for the Christian to consider the possibility of his "glory" before the sight of God, and our Lord Himself rebuked the idea that a man can do more service to God than is his duty (S. Luke xvii, 10).

"This then is the way, that thou shalt keep this fast": It is pleasing to observe that in his zeal for the outward discipline of self-humiliation Hermas does not forget to emphasize that fasting is not an end in itself. It is only of virtue when it springs from a desire for inward purity, and what is saved by fasting should be used for practical good. It is interesting to observe the practical detail that the Christian fast is not a total one; bread and water may be taken.

"He that hath received from thy humiliation . . . may pray for thee to the Lord": For an expansion of this, see Parable ii.

4. "Asketh understanding of Him": Compare S. James i, 5, 6.

5. "The estate is the world": We here have a reminiscence from another of our Lord's parables, that of the Wheat and Tares (S. Matt. xiii, 38).

"The servant is the Son of God": The "interpretation" of Hermas' original parable serves to make it most obscure! The first point about fasting is now rather confusingly dropped, and the parable adapted to illustrate the doctrine of the Incarnation. The "servant" in the Parable now ceases to be the believer, whose reward is to be made "joint-heir with Christ," and becomes the Son of God Himself, who is the Lord of the vineyard, the Church. Yet in the next chapter Hermas further contradicts himself by saying that the parable does not present the Son of God in the guise of a servant, but as in a position of great power!

"And the vines are this people whom He Himself planted": Compare Isaiah v, 7.

6. "The Son of God is not represented in the guise of a servant": There would seem to be a reminiscence of S. Mark x, 45, here. Hermas' expression is confused, but his sense would appear to be that the suffering and humiliated divine Son, who has redeemed the vineyard of the Church at the price of His agony, is only apparently a "servant." Actually, He is the divine Lord.

"And the Son placed the angels in charge of them": Hermas thus teaches that the angels are co-workers with the suffering Son of God in the redemption of the Church. Yet it is to be observed that he does not say that the angels suffered together with the Son. They are apparently cooperators in the work of redemption accomplished by the Son, not subsidiary co-redeemers. This is an important and sound distinction.

"Having Himself then cleansed the sins of His people": Compare Hebrews i, 3.

"He showed them the paths of life": Compare Psalm xvi, 11.

"The law which He received from His father": Compare S. John x, 18.

"Having received all power from His father": Compare S. John xvii, 2.

"The Holy Pre-existent Spirit, which created the whole creation, God made to dwell in flesh that He desired.... When then it had lived honourably in chastity.... He chose it as a partner with the Holy Spirit": After the changes and confusions of Hermas' Parable, we are hardly surprised to find that the application of the details of his story to the doctrine of the Person of Christ entangles him in still more serious confusion! At no point is Hermas' inexpertness as a theologian more clearly exemplified than in this celebrated passage, which has received far more than its due share of attention. Hermas appears to teach that Jesus was a man who lived a life of exemplary righteousness, in consequence of which the divine Holy Spirit came upon him in a unique manner. This is apparently regarded as a doctrine of the Incarnation. This is clearly a most inadequate statement, and on the face of it answers to the heresy of Adoptionism. It completely confuses the divine Son with the Holy Spirit (as also in Parable IX, 1), and makes our Lord no more than the perfect climax of inspired men. Adoptionism was at that time already branded as a definite heresy, and indeed had been so as early as the composition of S. Mark's Gospel, where the citation of Psalm ii, 7, by custom applied to Christ as "messianic" (cf. Heb. i, 5), is in S. Mark i, 11, carefully reproduced without the clause "this day have I begotten Thee" to avoid the implication that at His Baptism our Lord "became" the Christ by the descent of the Holy Spirit. We cannot say with certainty any more than that the language of Hermas does not conform to the orthodoxy of his time at this point. It is just possible, however, in view of the changes in the train of argument in chapters 5 and 6, that Hermas may be thinking back to the first application of his Parable, in chapters

2 and 3. In this case it could perhaps be argued that "the flesh" in which the Holy Spirit comes to dwell is that of "the faithful servant" of Chapter 2, who did more than his duty. This would make the descent of the Holy Spirit to be upon the Christian believer, a much more orthodox position. This would accord with the general attitude of Hermas (see Parable IX, 12, with note). In all events, Hermas has shown himself in this whole Parable a careless literary composer, and a blundering theologian.

7. "See that it never enter into thine heart that this flesh of thine is perishable, and so thou abuse it in some defilement": The Parable closes with an affirmation of the doctrine of the resurrection of the body, with its important correlative that the body is the subject of Christian salvation, and therefore is to be kept pure.

"If thou defile thy flesh, thou shalt defile the Holy Spirit also": Compare 1 Corinthians vi, 17, 19–20. This comment serves as a warning that we must interpret with caution the vague language of Hermas, and not see "heresy" in it too quickly. Taken in isolation this passage reads like one of those which make "the Holy Spirit" no more than the higher aspect of man's natural faculties, yet it is based upon a great doctrinal statement of S. Paul. The admittedly vague language is presumably to be taken in the Apostle's "orthodox" sense.

Parable 6

1. 2. In this parable Hermas sees "the angel of self-indulgence" as a young shepherd in charge of a flock of well-fed and frisky sheep. That the self-indulgent are in a flock tended by a shepherd indicates that they are part of the Church. Hermas clearly feels that there are some in the Church of his time, apparently pastors as well as people, who are proud, irresponsible, self-indulgent, and lacking in discipline. The Parable divides these into two classes, the self-indulgent who are guilty of definite apostasy, for whom there is no repentance, and the careless who have not sinned so deeply, and for whom there is hope of restoration through penitential discipline (see also Parable IX, 18, 19, 26).

1. "Able to save a man's soul": Compare S. James i, 21.
"A young man, a shepherd, clothed in a light cloke": Avowedly this

figure is the symbol of self-indulgence. We surmise that he is also a symbol of the irresponsible, self-seeking, and flattering pastor.

2. "I comprehend not what means 'unto death,' and what 'unto corruption' ": Any writer on practical pastoral discipline is bound to make some such distinction as this, artificial though it may be in principle. None of the flock are perfect, so all need discipline, even though they are on the way to final salvation. Some are "all too human," though well meaning, and it is hard to exclude them from the hope of salvation. There are other more grievous faults, which seem to involve apostasy. There is no difference in principle between these sins and others, and in principle they can be forgiven to the sincerely penitent. But a puritan writer like Hermas is naturally shy of admitting this into the penitential system, lest men presume upon the divine mercy. So a practical distinction is here drawn, though as we have seen, Hermas cannot forbear to hope that even gross sinners may be saved by some extraordinary means, and at a great price (see Precept IV, 3).

"For the name of God is being blasphemed through them": Compare Heb. vi, 4–6.

2. 3. "A great shepherd like a wild man in appearance . . . This is the angel of punishment": We are now introduced to the wild and severe shepherd, who disciplines that section of the erring flock which is guilty only of what may be described as venial sins, so as to restore them to grace through repentance. Taylor traces the features of S. John the Baptist in this "angel of punishment."[1]

4. 5. The Parable closes with an intricate discussion of the relative severity of crime and punishment. It is disclosed that an hour of self-indulgence is to be punished with an "hour" of torment, but this hour "hath the power of thirty days," while the chastening memory of one of these "days" of punishment lasts for a whole year! The passage is interesting as giving light upon the tortuous mind of Hermas, but it also serves as a warning against the artificiality and unspirituality of attempts to mete out virtue and punishment quantitatively.

Parable 7

Hermas is forewarned that he must receive the grievous attention of "the angel of punishment," and requests that he be taken away. The

[1] C. Taylor, *The Witness of Hermas to the Four Gospels*, Cambridge, 1892, p. 32.

Shepherd shows that this is not possible, for Hermas is suffering on account of the sins of his family.

"Thy sins are many, yet not so many that thou shouldst be delivered over to this angel": So it is possible for a believer like Hermas to be rebuked as a sinner, yet to be less of a sinner than the more hopeful section of the erring flock handed over to the "angel of punishment." There are indeed many degrees of sinners in the Church, separated in a most artificial way. Here is another warning against quantitative schemes of judging sin and punishment.

"Thy house has committed great iniquities and sins . . . they cannot be afflicted otherwise . . . unless thou, the head of the whole house, be afflicted": Hermas is suffering more than he personally deserves, through the principle of the solidarity of the family. Also, he is in some sense responsible for the faults of his children (Vision I, 3).

"But if thou be prosperous, they can suffer no affliction": The presupposition seems to be that spiritually profitable affliction is likely to be temporal. Hermas appears to have a great fear of wealth, and a certain rather naïve confidence that hardship is good for the soul. This attitude clearly answers to his own experience in prosperity and adversity (Vision III, 6), but is hardly to be regarded as a general principle.

"Thinkest thou that the sins of those who repent are forgiven forthwith? Certainly not; but the person who repents must torture his own soul . . . and if he endure the afflictions which come upon him, assuredly He who created all things . . . will be moved with compassion": The spirituality and theology of Hermas is certainly to be criticized at this point. The confusion in his mind is between the spiritual principles of repentance before God, and of divine forgiveness, and that which can be the outward means of this grace, namely, penance and restoration to Church communion. Contrary to Hermas, our Lord taught that God does forthwith forgive the genuinely penitent sinner, and that He does not need to be moved to compassion (S. Luke xv, 11–32; xviii, 9–14). But man, who cannot see into the heart, cannot act like God. In matters of ecclesiastical discipline, those professing penitence must prove their sincerity by patiently undergoing their punishment for a while.

Parable 8

"The Shepherd" now shows Hermas the great willow tree of the Law of God, superintended by the angel Michael. There then follows a very involved allegory, full of pedestrian detail, pointing out the respective rewards received by various classes of the people, according to the degree of life retained by the willow wands with which each is supplied. The tower of the Church appears again, to which those who are approved are admitted. The theme is a union of the ideas of our Lord's Parables of the Vine and of the Talents, and the passage is chiefly interesting as an example of early Christian exegetical preaching from the Parables of Jesus. The example of Hermas shows that sermons were preached from the Parables. We trust that his work is not a good example, for this and Parable IX are models of how not to expound Christ's teaching! Nevertheless, one must be cautious in judgment, for it is well possible that the very different mentality of the ancient Church could see more of inspiration in these labyrinths of prosaic detail than can the modern reader.

3. "This Law is the Son of God preached unto the ends of the earth": S. Paul was inclined to place the Law and the Gospel as in some sense opposites to one another (Rom. vi, 14, etc.). It was however a common usage in the ancient Church to speak of the Gospel as "the New Law," as here. This is not necessarily inconsistent with the intention of S. Paul, and does not necessarily involve "legality." On the principle that the Church is "the New Israel," the purified and reconstituted People of God, new and yet continuous with the old Israel, the religion by which the Church lives may by analogy be described as "the Law" of the New Covenant, just as the Mosaic Law was the basis of the religion of the old community. The question as to whether the Christian Gospel is rightly understood is left open by the use of this title.

6. "It is that thou mayest see the abundant compassion of the Lord, how great and glorious it is, and He hath given His Spirit to those that are worthy of repentence. . . . To those, whose heart He saw about to become pure and to serve Him with all the heart, to them He gave repentance": Hermas' statements are not very clear, or theologically very satisfactory, but it would appear that his underlying intention is to express the two cardinal principles of salvation by divine grace, and of human cooperation with grace. We have stress upon the compassion of God, and that He "gives repentance." This is the idea of grace. God gives His grace to those who are "about to become pure." This is probably a clumsy way of saying that God gives His grace to those whose hearts are open to receive it (a sound position), and does not involve the error that God requires a man by his own effort to reform his character, before divine grace can be bestowed.

"That blasphemed the Lord in their sins": Compare James ii, 7.

"Ashamed of the Name of the Lord": Compare 1 Peter iv, 14, 16.

"For they were hypocrites, and brought in strange doctrines. . . . These then have hope of repenting": It is noteworthy that Hermas has a hope for the restoration of heretics.

7. "Life is for all those that keep the commandments of the Lord": Compare S. Mark x, 17–19.

"But in the commandments there is nothing about first places": Compare S. Mark ix, 35–45.

8. "These still have place for repentance, if they repent quickly": Compare Revelation ii, 5, 16.

9. "Yet they departed not from God, but continued in the faith, though they wrought not the works of the faith": It is notable in this context that "faith" has not its full sense of "obedient trust in Christ." It is "The Faith," that is, the Christian system of belief and practical discipleship (Eph. iv, 5, etc.). Hermas can therefore write of those who have a more or less nominal acceptance of "the faith," but who do not bring forth its practical fruits (cf. S. James ii, 17–20).

"The Gentiles": That is, the unbelievers, the Church being "the Israel of God."

10. "Still they never separated from God, but bore the Name gladly, and gladly received into their houses the servants of God": These are not perfect Christians, but were prepared to suffer persecution as Confessors of "the Name," and so are counted as in a state of penitence and grace (cf. 1 Peter iv, 16). We observe that to forsake "the Name" is to be separated from God.

11. "The Lord in His compassion sent me to give repentance to all, though some of them do not deserve it for their deeds": This is typical of the confused language of Hermas. In a passage giving a strong witness to the idea of divine grace, he can inconsistently write of some "deserving" to be saved.

"The Lord willeth them that were called through His Son to be saved": Compare 1 Timothy ii, 4–5.

Parable 9

In this still more extended and complex parable, Hermas is again shown the vision of the Church, in the form of a tower which is yet in the building. Various classes of believers, in their various states of Christian grace, are represented by various sorts of stones. The necessary discipline of each class, and the final acceptance or rejection of each, is figured in the treatment of the stones. This is manifestly exposition of the theme of S. Paul in Ephesians ii, 19–22, and iv, 15–16.

1. "The Holy Spirit, which spake with thee in the form of the Church.... For that Spirit is the Son of God": This is a good example of the inexact terminology of Hermas. He can use the phrase "Holy Spirit" almost in the same sense as "Angel," that is, the figurative symbol of a divine message. Thus he can say that the Spirit is the Son, almost as he can say that an angel is the Son. Similarly, the symbolical figure "the Church" also brings a divine message: so it can be said that the Spirit speaks here.

"Arcadia": Some have surmised that this mountainous district had been the birthplace of the Greek Hermas.

"Twelve mountains": These are the nations of the world. Thus the reference is probably to S. Matthew iv, 8, where Christ is placed on a high mountain, and shown the kingdoms of the world.

2. "The rock was loftier than the mountains": Compare Isaiah ii, 2; Micah iv, 1, a "prophecy" of the Church.

"The gate seemed to me to have been hewed out quite recently": This is a figure of Christ (see Chap. 12).

"Twelve virgins": These represent cardinal Virtues (see Chap. 15).

"Entreat the Lord, that thou mayest receive understanding": Compare S. James i, 5.

3. "There went up ten stones square and polished, (not) hewn from a quarry": Some commentators insert "not" into the received text at this point (see Lightfoot, p. 372, footnote). If this be allowed, then the allusion is probably to the "stone cut out without hands" of Daniel ii,

34, 45, which Irenaeus says is a figure of Christ, born of a Virgin (*Adv. Haer.*, III, xxi, 7). Taylor, observing that there are ten stones, and that the Greek figure for ten is iota, the first letter of the name Jesus in Greek, states that this foundation of ten stones is Christ.[1] Hermas, however, seems himself to hint at another construction (see Chap. 15, with note). It must be remembered that all these constructions are conjectural, for we cannot be sure of all Hermas' multiplicity of hidden meanings in this very detailed parable.

4. "Twenty-five stones": See Chapter 15.

5. "There was a cessation in the building": There is a significant pause after the laying down of the first four courses of stones, in the building of the Church, until the Master of the Church shall come and test the work. This pause may well represent the transition from the Church of the Old Covenant to that of the New, by the coming of Christ (see Chap. 15).

6. "A man of such lofty stature that he overtopped the tower": This strange figure may well represent God the Father, who has committed the Church and its members to the Shepherd (but see Chap. 12, with note).

7. The discipline and redemption of unworthy members of the Church is delivered by "the glorious man" to the Shepherd (Christ?): Compare S. Matthew xxviii, 18.

9. "Twelve women were called, most beautiful in form, clad in black . . . with their hair hanging loose": These black-clothed wantons represent twelve Vices (see also Chaps. 13, 15).

11. "Thou shalt pass the night with us . . . as a brother, not as a husband. . . . But I was ashamed to abide with them": The modest Hermas finds it necessary to discipline himself in continence even when in the company of the Virtues! However, as he sports with them he finds, "I had become as it were a younger man." The whole is an odd picture.

"I supped, Sir . . . on the words of the Lord the whole night through": Compare S. Luke iv, 4.

12. "This rock and gate is the Son of God. . . . The Son of God is older than all His creation . . . therefore also He is ancient. . . . He was

[1]*Hermas and the Four Gospels*, pp. 29–32.

made manifest in the last days of the consummation; therefore the gate was made recent": We have here a much more adequate doctrine of our Lord's divine nature and office than in Parable v. God the Son is preexistent, and the Agent of creation. He became incarnate in "the last days" to open the Kingdom of God to believers.

"That they . . . may enter through it into the Kingdom of God. . . . Man cannot enter into the Kingdom of God except through the gate itself": It is noteworthy that entrance into the Kingdom of God is by means of incorporation into the tower of the Church, through Christ, who is the door (S. John x, 7).

"Except he receive the name of His Son": Compare Acts iv, 12.

"But the gate is the Son of God; there is this one entrance only to the Lord": A parallel thought to the above: Christ the Door of the Sheep is the only way for man to come to God (S. Luke x, 22; S. John xiv, 6).

"The glorious man . . . is the Son of God": The symbolism is at this point very perplexed. The rock on which the Tower of the Church is built is the Son of God, and the new door is Christ. But the glorious Man who inspects the Tower, with its door, is also the Son of God! We are left wondering whether Hermas has forgotten what he has written, for the identification made in this passage brings confusion to the rest of his symbolism. The identification of the Man of "lofty stature" which best fits the scheme is that He represents God the Father (see Chap. 6).

13. "No man can otherwise be found in the kingdom of God, unless they shall clothe him with their garment": Compare S. Matthew xxii, 11–12.

"If thou bear the Name, but bear not His power": Compare S. Matthew vii, 22–3.

"They shall become one spirit and one body": Compare Ephesians iv, 4.

14. "This is the reason why there was also a cessation in the building, that, if these repent, they may go into the building of the tower": This is a reference to the time for repentance allowed by a merciful God before the Last Judgment.

"Because he had compassion on all that called upon His name, and sent forth the angel of repentance to us that had sinned against Him, and refreshed our spirit, and when we were already ruined and had no hope of life, restored our life": Here is a clear doctrine of divine grace, and of salvation by grace. It is to be noted that the sending of the Angel of Repentance is a work of grace, not merely of legal severity.

"The name of the Son of God is great. . . . If then all creation is sustained by the Son, what thinkest thou of those that are called by Him?": Here is a high doctrine of the Person of Christ, to set against some of the ambiguous statements of Hermas. The Son is the controller of the universe, and the foundation of the Church (cf. S. Mark xii, 10).

15. The names of the Virtues and Vices are then given. The name of the first Virtue is fittingly Faith, and the second, characteristically for Hermas, Continence. So with the list of Vices: the first is Unbelief, and the second Intemperance.

" 'But the stones, Sir,' say I, 'that came from the deep, and were fitted into the building, who are they'?": We now come to a somewhat obscure but theologically important section of the interpretation. The details are slightly confused, as is not uncommon with Hermas, but the general sense seems to be clear enough. We have a parable of the union of the Church of the Old Covenant with that of the New. The ten original stones forming "the first generation" of the Church are presumably the ten Patriarchs, from Adam to Noah (1 Chron. i, 1-4; S. Luke iii, 36-8). (For an alternative interpretation of the ten stones by Taylor, see note on Chapter 3.) If Noah is counted again as the beginning of the next Dispensation of the Church, the twenty-five stones of "the second generation of righteous men" extend to David (S. Luke iii, 31-6; though it is only twenty-four in 1 Chron. i, ii). The thirty-five stones of "God's prophets and His ministers" (the priesthood) presumably represent the pre-messianic kingdom of God's people. It does not appear that thirty-five generations can be fitted into the Biblical genealogies, so possibly this number is an arbitrary figure, designed to equal the total of the two previous Dispensations. The next and fourth course of forty stones, "the apostles and teachers of the preaching of the Son of God," apparently represents that original generation of Hebrew Christians in which the Old and New Israel overlap. This gives the transition to the fourth Dispensation of that Gentile Church which Hermas regards as his own.

"Wherefore . . . did the virgins give in these stones also for the building of the tower and carry them through the gate?": We observe that the Patriarchs and worthies of old Israel are joined to the Church only through Christ, the Door. This thought is developed in the next chapter.

"Because they . . . bore these spirits . . . till they fell asleep": The ancient worthies could be joined to the Church through Christ because all their days they walked in the spirit of the twelve Virtues.

16. "It was necessary for them . . . to rise up through water, that they might be made alive. . . . They could not enter into the kingdom of God [cf. S. John iii, 5], except they had put aside the deadness of their former life. So these likewise that had fallen asleep received the seal of the Son of God and entered into the kingdom of God": The first three courses of stones in the tower of the Church have "to rise up through water" because it is necessary for the Church of the Old Covenant to receive "the seal of the Son of God," that is, Holy Baptism, before they can rise to life and "enter into the Kingdom of God." An interesting double use of the word "water" appears, for it is the water of the sleep of physical death, as well as the water of Baptism. The idea of going down into the water as "dying with Christ" is close to hand here (Rom. vi, 3–5).

"The Apostles and the teachers . . . after they had fallen asleep in the power and faith of the Son of God, preached also to them that had fallen asleep before them, and themselves gave unto them the seal of the preaching": Here is an interesting and daring extension of the doctrine that our Lord Himself, after His death, carried His saving work back to righteous men who had lived in the ages before Him (1 Pet. iii, 18–21). Hermas teaches that the deceased Apostles carried on a parallel ministry of preaching and Baptism among the bygone generations in the unseen world. Thus in effect "the Great Commission" extends to the departed (S. Matt. xxviii, 19). Hermas teaches an unusual aspect of the doctrine of the Communion of Saints.

"But these went down alive . . . whereas the others that had fallen asleep before them went down dead and came up alive": The worthies of the Old Testament Church went down into the water of death spiritually dead, because until a man is baptized he is spiritually dead. However, in the unseen world they came up out of the water of Baptism alive. By contrast, the first Christian generation, the fourth course of forty stones, being baptized, went down into the water of death spiritually alive. So the Patriarchs came to the full knowledge of the Christian faith, and were built into the Church. We can hardly doubt that this strange doctrine belongs to the same circle of thought as the obscure "Baptism for the dead" mentioned by S. Paul in 1 Corinthians xv, 29.

17. An exposition of the twelve mountains which surround the plain on which the tower of the Church stands yields a doctrine of the catholicity of the Church.

"These twelve mountains are twelve tribes that inhabit the whole world. . . . And they are various in understanding and in mind": Hermas does not mean that different ethnic groups have different characteristics, and different talents which they can bring into the Church. The different degrees of understanding are various degrees of Christian faithfulness in humanity taken as a whole. Therefore although nominally it is the whole human race which is described as "twelve tribes," the thought is not far away that the one Church existing among every nation is the New Israel of God, "the Twelve Tribes of Israel" (S. Matt. xix, 28; S. James i, 1; 1 Pet. i, 1; Rev. vii, 4).

"All nations that dwell under heaven, when they heard and believed, were called by the one Name": Compare Ephesians ii, 11–14.

"So having received the seal, they had one understanding and one mind, and one faith became theirs and one love": Thus men of every nation are united into the one Church by the Name of one Lord, by one Creed, and one seal of Holy Baptism (cf. Eph. iv, 4–5).

18. "If then he that ought to do good committeth wickedness, does he not seem to do greater wickedness than the man that knoweth not God?": The theme of the great sin of apostasy is taken up again. The heathen that sin are held accountable. They are "condemned to death." This seems to indicate punishment rather than damnation. To "die eternally" is reserved for Christians who deliberately and knowingly commit a great sin, involving apostasy from Christ (compare S. Luke xii, 47–8; S. John xv, 22, 24).

"The Church of God shall be one body . . . one faith": Compare Ephesians iv, 4. We note that Hermas says "shall be," not that it is, with S. Paul. He is thinking of the future perfected Church on earth, after the Judgment, not of the ideal Church now existing in the mind of God, as in Ephesians.

"Show me the force and the doings of each one of the mountains": In a most confusing and inconsequential manner, quite typical of Hermas, the symbolism of the twelve mountains is now changed.

They become types of different classes of hearers of the Gospel, of differing degrees of faithfulness. Thus we have a long allegory of the same type as the interpretation of our Lord's Parable of the Sower. This Parable is actually referred to in an exhortation against worldliness in Chapter 20.

19. "For these there is no repentance": The definite apostate is beyond hope of redemption (Heb. iv, 4–6).

"These men have a name indeed, but they are void of the faith": Compare Revelation iii, 1.

"For these then repentance is offered": For the hypocrites in the Church, if not apostate, there is hope of restoration, if they repent quickly.

20. "The thorns are they that are mixed up in various business affairs": We now come to a plain reminiscence of the Parable of the Sower (S. Mark iv, 19).

"Shall hardly enter into the kingdom of God": A citation of S. Mark x, 23.

"It is difficult for such men to enter into the kingdom of God": A citation of S. Mark x, 24.

21. "And the part towards the root withered, and some of it dried up by the sun": Compare S. Mark iv, 5–6.

"The double-minded": Compare S. James i, 8.

"They have the Lord on their lips, but have Him not in their heart": Compare Isaiah xxix, 13.

"Their words only live, but their works are dead": Compare Revelation iii, 1.

"When they hear of tribulation": Compare S. Mark iv, 17.

"If they repent quickly, shall be able to live": Compare Rev. ii, 16.

22. "Desiring to know all things, and yet they know nothing at all": Compare 2 Tim. iii, 7.

23. "Propitiated"; ἵλεως (Lightfoot, p. 392): This word occurs in the New Testament in S. Matthew xvi, 22, where it is rendered "be it far from thee," and in Hebrews viii, 12, where it is rendered "merciful." The latter is a better sense than "propitiated," for the word is a cognate of ἱλαστήριον, "the means by which that which is offensive to God is cleansed" (rendered "mercy-seat" in the English Old Testament).

"Doth man, who is mortal and full of sins, bear a grudge against man?": Compare S. Matthew xviii, 32-3.

25. "Kept back no part at all for evil desire": Compare Acts xx, 20, 27.

26. "Deacons that exercised their office ill": One of the chief offices of the deacon in the Church was to distribute the alms to the poor.

"But if a man be found to have denied from the heart, I know not whether it is possible for him to live": The normal rule is that apostasy is the sin "which hath never forgiveness" (see Parable VI, 1, 2). However, despite his rigid disciplinary principles, Hermas cannot forbear to hope that in some uncovenanted way God will be able to restore even these (cf. Precept IV, 3). However, in this case Hermas would seem to have in mind apostates under the Old Covenant ("those who denied Him long ago"). There is not the same hope for those who have fallen away from the Christian faith.

"The words of such men poison and kill a man": Compare S. James iii, 8.

27. "Bishops, hospitable persons": 1 Timothy iii, 2. These are presumably "presbyter-bishops," as it does not seem that in the Roman Church of this time there was yet a clear distinction between a single ruling bishop and the assistant presbyters (see also Vision II, 2). A leading part of the function of the bishop in the local congregation is to receive fraternal visitors from other parts of the Church. Thus his office expresses the Catholic solidarity of the whole Church.

28. "All as many as ever suffered for the Name's sake are glorious in the sight of God, and the sins of all these were taken away . . . But ye that suffer for the Name's sake ought to glorify God, because God deemed you worthy that ye should bear this name, and that all your sins should be healed": The most fruitful of all disciples are those who have suffered martyrdom "for the Name," that is, expressly for being Christians (1 Pet. iv, 16). As with S. Ignatius (Ep. to the Romans, 5), martyrdom is the seal of discipleship, and brings the guarantee of forgiveness of sins (S. Mark viii, 35).

"But as many as . . . considered in their hearts whether they should deny or confess, and yet suffered, their fruits are less, because this design entered into their hearts": Hermas' argument is rather superficial here, for we cannot look into the heart, and measure the respective degree of virtue in those who suffered martyrdom with cheerful courage, and those who did so after anxious fear.

"Reckon yourselves blessed therefore": Compare S. Matthew v, 10–12.

"Yea, rather think that ye have done a great work, if any of you shall suffer for God's sake": There is indeed a sense in which this word of encouragement is not untrue, because to suffer martyrdom is a signal example of virtue. Nevertheless, we surmise that Hermas looks upon himself as one who has to some extent at least suffered for Christ, or at least as a member of a martyr Church. This spirit of mild self-congratulation is much less seemly than the attitude of S. Ignatius, who actually was a martyr (Ep. to the Romans, 5).

29. "Such ... dwell without doubt in the kingdom of God, because ... they continued as babes all the days of their life": Compare S. Matthew xviii, 3.

30. "Their riches have darkened and obscured them a little from the truth": Even substantially faithful Christians are apt to be contaminated by worldliness, from which those who would be perfect must resolutely abstain (see Parable I).

"He commanded their possessions to be cut from off them, yet not to be taken away altogether, so that they might be able to do some good with that which hath been left to them": Compare S. Matthew xix, 16–22. Here is our Lord's counsel of perfection prudently moderated in a spirit of common sense!

31. "Then they will fit into the Kingdom of God": Compare S. Matthew xix, 16–22.

"Blessed I pronounce you all to be—I, the angel of repentance—whoever of you are guileless as infants": Compare S. Matthew xviii, 3. The figure of the Angel of Repentance as Christ, calling upon men to be converted and become as little children, becomes a little clearer here.

"But if he find any part of the flock scattered, woe unto the shepherds": Compare Ezekiel xxxiv, 2, 5; S. John x, 12–13.

32. "Amend yourselves therefore, while the tower is still in course of building": The day of final judgment presses on, when God shall have filled up the number of His elect, and perfected the Church (see also Vision III, 5).

33. "I forgot, Sir": A lame touch in the story! Characteristically it comes as the climax of a tedious parable.

"The Lord saw that their repentance was good and pure": Repentance here is almost "penance" (see Precept XII, 1, 2, 3).

Parable 10

1. "The angel who had delivered me to the Shepherd": Upon the supposition that the Shepherd is a figure of Christ, it is a little incongruous that Hermas should be delivered to His authority by "an angel." Here is an objection to this interpretation. However, it is not an insuperable one, in view of the confused imagery of Hermas, and his frequent incongruities.

"If thou keep his commandments . . . success shall attend thee in every good undertaking": The notion that this is success in spiritual things is not excluded, but we are inclined to suspect Hermas of a somewhat more prudential attitude.

"Tell it out unto all men that he is held in great honour and dignity with the Lord. . . . To him alone in the whole world hath authority over repentance been assigned": Compare S. Matthew xi, 27; S. John xx, 21–3. Here are words which most fittingly apply to Christ.

2. "Each one becometh guilty of his own blood": Compare Ezekiel xxxiii, 4.

3. "For it is impossible that these commandments be kept without the help of these Virgins": Here we have another view of Hermas' doctrine of salvation by divine grace.

4. "Whosoever therefore shall walk in these commandments, shall live and be happy in his life": Compare S. Luke x, 25–8. The promise of "happiness" to the faithful believer is not a very Christian one.

"He then who knoweth the calamity of a man of this kind and rescueth him not, committeth great sin": Compare 1 John iii, 17.

VIII   An Apology: The Epistle to Diognetus

1. Character of the Writing

It is appropriate that the Apostolic Fathers should comprise among their customary number an interesting and beautiful writing which represents the transition to the next phase of Christian thought and literary composition. In introducing the subject of the Apostolic Fathers we have ventured the judgment that the early decades following upon the great creative New Testament period were years when the Church, as it were, "paused for breath" before rallying her energies and resuming her advance. In the company of the Apostolic Fathers we find some vigorous, heroic, and attractive Christian personalities, as well as some figures of lesser calibre. They have some memorable things to say, but in the main these are, theologically speaking, the reproduction of what we already find in the New Testament. The constructive work of the Apostolic Fathers is chiefly in the field of the institutions and discipline of the Church. This was clearly the necessary and providential development, as the Church ventured out from the shelter of Judaism into the wide and exposed mission field of the Gentile world. In the primitive Church there were, as S. Paul himself observes, "not many wise men after the flesh, not many mighty, not many noble" (1 Cor. i, 26). There were not many with the gifts, and perhaps still fewer with the interest, to attempt the intellectual clarification and development of Christianity, and the literary presentation of the same. The first Christians felt that they were called to make their witness by suffering, rather than by theological writing. However, in the providence of God, and under the guidance of the Spirit, a new phase was to come. The Church was destined to produce those who may properly be called Christian scholars and theologians.

The Christian Apologists form the first important school of these theologians. An "apology" is properly a literary defence of a position (in this case the Christian position), with the connotation that what is required in defence is chiefly clarification of what one's position actually is. An apology is addressed to the presumed basic fair-mindedness of the unconvinced, or partly convinced, on the plea that the dispelling of misconception will work the abatement of prejudice, and the growth of good will. The appeal is to the inherent reasonableness of the case. The early Christians commonly found themselves surrounded by populations possessed of prejudice against them, and often of bitter prejudice, to the point that outbreaks of mob violence and even persecution were not infrequent. False stories of disloyalty to the established order of society, and of obscene rites carried on in the secret Christian meetings, were widely believed. As the Christians increased in number and prominence, and were more and more of purely Gentile descent, outside opinion was increasingly able to distinguish the Church from the Jews. This increased the threat of violence, and of local governmental persecution, because the Jews, though an unpopular community, were recognizable and accepted as an ancient nation, while the Christians appeared in the guise of a secret society of dubious antecedents, and of no legal standing. On the other hand, the Church was now beginning to comprise in her membership at least a few men of intellectual and literary ability. The natural response, therefore, to growing popular pagan ill will was a first move of constructive theological thought. Writers set out as much as they could of the Christian position for the reading of unbelievers, explaining it in the way most likely to be understood by those having only a non-Biblical cultural background, and presenting the chosen part of Christian truth in the light which would be most likely to win sympathy from the outsider. So we have the rise of the Apologists.

Most of the Christian preaching recorded in Acts is addressed to Jews, to proselytes, or to the "devout persons" of Gentile background associated with the synagogue. This audience had at least some degree of understanding for, and sympathy with, Jewish religion and the Hebrew Scriptures. However, on two occasions S. Paul is represented as speaking to pagans, and then we see that his method interestingly prefigures that of the Apologists, who later were to address this same type of hearer. We have a sample Christian sermon to simple rustic pagans at Lystra (Acts xiv, 14–18), and to learned and sophisticated Greeks at Athens (Acts xvii, 16–32). In each case the approach is to argue from the order and goodness of nature the existence of one righteous God, and to display the consequent folly of idolatry. The

Apostle speaks not so much as a Christian, but as a Jew to pagans, laying down the essential preparation for the Gospel. The distinctively Christian doctrine of the crucified and risen divine Son is to some extent kept in reserve. The Apologists, seeking to address a similar audience, occupy similar ground.

In these books, written by Christians for pagans, the distinctive Christian doctrine is not usually declared so fully and uncompromisingly as it is in the Apostolic Fathers, which were books written by Christians for Christians. The being and goodness of God is argued from the order of nature, and the true nobility of the Christian life demonstrated from the elevated morality of the Christians. Thus the Christians sought to vindicate themselves as rational, dignified, and upright people, not the purveyors of an ignorant superstition, and as good citizens of the Roman Empire, not as members of a depraved and disloyal secret society. So far, the argument is hardly "Christian" at all. Thus in the Apologists we often have the Christian appeal rehearsed with the distinctive Christian Gospel of Christ crucified and risen "soft-pedalled." Experience showed that the essential Gospel could not really be appreciated except by hearers who had at least a minimum measure of instruction in the Christian background of Biblical and Hebrew thought. Without this, the preaching of the Cross was more likely to occasion uncomprehending ridicule than to evoke reverence and love. So the writings of the Apologists are largely an essay in "natural religion," which has ever been so important a part of the equipment of the missionary to the pagan world. We are often left with the feeling that these writers could have been a good deal more explicit regarding their doctrine of a divine Saviour, had they chosen to address fellow Christians. One is therefore warned against a too hasty judgment that they are "theologically inadequate," or "sub-Christian," as compared with the more dogmatic writers who went before them, and those who came after.

There was, however, one telling use which could be made of the Hebrew Scriptures to a pagan reader. This is a prominent mode of argument in the Apologists, and must for the sake of completeness be briefly noted here, even though it is not employed in the particular writing we are to consider. The Apologists commonly stress the argument from prophecy. The educated Greek, brought up to reverence his classical writers, was well accustomed to the notion that the more venerable the book, the more authoritative. In the Hebrew Scriptures there were books apparently older by far than the writings of the philosphers. They apparently forecast mysterious details about the life of Christ, which human imagination could never have guessed, and which marvellously came to pass centuries later. This proved to be a telling argument for the claim that the Hebrew Scriptures were inspired by God, with the implications that the Christ who was thus prophesied was from God, and that the Church which was manifestly founded upon these Scriptures likewise enjoyed a divine sanction.

Connected with this line of argument there is in the Apologists a developed theological venture, which contrasts markedly with their reserve upon some other subjects. This is the doctrine of Christ as the Word, or Logos, of God. This doctrine is based upon the connection between, and the contrast between, two important senses of the Greek term λόγος, in English letters logos. Λόγος is first "reason," a thought dwelling in the intelligent mind. This is a purely spiritual thing. Then λόγος is also "a word," that is, a thought proceeding out from one intelligent mind to others, by outward and material means. Thus "a word" is a symbol of that which is both spiritual and material, and can be used as a figure of the Incarnation of the divine Son. This is the doctrine of S. John i, 1–14, where it is taught that the divine Son is the creative Word of God, who in the beginning gave being and rational order to the universe. He, a spiritual Being, at the Incarnation took upon Himself a material form, as a man. So the creative Reason of God became the outspoken "Word" of God, the mind of God communicated to man. This Logos theology is admirably adapted to demonstrate the relationship of Christ, the supreme Teacher, to the teachers who went before Him, alike the Hebrew prophets and the Greek philosophers and poets, and to demonstrate, furthermore, the relationship of these two classes of teachers one to another. There was a certain measure of divine Reason (λόγος) in all men who taught something of the truth. This divine Reason became incarnate in Christ. It will be seen how well this accords with the interests of the Apologists. A place is found for the philosophers alongside the prophets as a preparation for Christ, and the Christian preaching is intelligibly set within the context of the general culture of the times. Furthermore, the doctrine gives an attractive and rational exposition of the telling

Christian "argument from prophecy." The difficulty is that the Logos theology answers better to the preaching of Christ as the Great Teacher, and supreme Revelation, than it does to the preaching of the crucified and risen Son of God. It is best adapted as a vehicle for the "natural religion" of the Apologists. It can easily entrap its exponents into a version of Christian doctrine minus the essential Gospel, though this failing is of course not necessary. Nevertheless, in its day this theology played a valuable part in the presentation of Christian truth to the world, and in the development of the doctrine of the Person of Christ. The theologically accomplished Epistle to Diognetus implies the Logos doctrine.

It is a characteristic of an apology that it is commonly addressed to some influential person. Thus the greatest of the Apologists, S. Justin Martyr (c. A.D. 105–166), addresses his Apologies to the Emperor Antoninus Pius himself, and to the Roman Senate. This was hardly with the idea that these august personages would themselves actually read a piece of Christian literature! Men of influence lower down in the scale, and nearer to the scene of conflict, were doubtless aimed at. The intention was similar to the old usage of dedications of books and works of art to patrons among the nobility and gentry. Here was the attempt to represent the Christian apology as very far removed from the illiterate scribbling of a despised conventicle in the lower quarters of the town. It was a claim that this was a responsible work, of which an educated gentleman might not be ashamed to take account. The Epistle to Diognetus is addressed in this way. It is addressed to a certain Diognetus, of whom nothing certain is known save that he must have been a person of standing and culture, the victim indeed of certain regrettable prejudices against the Christians, but a reasonable person nevertheless, and not proof against rational arguments in favour of the Christian case.

The Epistle to Diognetus owes its usual place among the Apostolic Fathers to the claim in the added appendix that its author is "a disciple of apostles" (Chap. 11). It is, however, later in date than this. It is in fact a short, beautiful, and ably written apology, and belongs to the class of Christian literature characteristic of the age succeeding that of the Apostolic Fathers. It fittingly brings the Apostolic Fathers proper to a close, and opens the door to a much larger school of Christian theology. The characteristics of the longer apologies may be seen in it, and it is to be understood in light of the general principles of this class of writing.

2. Authorship and Date

The Epistle to Diognetus carries no author's name and no date, nor is there any certain indication of these things from circumstantial evidence. The authorship and date have therefore long been an open subject for learned speculation. The most useful modern monograph on this Epistle is that of Henry G. Meecham, *The Epistle to Diognetus* (Manchester University Press, 1949), which gives an Introduction, a detailed linguistic commentary upon the Greek text, a translation, and an exhaustive bibliography (pp. 69–73). Meecham agrees with Lightfoot in preferring a relatively early date, about A.D. 150. Evidence for this is the "early" type of Christian thought, the lack of mention of heresies, the association of the writing with those of S. Justin, and the possibility that the reference to the emperor commissioning his son may have been suggested by the adoption of Marcus Aurelius into the tribunician power by Antoninus Pius in A.D. 147. Westcott places it as early as A.D. 117, Harnack possibly as late as A.D. 310.

As to authorship, the single Greek MS on which the text depends places it among works ascribed to S. Justin Martyr, but few modern scholars accept this. Meecham assembles a large number of small theological differences between the writer to Diognetus and Justin, which in total are impressive (pp. 61–2). The Epistle has been ascribed by different scholars to most of the known Christian writers of this period, and also to the heretic Marcion (*ibid.*, pp. 16–18). A notable recent contribution to this discussion is the learned and detailed work of Dom P. Andriessen, *L'Apologie de Quadratus conservée sous le titre d'Épitre à Diognète* (1946), which restates the theory that the Epistle is in reality the lost Apology of Quadratus, mentioned by Eusebius as presented to the Emperor Hadrian, and briefly cited in *H.E.*, IV, iii, 2. This would make "Diognetus" a veiled name for Hadrian. The difficulty is that the short quotation from Quadratus given by Eusebius does not appear in our text of Diognetus, and Andriessen has to defend the thesis that Eusebius happens to cite from the missing portion of the Epistle, in Chapter vii. He argues to show that the train of thought

AN APOLOGY: THE EPISTLE TO DIOGNETUS 275

of the Epistle before and after the break connects with the fragment in Eusebius. This may be so, but the theory appears if anything a little too ingenious. The multiplicity of theories indicates that the whole matter is one of speculation. It is generally agreed that chapters xi and xii are part of a different work, and most probably by a different author. The ground of this is the sudden change of subject matter and treatment, and also smaller disparities of theology and vocabulary. Some have attributed this section to S. Hippolytus (see Meecham, p. 66). Westcott and Lightfoot see the exposition as Alexandrian in tone, particularly the treatment of the Garden of Eden as an allegory of the Church. Lightfoot conjectures that this epilogue is the work of Pantaenus, the master of Clement of Alexandria. The ingenuity with which so many have tried to associate the Epistle with some illustrious name is a tribute to the inherent interest and value of this work.

3. Source

The Epistle to Diognetus is derived from a single Greek MS, the Codex Argentoratensis. This was probably copied in the thirteenth or fourteenth century, and contained five works falsely ascribed to S. Justin Martyr, some of them bearing names of works by Justin listed by Eusebius, but now lost (*H.E.*, IV, xviii, 3-5). This MS had been bought from the Carthusians by the great German humanist scholar Johannes Reuchlin (1455-1522), as stated on the back of the volume in a note in Reuchlin's own handwriting. Between 1793 and 1795 it arrived in the library of Strasbourg, where it perished by fire during the bombardment of the Franco-Prussian War of 1870. However, a transcript made by H. Stephens in 1586, for his first publication of the Epistle, still exists, and the readings of the original MS were also collated for Otto's editions of the works of Justin Martyr in 1843 and 1879.

4. Commentary on the Epistle to Diognetus

1. "Most excellent Diognetus"; κράτιστε Διόγνητε (Lightfoot, p. 490): This was a common title used in addressing men of high

official position, yet without too close association with their precise rank. Thus the word gives no information as to who Diognetus may have been. The name Diognetus ("born of Zeus") was a common one, and so again gives no clue as to whom the Epistle was dedicated. One of the tutors of Marcus Aurelius indeed bore this name, but it is a pure conjecture that the Epistle may have been addressed to him.

"What God they trust and how they worship Him": Diognetus would presume that Christianity was another new Eastern "mystery religion," and these are the natural questions which an inquiring man of the times would ask. We observe that, despite this implied opening offer to describe Christian worship ($\theta\epsilon o\sigma\epsilon\beta\epsilon\iota a$, Lightfoot, p. 490, a favourite word with the author), he pointedly does not do so. The emphasis rather is the typical Apologist's interest in commending Christianity as an elevated doctrine of God, and as an improving and moral discipline of life. This, it was doubtless felt, was the most hopeful way to make a good initial impression with an unbeliever. To describe the deeper matters of Christian faith and worship to such a man was not fitting, and would not help at this stage. Thus the true Christian "Mystery" is several times mentioned, but not expounded.

"They all disregard the world and despise death": The writer first fittingly fixes upon the two chief points which attracted pagan attention to Christianity, the first in a prejudiced and the second in an admiring way. The outsider objected that the Christians "disregard the world." They kept themselves aloof from general social life, communal amusements, public office, and from the communal religion which it was felt had to be maintained in order to bring good fortune to the particular city or state. The Christian reason for this was that with much justice they felt that the life of society was impure, and the common amusements debasing, while to enter public office or the army involved inevitable entanglement in communal pagan rites. In consequence, the Christians were misrepresented and disliked as "haters of the human race," and "atheists." Nevertheless, this strange world-denying attitude had another and impressive side. The unaccountable fortitude of Christian martyrs was the chief factor which made the unbelieving world feel, despite its prejudices, that there was something of power and of good in Christianity (cf. Ignatius, Ep. to the Romans, 2). That citizens of dignity and family pride should on occasion suffer heroically for the public cause was no new thing among the Romans, but that the Christian Faith should be able to put something of the spirit of Regulus into the ignorant and unprivileged lower classes, into women, and even into cringing slaves—this was astonishing!

"Take no account of those who are regarded as gods by the Greeks, neither observe the superstition of the Jews": As the writer has acknowledged that there is a social objection levelled at Christianity, so now he shows himself aware that there is a profounder religious objection to be encountered. In the ancient world religion was not, as so often with the modern man, treated as a matter of private opinion. It was inherently communal, and its purpose was to bring divine blessing and "good fortune" to the state, to a particular area or city, or to a nation, tribe, or family. To stand apart from this worship was more than to subvert the moral basis of society. It was to make of oneself a person whose presence in the community might well be dangerously offensive to "the gods," and bring "bad luck." Therefore the Romans were tolerant to all recognized and traditional national and civic religions, and paid respect to their institutions. This toleration could at a pinch be stretched even to cover the case of the unaccountable and intolerant religion of the Jews, for the Jews were a recognizable and ancient national group. However, as it became increasingly obvious to the pagan world that the Christians were not in fact a branch of the Jews, there was no provision to cover them. They appeared in the guise of an anomaly which could not be tolerated with safety, an illicit secret religious society improperly engaged in drawing folk away from their natural religious duties.

We find that the Christian response to this objection that the Church is an anomalous "peculiar People" is to glory in the fact that this is indeed the truth. Humanity is no longer divided, as of old, into two "races," the Jews and the Gentiles ("Greeks"), but into three (cf. Origen, *Contra Celsum*, i, 26). The writer to Diognetus hints at this principle here, and in several other passages. He goes into the counterattack by emphasizing the superior principle of brotherhood and of social morality which exists within the Church.

"Affection"; φιλοστοργία (Lightfoot, p. 490). This word has the connotation of "strong family love" (4 Macc. xv, 6, 9; cf. Rom. xii, 10). Here we have the favourable Christian construction placed upon that same characteristic which to the outsider appears to be an unwelcome and suspicious Christian "clannishness."

"This new development or interest": In a world where the chief claim of an institution for veneration was its age, the novelty of Christianity was felt to be an offence. If the magistrate felt that it was an antisocial outrage to proselytize folk away from their ancestral religion, the more learned critic of Christianity scornfully asked why, if this religion were indeed true, God should have waited so long to declare it! (Origen, *Contra Celsum*, iv, 7). The writer to Diognetus has to fall back upon the assertion that the Christian way is a divine Mystery, which man in his wisdom could never have discovered, but which God has at length made known according to His inscrutable counsel (chaps. vii, viii). This is an echo of S. Paul's doctrine, in Ephesians i, 9–10; iii, 9–10.

"I gladly welcome this zeal in thee": It has been observed that the conclusion of this chapter is on the style of Greek orations. This answers to the attempt to make Christian doctrine presentable in a literary sense to the pagan world, and is a natural part of the apologistic aim.

2. "Come then, clear thyself of all the prepossessions which occupy thy mind": Here is the other half of the typical Apologist's plea. He presupposes in his courteous introduction that his reader has a certain underlying sympathy, to which he can make appeal. However, he also realizes that he is writing to the unconvinced, to an intelligent pagan.

"The habit"; συνήθεια (Lightfoot, p. 490): This word can have the general sense of "custom," but in Clement of Alexandria it has the sense of the "habit" of idol worship. This would agree with the context here. The prejudice which makes it hard for the reader to accept the reasonable Christian case finds its focus and its strength in his attachment to a traditional system of worship, with which it is not easy to break.

"See not only with thine eyes, but with thine intellect also. . . . Are not all of these perishable matter?": The writer's case therefore fittingly opens with the argument of the self-evidenced illogicality and irrationality of idol worship. This mode of argument was not unknown to sceptical Greek thinkers, but the chief inspiration of this passage is the Old Testament case against idolatry. The argument is essentially that of irony and sarcasm, rather than an appeal to reasoned theological principles. The heathen had no real confidence in the power of the "gods" which they themselves have made, for they lock up the valuable images, lest they be stolen! No cognizance is taken of the circumstance that the instructed pagan could reply that he does not reverence the stone or the golden idol as such, but the divinities of which these are the visible symbols, and that there is in fact no logical inconsistency in guarding the valuable apparatus of religion.

"Did not the sculptor make one?": Compare Isaiah xliv, 10–19.

"Are they not all deaf and blind . . . and ye end by becoming altogether like unto them": Compare Psalm cxv, 4–8. The writer does approach the valid theological point that the worship of "god" under a false conception bemuses the mind of the worshipper, and fills him with an essentially irrational hatred of the truth.

"Ye reproach them by propitiating them with the blood and fat of victims . . . Nay, not so much as a single individual will willingly submit to such punishment, for he has sensibility and reason": The argument here is that of a not very profound sarcasm. A thinking man would not willingly expose himself to the reek of blood and smoking fat. To him it would be a "punishment." That the idols cannot prevent this treatment of themselves is a token of their powerlessness!

3. "The Jews then, so far as they abstain from the mode of worship described above, do well": It is to be admitted that the second of the "three races" into which mankind is divided does better than the Gentiles, because Jewish worship does not involve crude idolatry, and the Jewish creed confesses one all-sovereign God. However, the apologistic argument is a "war on two fronts," and places the Christian writer under the necessity also of sharply dividing himself from the Jew. Thus the present Epistle objects that though the Jews have no idols, they worship God with ceremonial not dissimilar from that of paganism. Irrationally they behave as though the Lord of all things needs gifts from man. It is to be noted that at this time the Jerusalem sacrifices had in fact ceased, though the author writes as though they were continuing. He is writing theologically rather than historically.

"For He that made the heaven and the earth and all things": Compare Acts xvii, 24–5.

"He . . . cannot Himself need any of these things which He Himself supplieth to them": This is the thought of Psalm l, 7–14, and illustrates that the writer's point of view is not necessarily a sound comment upon Hebrew religion. There is in the Old Testament itself an answer to the objection raised. The Jewish sacrifices were essentially symbolical means of self-offering to God, and of communion with Him. They were not necessarily regarded crudely as gifts with which it was hoped to purchase the good will of God, though doubtless the less thoughtful of the Jewish people at times misunderstood them in this way. The same objection, that God does not "need" our gifts, which are in any case derived from Him, may be made with equal force against Christian worship. Christian rites may likewise be misunderstood in an unspiritual manner by superficial minds.

"In no way different from those who show the same respect towards deaf images": This passage introduces us to the markedly hostile view of Jewish religion taken by this writer. The instinct of the best Christian theology has always been to balance two contrasted thoughts. On the one hand there is the continuity of Christianity with its Hebrew background, in token of which the Hebrew Scriptures are read as Christian Scriptures. On the other then, there is its newness, in that the Christian faith is based not upon a mere revision of the Law of Moses, but on a unique historic act of redemption in Christ, which took place at the end of the Jewish Dispensation. A Christian, therefore, is never on the soundest ground when he is assailing Judaism. He may obscure the principle of continuity. This tendency in the writer to Diognetus is the main blemish remaining upon an otherwise admirable work. However, it is not on this account that the writer so markedly does not quote the Old Testament to Diognetus, or base himself upon the argument for prophecy. The writer of the Epistle of Barnabas is even more anti-Jewish in tone, and yet can fill his work with quotations from the Jewish Scriptures. The reason is that this Apologist chooses not to argue explicitly from Scripture to a reader who cannot be presumed to acknowledge the sanctity of the Christian Bible. He makes his initial approach on more general grounds. The question remains as to why this intelligent and humane writer should take a somewhat jaundiced view of Judaism. The likelihood is that the Jews, themselves an unpopular social group, at times yielded to the natural impulse to try to turn mob violence away from themselves on to the Christians, as scapegoats, and that some Christians equally naturally and equally regrettably responded in kind. This emphasized the sense of difference between the two originally kindred communities.

4. The writer's anti-Judaic polemic is extended to detail in this chapter, in which he pours scorn upon some aspects of Jewish cere-

monial. This not very good-natured passage does not in fact take the argument much further, for it can hardly be supposed that Diognetus needed to be warned against an inclination to Judaism. However, it is a part of the elaboration of the writer's case that the Christians are to be understood as "the third race," a community of divine foundation distinct both from Greeks and Jews. The strong anti-Jewish tone has led some scholars to advance the hypothesis that the writer to Diognetus was a Marcionite heretic, or a semi-Marcionite, or even Marcion himself! There is no need to go so far as this. In the sense that Marcionitism was extreme anti-Jewish Christianity, while this work shows some degree of anti-Jewish feeling, it may be maintained that the writer displays some of the instincts which gave rise to this heresy. However, Marcionite doctrine went much further than this Epistle, and advanced the theory that there were two "gods," the false god of severe legal justice and spiritual bondage of the Old Testament, and the true God of fatherly love, of the New. This involved much more than rejection of various Jewish ceremonial customs. It implied the rejection in principle of the whole Jewish religion, and its Scriptures, and the repudiation of all continuity between the Church and Judaism. The writer to Diognetus shows no trace of these theoretical considerations, and simply writes as a Christian who thinks that some Jewish customs are mistaken or absurd.

"The dissimulation of their fasting and new moons": It is to be noted that *Didache*, viii, is even stronger, and pronounces that the Jews fast and pray as "hypocrites."

"As if He forbad us to do any good thing on the sabbath day": The same spirit of opposition leads the writer to decry the keeping of the Jewish Sabbath. The reference is doubtless to our Lord's words, as in S. Mark iii, 4, though the spirit is hardly His.

"Again, they vaunt the mutilation of the flesh": This is a typical Gentile reaction of disgust at the custom of circumcision. That the Emperor Hadrian published a decree forbidding circumcision is treated by Andriessen as a ground for connecting "Diognetus" with Hadrian.

"And to watch for stars": The Jewish Sabbath and other holy days began, like all their days, at sunset, and the beginning of the new day was measured from the time when three stars were visible in the evening sky.

"But as regards the mystery of their own religion": The writer introduces us here to one of his favourite words, "Mystery," μυστήριον (Lightfoot, p. 493). The regular religious use of the word μυστήριον in the Greek world was of the cults into which one could be initiated by the performance of sacramental rites and the recitation of ceremonial words, so as to acknowledge the lordship of, and come under the protection of, some divinity, or to receive some oracle. To this answers the usage of the Greek Church, where μυστήριον became the word for "sacrament," and the equivalent for the Latin *sacramentum*. In contrast to the spurious pagan "Mysteries," which in their outward ceremonial kinship to the Christian sacred rites often appeared in Christian eyes as delusive diabolical copies of the Sacraments (for example, Justin, 1 *Apology*, lxii), the Church possesses her parallel true Christian Mysteries, ordained of the Lord. However, μυστήριον is also an important Pauline word, and is used to convey the conception of the Christian religion as a wonderful divine revelation. The divine plan of salvation is so marvelous that it could not have entered into the heart of man to conceive. Therefore it lay hid for ages in the secret counsel of God, but the divine secret is now an "open secret," for it has been made wonderfully known to man in Christ (Rom. xvi, 25; 1 Cor. ii, 7; iv, 1; Eph. i, 9; iii, 3, 4, 9; v, 32; vi, 19; 1 Tim. iii, 9, etc.). The writer to Diognetus regularly uses the word "mystery" in this Pauline sense. It is used of the revelation of God in nature (Chap. vii), in the plan of salvation (viii), and also of the system of Christian doctrine (x). The term is most useful in his argument as a means of answering the objection that if the Christian doctrine were indeed true, and from God, God would have made it known long ago.

5. As we pass from the negative to the positive side of the apologetic, and turn to the writer's vindication of the excellence of the Christian way of life, the tone becomes altogether more humane, and the style more elevated. We come now to the opening of the passage which has won general admiration, and established the reputation of the Epistle as an outstanding piece of ancient Christian writing. Furthermore, the argument at this point becomes more Scriptural, and Chapter 5 is largely a compendium and paraphrase of S. Paul's doctrine of the Church. In an Epistle not rich in Scriptural allusions, and with very few explicit quotations, this chapter is manifestly in debt to a variety of Pauline texts.

"For Christians are not distinguished from the rest of mankind either in locality or in speech or in customs": The difficulty of the Christian position in Roman society was that the Church was not a *religio licita*, that is, a recognizable national cult, the preservation of which was considered by the Romans necessary to the welfare of the appropriate region (so long as the nation in question loyally accepted also the Roman civic religion). The writer to Diognetus has to admit this, and seeks to turn the ground of offence to good effect. The Christians, he pleads, are not a social or racial group. They are a new phenomenon. They are "the third race," an international society marked by close internal brotherhood and elevated morality, and by a desire to do good to "all sorts and conditions of men." The conception of the Catholic Church is eloquently set forth in language derived from the New Testament, though without mentioning the name of "Church." Here is an example of the principle of apologistic "reserve." It is not the whole Christian doctrine which is here explicitly declared, but that part of the doctrine which serves as a preparation for the rest, and in such language as will appeal to an outsider.

"Nor are they masters of any human dogma as some are": The Christians are not to be compared to the schools of Greek philosophy, nor to the eastern "Mystery Religions." That is, they are not the disciples of human teachers. "Dogma" $\delta \acute{o} \gamma \mu a$ (Lightfoot, p. 493) was the word used by the Stoics to denote the "principles" of their teaching, and this sense is apt here, where the philosophers are referred to. However, the word can be used in a more general sense of a decree or decision, as in S. Luke ii, 1; Acts xvii, 7.

"Citizenship"; $\pi o \lambda \iota \tau \epsilon \acute{\iota} a$ (Lightfoot, p. 493), is properly speaking a civic word, and clearly has this connotation here, though it can be used in the wider sense of "a way of life." As the Christians follow a doctrine not known to this world, so they have a new and remarkable heavenly citizenship (cf. Phil. iii, 20).

"They dwell in their own countries, but only as sojourners . . . every fatherland is foreign": The Christians are, indeed, not altogether of the community, as their detractors maintain. They are foreigners in their native land. (Cf. Eph. ii, 19; Heb. xi, 9; 1 Pet. ii, 11.)

"They share in all things as citizens . . . they obey the established laws, and they surpass the laws in their own lives": Compare Rom. xiii, 5-7. The Apologist pleads that the "foreign" character of the

Christians by no means involves that they are lacking in civic spirit, as was commonly supposed. Their superior morality marks them out as model citizens. In citizenship they go beyond the usual requirements of the law. We may observe that this did not quite overcome the difficulty that Christians were known to avoid service in public office and the army, on account of the compromise with idolatry involved.

"They marry like other men . . . but they do not cast away their offspring": To marry and bring up a family was clearly a mark of responsible citizenship. In the Roman Empire there was at times nervousness at the decline in the birth rate, and attempts on the part of government to encourage the raising of families. It is notable that the writer does not teach that celibacy is a part of the Christian discipline. An inclination in this direction, going back to S. Mark x, 29; S. Matthew xix, 12; I Corinthians vii, 26–7, and perhaps Revelation xiv, 4, was early manifested in some circles of Christian opinion. If this writer knows anything of it he chooses to keep it in reserve from Diognetus. The exposure of unwanted infants was not unknown in the ancient world.

"They have their meals in common, but not their wives"; τράπεζαν κοινὴν παρατίθενται, ἀλλ' οὐ κοιτήν (Lightfoot, p. 493), more literally rendered by Meecham, "A common table they provide, but not (a common) marriage-bed." (Note, the MS reads κοινήν conjecturally emended to κοιτήν.) Here is an excellent example of the author's epigrammatic style. S. Justin Martyr (*Apology* i, 14) uses τράπεζα κοινή in the sense of the primitive "community of property" or liberal charity of the primitive Church (cf. Acts ii, 44). This may be what is meant here. In any case, the allusion is to the common slander that the secret Christian common meal was followed by promiscuous sexual intercourse. However, there may in this "table" be a veiled allusion to the Christian "love feast" (in which case the denial of sexual irregularity is apt), or even to the Eucharist.

"They find themselves in the flesh, and yet they live not after the flesh": S. Paul's antithesis between life "in the flesh" and "in the Spirit" (Rom. viii, 4–13; Gal. v, 16–25) is aptly taken up to vindicate the position in the world of the persecuted Christians. "The spirit" in man is that which rebukes "the works of the flesh." This is a salutary but necessarily irksome discipline. The superior social morality of the Christians has this same salutary effect upon the order of society, and is just as naturally and inevitably the occasion of ill will and persecution (Chap. vi). This is a fitting retort to the popular supposition that the Christians merited persecution for their "crimes." In fact they are persecuted for their goodness, a natural but quite irrational phenomenon.

"They love all men, and they are persecuted by all." "Being punished they rejoice, as if they were thereby quickened by life": The argument fittingly moves into a beautiful and eloquent demonstration of what is the most telling apologetic for the Christian Faith in the ancient world. The writer points to the strange spectacle of the martyr Church; of plain men and women irrationally persecuted on account of their goodness, doing good to their persecutors and invoking blessing upon them sustained in their sufferings by the confident expectation of a heavenly reward, and increasing in numbers and influence through the very measures designed to destroy them.

"They are in beggary, and yet they make many rich": This whole passage is manifestly based on 2 Cor. vi, 9–10.

"And yet they are vindicated"; δικαιοῦνται, "justified" (Lightfoot, p. 494). Meecham (p. 112) prefers to construe this as referring to the vindication of the martyr Church before men. It is proved to be in the right by the victory of its sufferings, and by its divinely appointed growth. However, the writer uses the same word in its theological sense in Chapter ix, of man's justification in Christ before God. We cannot exclude something of this sense here too. A leading theme of the whole passage is that the Christian travail through this evil world is the appointed occasion of growth in spiritual things, until he come to heaven. As he looks at the martyrs the writer has a weightier matter in view than the preservation and increase of the Church on earth. He sees that those who suffer with Christ, and in the Christian way, are "right with God."

"They are reviled, and they bless": Compare 1 Corinthians iv, 12.

"And yet those that hate them cannot tell the reason of their hostility": The persecutors would doubtless have denied this, but in the last issue the gibe is true. Those who were persuaded that the Christians were evil and socially dangerous men clung to their delusion in face of all the evidence to the contrary, such as is surveyed in the Epistle. They did so under the influence of the irrational reaction of those who find their accustomed way of life challenged by a strange new force, and who discover that their common human frailty is brought to judgment by an inconvenient moral example. This has ever been the experience of "Christianity in earnest." Those who are genuinely faithful can never expect to be popular (S. Luke vi, 22, 23, 26). The writer could appropriately have gone on to say that it was natural that the Christians should suffer in this way, because they were the followers of a divine Lord who Himself was persecuted on account of His goodness. He does draw near to this point at the conclusion of the next chapter. However, from the time of the Apostles onward this has ever been that part of the Christian message which the men of this world find it the most difficult to take seriously (1 Cor. i, 23), so contrary is it to human pride and every natural prejudice. It is not the Apologist's purpose to declare the heart of the Christian "Mystery" plainly at this point, to a man who is not yet prepared in heart and mind to receive it.

6. "What the soul is in a body, this the Christians are in the world": This is hardly the Biblical way of speaking of human nature, though the fact is disguised from the general Christian reader by the circumstance that the New Testament speaks of the $\psi v \chi \acute{\eta}$ of man (familiarly rendered "soul": cf. S. Matt. xvi, 26; S. Luke xii, 19; Heb. x, 39, etc.), and we instinctively assume in reading that this term indicates the nonmaterial part of man's nature, as opposed to the body. This is an error, for the "soul" here is the whole "self." The familiar division of human nature into a higher nonmaterial soul and a lower material body is a distinction drawn from Greek thought, though it does not follow from this that it is illegitimate as a part of Christian theology. The Bible, by contrast, looks upon human nature from a nonspeculative point of view as unitary. The living man, material and nonmaterial together, is the "self." The notion of the body as "the prison-house of the soul" is a common Greek theme, and has often been incorporated into Christian theology, though counterbalanced by the Biblical and Hebraic idea of the salvation and resurrection of the body. This is what has happened here. The essentially non-Biblical idea of the invisible soul as the "spiritual" and the material body as the "unspiritual" parts of man makes an appropriate parallel to the conception of the Christians, with their "invisible" and spiritual worship and hope, surrounded by the visible "body" of persecuting pagan society.

"And yet they are not of the world": Compare S. John xvii, 11, 14.

"And yet their religion remaineth invisible": A common taunt aimed at the Christians was that they had no idols, and therefore no worship. They were "atheists." This taunt is most neatly thrown back. The "invisibility" of the Christian religion is a mark of its true spirituality. We should not infer from this, however, that the writer to Diognetus is hostile to the Christian sacramental rites, even though they are "visible."

"Christians love those that hate them": Compare S. Matthew v, 44.

"Christians are kept in the world as in a prison-house, and yet they themselves hold the world together" (or "restrain the world" συνέχουσι, Lightfoot, p. 494). This is the climax of the argument concerning the relation of the Church to society. To a certain extent there appears to be a double meaning attached to the term "world," κόσμος (Lightfoot, p. 494), which occurs fourteen times in the Epistle, and eight in this chapter. The dominant sense is that of the New Testament, where "the world" is the world of human affairs arrayed in hostility to God (as in S. John xiv, 17). This sense answers to that of the contrast between the Church and the human society which persecutes it. Yet the classical sense of κόσμος as the ordered system of the universe is not far away here, for "the world" is that which is held together. Nevertheless, we judge that the intention of the present passage is not so much that Christian social morality is a saving "salt" which prevents the community from going to corruption. The writer would hardly have claimed so much influence for Christianity in the affairs of men! The connotation is rather that of Abraham pleading with the Lord to spare Sodom and Gomorrah, and the merciful reply, "If I find in Sodom fifty righteous within the city, then will I spare all the place for their sakes" (Gen. xviii, 26). This is certainly the accustomed argument of such writers as S. Justin (*Apol.*, i, 45; ii, 7), Tertullian (*Apol.* 32, 39), Clement of Alexandria (*Quis dives salv.*, 36), and Origen (*Con. Cels.*, viii, 70). So Meecham perhaps rightly renders συνέχουσι as "they restrain" (p. 81). The sense is similar to the cognate ὁ κατέχων, "he that restraineth" the working of the mystery of iniquity (2 Thess. ii, 7).

"They look for the imperishability which is in the heavens": Compare 1 Corinthians xv, 53.

"So Christians when punished increase more and more daily": The argument fittingly moves to its climax in a return to the point made in Chapter 5. Compare Tertullian, *Apologeticus*, 50: "The oftener we are mown down by you, the more in number we grow; the blood of Christians is seed."

"So great is the office for which God hath appointed them": This persecution is by no means a miscarriage of the divine government of the world. It is a part of God's "Mystery." The Christians are divinely called to take their part in it, and must not seek to escape. Indeed, they must rejoice in their sufferings, for martyrdom is the Christian's glory. Here is the essential philosophy of the Christian way of life, put in a masterly way by one who as a member of a martyr Church had a moral right to say what he did. It is interesting that one who can rise to this height should not be able to take a more sympathetic attitude toward Hebrew religion, and toward the great figures of Greek philosophy. S. Justin Martyr is in this a broader and a deeper Christian, and in the last resort a better, though hardly a more eloquent, Apologist.

7. "For it is no earthly discovery": The heavenly "Mystery" or divine revelation, which is the basis of the Christian way of life, is now more directly disclosed as the Incarnation of the divine Son, to be the personal representative of God with man, and the teacher and Saviour of mankind. Some students have found the Christology vague and unsatisfying, and have even advanced this as a reason why so eloquent and forceful a writing was given so little notice in the Church of later times. Admittedly, the passage does not make orthodoxy explicit. Nevertheless, it shows considerable power of discriminating thought, and a sense for the values of the Christian Gospel. It is therefore hard to suppose that the vagueness is due either to unorthodoxy or to superficiality of thought. The writer to Diognetus is not a theological bungler, but an accomplished theologian who in the present work chooses not to declare too explicitly the most sacred mysteries of the Faith. He will not cast his pearls before swine, and speak of the crucified and risen divine Son to one who is more likely to be moved to ridicule thereby, and to have his incipient sympathy with Christianity destroyed. So we have a careful but very reticent statement of the Logos doctrine, and then with this preparation duly made, a brief and equally reticent allusion to the general idea of

Atonement. The matter is then left, until the Apology has done its work, and the reader comes back as a seeker.

"The dispensation of human mysteries": Compare 1 Corinthians ix, 17.

"The invisible God Himself from heaven planted among men": Meecham observes (p. 118) that the phrase ἀπ' οὐρανῶν (Lightfoot, p. 495) "from heaven" should probably be taken not with αὐτός but with ἐνίδρυσε, to read "God established from heaven." This indicates the source of the divine action and the origin of the truth so established.

"The holy teaching (λόγον) [Lightfoot, p. 495] which surpasseth the wit of man," or as Meecham translates, "the holy and incomprehensible word": This passage admirably exemplifies the subtle and various apologistic aptitude of the word λόγος. This can equally well be rendered by the neutral "teaching," claiming for Christianity no more than the place of one divine doctrine among many, or by the stronger "word," reminiscent of the Biblical "word of the Lord," or by the explicitly Christian and theological "Word," being a title of the divine Son, as in S. John i. In this reticent passage the usage is quite fluid. At the lowest, the λόγος which God has established from its heavenly source is a doctrine. God has made known to man a part of that divine Reason which gives rational order to the cosmos, and which is the agent of creation. However, it is hard to think that no more than this is implicit. An heavenly being who might fittingly bring to mankind a superior system of doctrine would be an ὑπηρέτης, a ministering spirit, "a subaltern or angel or ruler." This is carefully excluded. The One who came was in a more express degree than this the personal representative of the Majesty on High, and of similar rank to God the King. Therefore we can hardly doubt that the λόγος mentioned in this passage is not an impersonal Rational Creative Principle, but a preexistent personal divine Word, who became incarnate. Yet this claim is not put in such a way as to affront a cultured pagan reader.

"Not an angel or ruler": The idea of ruling angels is common in early Christian literature, and in later times, being carried over from the original tradition of Jewish religion. The title ἄγγελος could also in the primitive Church be applied to Christ. Thus S. Justin Martyr can say: "The Word of God is His Son . . . and He is called Angel and Apostle" (*Apology* i, 63). The basis of this doctrine is Scripture. The Old

Testament theophanies were viewed by the Christians as "prophecies of Christ." In particular, Isaiah lxiii, 1–9, is responsible for language such as that used by Justin. The opening verses of this passage invite a Christian application of the prophecy to the blood-stained Crucified One, and the oracle closes with "in all their affliction he was afflicted, and the angel of his presence saved them." However, it was gradually realized that it was theologically unsatisfactory to describe the divine Son as an angel, as this led to confusion with the created ministers of God. Doubtless reaction against incipient Gnosticism was largely responsible for this, in order to distinguish orthodox Christology from "emanationism." It is significant that the writer to Diognetus has taken this decisive step, and has repudiated the title of "angel" for Christ. However, he does not write as though he faced a Gnostic adversary.

"The very Artificer and Creator of the Universe Himself ... Him He sent unto them": The Logos is the personal and rational Agent of creation, and of divine providence. This answers to the thought of S. John i, 1–3; Colossians i, 15–17; Hebrews i, 2–3.

"To establish a sovereignty, to inspire fear and terror": Possibly Diognetus had heard some rumour that the Christians have a doctrine of the coming of "the Kingdom of God." The natural construction which an outsider would put upon such a phrase is rebutted. When God exerts His sovereignty upon earth, it is not "as a man might conclude, to rule in tyranny and terror and awe" (Meecham, p. 83). The sovereignty to be established is one of love and gentleness, a Kingdom to be administered by the meek (cf. S. Matt. v, 5; S. John xviii, 36).

"As a king might send his son who is a king": The reference here is doubtless to the dynastic arrangements of certain of the Roman emperors, who would on occasion secure the succession and strengthen the administration by nominating the heir to the Purple from the imperial family, and by appointing him as a co-emperor. Thus the undivided sovereignty of the empire might be fully wielded by each of two related persons. This is certainly not a perfect presentation of later Trinitarian orthodoxy, but it is a much more adequate illustrative analogy than most of those adduced in the ancient Fathers of the Church. For it to occur at this early date reflects real theological insight.

"As sending God"; ὡς Θεὸν ἔπεμψεν (Lightfoot, p. 495). We have not quite such a definite piece of Christian dogma here as might appear to the modern reader of a translation. We are accustomed to the Biblical idea of one sovereign God, and of a great gulf of being fixed between "God" and His creation, which is "not-God." The mind of the ancient pagan world was not so clear upon this point, and could speak both of ‘Ο Θεός, "God" in the full and proper sense, the Supreme Being, and also of θεός, "god," divinity in a lower and more general sense. A pagan reader could take this passage as conveying no more than that the Teacher of the Christians was "a divine man" or supernatural hero. Yet it can so easily mean so much more, and the context makes this natural.

"As using persuasion, not force": From a discreet declaration of the Incarnation we naturally pass to an equally discreet but quite distinct reference to the Atonement. The two cardinal doctrines are most appropriately linked by the paradoxical conception of the gentleness of God, for it is God's respect for the human personality which He has Himself created that requires that the victory of the Sovereign Potentate over evil shall be essentially a moral victory, and a victory of suffering love. The illuminator of this passage is S. Irenaeus, who teaches a carefully developed doctrine that God uses persuasion and not force to save man.[1] The basic idea of this is that man must be rescued from his spiritual enemies, from Satan, sin, and death, by morally fitting means, and not, as he conceivably could be, by the mere fiat of divine omnipotence. Irenaeus plainly grasps that it is necessary both that God's just government of the world be vindicated in man's salvation, and that man's free will and moral responsibility be safeguarded. These considerations are the mainspring of every worthy theology of the Atonement. This doctrine is implicit here in the Epistle to Diognetus. The supposition has indeed been advanced that S. Irenaeus borrowed the idea from this Epistle, or even that the Epistle is dependent upon Irenaeus, which would make a later, rather than the usually accepted, date (Meecham, pp. 121–2).

"As loving, not as judging": In confirmation of the association of this passage with the Atonement, we find, first, a distinct allusion here to S. John iii, 17, and then a return to the theme of the victory of the Cross in the Christian martyrs.

[1] Particularly *Adv. Haer.*, V, i, 1. See also Lawson, *The Biblical Theology of S. Irenaeus*, pp. 197–8.

"For He will send Him in judgment, and who shall endure His presence": παρουσίαν (Lightfoot, p. 495). There is here brought out that contrast, which is so essential an element of Christian thought, between the first Parousia, the first "Royal Presence" of our Lord, when He came to His world in gentleness and meekness and "in great humility," and that awesome promised occasion when He shall make known the same "Presence," but "in His glorious majesty, to judge both the quick and the dead."

It will be observed that there immediately follows a lacuna, or break in the text. We have no idea of the contents of the text missing at this point, unless with Andriessen we conveniently fit into it the citation of Quadratus in Eusebius. There is some kinship of sense between the fragment of Quadratus and this context, but it is not sufficiently close to make the association of the two compelling. The fragment is speaking about the sick, not the martyrs, as is the Epistle. Thus those who are raised from the dead are the sick, and the miracles which prove the Gospel are healing miracles in Quadratus, not the miraculous endurance of the martyrs of which this writer speaks.

"They are the power of God; they are the proofs of His presence": The writer returns to his argument that the growth of the Christians under persecution indicates that the Church is more than a human institution. The question is raised whether the Presence or Parousia mentioned here is the same as that referred to just before the break in the text. Meecham prefers the construction that the triumph of the martyrs is the token of the general and abiding presence of God, or of Christ, with the Church (p. 123). However, it is a standard Scriptural reference, and one adopted by our Lord Himself (as in S. Matt. xxiv, 9), that an outbreak of wickedness in the world, and of persecution for the Saints, is an eminent mark of "the End of the Age." Therefore it is also quite appropriate to read this passage as teaching that the endurance of the martyrs is a seal of the vivid Advent hope of the Church.

8. "For what man at all had any knowledge what God was, before He came?" At this point the writer moves to the defence of Christianity against a further objection, which has already been hinted at in the opening of the Epistle. We have already observed that the practical man of affairs took offence at the novelty of Christianity. It did not fit in to the system of traditional and allowable communal religions. The writer realizes that the more philosophic mind feels in a somewhat different way the force of this objection of the newness of the Christian doctrine. He asks: "If it is indeed true, why has God, who by definition is always the same, not made it known from the beginning?" This is an objection which the modern mind finds it hard to appreciate, for modern evolutionary thought has accustomed us to the idea of "progressive revelation." Indeed, the prejudice of the modern man is likely to be that the new doctrine is more to be regarded as the truth than is the old. It must be remembered that the scholarship of antiquity tended to proceed upon the opposite principle of authority. It was the venerable teachers of old time who were presumed to have the more mature wisdom. This idea answers both to the social custom of honouring the old men of the clan as its instructors and bards, and also to the conception that truth is discovered not so much by prolonged research and experience, but by revelation. It is to be presumed that God spoke more clearly to the men of "the good old days" than to their degenerate successors. This fits in well with the doctrine of philosophy that God is always the same. If He has truth to declare, He must have declared it throughout all time. The social objection to the novelty of Christianity has been met by the writer to Diognetus with the doctrine that the "third race" is founded upon a "Mystery," a divine revelation. This train of argument is taken a stage further here. The full Christian answer to the objection of the "novelty" of Christianity is that the Gospel is not a philosophy or a body of teaching, but the news of an historic act of God in Christ. The world therefore had to be prepared by a long historic process, before God could fittingly act "in the fulness of time" (Gal. iv, 4).

Here we have concrete Biblical and Hebraic thought impinging upon the presuppositions of Greek thought. S. Irenaeus treats this important point explicitly, and turns the "novelty" of Christianity to gain. The doctrine of Christ, he allows, had been declared beforehand and from the beginning by the ancient prophets, but "know ye that He brought all novelty, by bringing Himself who had been announced" (*Adv. Haer.*, IV, xxxiv, 1; cf. IV, xx, 10).[1] This is a witness to the important principle that Christ, who is the climax of revelation, is also much more than a revelation. He is a divine saving act. A revelation

[1] See also Lawson, *Biblical Theology of S. Irenaeus*, pp. 238–40.

declares truth, which is timeless. An act takes place in history. So the Christian "Mystery" took place in time, and before that time it was not. The writer to Diognetus occupies the same ground as Irenaeus, though once again he is less explicit. In the previous chapter he has enunciated something of the doctrine of the Incarnation. He now proceeds to the claim that the revelation in Christ, declared at a certain time according to the will of the Father, is inherently superior to all human philosophies which went before. In the next chapter he brings the argument to its fitting climax by a declaration, reticent as always, that Christ is an atonement for sin: that is, He performed a divine saving act. The immediate consequence is that the writer to Diognetus joins with Irenaeus in a more conservative view of Greek philosophy than that notably held by S. Justin. Justin was to use the doctrine of "the spermatic word" (that is, of the divine Reason distributed to some extent as a seed in the minds of all truly rational and truth-seeking men) to support his broad, humane, and scholarly proposition in relation to the Greek philosophers, that "Whatever things were rightly said among all men, are the property of us Christians" (2 *Apology*, xiii). Greek philosophy at its best contained part of the Christian truth, and so was a preparation for Christ, even as were the prophets. The writer to Diognetus, cultured and eloquent author though he is, will not allow this. No religious knowledge of any worth is to be found outside God's "Mystery" (cf. *Adv. Haer.*, III, xxv, 1). The philosophers are therefore severely criticized.

"Some said that God was fire . . . and others water": Heraclitus had taught that the primal element of the world was fire, Thales that it was water.

"The elements"; στοιχεῖα (Lightfoot, p. 496): For S. Paul's use of this word see Galatians iv, 9. The elements from which all things were made were often traditionally enumerated as "earth, air, fire, and water."

"And He revealed Himself by faith, whereby alone it is given to see God": Compare Hebrews xi, 27. In this passage, therefore, "faith " is that faculty which enables man to receive a revelation. Taken by itself this is somewhat less than the full Pauline sense of faith as loving and trustful self-identification with Christ. "Faith" is here reverent and trustful acceptance of the truth. It does not necessarily follow, however, that the writer has departed from the doctrine of S. Paul, or that he is disloyal to vital Christian truth. Reverent acceptance of the Revelation is a genuine part of full Christian "saving faith." It is the essential initial stage, for God must make Himself known as trustworthy, and this truth must be accepted, before man can begin to live by personal trust (Heb. xi, 6). Yet the writer is by no means limited to this. He goes on in the next chapter to show that Christianity is more than a doctrine, and gives a doctrinally reserved yet quite effective exposition of the saving act of God in Christ. When after this he again comes to speak of faith, the term carries with it much more of the sense of personal trust. It is therefore hazardous to say, as not a few scholars have done, that the writer to Diognetus does not understand what S. Paul means by saving faith, and moves at a lower spiritual level than the New Testament.

"But also long-suffering"; $\mu\alpha\kappa\rho\acute{o}\theta\mu o\varsigma$ (Lightfoot, p. 496): This is a word of Biblical association (Exod. xxxiv, 6; Rom. ii, 4). This word, as expressing an aspect of God's goodness and mercy, is well adapted to a discussion of the long delay in the coming of Christ. God does not act as a sovereign Potentate upon passive humanity. His grace is content slowly to educate men to cooperate with His purpose. This places God's revelation in the category of an action in history, not of the revelation of a doctrine only.

"And He alone is good": Compare S. Mark x, 18.

"And having conceived a great and unutterable scheme He communicated it to His Son alone": The doctrine that the Father took counsel with the preexistent divine Logos is implied in S. John i, 1–3, and was fancifully seen by many ancient exegetes in the "Let us make" of Gen. i, 26. It is taught in *Hermas*, Parable ix, 12; *Epistle of Barnabas* v, 5; and Theophilus, *To Autolycus*, ii, 18, 22.

"To His Son [lit. 'Child'] alone"; $\pi\alpha\hat{\imath}\varsigma$ (Lightfoot, p. 496): The term $\pi\alpha\hat{\imath}\varsigma$ as a title for Christ is an interesting New Testament usage (Acts iii, 13, 26; iv, 27, 30), which later dropped out and was displaced by "Son." It is also used of Christ in *Didache* ix, and *Barnabas* vi, 1; ix, 2 (Lightfoot, pp. 221, 248, 253). $\Pi\alpha\hat{\imath}\varsigma$ can be translated either "child" or "son," as here, or "servant." Its currency in the ancient Church as a name for Christ is doubtless due to the circumstance that our Lord had applied to Himself "the Song of the Suffering Servant" (Isaiah liii), in S. Luke xxii, 37. Thus it is perhaps not without significance that in approaching the doctrine of the Atonement the writer to Diognetus uses a title with these associations, though later on he slips back to the more usual name of "Son."

"For so long as He kept and guarded His wise design as a mystery, He seemed to neglect us and to be careless about us": The writer comes back to the Pauline doctrine of the Gospel as a divine "Mystery" (Chap. 4). As this doctrine is the explanation of why it is possible for a new revelation to be true, so also it is the explanation why the saving act of God in Christ had to wait so long in history.

"But when He revealed it through His beloved Son, and manifested the purpose which He had prepared from the beginning, He gave us all these gifts at once": The point of the preceding chapter is now made more explicit. The One who, being sent to earth, was more than a Teacher, and who is the personal representative of God with man, "like the King's son," is in fact the beloved "Child" Παῖς (Lightfoot, p. 496) of God. His coming was the bringing into effect of the age-long purpose of God, and is the supreme declaration of the Revelation. The central point of the "Mystery" regarding which the Father took counsel with His Servant before the ages, and which He has at length made known, is now to be described. It is the divine act of the Atonement, the long-foretold but mysterious vicarious death of the Suffering Servant.

"The sight and understanding which none of us ever would have expected": That the supreme "wisdom of God" should have been the crucified Son of God is a thing no man could have dreamed of. The central mystery of the Faith is contrary to all the presuppositions of the men of this world (1 Cor. i, 18–25). The Gospel of the Cross is the ultimate of revelation (1 Pet. i, 10–12).

9. "Having thus planned everything . . . with His Son": Again we have the doctrine of the Father's heavenly counsel with the Son (Chapter 8).

"He permitted us . . . to be borne along by disorderly impulses as we desired . . . not at all because He took delight in our sins, but because He bore with us": Compare Romans i, 24. This passage expresses the thought of S. Paul in Romans xi, 32: "for God hath concluded them all in unbelief, that He might have mercy on all." God has allowed man to continue long in disobedience, and to wander into the far country, so that the knowledge of his own guilt and weakness may come home to him, and so he may "come to himself." It is a mark not of God's lenience with sin, or of indifference to wrong, but of His gracious long-suffering with man.

"Not because He approved of the past season of iniquity . . . but that, being convicted in the time past by our own deeds": This passage is cited by Andriessen as a parallel to S. Paul's speech at Athens (Acts xvii, 30).

"Our inability to enter into the kingdom of God of ourselves": Compare S. Mark x, 27; S. John iii, 5.

"Might be enabled by the ability of God. . . . O the exceeding great kindness and love (ἀγάπη) [Lightfoot, p. 497] of God, He hated us not . . . but was long-suffering and patient": Here we come to a clear doctrine of divine grace, and of salvation by grace.

"Kindness and love of God": Compare Titus iii, 4.

"He took upon Himself our sins, and Himself parted with His own Son": The statement of the doctrine of salvation by grace is appropriately followed by a highly Scriptural statement of the doctrine of the Atonement. The doctrinal adequacy of it is the more impressive, in view of the principle of apologistic "reserve" which governs the treatment of this subject, as of others in the Epistle. Thus we do not have the Cross mentioned, or the death of Christ expressly described as a sacrifice. The New Testament doctrine is to some extent rendered into other terms. Yet it is substantially there. From the point of view of a treatment of the doctrine of salvation in Christ, the Apostolic Fathers come to one of their high points in this passage. It is to be noted that the writer to Diognetus has firmly grasped the essential principle that for God to give His Son to suffer is a mark that the Deity Himself is taking upon Himself the sin of man. The Atonement does not betoken some kind of division within the Godhead, but is the action of God as man. Here is the thought of such a leading text as 2 Corinthians v, 19.

"As a ransom"; λύτρον (Lightfoot, p. 497): Compare S. Mark x, 45. In view of its context we may have some degree of confidence in taking this word in its New Testament sense. It conveys the general idea of "a means of emancipation," and is not limited to the original and narrower connotation of a price paid down to some party. This allusion to our Lord's word then leads to an enunciation of the doctrine of vicarious suffering.

"The just for the unjust": In a writing containing few express citations we here come to a most fitting one of 1 Peter iii, 18.

"For what else but His righteousness would have covered our sins?" The thought is surely not far away that it is by self-identification with the Righteous One that the sins of believers are "covered." This is an important aspect of the doctrine of Justification, with which this passage now deals. By being joined to Christ in faith, sinners share His righteousness, δικαιοσύνη (Lightfoot, p. 497), and so they are justified, that is, forgiven. For the "covering" of sin as a Scriptural phrase for forgiveness, see Psalm xxxii, 1, and S. James v, 20.

"Ungodly men . . . have been justified"; δικαιωθῆναι (Lightfoot, p. 497), The allusion is to Romans iv, 5. For God to "justify the ungodly," or, to retranslate into less conventional words, for Him to "acquit the guilty," is S. Paul's historic way of saying in legal terminology that the God of grace in Christ freely forgives the penitent sinner who cannot deserve to be forgiven (cf. S. Luke xviii, 14).

"That the iniquity of man should be concealed (κρυβῇ, Lightfoot, p. 497) in One Righteous Man": Compare Romans v, 12 f. Although there is no express citation, the contrast of the one Righteous and the many sinners takes our minds to this text, where S. Paul sets out the doctrine of Adam and Christ as the two "Federal Heads" of mankind. In S. Paul's theology Adam, who sinned and who therefore died, is "the man." He is the figure who typifies what the whole human race collectively had done, and every individual in it (Rom. v, 12). God's Son made man is "the New Man," who at a great price obeyed, and who lives, reversing in principle what Adam did (1 Cor. xv, 22). Those who by faith make themselves one collectivity with Christ share in His victory, for He is their Head and their Type. Some such conception of the collectivity of the human race is necessary to render intelligible any doctrine of vicarious suffering. We may surely find it here, in this most Pauline passage of the Epistle.

"The righteousness (δικαιοσύνη) [Lightfoot, p. 497] of One should justify (δικαιώσῃ) many that are iniquitous": God's righteousness, that is, the action which He takes to uphold and vindicate the cause of right in the human heart, and in the world of men (Isaiah li, 5, etc.), is seen in the action which makes forgiveness possible.

"The inability of our nature to obtain life . . . a Saviour able to save": We have here a clear demonstration of the doctrine of salvation by grace.

"He willed that . . . we should believe (πιστεύειν) [Lightfoot, p. 497] in His goodness": It is difficult to resist the conclusion that this manner of "faith," to which those who would share the benefits of Christ are called, is much more than reverent acceptance of the divine revelation, as in Chap. 8. We are to look to the Saviour as our "father" and our "strength." We find in the next chapter that the power to imitate Him depends on love, which love is our response to His love for us. The language is not precise, but the thought answers to that personal trust in Christ, and personal union with Him, which is the true and saving "faith that works by love."

"And have no anxiety about clothing and food": Compare S. Matthew vi, 25, 28, 31. This final clause is considered by Lightfoot to be an addition which breaks the sense.

10. The MS text of the first sentence lacks its conclusion, and as it stands reads: "If you also long for this faith and first obtain knowledge of the Father" (Meecham, p. 87). Lightfoot and others emend λάβῃς to κατάλαβε (p. 497), which makes the sentence read: "This faith if thou desirest, apprehend first full knowledge of the Father." This is the converse to the proposition in Chapter 8, where faith is the faculty by which man sees God. However, both propositions are in their own way true. Contact with God evokes faith. Faith in God enables man to know more of God. This is the cooperation of the human spirit with the divine initiative of grace. The contradiction, therefore, between Chapters 8 and 10 is only a superficial one. Lightfoot's emendation at least agrees with the context, which continues in the theme that it is the recognition of the love of God which kindles love and obedience in the heart of man.

"For God loved": A quotation of S. John iii, 16.

"For whose sake He made the world": This highly Scriptural passage is a recapitulation of the argument hitherto. The love of God is demonstrated in the creation of the world, the making of man in the image and likeness of God, the redemption by the incarnate Son, and the promise of the Kingdom. Those who recognize this wonderful "Mystery" will surely love God. This will fill them with joy and enable them to obey.

"He subjected all things": Compare Genesis i, 28.

"To whom He gave reason," λόγος (Lightfoot, p. 498).

"Whom He created after His own image": Compare Genesis i, 27.

We note that one aspect of the "image of God" in man is his reason, which is an image of the creative Logos.

"He sent His only begotten Son": A quotation of S. John iv, 9.

"To whom He promised the Kingdom": Compare S. Matt. xxv, 34.

"Will give it to those that have loved Him": Compare S. James ii, 5.

"With what joy thinkest thou that thou wilt be filled?": Compare 1 John i, 4.

"Wilt thou love Him that so loved thee?": Compare 1 John iv, 19.

"And loving Him thou wilt be an imitator of His goodness. . . . He can, if God willeth it": Here is the doctrine of sanctification by divine grace. Man is to model himself upon the character of God (cf. S. Matt. v, 48). Yet he can only hope to do this if God takes the initiative, and supplies His grace. And this initiative is that God shows the divine love which kindles human love in return.

"For happiness consisteth not in lordship over one's neighbours": Compare S. Mark x, 42. The second Great Commandment follows from the first. In creation and redemption the sovereign God of incomparable power has Himself shown the perfection of unselfish love. The sons of divine grace, who have something of this quality of love kindled in their hearts, will show it practically in a "God-like" humble and charitable attitude toward their fellow men.

"Taketh upon himself the burden of his neighbour": Compare Galatians vi, 2.

"Not in lordship": Is this a word for Diognetus, who is possibly a magistrate?

"God liveth in heaven": Compare Ephesians vi, 9. "Liveth," πολιτεύεται (Lightfoot, p. 498); a rare word to apply to God. The initial meaning is "to live the life of a citizen," and so can mean "to rule." This may be the sense here. In any case, the argument is that those who by "the faith which works by love" live "as seeing Him who is invisible" (Heb. xi, 27) are a part of the Kingdom of Heaven on earth. This is the true nature of the remarkable fellowship and brotherhood of the persecuted "third race."

"Then shalt thou begin to declare the mysteries of God; then shalt thou both love and admire those that are punished because they will not deny God": If Diognetus submits to the challenge of the Faith, and by faith unites himself to Christ and the Church, he will do more than understand the "Mystery." He will himself become a witness to it, because he will be a part of the martyr Church, and the suffering of the martyrs is the central point of the Christian witness (cf. S. Ignatius, Ep. to the Romans, 2).

"When thou shalt fear the real death": It is observable that the life of "the faith that works by love" by no means excludes the wholesome "fear of the Lord" (cf. Collect, Second Sunday after Trinity). This answers to our Lord's word in S. Matthew x, 28.

"Eternal fire": Compare S. Matt. xviii, 8; xxv, 41.

"Then shalt thou admire those who endure for righteousness' sake": We come to the most Christian conclusion to the vindication of the martyr Church: "He that loseth his life for My sake shall find it" (S. Matt. x, 39, and so on).

The original MS had a note observing that there was a gap in the text here. It is not likely, however, that much of the original is lost at this point, for the argument is apparently substantially complete. The three objections to Christianity have been met, and the appeal to Diognetus made. It is generally agreed that the two succeeding chapters are part of a different work, and by a different hand. Notes upon this section are given after the doctrinal summary of the Epistle.

5. Summary of the Theology of the Epistle to Diognetus

Together with S. Ignatius of Antioch, the writer of the Epistle to Diognetus is clearly the ablest theologian of the first period of the Church, following the New Testament. In the first place, not one of his fellow writers is more essentially and unambiguously a New Testament theologian. Though he incorporates very few verbal citations, his more theological passages are very fully derived from the Gospels and Epistles. Indeed, he is almost too much of a New Testament Christian! He is singularly free from any immediate dependence upon the Jewish Scriptures, which it must be remembered were at the probable date of the composition of the Epistle still to an eminent degree "the Scriptures" in the Christian Church. He alludes to the Old Testament only occasionally, and in this presents a strong contrast to most ancient Christian writing. The author is scornful of Jewish religion in a way which is not at all to our modern taste, though not more so than some other of these writers, such as those of the Epistle of Barnabas, and of *Didache*. The extreme position of the writer to Diognetus in this respect is that he seems to have no place for the Jewish religion as a preliminary divine Dispensation. He does not dwell upon the characteristic proof of the Christian Faith from prophecy, or adduce the institutions of Old Testament religion as types of Christian institutions. This is significant, and places the writer in this respect somewhat outside the general track of orthodox Christian tradition. To some extent this is perhaps due to the circumstance that he is writing to a pagan, who may be presumed not to be moved by veneration for Hebrew institutions and Scriptures. However, most ancient Christian writers of undeniably Gentile antecedents do notably make this Old Testament appeal, and the tenacity with which the Church clung to the Old Testament as Christian Scripture is a token of the proved value of this appeal. We cannot exclude the possibility that the writer displays to a restrained and moderate degree that mentality which notoriously came to extreme expression in Marcion and his followers.

This is certainly not to say that this accomplished and substantially orthodox writer was a "moderate Marcionite," though some have expressed this view. The writer to Diognetus parts company with Marcion at the heretic's characteristic and essential point, namely, that there were two "gods," the Old Testament god of severe legal justice, and the New Testament God of love and mercy. In this Epistle the God of creation is Himself the God of love, while the God of redemption is still the God of righteous judgment. The essential Christian position is preserved. Nevertheless, whenever there has been an outbreak of definite heresy it has not been an isolated phenomenon. The essential principle of heresy is unbalance, the emphasis of one truth at the expense of other and counterbalancing truths. Therefore it is natural to find that there have usually been some in the Church, who have passed as substantially orthodox, who yet have showed to some degree the tendency which served to make the heresy attractive to others who were less discerning or balanced than they were themselves. The writer to Diognetus is possibly an orthodox theologian who stands in this relationship to Marcion. Here is perhaps a reason why this Epistle, so attractive to us, was passed over in such strange neglect by the Fathers, when apparently inferior work of this period was almost canonized. The official guardians of the Church have preferred always to appear as different as possible from whatever adversary seemed most to threaten at the moment. They have approved of "the good party man," who gives away nothing to the other side! At a time when the Church was struggling with Marcionitism, which was one of the best-disciplined, most tenacious, and formidable of heresies, it must have hung as rather a cloud over the Epistle to Diognetus that it was, to say the least of it, not sufficiently anti-Marcionite to be fully useful and attractive.

However, apart from this minor aberration, regrettable in one way to the ancient Fathers, and in another way to us, the writer to Diognetus is an accomplished orthodox theologian, alike splendidly catholic and splendidly evangelical. Though we have only this short writing from his pen, none of the Fathers of the first period has a clearer view of the Church as an international and universal brotherhood, a People of God of divine foundation, who possess by divine revelation an authoritative doctrine. The Church is called to suffer with Christ, and is adorned with the virtue of martyrs. She witnesses to, restrains, and preserves the general body of the community, and rejoices in the inheritance of a promise that as the earthly representative of the Kingdom of Heaven she will endure in the world till the Coming of the Lord. S. Ignatius himself can hardly say more than this. Yet, significantly, there are things which Ignatius of Antioch adds, about which this writer is strangely silent. Though he speaks of the authoritative doctrine, he has no word about the authoritative Ministry which interprets and preaches it, and he is silent concerning the worship and Sacraments of the Church. Yet he certainly does not write as the individualist type of mystic, who cares for nothing but the "inward." The Church of which he speaks is manifestly a world-wide, unified, visible disciplined body. Yet he does not use the word "Church." He teaches the idea of "catholicity," but leaves the word to S. Ignatius. We can only presume that this is the outcome of his cautious apologistic approach. He will avoid strong dogmatic words which the pagan reader may have heard used, but heard used only in a prejudiced sense. He will express himself in more devious ways. Furthermore, he is only giving preliminary teaching, and declaring a part only of the Christian message in order to evoke good will for the rest. He therefore depicts in the best possible light the outward and practical life of the

Church, as it faces the world, and says nothing about the inward sacramental aspect of the "Mystery."

The same is true of the evangelical side of the teaching of this Epistle. We have the Gospel of redemption declared in a manner which the great Apostle of Grace himself could hardly have impugned. In the doctrine of this writer, man is a fallen and sinful creature. God patiently disciplined him until he was thoroughly humbled, and had realized that he could not save himself by his own doctrines and devices. Then in love divine the creative Word became incarnate as the personal representative of God with man. As man the Suffering Servant of the Lord died as a ransom for mankind, and all those who in faith make themselves one with their Head can share in the merit of His suffering. Thus they are justified, forgiven: and this salvation is by grace. Those who respond aright to the love of God in Christ will be filled with love, and this "faith that works by love" it is which kindles love to brother man in the heart of the believer, and gives him the power to obey God's law of love. So by this loving faith he is joined to the martyr Church, and learns what it is to suffer and to triumph with Christ, confidently expecting eternal life with God, and awaiting the Last Judgment.

As before, we have the implied doctrine, but not the hallowed dogmatic formulae. Thus Christ's true humanity is affirmed, but the facts of His earthly life are passed over. Nothing is said about the Sacrifice of the Cross, though the underlying principle is taught. The fact of the Resurrection of Christ is not mentioned, though the correlative of "rising to new life with Christ" is plainly stated. The work of the Holy Ghost is described, but no exposition given of His Person or divine procession. The General Resurrection and the Second Advent are not expressly mentioned, but the practical effect of these doctrines in present experience is clearly emphasized. At every point we see the Apologist's indirect and undogmatic approach to dogma. He avoids the vivid and dramatic Biblical words which at Athens made cultured pagans scoff at S. Paul (Acts xvii, 30–32), but he leads up to their substance and intention. The writer is studying to bring Diognetus round to the point where he may find it in his heart to believe, when on some future convenient occasion the fuller nature of God's "Mystery" shall be more pointedly declared to him.

It is with insight that Dr. Telfer observed to the present writer that the argument of the writer is often of the nature of the *double entendre*. A statement is made which Diognetus can accept, because taken in one sense it is in accord with his pagan thought forms. Yet it also bears a higher Christian sense, which Diognetus will come also to accept, if and when his eyes are opened to the majesty of the Christian revelation. An example cited by Dr. Telfer of this principle is the statement that God "gave up His own Son as a ransom" (Chapter 9). To a pagan this might convey no more than the notion of a theophany of the divine Logos, which provided the manumission price delivering man from the bonds of habitual sinning against the divine law in Nature. But if he became a Christian it would be read as a specific dogmatic declaration of Atonement by the crucifixion of the divine Son. The classic example and Scripture precedent for this method of the evangelistic *double entendre* is the word of the Roman centurion at the Cross (S. Mark xv, 39).

Herein may lie another reason for the relative neglect of this writing. We commonly find that antiquity wrote for one reason, but posterity has valued and preserved that which was written for another. Thus S. Paul wrote to the Romans to expose misconceptions about himself, and to answer detractions, in anticipation of his visit to the Church at Rome. His Epistle has been valued as the sheet anchor of "justification by faith"; a legitimate use, but one which might well have surprised him. S. Ignatius wrote to exhort, to bless, and to thank the Churches which had ministered to him in his journey. His letters have been remembered down the centuries as a chief cornerstone for the structure of Catholic episcopacy, and as a personal portrait of one of the Saints. Unfortunately for himself, however, the almost too circumspect writer to Diognetus does not leave in his work much which is of this secondary preservative value. He fails to give in passing any precious glimpses of the organization and history of the Church of the second century. He leaves no biographical or autobiographical sketch. No formula hallowed in later Catholic dogma finds its first interesting mention in his Epistle, to make of him an authority to be eagerly adduced in later controversy. His writing was useful only for the purpose for which he intended it, and so he has paid the penalty of his discretion. As times changed, and there were fewer cultured pagans in Diognetus' frame of mind to be wooed and won, the Epistle was increasingly outmoded. We may be thankful that a solitary precious manuscript by accident lingered through the wreck of ages to be read in the modern world, and in the modern world to perish.

6. Commentary on the Appendix to the Epistle to Diognetus

The MS had a break in the text at the end of Chapter 10, together with a marginal note "and here the copy had a break." Most scholars agree that the last two chapters are a different work, or part of a work, and by a different hand. The chief reason for this is the distinct difference of approach. In particular there is an example of allegorism of the Old Testament in the Alexandrian manner, which contrasts strongly with the pointed avoidance of argument from the Old Testament in the Epistle. It is possible to argue that this is due to a difference of aim, the Epistle being addressed to a reader who will not be moved by an appeal to the Old Testament Scriptures, while the Appendix seems from the opening of Chapter 11 to be addressed to catechumens, that is, to believers. Thus the two parts might be the work of the same hand, and some have even argued that the Appendix was addressed to Diognetus after he had responded to the extent of becoming a catechumen. However, there seems also to be a more generous attitude toward the Jewish religion than in the Epistle, for the Mosaic ordinances are not ridiculed, and the Law is quoted alongside the Gospels and Apostles as a source of divine truth, in the usual Christian manner. Furthermore, 1 Corinthians viii, 1, is cited with the formula "the apostle says," which would seem to make it a stage nearer to canonical New Testament Scripture than the allusive treatment in the Epistle. Some have also argued that there are small stylistic differences in the Greek (see Meecham, pp. 65-6). However, the Appendix is short for the making of a judgment of this sort, and there is a difference of subject, which makes comparison harder. Some scholars, from Bunsen onward, have claimed that these chapters are the work of S. Hippolytus. Others have been chiefly impressed by the allegoristic exegesis of the story of the Garden of Eden as a type of the Church, and have affirmed on this ground that the Appendix is Alexandrian work. Westcott assigned the fragment to a Jewish convert of Alexandria writing about A.D. 140-50, while Lightfoot suggested

Pantaenus (c. A.D. 180–210) as the author (pp. 488–9). He observes that Pantaenus, the first distinguished figure in the catechetical school of Alexandria, is singled out with two or three other early Fathers by Anastasius of Sinai as giving this treatment to the story of the Garden of Eden. It is impossible to judge in these matters with any certainty. There is, however, a more explicitly dogmatic attitude in this Appendix than in the Epistle. This may bespeak, but does not require, a different author, but it does indicate that it is at least part of a different work.

11. "Having been a disciple of Apostles": The word "apostle" has two related New Testament meanings. There is the original sense of one appointed and sent by the Lord as a witness to Himself, with consequent authority in the Church (S. Matt. x, 1–5, and so on, Acts i, 15–26). However, as these witnesses characteristically became travelling missionaries and founders of Churches, the word "apostle" can also be used in the derived sense of a travelling Christian preacher (Acts xiv, 4; Rom. xvi, 7). The former use is usual in the Apostolic Fathers, apart from *Didache*, which notably employs the latter (Chap. 11). The Appendix itself speaks of S. Paul as "the Apostle," which answers to the first usage, and therefore it is natural to read in this sense in this passage also. It is this apparent claim by the writer that he is a second-generation teacher which has placed the whole Epistle to Diognetus by custom among the number of "the Apostolic Fathers." However, he may mean no more than that he rests himself upon the genuine Apostolic tradition.

"The lessons which have been handed down"; τὰ παραδοθέντα (Lightfoot, p. 499): This phrase answers to the idea that the Christian doctrine is a tradition, παράδοσις, something "handed down" as a fixed, authentic, and precious deposit of truth from the Lord, and from the first days of the Church (cf. 1 Cor. xi, 23; xv, 3; Gal. i, 8, 9, 11, 12; 2 Peter i, 16–21).

"The Word": The context makes it clear that the λόγος in this Appendix is explicitly Christ, and not just the principle of divine Reason (cf. Chapter 10). This is an example of the more markedly dogmatic attitude of the Appendix.

"To whom the Word appeared": Compare S. John i, 14.

"Not perceived by the unbelieving": Compare S. John xx, 27. The disciples who are "reckoned faithful" are those who have accepted the divine revelation, that is, "the Mystery." This appears to answer to the idea of faith as acceptance of the Creed, rather than the full evangelical sense of "faith-union," particularly as the passage goes on to cite a creedal form.

"The mysteries of the Father . . . believed in by the Gentiles": This striking passage appears to be based on 1 Timothy iii, 16, a passage which is in turn probably based on a primitive Christian hymn or creed form (cf. also 1 Cor. xv, 3–4).

"This Word, who was from the beginning": Compare S. John i, 1; 1 John ii, 13–14.

"Who appeared as new and yet was proved to be old": Compare Rev. i, 8. This is the same thought as Chapter 8. There is hardly here a speculative doctrine of the Incarnation, as a divine progress from λόγος ἐνδιάθετος to λόγος προφορικός. Rather is it the practical doctrine that the relatively recent revelation of Christ was the revelation of a preexistent divine Logos.

"Engendered always young in the hearts of saints": Compare Rev. xxi, 5. We have here the Pauline and Johannine conception; the mystical indwelling of the believer by Christ (Rom. viii, 1 John xiv, 20).

"Who today was accounted a Son"; ὁ σήμερον υἱὸς λογισθείς (Lightfoot, p. 499): This somewhat obscure phrase probably rests upon Psalm ii, 7, which was to the Christians a leading messianic prophecy.

"Through Whom the Church is enriched": Compare Ephesians iv, 8 ff.

"Which announces seasons"; διαγγέλουσα καιρούς (Lightfoot, p. 499): This obscure phrase probably refers back to the Word of God, who is new and yet old. Grace enables the believer to recognize the coming of Christ as "the fulfillment of the time" (cf. S. Mark i, 15), and to look for the promised Advent in glory.

"The pledges of faith"; ὅρκια πίστεως (Lightfoot, p. 499): These are doubtless the Sacraments, particularly the Baptismal vow.

"The boundaries of the fathers"; ὅρια πατέρων (Lightfoot, p. 499): These are presumably the standards of belief fixed by the Apostles, and naturally associated with Holy Baptism. The reference is doubtless to the tradition, to which reference has already been made, and may even indicate that the Church has an incipient Creed form, or "Rule of Faith." It is to be noted that grace is given by God through the Church. It is "multiplied among the saints," and granted to those who honour the Sacraments and tradition of the Church.

"Whereupon the fear of the law is sung, and the grace of the prophets is recognized": This is an appropriate comment upon the religion of the Old Covenant, the two aspects of which are represented by the Mosaic Law and the Prophets. The Law, with its ritual and prohibitions, answers chiefly, though not exclusively, to God's rule by means of rewards and punishments, that is, by means of "fear." The greatest passages in the Prophets represent the inward and spiritual, and the moral aspects of religion. To a Christian the Prophets point forward to the Saviour. Hence they answer to the idea of "grace." It will be noticed that the Old Covenant stands in parallel to the New. The Law and the Prophets lead into the Gospels and the Apostolic tradition. This is the typical and orthodox Christian position, and reflects a much more favourable judgment upon Jewish religion than does the main body of the Epistle. Here is a leading argument that the Appendix is a work by a different author.

"The Gospels": It is to be noted that the word is plural, and refers to holy books which may be compared with the Hebrew Scriptures. This is a witness to an important stage in the formation of a New Testament canon of Scripture (cf. Justin Martyr, *Apology*, i, 66).

"The joy of the Church"; ἐκκλησίας χάρις (Meecham, p. 88): "The grace which works in the Church" (Meecham, p. 139).

12. "A Paradise of delight": We have here an interesting allegorical exegesis of the Genesis story, in which the Garden of Eden is a type of the company of those who believe in Christ, that is, of the Church.

"A paradise of delight": Compare Gen. ii, 15.

"A tree bearing all manner of fruits": Compare Rev. xxii, 2.

"A tree of knowledge and a tree of life": Compare Gen. ii, 17; iii, 22.

"The tree of knowledge does not kill": This would appear to be a correct interpretation of the Genesis story. In all events, it leads up to the doctrine that Christ is the Life of man.

"Revealing life through knowledge . . . For neither is there life without knowledge": This is a distinct reflection of Johannine doctrine; compare S. John viii, 12; xvii, 3. The "Tree of Knowledge" is taken in a good sense here. It is a type of the divine truth made known in Christ to the Church. The "Tree of Life" likewise is a type of the life in Christ. The door to this, once closed through disobedience, is now open to the faithful and obedient.

"The Apostle": S. Paul is here fully included in the company of the Apostles; compare Ignatius, Epistle to the Romans, iv, 3.

"Knowledge puffeth up, but charity edifieth": 1 Corinthians viii, 1. In contrast to the usage of Chapters 1–10, we come to an express citation of the New Testament.

"The man who supposes that he knows anything without the true knowledge . . . is ignorant": Compare 1 Corinthians viii, 2. Those who in the Church accept the authentic tradition based upon the Gospels partake of spiritual life. Those who wander away into other and heretical doctrines partake of the death which comes to the disobedient, prefigured in Genesis ii, 17.

"True reason"; λόγος (Lightfoot, p. 500): "Logos" is here "teaching," not "the Word."

"Neither is Eve corrupted, but is believed on as a Virgin": We have the same doctrine, more fully expanded and made explicit, in S. Irenaeus, *Adv. Haer.*, III, xxii, 4; V, xix, 1, and *Demonstration of Apostolic Preaching*, 33.[1] The obedience of the Blessed Virgin (S. Luke i, 38) has been used by God as a part of the divine plan of *Christus Victor* to undo the effect of the disobedience of the virgin Eve.[2] So it is implied in this passage that Eve is a type of the Virgin. The Virgin is, however, an "Eve" who has remained virgin, that is, who has remained perfectly obedient to God, unlike the first Eve. The reference to faith in the "virginity" of our Lord's Mother is therefore here primarily a belief in her moral obedience and purity, but the doctrine of the Virgin Birth of our Lord is doubtless not far from the writer's mind.

"Filled with understanding"; συνετίζονται (Lightfoot, p. 500): This word can be taken in two senses: (i) the Apostles were inspired with the knowledge of the truth, so that the authentic tradition is to be accepted; (ii) the Apostles are "made intelligible," that is, their writings are interpreted to the Church. This later construction makes the sentence look forward to the succeeding mention of the Christian Passover, or Eucharist, at which the writings of the Apostles were read and expounded (Justin Martyr, 1 *Apol.*, lxvii).

[1] See also Justin Martyr, *Dial.*, 100, and Tertullian, *De Carn. Christi*, 17.
[2] See Lawson, *Biblical Theology of S. Irenaeus*, pp. 150–2.

"The passover of the Lord goes forward": This is the Eucharist, which is the Christian continuation of the Jewish Passover (S. Luke xxii, 15).

"And the congregations are gathered together" (Lightfoot), or, "And the seasons are gathered together" (Meecham, pp. 90–91). The MS reads κηροί. Some emend to κλῆροι, which gives Lightfoot's translation of "congregations," others to καιροί, which gives "seasons." This might be an early reference to the seasons of the Christian year.

I Index of Subjects

Abstinence, 240
Abraham, faith of. *See* Faith
Acts of the Apostles, 76
Adam, 298
Adoptionism, 60, 252
Advent, Christ's First and Second. *See* Christ
Advent Hope, 87-8, 100, 112, 144, 151, 175, 192, 215, 229, 292
Advocate. *See* Christ
Agape, 85-6, 89-90, 91, 94, 142, 148, 284
Alexandria, Church of. *See* Church
Alexandrinus, Codex, 26, 27
Allegory of Scripture. *See* Scripture
Alms, 95, 124-5, 191-2, 249, 265, 266
Altar, 109
Anabaptists, 10
Anastasius of Sinai, 307
Andriessen, P., 274-5, 281, 292, 297
Anencletus, 26, 27
ANGELS: 45, 138, 147, 289; place in redemption, 252. *See also* Hermas
Anicetus of Rome, 156
Antichrist, 202, 205, 214
Antinomianism, 204
Antioch, Church of. *See* Church
Antoninus Pius, 273, 274
Apocalyptic, 232
Apocrypha, Biblical, 212
Apocryphal Gospels. *See* Gospels
Apocryphal and unknown writings cited, 5, 35, 37, 40, 55, 75-6, 137, 182, 184, 187-8, 191, 204, 208, 209, 211, 212, 216, 229
Apologists, the, 269-70
Apology, Christian, its method, 270, 271, 272, 273, 276, 278, 280, 282, 283, 288, 297, 305
Apostasy, 197, 237, 238, 253, 254, 257, 263, 264, 265
Apostle, Office of, 1, 6, 25, 49, 66, 74, 92, 153, 209, 230, 307

"Apostles" (traveling preachers), 92, 93, 94-5
Apostles' Creed, 237
Apostolic Constitutions, 75
APOSTOLIC FATHERS: authority, 161; definition of, 1, 6, 17, 19, 20, 200; spiritual insight of, 2, 16, 60; status and work of, 6, 9, 11, 269; writings of, 134, 164, 193
APOSTOLIC WRITINGS: 1, 6, 26, 30, 36, 74, 83, 158, 179, 185, 190, 198, 222, 306, 307, 310; authority of, 25, 30, 46, 153, 185
Apostolical Succession. *See* Succession
Asia Minor, Church of. *See* Church
Asiarch, 172
Asceticism, 231
Assurance, Christian, 192
"Atheists" (Christians), 287
Athos, Mt., MS., 226
Atonement, 18, 32-3, 37, 56, 117, 123, 127, 206. *See also* Christ, saving work of
Augustine of Hippo, S., 86, 227
Augustinianism, 58
AUTHORITY: apostolic, 3; appeal to, 293. *See also* Christ, Councils, Ministry, Testament, New; Testament, Old

BAPTISM, HOLY: 78-9, 87, 91, 116-17, 130, 131, 142, 145, 148, 150, 172, 185, 186, 207, 211, 230, 237, 262, 263, 308; Believer's, 81; of blood, 130; for the dead, 263; Infant, 81, 172, 207; our Lord's, *see* Christ; by pouring, 80
BAPTISMAL: Confession, 79, 80, 124; Creed, 79; fasting, 81; Formula, 79, 80; immersion, 79, 80; Order, 73, 79-81; Regeneration, 212, 237, 238; ritual, development, 80
BARNABAS, EPISTLE OF: accounted canonical, 63, 180, 198-9; character and

313

INDEX OF SUBJECTS

BARNABAS, EPISTLE OF (cont.)
purpose, 193-4; charismatic ministry, see Ministry; date, 75, 200, 201, 205; and Ep. of S. Polycarp, 159; relation to *Didache*, 200, 217; exegesis in, 198-9, 200, 202, 203, 205, 207-8, 211, 212, 213, 216; and Ep. to Hebrews, 198; MS. of, 201; Pauline thought in, 205, 214-15; theology of, 211; "The Two Ways," 75, 200, 216

BISHOP: apostolic appointment, 155; development of Episcopate, 8, 39, 62, 104, 155, 224, 225, 228, 229, 231, 265, 305; election of, 54, 136; office of, 23-4, 48, 49, 54-5, 62, 98, 101, 103, 104, 108, 109, 110, 120, 121, 124, 132, 133, 134, 140, 141, 142, 144, 145, 148, 192, 230. See also Episcopate, Historic; Presbyter-Bishop; Succession

Body, salvation of, 57, 253
Breaking of Bread, 97
"Brother" (and "Sister"), as Christian title, 143, 188
Bryennios, P., 27, 63, 201
Bunsen, 306

Caesar, "Genius" of, 168, 170, 171, 184
CANON: Apostolic Fathers as canonical (refer to names of various writings); Muratorian, 223, 224, 225; Old Testament, 212. See also Scripture.
Caryé, F., 70
Catechism, 71, 79
Catechumens, 91
Catholicity. See Church
Celibacy, 144, 188, 284
Charismatic Ministry. See Ministry
"Charters," the, 134
Chastity (continence), 188, 220, 231, 236, 259, 261
CHRIST: Adam, the New, 298; Advent, 135, 308; Advent, Second, 88, 90, 204, 205, 214, 215, 238, 292, 303, 304, 308; Advocate, 186; "Angel," the, 100, 179, 201, 202, 239, 289-90; Baptism of, 60, 116; "Bishop" of the Church, 132; Body of, see Church; Bread of Life, 86, 87, 90; "Christus Victor," 310; confession of, 184; Cross of, 32, 33, 56, 84, 89, 127; Descent into Hell, 123, 127; divinity of, 8, 114, see also God the Son;

ethical teaching, 36-7, 73, 74, 78; genealogies, 115; High Priest, 45-6, 60, 135, 164; humanity, 147, 304; Incarnation, see Incarnation; Logos, the, 19, 122, 146, 272, 288, 289, 290, 295, 299, 307, 308; Messiah, 86, 90, 114, 115, 118-19, 147; Name of, 257, 260, 263, 265; obedience of, 37, 84; Person of, 191, 252, 261, 273; prophecies of, 86, 135, 136, 140, 147, 194-5, 206, 233-4, 289-90, 308, 309; resurrection, 40, 117-18, 137, 163, 206, 304; resurrection-body of, 137, 140; as a revelation, 46, 294; saving work of, 18, 32, 33, 34, 35, 37, 45-6, 57, 61, 89, 116-17, 123-4, 127, 135, 138, 140, 142, 147, 150, 163, 182, 198, 203, 206, 208, 211, 213, 251-2, 259, 273, 289, 291, 294, 295, 296, 297, 299, 304, 305; sayings of, not in Gospels, 30; "Son," or "Child," 86, 87, 295-6; Son of David, 126, 212; Son of Man, 118-19, 212; "Suffering Servant," 295, 296, 304; sufferings of, 111, 130; as Teacher, 272; two Natures, 8-9; "Types" of, 31, 35-6, 41, 197, 208, 210-11, 212, 259, 301, 309; "Vine," the, 86-90; Virgin Birth, 115, 116, 117, 137, 147, 195, 259, 310; words, authority of, 30, 36, 55, 61, 74, 147, 161, 185, 189, 190, 193, 206; words, quotation of, 36, 41, 74, 147

CHRISTIANITY: appeal of, 42; "novelty" of, 278, 292-3; popular, 179-80, 181
Christians, "the Third Race," 277, 281, 300
Chrysostom, S. John, 63

CHURCH: Alexandria, 199, 306; Antioch, 124, 136, 145; Apostolic, 1, 25, 175-6, 179, 181, 192-3; apostolic foundation, 56, 230; Asia Minor, 104, 105, 153, 155; authority of, 17, 37, 46, 51, 60, 209, 210, 242, 303; Body of Christ, 8, 46, 120, 144, 153, 189, 190, 191; Catholic, 141, 167, 170; catholicity, 1, 18, 23, 24, 28, 38, 44, 48, 51-2, 61, 66-7, 105, 109, 111, 124, 127, 132, 135, 136, 141, 148, 149, 151, 166-7, 181, 199, 216, 263, 265, 283, 303; Christ's promise to, 9, 181, 303; Corinth, 23, 25, 32, 39, 55; Councils

INDEX OF SUBJECTS 315

CHURCH (cont.)
of, 8–9, 17, 25, 145; deputations in, 60; discipline, 1, 10, 11, 21, 22, 23, 36, 39, 47, 48, 49, 51, 52, 58, 64, 67, 77, 93, 94, 96, 108, 109, 110, 134, 136, 140, 141–2, 144, 148, 151–2, 164, 219–20, 222, 225, 227, 236, 237, 239, 243, 253, 269 (see also Discipline); divisions, 51–2, 81, 222–3; "fall" of, 10–11, 22, 66; "Family of God," 56; "Flock of God," 234; founded by Christ, 9, 22, 259; freedom of, 24; Gentile, 38, 183, 189, 193–4, 216, 250, 261, 269, 270; government of, 21–2, 95, 148–9; guided by Holy Spirit, 7, 20, 22, 134, 149, 152; Ideal, the, 189, 190, 229, 263; integrity of, spiritual and theological, 9–10, 15–16, 19, 20, 22, 52, 61, 67, 101, 108, 134, 136, 151, 180–81, 219, 222, 223, 239, 244, 269; Jewish, 19, 193, 261; millennial, 190, 263; "New Israel," 22, 29, 31, 34, 45, 47, 51, 58, 59, 61, 122, 123, 183, 189, 190, 193, 196, 203, 206, 209, 213, 228, 250, 256, 263; New Testament, 225; Old Testament, see Israel, Old; organic unity, 8; Philippi, 158, 160, 162, 164–5; Philomelium, 166; ROMAN —apostolic foundation, 25, 27, 31, 128, 130, 149, authority, 24, 25, 31, dignity, 69, 128, episcopate of, 24, 27, 104, 128, 132, 149, 162, 224, gift of government, 23, 46, 62, influence, 128, moral discipline, 219; Smyrna, 167; theology of, 13fn., 189, 191, 229–31, 232, 256, 258, 259, 260, 263, 283, 292, 300, 303, 309; unity, 30, 34, 40, 46, 51–2, 53, 55–6, 60, 86, 87, 90, 108, 109, 127, 132, 136, 142, 144, 148, 150; worldliness in, 220
Churches, dedication of, 176
CIRCUMCISION: in Church, 133; among Gentiles, 210; question, 8, 13, 15, 83; Roman attitude, 281; spiritual, 209, 210
Clement, in *The Shepherd*, 225
Clement of Alexandria, 70, 199–200, 201, 221, 275, 278, 287
CLEMENT OF ROME, S.: Bishop, 21, 27, 62; character, 21, 27, 102, 181; on Church government (see under Church, Minis-try, Ministerial Order, Succession); doctrine, summarized, 60–2; on faith, 40; on grace, 29, 30, 35, 44; Hebrews, use of, 45–7; on humility, 34; identity, 26; Johannine thought, 57; New Testament, use of, 56; Pauline thought, 28, 30, 32, 35, 37, 40, 44, 45, 47, 55, 56, 57, 61; Scripture, use of, 29–30, 37; as writer, 21
CLEMENT, FIRST EPISTLE: authorship, 26; character and style, 21, 60; comparison with S. Paul's Epistles, 21; date, 26, 29; MS. sources, 27, 63; occasion of writing, 23, 25; quasi-canonical, 26
CLEMENT, SECOND EPISTLE: 63, 179, 181–2; date, 182; theology of, 191
Community of property, 284
Confession, baptismal. See Baptism
Confession, penitential, 144
Confessor, 102, 104, 112, 124, 145, 150, 167, 257
Constantinopolitan MS., 27, 63, 201, 208
Continence. See Chastity
Corinthians, S. Paul's Epistles to, 55
Councils. See Church
COVENANT: New, 204, 205, 256; Old, 205, 213; Old and New, 36, 135, 198, 213, 259, 309. See also Testament
CREATION: "days" of, 214; divine, 45, 194, 299; doctrine of, 146; the New, 215
CREED: 79, 85, 137, 170, 194, 263, 308; development of, 127, 147; Old Roman, 79
Cremation, 176
Crocus, 132
Cyril of Jerusalem, S., 91

Danaids and Dircae, 32
Davies, R. E., 13fn.
DEACON: 48, 49–50, 62, 69, 95, 99, 148, 230, 265; office of, 50, 108, 124, 125
DEAD: burial of, 130; salvation of, 34, 123, 262–3
Dead Sea Scrolls, 63
Deists, 10
Depravity, Entire, 14
DIDACHE: Agape in, 89–90; authorship, 64; baptismal Order, 79–81 (see also Baptism); "Charismatic" ministry,

INDEX OF SUBJECTS

DIDACHE (*cont.*)
evidence of, 67–70, 92–6; Christ's words quoted, 74; Church background, 70; a Church Order, 71; contents, 64; date, 68, 70; Eucharist in, 86–91 (*see also* Eucharist); the Fathers, quoted by, 70; Jewish thought in, 71, 73; Judaism, attitude to, 81, 281; MS. source, 63–4; moral law in, 73; name, 63fn.; orthodoxy of, 68, 69, 70; Pauline thought in, 78; place of composition, 70–1, 81, 86–7; Scripture, quoted in, 69–70; Scripture, rejected as, 63; "The Two Ways," in Barnabas and *Didache*, 64, 71, 73–4, 74–5; value of, 67–8

Diocese, 141

Diognetus, identity of, 273, 275–6, 300

DIOGNETUS, EPISTLE TO: appendix to, 275, 306; authorship, 273, 274, 309; character of, 273–4, 305; date, 274; Judaism, attitude to, 280; MS. source, 275, 301, 305–6; on martyrdom, 229, 285–6, 288, 291, 292, 301; New Testament in, 301; Pauline thought in, 278, 282, 284, 294–5, 296, 297, 298, 304; and S. Ignatius, 303; style, 278, 284, 306; theology of, 288, 306, 301

Dionysius of Corinth, S., 26

Discipleship, Christian, 165, 184. *See also* Ignatius, S.

DISCIPLINE: ecclesiastical (*see* Church); moral, 71, 76, 245; penitential, 77, 97, 134, 144, 221, 222, 235, 238, 244, 253–4, 254, 255

Divorce, 236

Docetism, 124, 126–67, 137, 138, 147, 162, 187

DOCTRINE: development of, 7–9, 17, 18, 19, 20, 22, 24, 47, 48, 51, 60, 61, 111, 139, 146, 151, 269, 270; formulation of, 7, 8, 10–11

Dogma, the term, 283

Domitian, 26, 29, 204

Dualism, Gnostic, 126, 129

Easter, date of, 155–6

Ebionism, 121, 122, 123, 133

Ecclesiastical discipline. *See* Church

Ecumenical movement, 1

Eden, Garden of, 309

Eldad and Modat, Book of, 40, 229

Elect, the, 58, 267

Election, divine, 14, 34, 42, 45, 58–9, 230

Election, of officers, 98

"Elements," the, 231–2, 294

Emperor, Roman, 290

Empire, Christian loyalty to, 164, 172

Enoch, Book of, 204, 216

Ephesians, Epistle; authorship, 13fn.

Epiphany, the, 118

Episcopal Succession. *See* Succession

Episcopate, historic, 53. *See also* Bishop

Epistles, circulation, 177

Esther, 58

Eternal life, 304

EUCHARIST: 22, 48, 82–6, 97, 113, 119, 126, 140, 142, 148, 284; and the Atonement, 89–90; the baptized partake, 87, 91; Christian Passover, 311; Christ's Ordinance, 83–4; Messianic, 87; profanation of, 48–9; Words of Institution, 83, 84, 85, 89, 91

EUCHARISTIC: doctrine of intention, 19; Real Presence, 119, 139–40; ritual, 18, 84–5, 87–8, 89; sacrifice, 46, 47, 54–5, 84, 97; symbolism, 84; theology, 90–1, 109, 119, 132, 138–40, 150

Eusebius, 26, 63, 68, 102, 103, 104, 154, 155, 159, 166, 221, 224, 232, 274, 275, 292

Eve, disobedience of, 116; a virgin, 310

Evodius, 102, 103

Exorcism, 93–4

FAITH: 44, 114, 205, 212, 240, 241, 261, 295, 298, 299; of Abraham, 35, 41, 44; as fidelity, 34, 35, 44, 45, 61; in God, 42; Justification by, 7, 12, 13, 15, 16, 42–4, 45, 83, 130, 135, 298, 305; in Old Testament, 37, 133; salvation by faith, 161, 231, 233, 246–7, 300; saving, 34, 35, 40, 41, 42, 56, 61, 113, 136, 137, 151, 160, 191, 202, 241, 244, 248, 294, 299, 304, 308

Faith, The, 22, 40, 73, 114, 118, 137, 161, 257, 296, 308

Fasting, 78, 81, 82, 191, 250, 251

Flesh, The, 111, 164, 284

Florinus, Epistle to, 154

Gentiles, 228, 250, 257, 277

INDEX OF SUBJECTS

Germanicus (martyr), 168
Gnosis, Christian, 202–3, 204
Gnosticism, 124, 126, 127, 135, 137, 138, 147, 162, 187, 193, 196, 242, 290
GOD: Biblical doctrine, 195, 196, 291; the Father, 259, 302; fear of, 39, 202, 240, 244, 300, 309; image of, 207, 299–300; impassibility, 143; Kingdom of, *see* Kingdom; the "Living," 195–6; love of, 56, 300; Name of, 87; pagan doctrine, 291; philosophical doctrine, 293; providence, 38, 169, 172; righteousness of, 298; sovereignty, 240; wrath, 112. *See also* Son, Spirit, Trinity
Good works. *See* Works
GOSPEL: a book, 99, 134, 309; and Law, 256
GOSPELS: apocryphal, 5; authenticity, 221; authority, 4–5; the Four, 3, 140, 231–2, 242–3
Governors, 61, 164. *See also* Empire
GRACE: in Apostolic Fathers, 15; divine, 28, 33, 35, 42, 45, 56, 59, 113, 182, 185, 191, 194, 202, 241, 254, 255, 257, 258, 259, 260–61, 295, 297, 299, 304, 309; doctrine of, 12, 15–16, 28, 30, 39, 40, 43, 47, 60, 112, 114, 118, 119, 245, 246–7; to Gentiles, 34; infused, 29, 202; and Law, 120; means of, 54, 236, 238, 241, 244, 247, 308–9; New Testament doctrine, 12–13, 14, 15, 118; under Old Covenant, 122; Old Testament doctrine, 15, 34–5; Pauline doctrine, 28; Reformation doctrine, 12; salvation by, 12, 16, 47, 57, 77–8, 123, 138, 148, 151, 160, 163, 168, 180, 182, 183, 186, 187, 188, 206, 214, 217, 223, 229, 235, 236, 238, 241, 244, 245, 246–7, 248, 255, 256–7, 258, 261, 267, 297, 298, 300, 304; uncovenanted, 265; universal, 111
γραφή, 221
Grapte. *See* HERMAS, THE SHEPHERD
Greek thought. *See* Hellenic thought
Grosseteste, R., 107

Hadrian, 104, 200, 215, 274, 281
Harnack, A. von, 10, 274
Harrison, P. N., 157, 159
Heaven, 173

Hebraic thought. *See* Judaic thought
HEBREWS, EPISTLE TO: quoted, 76; theology of, 197
Hell, Descent into. *See* Christ
Hellenic thought in Christianity, 11, 16, 19–20, 23, 28, 111, 139, 143, 146, 174, 187, 195, 196, 197, 201–2, 272–3, 286, 294
Heraclitus, 294
HERESY: 101, 114, 146, 154, 162, 187, 310; nature of, 11–17, 20, 68, 110, 123, 126, 138, 193–4, 195–6, 242, 253, 302
Heretic, restoration of, 137, 257
HERMAS: In Arcadia, 225, 258; biographical details, 227, 230–1, 235, 258; character of, 219, 220, 225, 227, 231; as expositor, 220, 232, 250, 251, 256, 258, 263–4; family, 228, 255; identity, 224; use of New Testament, 220; use of S. James, 220, 230, 235, 239; Pauline thought in, 238, 256, 263; and Rhoda, 225, 227; Roman Catholic judgment, 223; as theologian, 229, 233, 236, 239, 240, 242, 245, 253, 257–8
HERMAS, "THE SHEPHERD" OF: Angel—Evil, 209; of Punishment, 254, 255; of Repentance, 229, 233, 234, 243, 246, 247, 261, 266; of Self-Indulgence, 253–4; Angels, doctrine of, 230; authorship, 224; character of, 219, 221, 222; cheerfulness, 241, 242; the Church, 228; circulation of, 221; Clement, 229; date, 225; Grapte, 229; MS. sources, 198–201, 225–6; Maximus, 229; not in Canon, 63, 180, 221, 223; occasion of writing, 219; outline of contents, 226; penitence, 223 (*see also* Discipline, penitential; Penance); as "Scripture," 221, 232, 235; "The Shepherd," identity of, 233–4, 238, 239, 247, 259, 267; Sibyl of Cumae, 227, 229; "Vices," the, 259, 261; "Virtues," the, 258, 259, 261, 262, 267
Herod (Roman official), 169
Hierarchy, 49, 53, 121, 140, 148
Hippolytus, S., 85, 91, 275, 306
Homiletics, early Christian, 37, 111, 192, 244, 256

Hope. *See* Advent Hope
Humility, 34, 36, 38, 47, 57–8, 110, 125

"Ideas," Platonic, 198
IDENTIFICATION: of Christ with man, 116; of man with Christ, 32, 44, 117, 127, 131, 132, 138, 150, 163, 173
IDOLATRY, 78, 183, 184; folly of, 38, 278–9
IGNATIUS OF ANTIOCH, S.: Bishop of Antioch, 102–3; character, 101, 129, 131, 132, 133, 145, 181; contrasted with S. Paul, 108, 111, 120; on discipleship, 107, 125, 127, 129, 137–8, 229; how far representative?, 146; martyrdom, 103, 128; New Testament, use of, 147; Pauline thought in, 113, 118, 121–2, 123, 130, 135, 143, 144, 145, 147–8; as a theologian, 96, 145–152; Theophorus, 107
IGNATIAN EPISTLES: collection of, 158, 165; date, 103, 104, 132; form of, 151; genuine Recension, 106; Long Recension, 106; MS. sources, 63, 106–7; order of, 105–6; writing of, 105, 124, 128
Image of God. *See* God
INCARNATION, the, 34, 56–7, 116, 117, 126, 189, 260, 272, 288, 291; doctrine of, 110–111, 114, 142, 146, 187, 206, 251, 252, 304, 308
Incorruptibility, 174
Irenaeus, S., 26, 37, 67, 79, 116, 126fn., 135–6, 153–4, 155, 196, 197, 206, 207, 221, 232, 235, 259, 291, 293, 310
ISRAEL: the New (*see* Church); the Old, 19, 45, 135, 136, 190, 193, 196, 261–2, 277 (*see also* Law); the Old and New, 19, 30, 42, 47, 203, 261

James, M. R., 5fn.
JAMES, S., on justification, 43–4; used by Hermas, *see* Hermas
Johannine thought, 308, 309
John, S., 153, 155
John the Baptist, S., 254
JUDAISM: anti-Jewish sentiment in Church, 81, 122, 133, 199, 279, 280; Jewish ceremonial, 280–81; Jewish Christians (*see* Church); Jewish Law (*see* Law); Jewish Prayer (*see* Prayer); Jews (*see also* Israel), as persecutors, 170, 173; Judaic thought in Church, 16, 19, 59, 64, 71, 73, 100, 121, 133, 140, 144, 185, 187, 195, 228, 271, 286, 293, 304; Judaism and Christianity, 123, 156, 280, 301–2, 306, 309; Judaizing Christians, 134, 135, 147
JUDGMENT: 207, 228, 249–50, 287; the Last, 41, 43, 100, 162, 186, 187, 191, 204, 205, 214, 215, 250, 260, 266, 292, 304
Judith, 58
JUSTIFICATION: definition of, 42–3, 205, 214–15, 239, 285, 298, 304; by Faith (*see* Faith); Roman Catholic doctrine, 43fn.; in S. James, 42–3
Justin Martyr, S., 3, 19, 50, 70, 79, 84, 97, 118, 173, 273, 274, 275, 282, 284, 287, 288, 289, 294, 309, 310fn.

Kelly, J. N. D., 79
Kerygma, 36, 74
KINGDOM: of God, 9, 72, 86, 87, 88, 116, 185, 188, 260, 262, 266, 290, 299, 300; millennial, 100, 188, 214
Kirk, K., 71

LAW: ceremonial, 72; Jewish (and Mosaic), 15, 72, 213, 256, 306, 309; of meats, 73; moral, 42, 71, 72, 73; New, 203, 256; Old and New, 280; preaching of, 72
Layman, 48
Legality, 78, 121–2, 191, 192, 203, 205–6, 217, 222, 223, 227, 245, 246, 256
Liberty, Christian, 78, 222
Lightfoot, J. B., 70, 106, 201, 275, 307, and throughout, where the Greek text is cited
Linus, 27
LOGOS: creation by, 41; Doctrine (*see* Christ); endiathetos and prophorikos, 308; spermatic, 294; the term defined, 289, 310
Lord's Day, the, 82, 85, 97, 113, 122, 215
LOVE: Christian, 56, 57, 61, 76, 120, 137, 138; gift of, 45, 55–6, 113, 161; to God, 240, 299, 300
Love-Feast. *See* Agape
Loyalty of Christians. *See* Empire
Lucian, 166

INDEX OF SUBJECTS

Luther, 13, 14
Lutheran doctrine, 16, 43fn.

Maccabees, 4, 277
Magic, 76, 118, 119
Maranatha, 88
Marcianus, 177
Marcion, 193, 243, 274, 281, 302
Marcus Aurelius, 274
Marriage, Christian, 144, 148, 236, 238
MARTYR, THE: "Acts" of, 165; burial, 176; figure of, 101; honor paid to, 158, 176; relics, 130, 176; trial of, 171
MARTYRDOM: calling of, 32, 107, 108, 112, 113, 117, 125, 127, 129, 130, 131, 151, 167–9, 173–4, 177, 184, 229, 265–6, 276–7, 285, 286, 288, 291, 292, 301, 303, 304; of S. Ignatius (see Ignatius); psychology of, 102, 125, 167–8, 169, 170–71, 174–5; of S. Polycarp (see Polycarp); of SS. Peter and Paul, 31, 32; witness of, 129, 130
Meecham, H. G., 274, 284, 285, 287, 290, 291, 292, 299, 306, 309, 311
Merit of good works, 14, 95, 144, 251
MESSIAH (see also Christ): Jewish, 212
Michael (angel), 256
Millenarianism, 100
Millennium. See Kingdom
MINISTERIAL ORDER, 24, 51, 52, 61–2, 95, 120–21, 125, 132, 133, 140, 141–2; Succession, see Succession
MINISTRY: Apostolic, 48, 49–50, 54, 61, 65–6, 68, 96, 99, 103, 105, 108, 121, 125, 126, 134, 148; authority, 24, 49, 53, 54, 126; "charismatic," 65–7, 69, 92–6, 133, 149, 239; development of, 10, 54, 62, 134, 141, 149; doctrine of, 53, 54; dominical foundation, 51. See also Bishop, Deacon, Hierarchy, Monepiscopacy, Presbyter, Presbyter-Bishop
Miracles, 165, 174–5
Monepiscopacy, 149
Monotheism, 41–2
Montanism, 68–9, 92, 94
MORAL: discipline, see Discipline; Law, see Law
Moralism, 77, 160, 244
MORALITY: Christian, 43, 77, 189, 222, 227, 228, 234, 237, 240, 241, 242, 244, 246, 247, 249, 251, 271, 276, 277, 284; pagan, 58, 76
MYSTERIES: Christian, 91, 113fn., 124, 282; pagan, 10, 47, 276, 282, 283
Mystery, 282, 286. See also Revelation
Mysticism, 303

Natural Order, 38, 40
Natural Religion. See Religion
Nero, 32, 205
New Testament. See Testament
Nicaea, Council of, 156

OBEDIENCE: 45; of Christ (see Christ, Sacrifice); inward, 76
Old Testament. See Testament
Onesimus, 108
Oracles, pagan, 118
Order. See Ministry, Sacramental Order
Ordination, 54, 98–9
Origen, 70, 200, 221, 224, 277, 278, 287
ORTHODOXY: 12, 126, 132, 148, 194, 303; nature of, 17, 18, 19, 110–11, 151, 162, 242, 243
Owen, E. C. E., 32fn., 130fn.

Pantaenus, 275, 307
Parousia, 292. See also Christ, Advent
Pastoral duty, 143
Pastoral Epistles, 159
Patriarchs, 209, 261, 262
Paul, S., 25, 31, 55, 307, 310
Pauline language in Apostolic Fathers, 107, 112–13, 114, 174
PAULINE THOUGHT: 12, 13–14, 42–3, 78, 87, 111; in Apostolic Fathers, 108, 308 (see also Clement, Hermas, Ignatius, Polycarp); in Church, 10, 140–1, 44, 72, 122, 180, 222, 282
Penance, 223, 236, 238, 255, 267, 297
Penitential discipline. See Discipline
Perfection, Christian, 57, 108
Perpetua and Felicitas, SS., Passion of, 32, 130
PERSECUTION: 86, 112, 136, 168, 172, 184, 220, 270, 288, 292; grounds of, 171, 173, 277, 285; by Jews, see Judaism
PETER S.: 25, 31, 103, 158; 1st *Epistle*, cited by S. Clement, 56; cited by S. Polycarp, 159

Philippi, Church of. *See* Church
Philippians, Epistle to, 161, 163
Philo, 197
PHILOSOPHY: Greek, 195; preparation for Christ, 294
Phoenix, 41
Pionius, 175, 177
Pius of Rome, 224
Pliny the Younger, 85
POLYCARP OF SMYRNA, S.: 119–20, 143, 154, 155, 156–7, 181; character, 153, 154; date of martyrdom, 153; Epistles, theory of two, 157–8; evangelical theology, 163; as exegete, 163; martyrdom, 165–6, 169; Pauline thought, 158, 164; I Peter quoted, 158; and S. John, 153
POLYCARP, S., "ACTS" OF: 165–6, 177; authenticity of, 166, 170; MS. sources, 166
POLYCARP, S., EPISTLE OF: 155, 157; and Epistle of Barnabas, 159; date, 165; MS. sources, 159, 201; style, 158
Poor, righteous, 249
Poverty, religious, 93
PRAYER: early Christian, 59, 89, 170, 173; ejaculatory, 87; Jewish, 82; the Lord's, 82; power of, 109, 113, 150; responsive, 85, 86
Preaching, early Christian, 179, 182, 192, 270
Predestination, 78, 230
Premillenarianism, 100, 214
Preparation, Day of, 169–70
Presbyter, 141, 148, 192. *See also* Ministry
Presbyter-bishop, 24, 27, 29, 39, 48, 49, 50, 53, 54, 62, 65, 68, 69, 88–9, 95, 99, 103, 104, 105, 121, 140–1, 149, 155, 224, 230, 265
Presbytery, the, 54, 108, 124, 228, 231
Pride, 110
PRIESTHOOD: Christian, 47, 48, 95; universal, 48, 109, 150
PROPHECY: argument from, 115fn., 194–5, 271, 273, 302; of Christ (*see* Christ); Old Testament, 36, 39, 196, 202, 258
PROPHETS: Christian, 65, 66, 76, 88–9, 92–3, 94, 95, 99, 118, 239 (*see also* Ministry, "charismatic"; Old Testa-ment, 132–3, 135, 146, 147, 309; "signs," 94
Propitiation, 227–8, 264
Providence, divine. *See* God
Purgatory, 223

Quadratus, Apology of, 274–5, 292
Quartodeciman controversy, 156–7. *See also* Easter

Rachia, 208
Ransom, 297, 305
Real Presence. *See* Eucharist
Reconciliation, 55
Reformation theology, 12, 14, 15, 16
Regulus, 277
Religio licita, 283
RELIGION: civic, 277; natural, 38, 72, 271, 273; pagan, 277; Roman attitude to, 283
REPENTANCE: 33, 57, 186–7, 228, 236, 247, 253, 255, 257, 266, 267; Angel of, *see* Hermas. *See also* Discipline, penitential; Penance
"Reserve," doctrinal, 38, 73, 79, 90, 91, 271, 283, 297, 303, 304
RESURRECTION: of the Body, 174, 187, 253; general, 40–1, 57, 100, 162, 304
Reuchlin, J., 275
REVELATION: divine, 87, 112–13, 114, 117, 146–7, 273, 282, 289, 293, 295; historic, 4–5, 147; "the Mystery," 108–9, 112, 113, 122, 123, 124, 135, 146–7, 276, 278, 288, 293, 294, 296, 299, 300–1, 303, 307–8; progressive, 196, 293
Revelation of S. John, 102
Revelations and visions. *See* Visions
Rhoda. *See* Hermas
Riches, 249
Roman Church. *See* Church
Rufinus, 166
Ruinart, 107

SABBATH: Jewish, 82, 122, 213, 281; a "type," 170
SACRAMENTS: 33, 308; Gnostic, 138
SACRAMENTAL: doctrine, 119, 126; order, 51, 52, 109; Real Presence, *see* Eucharist

INDEX OF SUBJECTS

SACRIFICE: Biblical doctrine, 97; Commemorative, *see* Eucharist; Eucharistic, *see* Eucharist; Jewish, 279; of obedience, 45–6, 84, 89, 116, 208; Old Testament, 208, 280; pagan, 184
Saints, Communion of, 112, 176–7, 262
Saints' days, 176
Sanctification, 45, 77, 108, 183, 300
SATAN (Satanic powers): 125, 127, 147, 185, 217, 238–9, 240, 246; Antichrist powers overthrown, 18, 113, 118, 204, 247, 248
Scapegoat, 208
Schaff, 101
Schism, 101, 120–1, 146
SCRIPTURE: allegory of, 196–7, 198, 199, 204, 207, 208, 209, 232, 275, 306, 309; Apocrypha, 30, 75; authority of, 6; canon, 190, 204; "difficulties" in, 194, 199; exegesis of, in ancient Church, 36, 98, 100, 114, 134, 135, 194, 197, 199, 204, 207, 210, 295, 306; "inspiration of, 6, 36, 147, 195, 272; "types," 31, 35, 47, 98, 114, 116, 190, 196–7, 198, 207
Self-righteousness, 144
Septuagint, 27–8, 30, 50, 75, 207
Service, Christian, 145
Shepherd, The, of Hermas. *See* Hermas
Sibyl of Cumae. *See* Hermas
Sinaiticus, Codex, 198, 201, 208, 225–6
SIN: 304; "against the Holy Ghost," 94; in believers, 221–2, 228, 264; forgiveness of, 89, 134, 227, 237, 298 (*see also* Repentance); judgment on, 187; postbaptismal, 186, 229, 237; punishment, 254–5
"Sister" (title of Christian), 165, 227. *See also* Brother
Slavery, 76–7, 143
Society, Christian attitude to, 227, 276, 284
SON: eternal generation, 111; God the, 252, 258, 259–60, 261, 289, 296, 305. *See also* Christ
Son of Man. *See* Christ
Soul, 286
Spirit, the Holy, 120, 146, 239, 241, 242, 243, 252, 258, 304
Spiritual gifts, 21–2, 65, 93, 95, 96
"Stations," 82, 250

Stoics, 283
SUCCESSION: Apostolical, 53, 110, 121, 148, 155; episcopal, 23, 103, 155; ministerial, 23, 50–1, 53–4
Supererogation, works of. *See* Works

Tacitus, 32
Taylor, C., 220, 232, 254, 259, 261
Teachers, order of, 99
Teaching of the Twelve Apostles. *See* Didache
Telfer, W., 304–5
Temple (Jerusalem), 215
Temple coinage, 121
Tertullian, 79, 176fn., 219, 221, 287, 288, 310fn.
TESTAMENT, NEW (*see also* Scripture): authority of, 2, 4, 5, 7, 9, 15, 68; canon of, 2, 3, 6, 63, 180, 199, 220, 306, 309; formation of canon, 4, 7, 159, 182; inspiration, 2, 5, 9; use of, by Apostolic Fathers, 74, 158. *See also* the writers by name
TESTAMENT, OLD (*see also* Scripture): authority of, 37, 72, 147; as Christian Scripture, 30, 74, 190, 193–7; devotional use, 196; "difficulties" in, 196; exegesis, modern, 136; Scripture, 3, 30, 34, 46, 57, 61, 134, 138, 146, 164, 185, 193–4, 196, 301; use by Apostolic Fathers, 193
Thales, 294
Theophanies, 289–90
Theophilus of Antioch, S., 295
Theophorus. *See* Ignatius
Titus (Emperor), 200, 204, 215
Toleration, 171
"Tongues," gift of, 65–7, 92–3, 118. *See also* Ministry, "charismatic"
Torrance, T. F., 15, 16, 28, 29, 33, 42, 44, 71, 89, 101, 192, 202, 210, 223
TRADITION: appeal to, 92, 194; in Church, 153, 307, 308, 310; unwritten, 154, 158, 161, 201
Trajan, 85, 103
Transubstantiation, 138
"Tree of Knowledge," 309–10
Trent, Council of, 43fn.
TRINITY: the Holy, 55, 58, 80, 290; prophecy of, 206
Truthfulness, 235

INDEX OF SUBJECTS

Trypho, Dialogue with, 173
"Two Ways." *See* Barnabas, *Didache*
"Types": of Christ (*see* Christ); Scripture, 31, 35, 47, 98, 114, 116, 190, 196–7, 198, 207

Ussher, 107

Valens, 164
Vespasian, 204
Vicarious suffering, 298
"Vices," the. *See* Hermas, *The Shepherd*
Victor of Rome, 155, 156
Virgin, the Blessed, 111, 116, 310
Virgin Birth. *See* Christ
"Virtues," the. *See* Hermas, *The Shepherd*
Visions, 125
Vokes, F. E., 68, 69, 70, 75, 90, 97, 200
von Harnack, A. *See* Harnack, A. von

Voss, 106

Wealth, danger of, 255
Westcott, 274, 275, 306
Whittaker, M., 225fn.
Widows, Order of, 142, 143, 161
Words of Institution. *See* Eucharist.
WORKS (*see also* Merit): good, 39, 44, 45, 113, 150, 184, 186, 205, 223, 246, 248, 249, 256, 257, 266; justification by, 42–3; of supererogation, 250–51
World, the, 287
Worldliness, 93–5, 227, 230, 242, 248, 250, 264, 266
WORSHIP: Christian, 85, 276; Jewish, 279
Wrath of God. *See* God

Year, the Christian, 311

II Index of Scripture References

This Index includes the Scriptural quotations, allusions, and references made by the Apostolic Fathers, and also those made by the writer in the composition of the notes.

GENESIS	Page
i, 1	235
i, 1ff.	41
i, 9	38
i, 23	40
i, 26	206, 295
i, 27	190
i, 28	207, 299
i, 26, 28	207
i, 26, 27, 28	45
ii, 2	214
ii, 15	309
ii, 17	309, 310
ii, 23	32
iii, 1–21	116
iii, 22	309
iv, 3–8	30
xii, 1–3	35
xiii, 14–16	35
xv, 5	44
xv, 5, 6	35
xvii, 5	213
xviii, 26	287
xviii, 27	37
xxii, 17	44
xxv, 21–3	213
xlviii, 11, 19	213
xlviii, 14, 18, 19	213

EXODUS	
ii, 14	31
iii, 11	37
iii, 13–15	87
iv, 10	37
xiv, 23, 26, 28	57
xv, 19	57

	Page
xvii, 8–16	212
xvii, 14	212
xx, 7	217
xx, 8	214
xx, 13–17	76
xx, 14	217
xxiv, 5–7	87
xxiv, 18	213
xxxi, 18	205, 213
xxxii, 7	205
xxxii, 7, 8, 19	213
xxxii, 32	57
xxxiii, 1, 3	207
xxxiii, 12–23	87
xxxiii, 20	206
xxxiv, 6	295
xxxiv, 28	205

LEVITICUS	
xi, 5	211
xi, 7, 10, 13–15	211
xvi, 7, 9, 8	208
xvi, 8	208
xix, 17–18	76
xix, 26	76
xxiii, 29	208

NUMBERS	
xii, 7	37, 50
xvi, 1–50	50
xvii, 1–10	50
xviii, 27	42
xix, 1–10	209

DEUTERONOMY	
iv, 34	42
vi, 4, 14	235
vi, 5, 13	217
vii, 6–9	42
ix, 12	205
ix, 12–14	57

DEUTERONOMY (cont.)	Page		Page
x, 16	209	iv, 4	164
xiii, 18	59	xii, 3–5	37
xiv, 6	211	xvi, 11	252
xiv, 12–14	211	xviii, 25–6	55
xvi, 5–6	48	xviii, 44	209
xxvii, 15	212	xix, 1–4	41
xxvii–xxx	73	xxii, 6–8	37
xxx, 19	121	xxii, 16	207
xxxii, 8–9	42	xxii, 18	207
xxxii, 15	30	xxii, 20	207
xxxii, 39	59	xxii, 22	207
		xxiii, 4	41
JOSHUA		xxiv, 1	58
ii, 3ff.	35	xxiv, 2	230
		xxiv, 4	214
1 SAMUEL		xxviii, 6	41
ii, 6–7	59	xxx, 1, 2	57
xii, 14	38	xxxii, 1	298
		xxxii, 10	40
1 KINGS		xxxiii, 9	113
ix, 4	59	xxxiii, 10	59
		xxxiv, 11–17, 19	40
2 KINGS		xxxiv, 12–13	209
xix, 19	59	xxxvii, 11	76
		xxxvii, 35–7	37
1 CHRONICLES		xli, 9	169
i, 1–4	261	xlii, 2	207
xxix, 14–15	249	xlix, 15	57
		l, 7–14	279
ESTHER		l, 14–15	57
iv–v	58	l, 16–23	45
		li, 3–19	38
JOB		li, 17	57
i, 1	37	li, 19	203
iv, 16–v, 5	47	lv, 22	231, 233
v, 11	59	lxvii, 1	59
v, 17–26	58	lxvii, 4	37
xi, 2, 3	44	lxviii, 36, 37	37
xi, 7	114	lxix, 30–2	57
xv, 15	47	lxxii, 16	87
xix, 26	41	lxxix, 13	59
xxxviii, 11	38	lxxxix, 20	38
		c, 3	59
PSALMS		civ, 4	46
i, 1	211	civ, 15	241, 246
i, 3	124	cx, 1	46, 213
i, 3–6	212	cxv, 4–8	279
ii, 7	308	cxviii, 12	207
ii, 7–8	46	cxviii, 18	58
ii, 11	160	cxviii, 19, 20	55
iii, 5	41		

PSALMS (cont.)	Page
cxviii, 22, 24	207
cxviii, 26	94
cxix, 114	59
cxxxix, 7–10	42
cxli, 5	58
cxlv, 18	60

PROVERBS	
i, 17	206
i, 23–33	58
ii, 21, 22	37
iii, 12	58
iii, 28	163
iii, 34	42, 110
vii, 3	30
x, 12	191
xviii, 17	124
xx, 27	39

ISAIAH	
i, 2	209
i, 10	209
i, 11–13	203
i, 13	215
i, 16–20	35
ii, 2	258
iii, 5	30
iii, 9–10	207
v, 6	242
v, 7	251
v, 21	205
v, 26	137
vi, 3	45
x, 33	59
xi, 1	86
xiii, 11	59
xiii, 22	40
xvi, 1, 2	211
xxvi, 20	57
xxviii, 16	207
xxix, 13	37, 184, 264
xxxiii, 13	209
xxxiii, 16–18	212
xxxiv, 4	191
xl, 3	209
xl, 10	45, 218
xl, 11	234
xl, 12	215
xlii, 6, 7	213
xliii, 5–9	86

	Page
xliv, 10–19	279
xlv, 1	213
xlv, 2, 3	212
xlix, 6, 7	213
xlix, 17	215
xlix, 22	137
l, 6, 7	207
l, 7	207
l, 8, 9	207
li, 5	298
lii, 5	126, 163, 189
liii, 1–12	37, 295
liii, 5	206
liii, 11–12	184
liv, 1	183
lvii, 15	59
lviii, 4–10	203
lviii, 5–7	250
lviii, 9	191
lix, 14	30
lx, 17	50
lxi, 1, 2	213
lxii, 11	45
lxiii, 1–9	290
lxiii, 1–10	233
lxiii, 2	175
lxiv, 4	45, 168
lxv, 2	212
lxvi, 2	37, 76, 217
lxvi, 18	123, 192
lxvi, 24	186

JEREMIAH	
ii, 12, 13	211
iv, 4	209
iv, 34	209
v, 4	164
vii, 11	189–90
vii, 22, 23	203
ix, 23, 24	36
ix, 26	209
xvii, 24	214
xviii, 1–6	186
xxi, 8	75
xxiv, 7	241

EZEKIEL	
iii, 21	191
iv, 1–17	94
vi, 1	59

INDEX OF SCRIPTURE REFERENCES

EZEKIEL (cont.)	Page
xi, 19	207
xiv, 14, 18	185
xxxiii, 4	267
xxxiii, 11	35
xxxiv, 2, 5	266
xxxiv, 4	162
xxxvi, 26	207
xxxvii, 12	57
xlvii, 1, 7, 12	212
xlviii, 12	42

DANIEL
ii, 34, 45	259
iii, 25–7	175
vi, 22	233
vii, 7	200
vii, 8	205
vii, 10	45
vii, 24	204
ix, 24	216

MICAH
iv, 1	258

ZECHARIAH
viii, 17	203
xiii, 7	207, 234
xiv, 5	100

MALACHI
i, 11, 14	97, 98
iii, 1	40
iv, 1	191

4 ESDRAS
v, 5	212

TOBIT
iv, 10	163
iv, 15	75

JUDITH
viii–xiii	58
ix, 11	59

WISDOM
ii, 24	30
xi, 22	41
xii, 12	41

ECCLESIASTICUS	Page
ii, 11	59
iv, 31	76, 217
xii, 13	241
xvi, 18, 19	59

MATTHEW
ii, 2, 9–10	118
iii, 13–17	116
iii, 15	137
iv, 8	258
v, 3, 10	161
v, 5	76, 290
v, 7	36
v, 10–12	130, 266
v, 21–30	76
v, 25	227
v, 26	75
v, 27–9	188
v, 39–42	15
v, 44	164, 287
v, 44, 46	75
v, 48	300
vi, 5	82
vi, 8	191
vi, 9–13	82
vi, 13	162
vi, 13	192
vi, 14	36
vi, 20	248
vi, 24	185
vi, 25, 28, 31	299
vii, 1, 2	36
vii, 6	76, 87
vii, 7	40
vii, 13–14	73
vii, 21	44, 184
vii, 21–3	43
vii, 22–3	186, 260
viii, 11	86
ix, 13	183, 206
x, 1–5	307
x, 10	95
x, 16	143, 234
x, 22	192
x, 23	169
x, 28	301
x, 32	184
x, 39	301
xi, 27	267
xii, 28–9	247

INDEX OF SCRIPTURE REFERENCES

MATTHEW (cont.)	Page
xii, 33	113
xii, 36–7	43
xii, 50	187
xiii, 3	41
xiii, 24–30	250
xiii, 38	251
xiii, 43	250
xvi, 22	264
xvi, 26	185, 286
xviii, 3	266
xviii, 6	55
xviii, 8	301
xviii, 17	144
xviii, 32–3	265
xviii, 23–35	112
xix, 9	236
xix, 10, 12, 21	78
xix, 12	138, 144, 284
xix, 16–22	266
xix, 21	230
xix, 28	209, 263
xx, 16	207
xxi, 9	94
xxii, 11–12	260
xxii, 14	206
xxii, 17–21	121
xxii, 37, 39	75
xxii, 44	213
xxii, 45	213
xxiii, 14, 23	191
xxiii, 25	188
xxiv, 9	292
xxiv, 10, 11, 12, 13, 24, 30	100
xxiv, 31	87
xxiv, 44	192
xxv, 13	100
xxv, 21	187
xxv, 31–46	41, 43, 186
xxv, 34	300
xxv, 34ff.	161
xxv, 41	301
xxv, 44	192
xxvi, 24	55, 233
xxvi, 31	207
xxvi, 39, 42	174
xxvi, 41	162
xxvi, 55	170
xxvii, 28	208
xxviii, 18	259
xxviii, 19	49, 80, 262

MARK	Page
i, 15	188, 234, 308
ii, 17	110, 183
iii, 4	281
iii, 28–30	94
iv, 3	41
iv, 5–6	264
iv, 17	264
iv, 17–19	230
iv, 18–19	242
iv, 19	249, 264
vi, 34	234
vii, 12	184
viii, 34	107
viii, 34–5	121
viii, 34–8	117
viii, 35	131, 167, 265
viii, 36	130, 185
ix, 35	161
ix, 34–45	257
ix, 36	107
ix, 42	55
x, 17–19	257
x, 18	295
x, 23	264
x, 24	264
x, 27	297
x, 29	284
x, 29–30	249
x, 38–9	174
x, 42	300
x, 45	184
xi, 24	241
xii, 1–9	207, 250
xii, 6–7	250
xii, 10	261
xii, 25	188
xii, 28–31	235
xii, 41–4	249
xiii, 3–13	229
xiii, 32–7	214
xiv, 21	55, 233
xiv, 27	234
xiv, 62	118, 192, 212
xv, 39	305

LUKE	
i, 1–4	92
i, 38	116, 310
ii, 1	283
iii, 22	175

INDEX OF SCRIPTURE REFERENCES

LUKE (cont.)	Page
iii, 23–38	115
iii, 31–6	261
iii, 36–8	261
iv, 4	259
vi, 20	249
vi, 20–6	73
vi, 22, 23, 26	286
vi, 27, 28, 32, 33, 35	75
vi, 29–30	75
vi, 30–5	76
vi, 31, 36–8	36
vi, 32–5	189
viii, 5	41
ix, 48	58
x, 7	93
x, 22	260
x, 25–8	267
xi, 20–2	247
xii, 8	184
xii, 19	286
xii, 20	248
xii, 4–5	240
xii, 32	234
xii, 35, 40	100
xii, 47–8	263
xv, 11–32	255
xvi, 9	249
xvi, 10–11	187
xvi, 13	185
xvi, 25	187
xvii, 1, 2	55
xvii, 10	246, 251
xvii, 20	188
xviii, 1–8	241
xviii, 9–14	255
xviii, 12	82
xviii, 14	298
xxi, 24	216
xxi, 33	92
xxii, 22	55
xxii, 37	37, 295
xxii, 41–4	242
xxii, 42	84
xxiv, 39	137
xxiv, 41–3	137

JOHN	
i, 1	41, 122, 308
i, 1–3	290, 295
i, 1–14	272, 289
i, 14	307
i, 18	207
iii, 5	262, 297
iii, 8	133
iii, 14–15	212
iii, 16	56, 299
iii, 17	291
iv, 9	300
v, 19	121
v, 22	192
v, 29	174
vi, 30–35, 48–58	86
vi, 51	212
vii, 17	52
viii, 12	309
x, 7	260
x, 11, 12	247
x, 11–16	233, 234
x, 12–13	266
x, 18	252
xii, 50	121
xiv, 6	260
xiv, 17	287
xiv, 20	308
xv, 1ff.	86
xv, 22	228
xv, 22, 24	263
xvi, 12–14	92
xvii, 2	252
xvii, 3	309
xvii, 11, 14	287
xviii, 36	290
xix, 14	169
xx, 21–3	49, 267
xx, 27	307

ACTS	
i, 6	88
i, 8	49
i, 15–26	307
i, 21–2	3, 49, 92
i, 25	121
ii, 1–13	49
ii, 24	160
ii, 38	80
ii, 42, 46	97
ii, 44	284
iii, 13, 26	295
iv, 12	260
iv, 27	86

INDEX OF SCRIPTURE REFERENCES

ACTS (cont.)	Page
iv, 27, 30	295
iv, 32	75, 76, 217
vi, 1–6	50
vi, 7	40
viii, 26ff.	50
viii, 30–5	37
viii, 37	80
ix, 17	143
x, 42	160
x, 48	80
xiv, 4	307
xiv, 14	92
xiv, 14–18	72, 270
xiv, 15–17	38
xiv, 23	49
xiv, 27	241
xv, 1–29	7, 15
xv, 23–29	145
xv, 29	25
xvii, 7	283
xvii, 16–32	270
xvii, 22–31	38, 72
xvii, 24–5	279
xvii, 30	297
xvii, 30–2	304
xix, 31	172
xx, 7	97
xx, 17, 28	49
xx, 20, 27	265
xx, 35	29, 74, 161
xxi, 14	170
xxi, 20	143
xxiv, 25	72
xxvi, 18	59

ROMANS	
i, 7	28
i, 17	13
i, 21–3	183
i, 24	296
ii, 4	295
iv, 1–16	133
iv, 11	213
v, 12f.	298
v, 21	206
vi, 3–5	262
vi, 3–6	117
vi, 4	118
vi, 14	256
viii, 4–13	284

	Page
viii, 5	111
viii, 10	308
viii, 17	250
xi, 32	296
xii, 9	75, 77, 217
xii, 10	163, 277
xiii, 1–7	164, 172
xiii, 5–7	283–4
xiv, 10–12	162
xv, 6	164
xvi, 7	307
xvi, 14	224
xvi, 25	282

I CORINTHIANS	
i, 18–25	296
i, 20	114
i, 23	286
i, 26	269
ii, 1–16	108–9
ii, 6–8	118
ii, 7	113, 282
ii, 8	127
ii, 9	45, 168, 188
	191
iii, 9–15	230
iii, 12–13	233
iv, 1	282
iv, 4	130
iv, 8–13	112
iv, 10–13	114
iv, 12	285
vi, 2	164
vi, 6	143
vi, 9	132, 240
vi, 9, 10	114, 161
vi, 11	183
vi, 15	191
vi, 15–17	144
vi, 17, 19–20	253
vi, 19	187
vii, 6–9	78
vii, 7–9	144
vii, 7–9, 26–35	188
vii, 20–3	143, 227
vii, 20–4	77
vii, 25	74
vii, 25–31	144
vii, 26–7	284
vii, 26–40	238

1 CORINTHIANS (cont.)	Page		Page
viii, 1	306, 310	xii, 1–4	125
viii, 1–13	78	xii, 9	118
viii, 2	310		
viii, 5–6	184	GALATIANS	
ix, 4–6, 15	78	i, 1	164
ix, 5	143	i, 8	92
ix, 17	289	i, 8, 9, 11, 12	307
ix, 24–7	182, 186, 193	i, 23	114
x, 11	31	ii, 11	103
x, 17	87	ii, 20	33
xi, 20–34	88	iii, 1	30
xi, 21	85	iv, 3	118
xi, 23	92, 307	iv, 4	293
xi, 23–6	84	iv, 9	231, 294
xi, 24	97	iv, 26	161
xii, 3	241	v, 1–4	122
xii, 4ff.	65	v, 4	120
xii, 14–21	109	v, 15	231
xii, 27	190	v, 16–25	73, 284
xiii, 10	57	v, 17	161
xiii, 13	202	v, 21	114
xiv, 1–25, 29–32	93	v, 22	240
xiv, 1–10	65, 69	vi, 2	300
xiv, 16	48, 97	vi, 7	161
xiv, 18	133		
xv, 1–58	40	EPHESIANS	
xv, 3	92, 307	i, 3	164
xv, 3, 4	79, 308	i, 4, 5	189
xv, 8–9	132	i, 9	282
xv, 20–2	206	i, 9–10	278
xv, 22	298	i, 10	207fn.
xv, 25	192	i, 23	190
xv, 29	263	ii, 5	118, 202
xv, 32	107	ii, 8–9	160
xv, 42, 50, 52–4	174	ii, 11–14	263
xv, 53	287	ii, 19	283
xv, 58	163	ii, 19–22	258
xvi, 22	88	ii, 20–22	230
		iii, 3, 4, 9	282
2 CORINTHIANS		iii, 3, 9, 10	113
i, 3	164	iii, 5, 6	189
iii, 2	164	iii, 9–10	278
iv, 6, 10	30	iii, 9–11	189, 229
iv, 14	160	iii, 11	230
v, 19	297	iv, 4	260, 263
v, 20	255	iv, 4–5	263
vi, 9–10	285	iv, 5	40, 118, 257
vii, 1	202	iv, 5, 13–15	92
viii, 21	162	iv, 8ff.	308
xi, 31	164	iv, 15–16	258

EPHESIANS (cont.)	Page		Page
iv, 26	164	iii, 1–13	69
iv, 30	236	iii, 2	265
v, 23–32	232	iii, 6	120
v, 25–32	190	iii, 9	282
v, 29	144	iii, 16	308
v, 32	282	iv, 14	54
vi, 5–7	143	iv, 15	164
vi, 5–9	77	vi, 7, 10	161
vi, 9	300		
vi, 11	145	2 TIMOTHY	
vi, 12	118, 125	i, 6	49
vi, 13, 16	232	ii, 4	145
vi, 16	241	ii, 12	161
vi, 18	164	iii, 7	264
vi, 18–19	108–9	iv, 7, 8	186
vi, 19	282	iv, 10	163
		iv, 21	27
PHILIPPIANS			
i, 1	50, 69, 99, 230	TITUS	
ii, 4	167	iii, 1	30
ii, 5–11	30, 37	iii, 4	297
ii, 10–11	160		
ii, 11	170, 192	HEBREWS	
ii, 16	163	i, 2–3	290
iii, 18	164	i, 3	46, 252
iii, 20	283	i, 3, 4, 7, 5, 13	46
iv, 3	26, 112	ii, 9–18	45
		iii, 5	50
COLOSSIANS		iv, 3–10	170
i, 15–17	290	iv, 4–6	264
i, 23	112	iv, 15–16	45
i, 24	168	v, 5	164
ii, 14–15	127	v, 7	242
ii, 15	118	v, 7–9	45
iii, 5	164	vi, 4–6	186, 254
iii, 16	202	vi, 4–7	237
		vii, 14	114
1 THESSALONIANS		vii, 26	60
iii, 2	112	viii, 1	60
		ix, 14	208
2 THESSALONIANS		ix, 24	46
i, 4	164	x, 9	205
ii, 3–12	204	x, 21	60
ii, 7	287	x, 23	188
iii, 15	164	x, 26–31	187
		x, 39	286
1 TIMOTHY		xi, 1–40	34
i, 15	192	xi, 6	295
i, 17	60	xi, 9	283
ii, 2	164	xi, 13	133
ii, 4–5	258		

INDEX OF SCRIPTURE REFERENCES

HEBREWS (cont.)	Page
xi, 13–14	248
xi, 27	294
xi, 31	35
xi, 33	233
xi, 35	192
xii, 11	192
xiii, 7	75, 76, 217

JAMES	
i, 1	263
i, 5	258
i, 5, 6	251
i, 6	241
i, 8	239, 264
i, 13–15	239
i, 15	245
i, 21	254
i, 27	235, 240, 249
ii, 5	230, 249, 300
ii, 7	257
ii, 14–26	43–4
ii, 17–20	257
iii, 2	245
iii, 5–8	235
iii, 8	265
iii, 13–18	240
iii, 15	243
iii, 17	243
iv, 1–7	240
iv, 4	185
iv, 6	42, 110
iv, 7	245, 248
iv, 11	235
iv, 12	248
iv, 13–14	248
v, 4	231
v, 7–8	193
v, 16	249
v, 19	44
v, 20	298

1 PETER	
i, 1	263
i, 2	28
i, 7	233
i, 8	160
i, 10–12	296
i, 13	160
i, 21	160
ii, 2	207

	Page
ii, 5–8	230
ii, 9	29, 48, 109
	154
ii, 11	248, 283
ii, 12	163, 188
ii, 13–17	172
ii, 17	163
ii, 22–4	163
ii, 25	234
iii, 9	161
iii, 18	297–8
iii, 18–21	262
iii, 19–20	34, 123
iii, 20	230
iv, 6	265
iv, 7	162
iv, 8	56, 191
iv, 12–16	172
iv, 14–16	257
iv, 16	257
v, 2, 4	234
v, 3	54, 145
v, 5	42, 110, 124
	163
v, 7	231, 233

2 PETER	
i, 16	92
i, 16–21	307
i, 17	35
ii, 20–2	192
iii, 8	201, 214
iii, 10, 12	233

1 JOHN	
i, 4	300
ii, 1, 2	186
ii, 13–14	308
ii, 27	235
iv, 2–3	126, 162
iv, 7, 8	56
iv, 12, 17, 18	57
iv, 18	87
iv, 19	300

JUDE	
3	40, 92, 114
14	216

REVELATION	
i, 7	208

REVELATION (cont.)			Page
i, 8	308	xviii, 8	230
i, 13–17	234	xviii, 20, 21	192
ii, 5, 16	257	xix, 11–16	192
ii, 16	264	xix, 13	208
iii, 1	264	xx, 1–7	100
iii, 9	133	xx, 1–8	214
v, 1	231	xxi, 1	215
vi, 2–5	232	xxi, 2	232
vii, 4	263	xxi, 5	308
x, 1	97	xxi, 14	230
xiii, 8	230	xxii, 2	309
xiv, 4	284	xxii, 12	45, 218

III Index of References to Ancient Writers of the Church

	Page
AUGUSTINE, S.	
Confessions, vi, 2	86
CLEMENT OF ALEXANDRIA	
Miscellanies	
ii, 6, 7, 15, 18, 20	200
v, 10	200
vi, 8	200
EUSEBIUS	
Chronicle, ii	103
Church History	
III, iii, 6	224
III, xv	26
III, xxii	102
III, xxv, 4	63, 224
III, xvi	26
III, xxvii	121
III, xxxvi, 2	103
III, xxxvi, 13–15	159
IV, iii, 2	274
IV, xv	166
IV, xviii, 3–5	275
IV, xxiii, 11	26
V, i–iii	166
V, viii, 7	221, 232
V, xvi	68
V, xviii, 13	94
V, xx, 5–7	154
V, xx, 8	155fn.
V, xxiv, 12–17	155
IRENAEUS, S.	
Adversus Haereses	
III, i, 1	3
III, ii, 8	232
III, iii, 3	27
III, iii, 4	155
III, xxi, 7	259
III, xxii, 4	116, 310
III, xxv, 1	294
IV, xviii, 4–5	126
IV, xx, 2	221, 235
IV, xx, 10	293

	Page
IV, xxxiii, 11	37
IV, xxxiv, 1	136, 293
V, i, 1	291fn.
V, ii, 2	126
V, xiv, 1	207
V, xix, 1	116, 310
Demonstration of the Apostolic Preaching	
33	310
67, 69	37
69	206
JUSTIN MARTYR, S.	
Apology	
I, xiv	284
I, xlv	287
I, lxii	282
I, lxiii	289
I, lxvi	3, 84, 309
I, lxvii	50, 97, 310
II, vi	118
II, vii	287
II, xiii	20, 294
Dialogue with Trypho	
90	212
100	310fn.
ORIGEN	
Contra Celsum	
i, 26	277
iv, 7	278
viii, 70	287
TERTULLIAN	
Apologeticus	
32, 39	287
50	288
de Carne Christi	
xvii	310fn.
de Corona	
3	176fn.
THEOPHILUS OF ANTIOCH, S.	
ad Autolycum	
ii, 18, 22	295

334

www.ingramcontent.com/pod-product-compliance
Lightning Source LLC
Chambersburg PA
CBHW071228230426
43668CB00011B/1353